PENGUIN BOOKS
MALGUDI LANDSCAPES

R.K. Narayan was born in Madras and educated there and at
Maharajah's College in Mysore. His first novel *Swami and Friends*
(1935) and its successor *The Bachelor of Arts* (1937) are both set in the
enchanting fictional territory of Malgudi. Other 'Malgudi' novels
are: *The Dark Room* (1938), *The English Teacher* (1945), *Mr Sampath*
(1949), *The Financial Expert* (1952), *The Man-Eater of Malgudi* (1962),
The Vendor of Sweets (1967), *The Painter of Signs* (1976), *A Tiger for
Malgudi* (1983), *Talkative Man* (1986), and his most recent, *The World
of Nagaraj*. Other novels include *Waiting for the Mahatma* (1955) and
The Guide (1958)—which won the Sahitya Akademi award.

In 1980 R.K. Narayan was awarded the A.C. Benson Medal by
the Royal Society of Literature and was made an Honorary Member
of the American Academy and Institute of Arts and Letters. In 1989
he was made a member of the Rajya Sabha. As well as five collections of short stories (*A Horse and Two Goats, An Astrologer's Day and
Other Stories, Lawley Road, Malgudi Days* and *Grandmother's Tale*), he
has published two travel books (*My Dateless Diary* and *The Emerald
Route*), four collections of essays (*Next Sunday, Reluctant Guru, A
Writer's Nightmare* and *A Story-teller's World*) translations of Indian
epics and myths (*The Ramayana, The Mahabharata, Gods, Demons and
Others*) and a memoir (*My Days*).

S. Krishnan taught English literature at the Madras Christian
College and at Annamalai University. He later spent many years
with the United States Information Agency in their educational and
cultural programme. He is an editor and freelance writer and lives
in Madras.

MALGUDI LANDSCAPES
The Best of R.K. Narayan

Edited with an Introduction by
S. Krishnan

PENGUIN BOOKS

PENGUIN BOOK

Published by the Penguin Group

Penguin Books India Pvt. Ltd, 11 Community Centre, Panchsheel Park, New Delhi 110 017, India

Penguin Group (USA) Inc., 375 Hudson Street, New York, New York 10014, USA

Penguin Group (Canada), 90 Eglinton Avenue East, Suite 700, Toronto, Ontario, M4P 2Y3, Canada (a division of Pearson Penguin Canada Inc.)

Penguin Books Ltd, 80 Strand, London WC2R 0RL, England

Penguin Ireland, 25 St Stephen's Green, Dublin 2, Ireland (a division of Penguin Books Ltd)

Penguin Group (Australia), 250 Camberwell Road, Camberwell, Victoria 3124, Australia (a division of Pearson Australia Group Pty Ltd)

Penguin Group (NZ), cnr Airborne and Rosedale Roads, Albany, Auckland 1310, New Zealand (a division of Pearson New Zealand Ltd)

Penguin Group (South Africa) (Pty) Ltd, 24 Sturdee Avenue, Rosebank, Johannesburg 2196, South Africa

Penguin Books Ltd, Registered Offices: 80 Strand, London WC2R 0RL, England

First published by Penguin Books India 1992

Copyright © R.K. Narayan 1992

Introduction copyright © S. Krishnan 1992

All the extracts in this selection, except for 'A Writer's Nightmare', 'Reluctant Guru', 'Misguided Guide', 'When India was a Colony' (*A Writer's Nightmare*, Penguin India); 'Sringeri', 'Cruelty to Children' (*A Story-teller's World*, Penguin India) and 'Westward Bound', (*My Dateless Diary*, Penguin India), were published by Indian Thought Publications, Mysore—*Swami and Friends*, 1935; *Bachelor of Arts*, 1937; *Dark Room*, 1938; *The English Teacher*, 1945; *Mr. Sampath* 1949; *The Financial Expert*, 1952; *Waiting for the Mahatma*, 1955; *The Guide*, 1958; *The Man-Eater of Malgudi*, 1962; *The Vendor of Sweets*, 1967; *The Painter of Signs*, 1976; *A Tiger for Malgudi*, 1983; *Talkative Man*, 1986; *The World of Nagaraj*, and *My Days*, 1976. The short stories, 'A Horse and Two Goats', 'Annamalai', 'Uncle' and 'A Breath of Lucifer', are taken from *A Horse and Two Goats*, 1970; while 'Selvi' is from *Stories Old and New*, 1981. The other excerpts are 'Yavati' (*Gods, Demons and Others*, 1964) 'The Wedding' (*The Ramayana*, 1972) 'Bride for Five' (*The Mahabharata*, 1978). 'Where is Malgudi' is excerpted from R.K. Narayan's acceptance speech of the fellowship of the American Academy and Institute of Arts and Letters. The publishers gratefully acknowledge the permission granted by the publishers of the above volumes and the author to reprint the selections in this book.

All rights reserved

15 14 13

For sale in the Indian Subcontinent and Singapore only

Typeset in Palatino Roman by dTech, New Delhi
Printed at Anubha Printers, Noida

Contents

IV: ESSAYS

V: TRAVEL

VI: LEGENDS AND MYTHS

VII: THE WRITER AS CITIZEN

VIII: ENVOY

Editor's Introduction

In the year 1942, when I was reading for my degree in literature at the Madras Christian College, one of my professors, Rev Dr J.R. Macphail, asked me if I had heard of R.K. Narayan. I should have, as his name was appearing in the *Hindu* and other publications, but I had not. Dr Macphail said that he had read a book called *Swami and Friends* by R.K. Narayan during home leave and found it exceptional in its treatment of theme and in its use of the English language. He asked me to try to get him a copy as he wanted to suggest to the Board of Studies that the book should be prescribed for non-detailed study for the B.A. degree. With all the brashness of a sixteen-year-old I wrote to Narayan himself, asking for a copy. He referred me to a friend of his in Madras from whom I borrowed the book. But nothing came of Dr Macphail's efforts as the book simply was not available—it was learnt later that most copies of Narayan's early novels were destroyed during the blitz. I eventually met Narayan in person during a balmy spring in New York in 1957. He was feeling very good and enjoying himself thoroughly in his own gentle fashion as he had finished writing *The Guide* during his stay in the U.S. As I write this, my thoughts go back to James Russell Macphail, scholar, teacher and friend, for opening Narayan's world to me.

Rasipuram Krishnaswami Ayyar Narayanaswamy—in his early years he signed himself R.K. Narayanaswamy, in the Tamil fashion, but at the time of the publication of *Swami and Friends,* he shortened it to R.K. Narayan on Graham Greene's suggestion—was born in 1906. He grew up in his grandmother's house in Madras until he entered his teens when he went to Mysore to live with his parents, his father being the headmaster of a prestigious school there. Narayan was not a particularly good student and he took longer than most of his peers to get a B.A. degree. But he was a voracious and eclectic reader (he can quote *Omar Khayyam* with the same facility as he can *Macbeth),* and he spent his time taking long walks in that idyllic city, reading, brooding and writing. His unwilling attempt to become a schoolteacher came to nought as he had neither the inclination nor the fortitude for it. Living with a large and affectionate joint family, he did not really feel the necessity to earn a living, although he made negligible amounts as a reporter of meetings and murders for a Madras newspaper, and through occasional contributions to various publications including one to *Punch*. Meanwhile he finished writing *Swami and Friends* and sent it to England for publication. Though rejected by several British publishers, the manuscript eventually reached the hands of Graham Greene who was sufficiently impressed by it to recommend it to Hamish Hamilton for publication. Greene found publishers for Narayan's next two books, *The Bachelor of Arts* and *The Dark Room*. All of them came out between 1935 and 1938, received good reviews in the British press, but sold negligibly. The intrusion of World War II in 1939 did not help either. The central, tragic event of Narayan's personal life occurred during this period. In 1933 he fell headlong in love with Rajam, an attractive girl in her late teens whom he had seen drawing water from a street-tap. Against tradition, against gloomy astrological predictions, and—let it be added—against a none too bright financial future, Narayan stood his ground, and married the girl of his choice. It was a happy marriage, Rajam blending in well with Narayan's joint family, and helping to run the household efficiently, with Narayan contributing whatever little he earned towards domestic expenses. The couple had a baby girl who constantly distracted Narayan from his writing. The happiness was not to last long as Rajam died of typhoid in 1939. To say that he was shattered would be an understatement; he went about like a zombie, doing nothing, relating to nobody except his three-year-old girl who was his only solace. For a change he went to Madras to stay with his sister, and there he had the psychic experiences which he describes in the second part of *The English Teacher*. Life and death began to hold a new meaning for him, and he returned to Mysore, a man in control of himself. He began writing again, and the result was *The English Teacher*, which Graham Greene, as a director of Eyre and Spottiswoode, published in 1944. The novel was an exercise in self-exorcism, though perhaps it was not consciously intended to be so. From hereon, Narayan's works do not delve into his persona though his writing gets richer, more broad-based and complex. He continues to use materials and characters experienced and explored personally, but he is always on the outside looking in.

The rest of Narayan's life is easily told. He produced and continues to produce novels on a regular basis, remarkable for their sustained quality and workmanship, short stories and essays, and retold myths and legends from the Indian background. Honours came crowding. He settled down in Mysore in a house he had built to his specifications, married off his only child, Hema, to her cousin, Chandru, and started travelling extensively in Europe, in the USA, in Australia. The best-known Indian man of letters, Narayan now divides his time between Mysore and Madras.

With the publication of *Swami and Friends,* a new voice, if one might use a cliché, came to be heard in the Indian world of letters, or at least in its English constituency. Hitherto, Indian fiction in English tended, by and large, to be philosophical, sentimental, political, or to ooze with an academic social consciousness. Naturally much of it was pretty unreadable, though chauvinist pride in the fact that we were using, moderately fluently, the language of the Englishman gave Indian writing in English a worth that was far from deserved. Narayan's clarity of style, his straightforward storytelling, his fully realized characters, and his unforced humour provided a clear new direction to Indian fiction. It is no one's case that other writers followed in Narayan's footsteps immediately, but certainly by the Fifties, Indian fiction in English tended to be less conventional and turgid. Consciously or otherwise his influence was being felt. At one level, *Swami* is the story of a small boy, and small boys are the same the world over, told with a tender fondness. But *Swami* is also full of relevant sharp insights, and the milieu of a small-town middle-class society is evoked effortlessly through deft descriptions and quick but well-rounded characterization. *The Bachelor of Arts,* whose hero, Chandran, is really Swami grown up, is appropriately enough crowded with adult characters, each one of whom has a specific role to play in Chandran's life. Narayan's gentle irony, which would have been out of place in *Swami,* is used to great effect in this novel, which he leavened with the humour that readers had already begun to expect of him. His next novel, *The Dark Room,* is totally different. It is a bleak, haunting story of a traditional Indian woman, ill-treated by her husband, wanting to rebel but in the end unable to do so. It is an early blow for women's liberation—it was written over fifty years ago when conventional orthodoxy was a miasma that enveloped the Hindu wife—and one cannot help the feeling that some real-life incident must have spurred Narayan into writing what is essentially a protest novel.

There was a break of several years before Narayan could get over his desolating sense of loss over his wife, and return to writing. The new book, *The English Teacher*, quite different, in that it is entirely autobiographical, with just a few details changed from real life to provide verisimilitude. Krishna, the protagonist who can be well seen as an adult Swami/Chandran, sets up house with his young wife and daughter after several months of enforced bachelorhood in the hostel of the college where he teaches. The happy and even tenor of his life is broken when his wife dies of typhoid. The rest of the book is given over to his efforts to reach her through psychical means. *The English Teacher* is a watershed in Narayan's writing. There was never to be any going back.

The novels which now followed in quick succession made an international reputation for Narayan, appearing not only in English but also in a number of foreign languages, ranging from Hebrew to Japanese, proving abundantly that his works have a universal appeal. Most of them had their core in an incident or a personality, developed into a full-fledged novel through Narayan's artistry. (How he would hate words like 'artistry'. But a critic is of necessity limited in his vocabulary.) *Mr Sampath* drew from Narayan's own experience in printing and publishing and from his keen observation of film-production when he wrote an occasional script for the Gemini Studio. The idea for *Financial Expert* was given to him by one of his brothers during the after-dinner sessions devoted to family conversation. The brother talked about an employee in his office, who, though dismissed, operated from outside the building as a middleman for rustics who needed money but did not quite know how to go about acquiring some. In *Waiting for the Mahatma*, one of his three unusual novels, the other two being *The Dark Room* and *A Tiger for Malgudi*, Narayan has Gandhiji himself playing a part, among other things, in the romance of a pair of young lovers. The novel received a mixed reception as the introduction of Gandhiji as a character in a novel offended some susceptibilities, but the novel is basically not about the Mahatma but about its sheltered protagonist, Sriram, and his coming of age.

The Guide marks another station-halt in the progress of Narayan as a storyteller. Undoubtedly the best-known of his books—it received a Sahitya Akademi award—it was inspired by rain-making efforts in drought-stricken Karnataka with which Narayan combined the theme of the sinner turned saint. While no novel of Narayan is casually constructed, *The Guide* is particularly noteworthy for carrying on a split narrative with technical perfection. The *Man-Eater of Malgudi* is something else again. Here Narayan takes one of those arrogance- of-power legends from Indian mythology—that of the *rakshasa*, Basmasura—and uses it as a perfect vehicle for his story of, not good and evil, but of good and gentle people pitted against a totally inconsiderate and brutal individual, who runs riot in a small community, upsetting its order and throwing everything into confusion. In the legend, Basmasura obtains a boon from Siva that enables him to burn to ashes anyone he wishes, whose head he touches. He is finally destroyed by Vishnu, appearing in the form of a beautiful damsel who promises to yield to him if he would repeat a dance she performs. He agrees, and naturally in the course of her dance she touches her own head, an action which he repeats and is immediately burnt to a cinder. Vasu, the man-eater of the title, is probably the only truly evil character Narayan has created who does not get from his creator that modicum of sympathy that the author doles out to his other villains. This is an extremely well-crafted novel. Narayan's subsequent novels explore unusual territory. In *The Vendor of Sweets*, Jagan, the sweetmeat vendor, conservative and philosophical by nature, has to come to terms with the fact that his only son has married a foreigner, and then again with the further fact that they are not actually married. The conflict between generations is the basic theme of the novel, and Narayan increases the tension by making father and son extreme representatives of their generations. *The Painter of Signs* is in some ways a radical departure for Narayan. Moving with the times, he provides Malgudi with Daisy, a birthcontrol propagandist with whom Raman, a sign-painter, falls desperately in love. After many vicissitudes, among which the attempted seduction of Daisy by Raman is a delectable one, the couple decide to get married only to be thwarted by the Government which posts Daisy to another town which has shown an increase of thirty per cent in population. In *A Tiger for Malgudi* Narayan breaks new ground again. He makes the tiger the narrator of the story, which took root in his mind when he read about a Swami at a famous festival in India who was accompanied by a tiger which followed him around faithfully, not hurting anybody. Raja, a circus tiger, breaks loose, and terrorizes the people of Malgudi (not because he particularly wants to but they fear him any way) until he meets a Swami who befriends him. Narayan's concern here is with the possibility that irrespective of outside appearances there may be common ground among all living beings. Narayan takes a giant leap into the last quarter of this century when he peoples his next novel, *Talkative Man*, with a westernized Indian who calls himself Rann and claims to be researching a project for the United Nations, and the wife he had deserted, a powerful lady named Commandant Sarasa. She comes to Malgudi in search of Rann, having read about him in a news item contributed by the Talkative Man who is the narrator and a journalist of sorts. The ensuing free-for-all is exactly the kind of farce Narayan revels in though there are undercurrents of seriousness to the story. Narayan's most recent novel, *The World of Nagaraj*, has a typical Narayan hero—Nagaraj, conservative, well-to-do, childless, leading a quiet and contented life with his wife and mother and planning his great opus on the age Narada. The even tenor of his life is rudely shattered with the arrival of his errant nephew, Tim, who is estranged from his father, Nagaraj's brother. Can Nagaraj support his nephew without antagonizing his elder brother?

The locale of all these novels and most of Narayan's short stories is Malgudi, the mythical town with which his name is inextricably associated. Two general assumptions must be immediately countered. One is that Malgudi is patterned after Mysore City. Nothing could be farther from this fact, and the dusty small town of Malgudi has no physical resemblance to princely, palace-filled Mysore. What is a fact is that Malgudi takes its contours from the sleepy little South Indian towns of those days, among which the inner city or the core part of Mysore can also be included. The other statement usually made about Narayan is to compare him with William Faulkner. The link is very tenuous and is sustained by no more than the circumstance that both writers created their own worlds and moved surely in them. Faulkner's Yoknapatawpha County, peopled by individuals with a sense of sin and horror underlying their lives, is a far cry from Narayan's Malgudi, a placid little backwater full of gentle and gently eccentric persons. The artistry of either writer by any standard is great as they were able to give 'to airy nothings a local habitation and a name', and to create a microcosm entirely out of their own experience. As John Updike has pointed out, both Narayan and Faulkner are 'writers immersed in their materials', though widely differing in their use of them. For the Narayan aficionado, Malgudi is a real place with which, as Graham Greene says, 'we have been as familiar as with our own birth place. We know, like the streets of childhood, Market Road, the snuff stalls, the vendors of toothpaste, the Regal Haircutting Saloon, the river, the railway'. The name Malgudi, Narayan has said, made its appearance in a sentence that suddenly flashed in his mind when he was working on *Swami and Friends:* 'The train stopped at Malgudi.' As happened the train did not stop at Malgudi in *Swami*, except at the end, though it does so in several later stories, notably in *The Guide* and *The English Teacher.* Narayan's own somewhat tongue-in-cheek answer to the question, Where is Malgudi? appears elsewhere in this volume. A particularly rewarding aspect of the Malgudi saga is the way characters keep reappearing in the various stories, sometimes in life-size roles. Swami was in a short story before he had a book to himself, and we had known Jagan long before his total apotheosis as the vendor of sweets.

It would be an exercise in futility to try to apply literary critical standards to Narayan's work. He is first and last the supreme storyteller, and the fully evolved story is more important to him than any other aspect of writing. His style derives from the stories themselves, reflecting their clarity, gentleness, and a totally unforced but puckish humour. Most Narayan stories would sound over-simple if ruthlessly summarized and it is his alchemical art that transforms them into a living experience in which the reader fully participates. It is perhaps for this reason that Narayan's stories have by and large not been successfully produced on the stage or the screen. The effort to have *The Guide* made into a film, and for that matter into a play, was a total disaster simply because the author's personality which pervades his writing could not be transferred to the other media. It is only when the producer has closely worked with Narayan at every stage that some of his works— *The Financial Expert* in its Kannada version, *Malgudi Days* in the Indian TV series—have achieved a measure of success. Not that this discourages producers—a Latin American group produced a Spanish version of *Lawley Road* and sold it to Columbia Pictures, though what happened to it afterwards remains something of a mystery. Currently Narayan is at work on a set of long short stories of which the first, *Grandmother's Tale*, has already appeared in serial form. While it is for the most part a true story from Narayan's own background, it has the curious distinction of being the only story of his that is not set in Malgudi, but any regret the loyal reader may feel over this is more than offset by the free-flowing and breezy nature of the story. The more important recognition that a writer might aspire for has come Narayan's way in full measure. In India, *The Guide* won the Sahitya Akademi award, the Government of India decorated him with a Padma Bhushan, and nominated him a

xiv *Malgudi Landscapes*

member of the Rajya Sabha (Upper House of Parliament) for a term.
Elsewhere, in Britain the Royal Society of Literature gave him the
A.C. Benson medal, while in the United States he received the
English Speaking Union's award, and was made a Fellow by the
prestigious American Academy and Institute of Arts and Letters,
only one of two Indians to be so honoured. His papers have been
acquired by the Department of Special Collections of Boston
University which will make them available to researchers. Graham
Greene, his staunch supporter and friend of more than fifty years,
once comparing Narayan to Turgenev and Chekhov, said:
'Narayan (whom I don't hesitate to name in such a context) more
than any of them wakes in me a spring of gratitude, for he has
offered me a second home. Without him I could never have known
what it is like to be an Indian.' To which it can be added that even
to Indians born and bred, he performs a similar service by revealing
truths about ourselves we have not been aware of.

I: AUTOBIOGRAPHY

Editor's note: This, Narayan's only effort at autobiography, came out in 1974 when he was in his late sixties. It is noteworthy for the gentle, almost lyrical, nostalgia with which he recreates his early years. It is also a straightforward account of his life until he 'arrives' as a writer, and it glosses over his years after the publication of *The Guide*, casually and not ruthlessly.

MY DAYS

Sighing over a pretty face and form seen on a balcony, or from across the street, or in a crowd, longing for love—in a social condition in which, at least in those days, boys and girls were segregated and one never spoke to anyone but a sister—I had to pass through a phase of impossible love-sickness. Perhaps the great quantity of fiction I read prepared my mind to fall in love with all and sundry—all one-sided, of course. Any girl who lifted her eyes and seemed to notice me became at once my sweetheart, till someone else took her place. Thus I had become devoted to a girl in a green sari with a pale oval face, passing down our street when we were living at Bojjanna Lines. She lived in the next street, the sister-in-law of an engineer, and I would have missed anything in the day rather than miss a glimpse of her. Sometimes I followed her quietly, like a slave, until she reached her gate and disappeared into her house without bestowing a single glance in my direction. I longed for some engineering business that might warrant a visit to her brother-in-law and then a gradual development of an acquaintance, the relationship maturing until I could freely propose to her, a la Victoria Cross or Marie Corelli. I was obsessed with her night and day, and I had no doubt that she would receive the impact of my thoughts, as Marie Corelli had taught me to believe that true love recognized no boundaries or barriers.

I lost sight of this girl suddenly—but found another, a little farther off, standing on the terrace of her home drying her hair—I noticed her at first on my way to the college, and then looked for her constantly on the way to and from; sure enough she would be there, a squat lumpy girl, but I loved her none the less. I think she was a flirt in her own way, ogling at every passer-by—not necessarily only me. I lost interest in her soon and bestowed it on another girl going to Maharani's College, who used to give me a smile and pass on. All this love for someone was necessarily one-sided and unspoken. But it made no difference. It gave me a feeling of enrichment and purpose. Among an inner circle of friends we always discussed girls and indulged in lewd jokes and enjoyed it all immensely. The blind urge to love went to fantastic lengths—I even fell in love with a lady doctor who had come to attend my mother because she spoke a few words to me whenever I greeted her; she was a British lady well past middle age, stout and married. But I saw great possibilities in her and read a significance in every glance. Love, especially one-sided, can know no bounds, physical, racial, of age, or distance. My most impossible infatuation was for a penfriend I had in England; we exchanged letters every week. She sent me her photograph and I sent her mine. I kept her photo in my breast pocket and hoped she did likewise with mine—five thousand miles away; even if I wished to reach her, it would mean a P&O voyage of four weeks. I wrote impassioned love-letters which she rejected outright; she wrote back impersonal letters describing a holiday in Brighton or her latest collection of stamps. Although she protested against the tone of my letters, she never stopped writing, and that seemed to me a hopeful sign. I continued to send her my unmitigated love in every letter, and treasured her cold, impersonal replies and the scent of her stationery for years—until I was married, when I threw them over the wall.

After the false starts, the real thing occurred. In July 1933, I had gone to Coimbatore, escorting my elder sister, and then stayed on in her house. There was no reason why I should ever hurry away from one place to another. I was a freelance writer and I could work wherever I might be at a particular time. One day, I saw a girl drawing water from the street-tap and immediately fell in love with her. Of course, I could not talk to her. I learned later that she had not even noticed me passing and repassing in front of her while she waited to fill the brass vessels. I craved to get a clear, fixed, mental impression of her features, but I was handicapped by the time factor, as she would be available for staring at only until her vessels filled, when she would carry them off, and not come out again until the next water-filling time. I could not really stand and stare; whatever impression I had of her would be through a side-glance while passing the tap. I suffered from a continually melting vision. The only thing I was certain of was that I loved her, and I suffered the agonies of restraint imposed by the social conditions in which I lived. The tall headmaster, her father, was a friend of the family and often dropped in for a chat with the elders at home while on his way to the school, which was at a corner of our street. The headmaster, headmaster's daughter, and the school were all within geographical reach and hailing distance, but the restraint imposed by the social code created barriers. I attempted to overcome them by befriending the headmaster. He was a book-lover and interested in literary matters, and we found many common subjects for talk. We got into the habit of meeting at his school after the school-hours and discussing the world, seated comfortably on a cool granite *pyol* in front of a little shrine of Ganesha in the school compound. One memorable evening, when the stars had come out, I interrupted some talk we were having on political matters to make a bold, blunt announcement of my affection for his daughter. He was taken aback, but did not show it. In answer to my proposal, he just turned to the god in the shrine and shut his eyes in a prayer. No one in our social condition could dare to proceed in the manner I had done. There were formalities to be observed, and any talk for a marriage proposal could proceed only between the elders of families. What I had done was unheard of. But the headmaster was sporting enough not to shut me up immediately. Our families were known to each other, and the class, community, and caste requirements were all right. He just said, 'If God wills it,' and left it at that. He also said, 'Marriages are made in Heaven, and who are we to say "Yes" or "No".' After this he explained the difficulties. His wife and womenfolk at home were to be consulted, and my parents had to approve, and so on and so forth, and then the matching of horoscopes—this last became a great hurdle at the end. He came down to a practical level one day, by asking me what I proposed to do for a living. Luckily for me, at about that time a small piece that I had written ('How to Write an Indian Novel', lampooning Western writers who visited India to gather material) had unexpectedly been accepted by *Punch* and brought me six guineas. This was my first prestige publication (the editor rejected everything I sent him subsequently) and it gave me a talking-point with my future father-in-law. I could draw a picture of my freelance writing for London papers and magazines and explain to him that when my novel was finished it would bring in income all my life and fifty years after. He listened to me with apparent interest, without contradicting me, but off and on suggested, 'I'm sure, if your father used his influence, he could fix you in a government job at Bangalore. Won't he try?' This always upset me, and I immediately explained my economic philosophy: how I spurned the idea of earning more than was needed, which would be twenty rupees a month or, with a wife, forty rupees, and I expected my wife to share my philosophy. Not a very politic statement to make to the bewildered and hesitant father of a girl, but I became headstrong in my conviction. However, while it distressed the gentleman it did not materially affect my progress toward matrimony.

What really mattered was not my economic outlook, but my stars. My father-in-law, himself an adept at the study of horoscopes, had consultations with one or two other experts and came to the conclusion that my horoscope and the girl's were incompatible. My horoscope had the Seventh House occupied by Mars, the Seventh House being the one that indicated matrimonial aspects. The astrological texts plainly stated that Mars in the Seventh House indicated nothing but disaster unless the partner's horoscope also contained the same flaw, a case in which two wrongs make one right.

The next few weeks were a trying period for me. The headmaster would have none of me. In very gentle terms he expressed his rejection of me, as also his resignation to such a fate, since he seemed to have been secretly in my favour. I lost the taste for food and company, and lay sulking in a corner of my sister's house on a gloomy easy chair. My mood was noticed by others with sympathy. I think I enjoyed a certain amount of self- dramatization and did all that one does when 'crossed in hopeless love'. I avoided going out in the direction of the street-tap, I avoided the headmaster and his school. Late in the evening when it became dark, I went out for a brisk walk, with my head bowed in thought, looking neither left nor right, but totally wrapped up in my own gloomy reflections, just enough initiative left to smoke two Gold Flake cigarettes and return home. My sister, being my hostess, tried to cheer me up in various ways. My pensive pose got on her nerves. At this period I remember writing a play; it kept me busy all the afternoon. The play was called 'The Home of Thunder'—a frightful tragedy in which all the principal characters are struck dead by lightning on a tower open to the skies, the play ending with a clap of thunder. It was a highly philosophical play examining the ideas of love, resignation, and death, the writing of which diverted my mind a great deal. I had great hopes for its future, and in due course sent it round to all kinds of producers and directors in every part of the civilized world. I had forgotten all about its existence till a few months ago, again when David Higham's office discovered and returned the manuscript while clearing out old papers.

The evil of my stars soon became a matter of discussion among the headmaster's astrological group. He sought me out and sent me here and there to meet his colleagues and talk it over with them and bring him their opinions and conclusions; finally he sent me along to meet an old man, living not far from us in the back of a coconut garden. His name was, strangely, 'Chellappa-sir', I don't know why—perhaps he was a retired teacher—and he was said to be an expert. I went to his house and explained my mission. He snapped at me, 'What do you want me to do? Am I Brahma to change your stars?' He looked angry for some inexplicable reason. 'Go and tell that headmaster one thing. I don't care whether his daughter gets married or not; I'll hold on to my views. I have spoken to that man again and again, but still he is full of doubts. If he knows better astrology than I do, he should not trouble me like this. If he listens to reason, he should go ahead and fix a date for the wedding, that's all. I see no harm in it. He hasn't noticed the moon's position in his daughter's horoscope, which neutralizes the Mars. But that man expects me to give him a guarantee that Mars will not harm his daughter's life. I can give no such guarantee. I am not Brahma.' He raised his voice to a shrieking pitch and repeated, 'I do not care whether that man's daughter is married or not. . . .'

In spite of all these fluctuations and hurdles, my marriage came off in a few months, celebrated with all the pomp, show, festivity, exchange of gifts, and the overcrowding, that my parents desired and expected.

Soon after my marriage, my father became bedridden with a paralytic stroke, and most of my mother's time was spent at his side upstairs. The new entrant into the family, my wife, Rajam, was her deputy downstairs, managing my three younger brothers, who were still at school, a cook in the kitchen, a general servant, and a gigantic black-and-white Great Dane acquired by my elder brother who was a dog-lover. She kept an eye on the stores, replenishing the food-stuffs and guarding them from being squandered or stolen by the cook. Rajam was less than twenty, but managed the housekeeping expertly and earned my mother's praise. She got on excellently with my brothers. This was one advantage of a joint family system—one had plenty of company at home. Yet with all the group life, there was still enough privacy for me and my wife. We had a room for ourselves and when we retired into it, we were in an idyllic world of our own. Within six months, she proved such an adept at housekeeping that my mother left her in complete charge, and we found the time to exchange pleasantries and intimacies only when she took a little time off during the day and came to my room or at night after everyone had retired and the kitchen door was shut. Presently I did not find too much time to spend at home either.

In order to stabilize my income I became a newspaper reporter. My business would be to gather Mysore city news and send it daily to a newspaper published in Madras called *The Justice*. The daily was intended to promote the cause of the non-Brahmin who suffered from the domination of the minority Brahmin class in public life, government service, and education. Though *The Justice* was a propagandist paper against the Brahmin class, it somehow did not mind having me as its correspondent in Mysore. I left home at about nine in the morning and went out news-hunting through the bazaar and marketplace—all on foot. I hung about law courts, police stations, and the municipal building, and tried to make up at least ten inches of news each day before lunchtime. I returned home at one o'clock, bolted down a lunch, sat down at my typewriter, and typed the news item with appropriate headings. I now had an old Remington portable (the double-barrelled one having been given away for twenty rupees, off-setting the bill for cigarettes and sweets at a shop) which was a present from my younger sister. It took me an hour or more to type the items, and then I signed and sealed the report in an envelope, and rushed it to the Chamarajapuram post office before the postal clearance at 2:20 p.m. If my youngest brother (Laxman, now a famous cartoonist) was available, he would be ready, with one foot on the pedal of his bicycle, to ride off to the post office for a tiny fee of a copper for each trip; but when he wasn't there, I practically sprinted along with my press copy. There was really no need to rush like that since most of the news items could wait or need not be published at all; but we were in a competitive society; I feared that other Madras papers like *The Mail* or the *Hindu*, whose correspondents had telephone and telegraph facilities, might get ahead of me. But those correspondents were lofty and did not care for the items I valued.

After the dispatch of the copy, I relaxed in my room; that was also the time when my wife could give me her company. I described to her the day's events, such as traffic accidents, suicides, or crimes, which were the grist for my mill; then I sank into a siesta for an hour and was ready to go out again at four o'clock after a cup of coffee. This time it would be a visit to the magistrate's court before closing time, to take down the judgement in a counterfeit case or murder conspiracy. On Saturday afternoons I sat at the municipal meeting, watching the city fathers wrangle over their obscure issues—all through the evening it would go on. In those days there were always a couple of lawyers on the council, and they never permitted the business to proceed beyond an examination of the procedure and the by-laws. No more than a couple of items in the voluminous agenda would be covered at the end of two hours. After a coffee break, I would suddenly clutch the agenda papers and leave, afflicted with a headache. Some days there would be academic matters to cover, a distinguished visitor lecturing at the university or a senate meeting. In those days there was a local League of Nations Union, which strove to establish peace in this world in its own way. The secretary of this union, who was a history professor, decreed that our reports should be scrutinized by him before we filed them. I resisted his order as an encroachment on the freedom of the press, and he threatened to disaccredit me as a correspondent (which could, in effect, only mean denying luncheon facilities) whereupon I declared that I would report him to our Journalists' Association, pass a resolution against him, and syndicate it to all the world's press and denounce him as an autocrat and enemy of freedom. He said, 'Do you know that I have powers to smash you and your papers. . . .' I walked out of the union meeting in protest, and so did a couple of my colleagues. I began to ignore its activities and boycotted its functions. I realized soon that this did not affect the prospect of world peace either way, nor provoke my news-editor to question why I was not covering the League of Nations Union.

Murders were my stand-by. From Nanjangud or Chamarajnagar, at the extreme south of Mysore District, the police brought in a steady stream of murder cases. On such occasions, I let myself go. I hung about the mortuary for the post-mortem verdict and the first police report. As long as I used the expression 'alleged' liberally, there was no danger of being hauled up for false reporting or contempt of court. I knew a lot of police officers, plainclothesmen, and informers—apart from presidents and secretaries of various public bodies (including the Pinjarapole, a home for aged or disabled animals) who craved publicity and sought my favour. Quite a number of wedding invitations came to me from fond parents hoping for a report and a photograph of the bridal pair in the paper. I should have gladly given all the space available to whoever wanted it, but my news-editor, when he did not reject it outright, mutilated and decimated my copy. He compressed my most eloquent descriptions into two lines. What did I make out of it all? Our contract was that I would be paid three rupees and eight annas per column of twenty-one inches. I fancied that the news I sent would cover at least fifteen inches each day and fetch me at least seventy-five rupees a month, but thanks to the news-editor's talent for abridgement, I had to crawl up each day by fractions of an inch. I measured my total 'inchage' with a scale at the end of the month and sent my bill; and they would invariably doubt and disallow my measurements and send me some arbitrary amount, never more than thirty rupees, often less.

But I enjoyed this occupation, as I came in close contact with a variety of men and their activities, which was educative. It lasted for about one year, and might have gone on, perhaps indefinitely, but for a letter I sent to the editor, which soured our relationship. They had withheld my payment for three months, and I wrote to say, 'I am a writer in contact with many newspapers and periodicals in America and England, who make their payments on precise dates; I am not used to delays in payments. . . .' To which the editor replied, 'If you are eminent as you claim to be, you should not mind a slight delay on our part; if, on the other hand, you could realize that after all you are a correspondent eking out your income with such contributions as we choose to publish, your tone is unwarranted by your circumstances.' I resented the tone of their reply, and decided to give up this work as soon as I could afford it.

Money was a big worry. When a cheque was delayed, it caused all kinds of embarrassments for me. My budget was precisely framed. I had to find money to pay for my share of the expenses at home, also for face powder or soap that my wife would ask for. I grandly promised her even a sari and bought her a green one on credit costing about sixty rupees, the shopman agreeing to take instalments of ten rupees on the fourth of every month. If I delayed, a bill-collector would appear on the morning of the sixth at our gate, demanding the instalment. He was a tall, gaunt man, with sunken cheeks and the expressionless face of a corpse. When I heard the clicking of the gate latch, I would tell myself, 'Here it cometh, my lord,' echoing Hamlet. I rushed forward to stop him before my wife or any one else could see him, and turned him back with soft words, promises, and a small tip for coffee; until I liquidated this debt, I felt guilty whenever I saw my wife in the green sari, as if I had given her a stolen present.

I continued to send in my reports of the turbulent city of Mysore, and off and on received a cheque from *The Justice*. But I voluntarily stopped this work on the day I received a cable from my friend

Purna, who was now at Oxford: 'Novel taken. Graham Greene responsible.' My friend and neighbour Purna, who used to hop over the wall and come to listen to my reading of *Swami and Friends*, had left in August 1931 for Oxford, promising to find a publisher for my book while he was there. When I had completed the novel, I faithfully dispatched it to Allen and Unwin and when it was returned, to another publisher and then another. I had got used to getting back my manuscript with unfailing regularity once every six weeks—two weeks onward journey, two weeks sojourn on a publisher's desk, and two weeks homeward journey with a rejection slip pinned to it; all in all it provided me with six weeks of hope! I had got used to this as an almost mechanical process and had shed all emotions surrounding a rejection. The last publisher to return it to me was Dent, and I had advised them in my covering letter to forward the manuscript when rejected to Purna at Exeter College, Oxford. I sent a parallel letter to Purna advising him to weight the manuscript with a stone and drown it in the Thames. Purna, however, seems to have spent much of his time visiting London and carrying the manuscript from publisher to publisher. After trying them all, he wrote to me, 'To the Thames? No need to hurry. Maybe never. Do not despair.' This went on while I was spinning out measurable news for *The Justice*. Graham Greene was living in Oxford at that time. Purna, by some instinct, approached him and gave him my manuscript. An introduction thus begun established a personal interest and friendship between us that continues to this day. Graham Greene recommended my novel to Hamish Hamilton, who accepted it immediately.

Purna's cable made me gasp with joy and surprise. I saw myself in a new role as a novelist. I could see the relief in my wife's face although she did not want to be too demonstrative about it. The first thing I did on receiving the cable was to write to *The Justice* that I would not be able to supply them any more news from Mysore, although the advance from the novel was twenty pounds (less fifty per cent tax).

Swami and Friends was published in the October of 1935. A few reviews were enthusiastic, but it had no sales; it appeared in the company of record-breaking best-sellers such as *Man the Unknown* and *Inside Europe*, and was simply flushed out of sight in the deluge. So much so that Hamish Hamilton rejected his option on my next novel, *The Bachelor of Arts*, with the words, '*Swami and Friends* was a failure. I don't think *Chandran (The Bachelor of Arts)* is going to do any better. I hope someone will prove me wrong some day.' Twenty years later I met Hamish Hamilton in London at a party in the office of *The Spectator*, where Graham Greene had taken me. It was a very interesting and cordial meeting. Egged on by Greene, Hamilton remembered his comments on my literary future, joked at his own expense, and then remarked, 'Remember, I was your first publisher, and I always feel happy at the thought of it.' Next morning he sent me a copy of his *Majority*, which has extracts to celebrate thirty years of his publishing firm, generously inscribed for me.

Thanks again to Graham Greene's recommendation, *The Bachelor of Arts* was published by Nelson, fulfilling a fancy I had entertained several years before when a Nelson representative had come from Edinburgh to see my father about the supply of books for our high-school library. I had confided to this salesman, 'If I write a book, will you ask your company to publish it?' 'Undoubtedly,' he had said and given me his card.

Change after February 1937. My father lived up to the last date of the month, as if to satisfy a technical need, and died leaving us to draw his pension for the full month. That was all the resources we were left with. My father had never believed in savings, property, and such things.

Now we feared a total economic collapse. But we managed. My elder brother, now back from Madras, as an experiment had opened a small shop in a new extension and called it National Provision Stores. Seenu had a government job and moved off to Bangalore. Mine was still a pure gamble. Sometimes I wished that I had not given up *The Justice*, but I was sustained by the gambler's inexhaustible hope and a Micawberish anticipation of something turning up. With a second novel published and a daughter added to the family, life seemed to be not so bad. Short stories were being accepted in India as well as abroad— Graham Greene helping me in London. So after all my claim to the editor of *The Justice* about contacts with London editors was being fulfilled, although it had, perhaps, been premature. The great gods who could view the past, present, and future as one bloc would have realized I had not been false!

My brother and I shared the household expenses. He looked after the supplies and miscellaneous items of expenditure, and I had to see that the house rent was paid; all aspects of shelter were to be my responsibility. 'Rama Vilas', in which we lived, was to be retained at any cost; there could be no question of our moving to another house. Fortunately our house-owner lived in Bangalore and only came down to Mysore once a month to collect the rent. I told him once, 'The rent is my responsibility. I have no fixed income. If my books sell, the royalty will come in only in December and June. So please permit me to settle the rent once every six months, although I will pay into your bank account whatever amount I'm able to earn meanwhile.' He was good enough to accept this arrangement. Now I had a scrappy, fitful income from various sources. In addition to other items I had to find money for baby food gripe-water, and toys. I did a variety of writing: humorous article every week for a *Merry Magazine* at ten rupees a week; a most taxing experience for me—to perform a thousand- word literary clowning week after week. I had also begun my third novel, *The Dark Room*. I took a pad and pen and disappeared every morning for three hours. I found it impossible to write at home now—there were far too many worrying distractions, and also the baby. She was just a little over a year old and I found it impossible to remain at my desk when she was around, since my wife often left her in my care while she was busy in the kitchen or in the garden gathering flowers for my mother's daily worship. I had also a routine duty to carry my daughter to let her watch the pink bougainvillaea flowers over the compound wall of Reverend Sawday's bungalow at the corner. She would gaze at the bunch of flowers for about ten minutes with rapt attention, and then I would have to lift her up to give her a glimpse of a white terrier that barked and frisked about inside the Reverend's compound. Only then would I be free to deposit her at home and leave. Before sending me out, my wife would give me a cup of coffee and sometimes whisper a warning: 'Don't make a fuss. Not enough coffee powder at home. Get some at the store when you return.' I set out to do my writing at the College Union, where the secretary had given me a room. I shut myself in for three hours, gazed on the green football field outside, across the street, and spun out the fate of Savitri—the heroine of *The Dark Room*. I was somehow obsessed with a philosophy of Woman as opposed to Man, her constant oppressor. This must have been an early testament of the 'Women's Lib' movement. Man assigned her a secondary place and kept her there with such subtlety and cunning that she herself began to lose all notion of her independence, her individuality, stature, and strength. A wife in an orthodox milieu of Indian society was an ideal victim of such circumstances. My novel dealt with her, with this philosophy broadly in the background. I wrote nearly a thousand words before I went back home for lunch, exhausted, but also feeling triumphant at having done my quota of work for the day.

The Dark Room, once again read and approved by Graham Greene, was published by Macmillan in 1938. I had the unique experience of having a new publisher for each book. One book, one publisher—and then perhaps he said to himself, 'Hands off this writer.' Hamish Hamilton, then Nelson, now Macmillan.

II: NOVELS

SWAMI AND FRIENDS

Editor's note: Swami is the most endearing character that Narayan ever created. He is about nine years old, fearful by nature and tending to take refuge in his grandmother's lap when the going gets too much for him, revelling in his friendship with physically bigger and more important classmates, and by the same token tending to look down on boys smaller than him in a kindly fashion. His life, as E.B. White said about his dog, is 'full of incident without accomplishment'. But he has his moments too.

Swaminathan had two different attachments: one to Somu, Sankar, and the Pea—a purely scholastic one, which automatically ceased when the school gates closed; his other attachment was more human to Rajam and Mani. Now that they had no school, they were free from the shackles of time, and were almost always together, and arranged for themselves a hectic vacation.

Swaminathan's one consuming passion in life now was to get a hoop. He dreamt of it day and night. He feasted on visions of an ex-cycle wheel without spokes or tyre. You had only to press a stick into the groove and the thing would fly. Oh, what joy to see it climb small obstacles, and how gently it took curves! When running it made a steady hum, which was music to the ear. Swaminathan thought that anybody in Malgudi would understand that he was coming, even a mile away, by that hum. He sometimes kept awake till ten-thirty in the night, thinking of this hoop. He begged everyone that he came across, from his father's friends to a municipal sweeper that he knew, to give him a cycle wheel. Now he could not set his eyes on a decent bicycle without his imagination running riot over its wheels. He dreamt one night that he crossed the Sarayu near Nallapa's Grove on his wheel. It was a vivid dream; the steel wheel crunched on the sandy bed of the river as it struggled and heaved across. It became a sort of horse when it reached the other bank. It went back home in one leap, took him to the kitchen, and then to his bed, and lay down beside him. This was fantastic; but the early part of the dream was real enough. It nearly maddened him to wake to a hoopless morning.

In sheer despair he opened his heart to a coachman—a casual acquaintance of his. The coachman was very sympathetic. He agreed that existence was difficult without a hoop. He said that he would be able to give Swaminathan one in a few hours if the latter could give him five rupees. This was an immense sum, which Swaminathan hoped to possess in some distant future when he should become as tall as his father. He said so. At which the coachman gave a convincing talk on how to get it. He wanted only six pies to start with; in a short time he would make it six annas, and after that convert it to six rupees. And Swaminathan could spend the five out of the six rupees on the hoop and the balance of one rupee just as he pleased. Swaminathan declared that nothing would give him greater happiness than giving that extra rupee to the coachman. If any doubts arose in Swaminathan's mind, they were swept away by the other's rhetoric. The coachman's process of minting higher currency was this: he had a special metal pot at home in which he kept all base copper coins together with some mysterious herb (whose name he would not reveal even if he were threatened with torture). He kept the whole thing, he said, buried in the ground, he squatted on the spot at dead of night and performed some yoga, and lo when the time came, all the copper was silver. He could make even gold, but to get the herbs for it, he would have to walk two hundred and fifty miles across strange places, and he did not consider it worth all that exertion.

Swaminathan asked him when he might see him again as he had to think out and execute a plan to get six pies. The coachman said that if the other did not get the money immediately he would not be available for weeks to come as his master was going away and he would have to go away too. Swaminathan cringed and begged him to grant him six hours and ran home.

He first tried Granny. She almost shed tears that she had no money, and held her wooden box upside down to prove how hard up she was.

'I know, Granny, you have a lot of coins under your pillows.'

'No, boy. You can search if you like.'

Swaminathan ordered Granny to leave the bed and made a thorough search under the pillows and the carpets.

'Why do you want money now?' Granny asked.

'If you have what I want, have the goodness to oblige me. If not, why ask futile questions?'

Granny cried to Mother: 'If you have money, give this boy six pies.' But nobody was prepared to oblige Swaminathan. Father dismissed the request in a fraction of a second, which made

Swaminathan wonder what he did with all the money that he took from his clients.

He now tried a last desperate chance. He fell on his hands and knees, and resting his cheek on the cold cement floor, peered into the dark space under his father's heavy wardrobe. He had a wild notion that he might find a few coins scattered there. He thrust his hand under the wardrobe and moved it in all directions. All that he was able to collect was a disused envelope musty with cobweb and dust, a cockroach, and pinches of fine dust.

He sometimes believed that he could perform magic, if only he set about it with sufficient earnestness. He also remembered Ebenezar's saying in the class that God would readily help those that prayed to him.

He secured a small cardboard box, placed in it a couple of pebbles, and covered them with fine sand and leaves. He carried the box to the puja room and placed it in a corner. It was a small room in which a few framed pictures of gods hung on the wall, and a few bronze and brass idols kept staring at Swaminathan from a small carved wooden pedestal. A permanent smell of flowers, camphor, and incense, hung in the air.

Swaminathan stood before the gods and with great piety informed them of the box and its contents, how he expected them to convert the two pebbles into two three-pie coins, and why he needed money so urgently. He promised that if the Gods helped him, he would give up biting his thumb. He closed his eyes and muttered: 'Oh, Sri Rama! Thou hast slain Ravana though he had ten heads, can't you give me six pies. . .? If I give you the six pies now, when will you give me the hoop? I wish you would tell me what that herb is. . . . Mani, shall I tell you the secret of getting a hoop? Oh, Rama! Give me six pies and I will give up biting my thumb for a year. . . .'

He wandered aimlessly in the backyard persuading himself that in a few minutes he could return to the puja room and take his money—transmuted pebbles. He fixed a time-limit of half an hour.

Ten minutes later he entered the puja room, prostrated himself before the gods, rose, and snatching his box, ran to a secluded place in the backyard. With a fluttering heart he opened the box. He emptied it on the ground, ran his fingers through the mass of sand and leaves, and picked up the two pebbles. As he gazed at the cardboard box, the scattered leaves, sand, and the unconverted pebbles, he was filled with rage. The indifference of the gods infuriated him and brought tears to his eyes. He wanted to abuse the gods, but was afraid to. Instead, he vented all his rage on the cardboard box, and kicked it from place to place and stamped upon the leaves and sand. He paused and doubted if the gods would approve of even this. He was afraid that it might offend them. He might get on without money, but it was dangerous to incur the wrath of gods; they might make him fail in his examinations, or kill Father, Mother, Granny, or the baby. He picked up the box again and put back into it the sand, the leaves, and the pebbles, that were crushed, crumpled, and kicked, a minute ago. He dug a small pit at the root of a banana tree and buried the box reverently.

Ten minutes later he stood in Abu Lane, before Mani's house, and whistled twice or thrice. Mani did not appear. Swaminathan climbed the steps and knocked on the door. As the door-chain clanked inside, he stood in suspense. He was afraid he might not be able to explain his presence if anyone other than Mani should open the door. The door opened, and his heart sank. A big man with bushy eyebrows stood before him. 'Who are you?' he asked.

'Who are you? Where is Mani?' Swaminathan asked. This was intended to convey that he had come to see Mani but was quite surprised to meet this other person, and would like to know who it was, whom he had the pleasure of seeing before him. But in his confusion, he could not put this sentiment in better form.

'You ask me who I am in my own house?' bellowed the Bushy-Eyebrows. Swaminathan turned and jumped down the steps to flee. But the Bushy-Eyebrows ordered: 'Come here, little man.' It was impossible to disobey this command. Swaminathan slowly advanced up the steps, his eyes bulging with terror. The Bushy-Eyebrows said: 'Why do you run away? If you have come to see Mani, why don't you see him?' This was logic absolute.

'Never mind,' Swaminathan said irrelevantly.

'Go in and see him, little man.'

Swaminathan meekly entered the house. Mani was standing behind the door, tame and unimpressive in his domestic setting. He and Swaminathan stood staring at each other, neither of them uttering a single word. The Bushy-Eyebrows was standing in the doorway with his back to them, watching the street. Swaminathan pointed a timid finger and jerked his head questioningly. Mani whispered: 'Uncle.' The uncle suddenly turned round and said:

'Why do you stand staring at each other? Did you come for that?
Wag your tongues, boys.' After this advice he stepped into the street
to drive away two dogs that came and rolled in front of the house,
locked in a terrible fight. He was now out of earshot. Swaminathan
said: 'Your uncle? I never knew. I say, Mani, can't you come out
now? . . . No? . . . I came on urgent business. Give me—urgent—six
pies—got to have it—coachman goes away for weeks—may not get
the chance again—don't know what to do without hoop. . . .' He
paused. Mani's uncle was circling round the dogs, swearing at them
and madly searching for stones. Swaminathan continued: 'My life
depends on it. If you don't give it, I am undone. Quick, get the money.'

'I have no money, nobody gives me money,' Mani replied.

Swaminathan felt lost. 'Where does your uncle keep his money?
Look into that box . . . .'

'I don't know.'

'Mani, come here,' his uncle cried from the street, 'drive away
these devils. Get me a stone.'

'Rajam, can you lend me a policeman?' Swaminathan asked two
weeks later.

'Policeman! Why?'

'There is a rascal in this town who has robbed me.' He related to
Rajam his dealings with the coachman. 'And now,' Swaminathan
said continuing his tale of woe, 'whenever he sees me, he pretends
not to recognize me. If I go to his house, I am told he is not at home,
though I can hear him cursing somebody inside. If I persist, he sends
word that he will unchain his dog and kill me.'

'Has he a dog?' asked Rajam.

'Not any that I could see.'

'Then why not rush into his house and kick him?'

'It is all very well to say that. I tremble whenever I go to see him.
There is no knowing what coachmen have in their houses. . . . He
may set his horse on me.'

'Let him, it isn't going to eat you,' said Mani.

'Isn't it? I am glad to know it. You come with me one day to tailor
Ranga and hear what he has to say about horses. They are sometimes more dangerous than even tigers,' Swaminathan said
earnestly.

'Suppose you wait one day and catch him at the gate?' Rajam
suggested.

'I have tried it. But whenever he comes out, he is on his coach. And as soon as he sees me, he takes out his long whip. I get out of his reach and shout. But what is the use? That horse simply flies! And to think that he has duped me of two annas!'

'It was six pies, wasn't it?'

'But he took from me twice again, six pies each time. . . .'

'Then it is only an anna-and-a-half,' Rajam said.

'No, Rajam, it is two annas.'

'My dear boy, twelve pies make an anna, and you have paid thrice, six pies each time; that is eighteen pies in all, one-anna-and-a- half.'

'It is a useless discussion. Who cares how many pies make an anna?' Swaminathan said.

'But in money matters, you must be precise—very well go on, Swami.'

'The coachman first took from me six pies, promising me the silver coins in two days. He dodged me for four days and demanded six more pies, saying that he had collected herbs for twelve pies. He put me off again and took from me another six pies, saying that without it the whole process would fail. And after that, every time I went to him he put me off with some excuse or other; he often complained that owing to the weather the process was going on rather slowly. And two days ago he told me that he did not know me or anything about my money. And now you know how he behaves—I don't mind the money, but I hate his boy—that dark rascal. He makes faces at me whenever he sees me, and he has threatened to empty a bucketful of drain-water on my head. One day he held up an open penknife. I want to thrash him; that will make his father give me back my two annas.'

Next day Swaminathan and Mani started for the coachman's house. Swaminathan was beginning to regret that he had ever opened the subject before his friend. The affair was growing beyond his control. And considering the interest that Rajam and Mani displayed in the affair, one could not foresee where it was going to take them all.

Rajam had formed a little plan to decoy and kidnap the coachman's son. Mani was his executive. He was to befriend the coachman's son. Swaminathan had very little part to play in the preliminary stages. His duty would cease with pointing out the coachman's house to Mani.

The coachman lived a mile from Swaminathan's house, westward, in Keelacheri, which consisted of about a dozen thatched huts and dingy hovels, smoke-tinted and evil smelling, clustering together irregularly.

They were now within a few yards of the place. Swaminathan tried a last desperate chance to stop the wheel of vengeance.

'Mani, I think the coachman's son has returned the money.'

'What!'

'I think. . . .'

'You think so, do you? Can you show it to me?'

Swaminathan pleaded: 'Leave him alone, Mani. You don't know what troubles we shall get into by tampering with that boy. . . .'

'Shut up or I will wring your neck.'

'Oh, Mani—the police—or the boy himself—he is frightful, capable of anything.' He had in his heart a great dread of the boy. And sometimes in the night would float before him a face dark, dirty and cruel, and make him shiver. It was the face of the coachman's son.

'He lives in the third house,' Swaminathan pointed out.

At the last moment Mani changed his plan and insisted upon Swaminathan's following him to the coachman's house. Swaminathan sat down in the road as a protest. But Mani was stubborn. He dragged Swaminathan along till they came before the coachman's house, and then started shouting at him.

'Mani, Mani, what is the matter?'

'You son of a donkey,' Mani roared at Swaminathan and swung his hand to strike him.

Swaminathan began to cry. Mani attempted to strangle him. A motley crowd gathered round them, urchins with prodigious bellies, women of dark aspect, and their men. Scurvy chickens cackled and ran hither and thither. The sun was unsparing. Two or three mongrels lay in the shade of a tree and snored. A general malodour of hencoop and unwashed clothes pervaded the place.

And now from the hovel that Swaminathan had pointed out as the coachman's, emerged a little man of three feet or so, ill-clad and unwashed. He pushed his way through the crowd and, securing a fine place, sucked his thumb and watched the fight in rapture. Mani addressed the crowd indignantly, pointing at Swaminathan: 'This urchin, I don't know who he is, all of a sudden demands two annas from me. I have never seen him before. He says I owe him that money.' Mani continued in this strain for fifteen minutes. At the end of it, the coachman's son took the thumb out of his mouth and remarked: 'He must be sent to the gaol.' At this Mani bestowed an approving smile upon him and asked: 'Will you help me to carry him to the police station?'

'No,' said the coachman's son, being afraid of police stations himself.

Mani asked: 'How do you know that he must be taken to the police station?'

'I know it.'

'Does he ever trouble you similarly?' asked Mani.

'No,' said the boy.

'Where is the two annas that your father took from me?' asked Swaminathan, turning to the boy his tear-drenched face. The crowd had meanwhile melted, after making half-hearted attempts to bring peace. Mani asked the boy suddenly: 'Do you want this top?' He held a shining red top. The boy put out his hand for the top.

Mani said: 'I can't give you this. If you come with me, I will give you a bigger one. Let us become friends.'

The boy had no objection. 'Won't you let me see it?' he asked. Mani gave it to him. The boy turned it in his hand twice or thrice and in the twinkling of an eye disappeared from the place. Mani took time to grasp the situation. When he did grasp it, he saw the boy entering a hovel far off. He started after him.

When Mani reached the hovel, the door was closed. Mani knocked a dozen times, before a surly man appeared and said that the boy was not there. The door was shut again. Mani started knocking again. Two or three menacing neighbours came round and threatened to bury him alive if he dared to trouble them in their own locality. Swaminathan was desperately appealing to Mani to come away. But it took a great deal more to move him. He went on knocking.

The neighbours took up their position a few yards off, with handfuls of stones, and woke the dogs sleeping under the tree.

It was only when the dogs came bouncing towards them that Mani shouted: 'Run,' to Swaminathan, and set an example himself.

A couple of stones hit Swaminathan on the back. One or two hit Mani also. A sharp stone skinned Mani's right heel. They became blind and insensible to everything except the stretch of road before them.

BACHELOR OF ARTS

Editor's note: This is the finest Indian novel in English written about the growing up of a young man into adulthood. Chandran, son of reasonably well-to-do parents, graduates from college, is not quite sure what he should do next—perhaps go to England, which is what affluent young people did in those days—but suddenly falls in love. This excerpt deals with the progress of Chandran's love and his parents' dismay when they come to know about it. There is enough autobiography here to make the episode particularly poignant.

It was on one of his river ramblings that he met Malathi and thought that he would not have room for anything else in his mind. No one can explain the attraction between two human beings. It happens.

One evening he came to the river, and was loafing along it when he saw a girl, about fifteen years old, playing with her younger sister on the sands. Chandran had been in the habit of staring at every girl who sat on the sand, but he had never felt before the acute interest he felt in this girl now. He liked the way she sat; he liked the way she played with her sister; he liked the way she dug her hands into the sand and threw it in the air. He paused only for a moment to observe the girl. He would have willingly settled there and spent the rest of his life watching her dig her hands into the sand. But that could not be done. There were a lot of people about.

He passed on. He went forward a few paces and wanted to turn back and take another look at the girl. But that could not be done. He felt that the scores of persons squatting on the sand were all watching him.

He went on his usual walk down to Nallappa's Grove, crossed the river, went up the opposite bank, and away into the fields there; but he caught himself more than once thinking of the girl. How old was she? Probably thirteen. Might be even fifteen or sixteen. If she was more than fourteen she must be married. There was a touch of despair in this thought. What was the use of thinking of a married girl? It would be very improper. He tried to force his mind to think of other things. He tried to engage it in his favourite subject—his trip to England in the coming year. If he was going to England how was he to dress himself? He had better get used to tie and shoes and coat and hat and knife and fork. He would get a first-class degree in England and come back and marry. What was the use of thinking of a married girl? Probably she was not married. Her parents were very likely rational and modern, people who abhorred the custom of rushing a young child into marriage. He tried to analyse why he was thinking of her. Why did he think of her so much? Was it her looks? Was she so good-looking as all that? Who could say? He hadn't noticed her before. Then how could he say that she was the most beautiful girl in the world? When did he say that? Didn't he? If not, why was he thinking of her so much? Chandran was puzzled, greatly puzzled by the whole thing.

He wondered next what her name might be. She looked like one with the name of Lakshmi. Quite a beautiful name, the name of the Goddess of Wealth, the spouse of God Vishnu, who was the Protector of Creatures.

That night he went home very preoccupied. It was at five o'clock that he had met her, and at nine he was still thinking of her.

After dinner he did not squat on the carpet in the hall, but preferred to go to his room and remain alone there. He tried to read a little; he was in the middle of Wells's *Tono Bungay*. He had found the book gripping, but now he felt it was obtrusive. He was irritated. He put away the book and sat staring at the wall. He presently realized that darkness would be more soothing. He blew out the lamp and sat in his chair. Suppose, though unmarried, she belonged to some other caste? A marriage would not be tolerated even between sub-sects of the same caste. If India was to attain salvation these watertight divisions must go—Community, Caste, Sects, Sub-sects, and still further divisions. He felt very indignant. He would set an example himself by marrying this girl whatever her caste or sect might be.

The next day he shaved with great care and paid a great deal of attention to his hair, and awaited the evening. When evening came he put on his chocolate-coloured tweed coat and started out. At five he was on the river-bank, squatting on the sand near the spot where he had seen the girl the previous day. He sat there for over two hours. The girl did not come. Dozens of other townspeople came to the river and sprawled all over the place, but not that girl. Chandran rose and walked along, peering furtively at every group. It was a very keen search, but it brought forth nothing. Why wasn't she there? His heart beat fast at the sight of every figure that approached the river clad in a sari. It was seven-forty-five when he set his face homeward, feeling that his brilliantine, shave, ironed tweed coat, were all wasted.

The next day he again went to the river and again waited till seven-forty-five in the evening, and went home dispirited. He tossed in bed all night. In moments of half-wakefulness he whispered the word 'Lakshmi', 'Lakshmi'. He suddenly pulled himself up and laughed at himself: it looked as if the girl had paid a first and last visit to the river, and it seemed more than likely that she belonged to another caste, and was married. What a fool he was to go on thinking of her night and day for three whole days. It was a ridiculous obsession. His sobriety ought to assert itself now. An idle brain was the devil's workshop. Too true. A brain given rest for over nine months brought one to this state.

He rose in the morning with a haggard face. His mother asked him if he was not well. Chandran felt that some explanation was due and said he had a terrible headache. His mother, standing two inches shorter than he, put out her hands, stroked his temples, gave him special coffee, and advised him to stay at home the whole day. Chandran felt that nothing could be better than that. He decided not to shave or comb his hair or wear a coat and go out. For he feared that if he went out he might be tempted to go on the foolish quest.

He stayed in his room all day. His father came in at mid-day and kept him company. He sat in the chair and talked of this and that. Chandran all of a sudden realized that he had better leave Malgudi. That would solve the problem.

'Father, will you let me go to Madras?'

'By all means, if you'd like a change.'

'I suppose it will be very hot there?'

'Must be. The saying is that Madras is hot for ten months in the year and hotter for two.'

'Then I don't want to go and fry myself there,' said Chandran.

'Try some other place. You can go to your aunt at Bangalore.'

'No, no. She will keep telling me what jewels she has got for her daughter. I can't stand her.' He decided that he would stay in the best place on earth, home.

Mother came in at about three o'clock to ask how he was feeling. Seenu came in at four-thirty, as soon as school was over, and stood near Chandran's bed, staring at him silently.

'What is it?' Chandran asked.

'Nothing. Why are you in bed?'

'Never mind why. What is the news in the school?'

'We are playing against the Y.M.U. on Saturday. After that we are meeting the Board School Eleven. What we can't understand is why the captain has left out Mohideen. He is bound to have a lot of trouble over that. People are prepared to take it up to the headmaster.'

He could not stay in bed beyond six-thirty. He got up, opened all the windows, washed his face, combed his hair, put on a coat (not the tweed one), and went out. What he needed, he told himself, was plenty of fresh air and exercise and things to think about. Since he wanted exercise he decided to avoid the riverside. The place, he persuaded himself, was stale and crowded. He wished today to take a walk at the very opposite end of the town, the Trunk Road. He walked a mile along the Trunk Road and turned back. He hurried back across Lawley Extension, Market Road, and the North Street, and reached the river. It was dark and most people had gone home.

Chandran saw her at the river-bank next evening. She was wearing a green sari, and playing with her little companion. Chandran saw her from a distance and went towards her as if drawn by a rope. But, on approaching her, his courage failed him, and he walked away in the opposite direction. Presently he stopped and blamed himself for wasting a good opportunity of making his person familiar to her; he turned once again with the intention of passing before her closely, slowly, and deliberately. At a distance he could look at her, but when he came close he felt self-conscious and awkward, and while passing actually in front of her he bent his head, fixed his gaze on the ground, and walked fast. He was away, many yards away, from her in a moment. He checked his pace once again and looked back for a fraction of a second, and was quite thrilled at the sight of the green sari in the distance. He did not dare to look longer; for he was obsessed with the feeling that he was being observed by the whole crowd on the river-bank. . . . He hoped that she had observed him. He hoped that she had noted his ironed coat. He stood there and debated with himself whether she had seen him or not. One part of him said that she could not have observed him, because he had walked very fast and because there were a lot of people passing and repassing on the sand. Chandran steadily discouraged this sceptical half of his mind, and lent his whole-hearted support to the other half, which was saying that just as he had noticed her in a crowd she was sure to have noticed him. Destiny always worked that way. His well-ironed chocolate tweed was sure to invite notice. He hoped that he didn't walk clumsily in front of her. He again told himself she must have noticed that he was not like the rest of the crowd. And so why would he not now go and occupy a place that would be close to her and in the direct line of her vision? Staring was half the victory in love. His sceptical half now said that by this procedure he might scare her off the river for ever; but, said the other half, tomorrow she may not come to the river at all, and if you don't start an eye friendship immediately, you may not get the opportunity again for a million years. . . . He was engaged in this internal controversy when he received a slap on the back and saw Veeraswami and Mohan, his old classmates, behind him.

'How are you, Chandran? It seems years since we met.'

'We met only last March, less than a year, you know,' said Chandran.

Mohan asked: 'Chandran, do you remember the evening we spent in your room, reading poetry?'

'Yes, yes. What have you done with your poems?'

'They are still with me.'

Chandran felt all his courtesy exhausted. He was not keen on reunions just then. He tried to get away. But Veeraswami would not let him go: 'A year since we met. I have been dying to see an old classmate, and you want to cut me! Won't you come and have a little coffee with us in some restaurant?' He locked his arm in Chandran's and dragged him along. Chandran tried to resist, and then said: 'Let us go this way. I promised to meet somebody. I must see if he is there. . . .' He pointed down the river, past the spot of green sari. They went in that direction. Mohan inquired three times what Chandran was doing and received no reply; Veeraswami was talking without a pause. Chandran pretended to listen to him, but constantly turned his head to his left and stole glances at something there; he had to do this without being noticed by his friends. Finally, when he passed before her, he looked at her for so short a space of time that she appeared only as a passing green blur. . . . Before leaving the river-bank he looked back twice only. He heartily disliked his companions.

'What are you doing now, Chandran?' Mohan asked, undefeated.

'Nothing at present. I am going to England in a few months.'

At this Veeraswami started a heated discourse on the value of going to England. 'What have we to learn from the English? I don't know when this craze for going to England will stop. It is a drain on the country's resources. What have we to learn from the English?'

'I may be going there to teach them something,' said Chandran. Even granted that she had not noticed him the first time, she couldn't have helped noticing him when he passed before her again; that was why he didn't look at her fully; he didn't want to embarrass her by meeting her gaze.

'Shall we go to the "Welcome"?' Veeraswami asked.

They had now left the river and were in North Street.

'Anywhere,' Chandran said mechanically.

'You seem to be worried over something,' Veeraswami said.

'Oh, nothing. I am sorry.' Chandran pulled himself up resolutely. Here were two fellows eager for his company, and he had no business to be absorbed in distant thoughts.

'Forgive me,' he said again.

They were now before the 'Welcome Restaurant', a small, smoky building, from which the smell of sweets and burning ghee assailed the nostrils of passers-by in the street.

They sat round an oily table in the dark hall. Serving boys were shouting menus and bills and were dashing hither and thither. A server came and asked: 'What will you have, sir?'

'What shall we have?'

'What will you have?'

'I want only coffee.'

'Have something with it.'

'Impossible. Only coffee.'

'Bring three cups of coffee, good, strong.'

Chandran asked: 'What are you doing, Mohan? Did you get through?'

'No. I failed, and my uncle cut me. I am now the Malgudi correspondent of the *Daily Messenger* of Madras. They have given me the whole district. They pay me three-eight per column of twenty-one inches.'

'Are you making much money?'

'Sometimes fifty, sometimes ten. It all depends on those rascals, mad fellows. Sometimes they cut everything that I send.'

'It is a moderate paper,' Veeraswami said jeeringly.

'I am not concerned with their policy,' Mohan said.

'What are you doing?' Chandran asked, turning to Veeraswami.

'It will take a whole day for me to tell you. I am starting a movement called the Resurrection Brigade. I am touring about a lot on that business.'

'What is the brigade?'

'It is only an attempt to prepare the country for revolution. Montagu-Chelmsford Reform. Simon Report, and what-not, are all a fraud. Our politicians, including the Congressmen, are playing into the hands of the Imperialists. The Civil Disobedience Movement is a childish business. Our brigade will gain the salvation of our country by an original method. Will you join it? Mohan is already a member.'

Chandran promised to think it over, and asked what they expected Mohan to do for the movement.

'Everything. We want everybody there, poets, philosophers, musicians, sculptors, and swordsmen.'

'What is its strength now?'

'About twenty-five have so far signed the brigade pledge. I expect that in two years we shall have a membership of fifty thousand in South India alone.'

They finished their coffee and rose. They went back to the river, smoked cigarettes, and talked all the evening. Before parting, Chandran promised to see them again and asked them where they lived.

'I am staying with Mohan,' said Veeraswami.

'Where do you live, Mohan?'

'Room 14, Modern Indian Lodge, Mill Street.'

'Right. I shall drop in some time,' said Chandran.

'I won't be in town after Tuesday. I am going into the country for six months,' said Veeraswami.

Chandran realized that friends and acquaintances were likely to prove a nuisance to him by the river. He decided to cut every one hereafter. With this resolution he went to the Sarayu bank next evening. He also decided to be very bold, and indifferent to the public's observation and criticism.

She was there with her little companion.

Chandran went straight to a spot just thirty yards from where she sat, and settled down there. He had determined to stare at her this evening. He might even throw in an elegant wink or smile. He was going to stare at her and take in a lot of details regarding her features. He had not made out yet whether she was fair or light brown; whether she had long hair or short, and whether her eyes were round or almond-shaped; and he had also some doubts about her nose.

He sat at this thirty yards' range and kept throwing at her a side glance every fifth second. He noticed that she played a great deal with her little companion. He wanted to go to her and ask whether the little companion was her sister or cousin and how old she was. But he abandoned the idea. A man of twenty-two going up and conversing with a grown-up girl, a perfect stranger, would be affording a very uncommon sight to the public.

This optical communion became a daily habit. His powers of observation and deduction increased tremendously. He gathered several facts about the girl. She wore a dark sari and a green sari alternately. She came to the river chiefly for the sake of her little companion. She was invariably absent on Fridays and came late on Wednesdays. Chandran concluded from this that the girl went to the temple on Friday evenings, and was delayed by a music master or a stitching master on Wednesdays. He further gathered that she was of a religious disposition, and was accomplished in the art of music or embroidery. From her regularity he concluded that she was a person of very systematic habits. The fact that she played with her young companion showed that she had a loving disposition. He concluded that she had no brother, since not a single soul escorted her on any evening. Encouraged by this conclusion, he wondered if he should not stop her and talk to her when she rose to go home. He might even accompany her to her house. That might become a beautiful habit. What wonderful things he would have to say to her. When the traffic of the town had died, they could walk together under the moon or in magic starlight. He would stop a few yards from her house. What a parting of sweetness and pain. . . ! It must be noted that in this dream the young companion did not exist, or, if she did, she came to the river and went home all by herself.

An evening of this optical fulfilment filled him with tranquillity. He left the river and went home late in the evening, meditating on God, and praying to Him with concentration that He would bless this romance with success. All night he repeated her name, 'Lakshmi', and fervently hoped that her soul heard his call through the night.

He had lived for over a month in a state of bliss, notwithstanding his ignorance. He began to feel now that he ought to be up and doing and get a little more practical. He could not go on staring at her on the sands all his life. He must know all about her.

He followed her at a distance of about half a furlong on a dark evening when she returned home from the river. He saw her enter a house in Mill Street. He paced before the house slowly, twice, slowing up to see if there was any board before the house. There was none.

He remembered suddenly that Mohan lived in Mill Street. Room number 14, Modern Indian Lodge, he had said. He went up and down the street in search of the hotel. At last he found it was the building opposite the girl's house. There was a signboard, but that could not be seen in the dark. Room number 14 was half a cubicle on the staircase landing. The cubicle was divided by a high wooden partition into Room 14 and Room 15.

Mohan was delighted to receive Chandran.

'Is Veeraswami gone?' Chandran asked.

'Weeks ago,' replied Mohan.

There was not a single table or chair in the room. Mohan lived on a striped carpet spread on the floor. He sat on it reclining against the wooden partition. There was a yellow trunk in a corner of the room, on which a shining nickel flower-vase was kept with some paper flowers in it. The room received its light and ventilation from the single window in Room 15, over the wooden partition. A bright gas lamp hung over the wooden partition and shed its greenish glare impartially on Room 14 and Room 15.

'Would you believe it? I have never been in this street before,' said Chandran.

'Indeed! But why should you come here? You live at the south end while this is the east end of the town.'

'I like this street,' Chandran said. 'I wonder why this is called Mill Street. Are all the people that live here mill-owners?'

'Nothing of the kind. Years ago there were two weaving mills at the end of the street. There are all sorts of people here.'

'Oh. Any particularly important person?'

'None that I can think of.'

It was on Chandran's lips, at this point, to ask who lived in the opposite house. But he merely said that he wished to meet his friend oftener in his room.

'I go out news-hunting at ten in the morning and return at about four, after posting my letters. I do not usually go out after that. You can come any time you please,' said Mohan.

'Have you no holidays?'

'On Sundays we have no paper. And so on Saturday I have a holiday. I spend the whole day in the room. Please do come any time you like, and as often as you like.'

'Thanks, thanks. I have absolutely no company. I shall be delighted to come here frequently.'

Through Mohan's co-operation Chandran learnt that his sweetheart's name was Malathi, that she was unmarried, and that she was the daughter of Mr D.W. Krishna Iyer, Head Clerk in the Executive Engineer's office.

The suffix to the name of the girl's father was a comforting indication that he was of the same caste and sub-caste as Chandran. Chandran shuddered at the thought of all the complications that he would have had to face if the gentleman had been Krishna Iyengar, or Krishna Rao, or Krishna Mudaliar. His father would certainly cast him off if he tried to marry out of caste.

Chandran took it all as a favourable sign, as an answer to his prayers, which were growing intenser every day. In each fact, that Mohan lived in the hotel opposite her house, that she was unmarried, that her father was an 'Iyer', Chandran felt that God was revealing Himself.

Chandran prayed to God to give him courage, and went to his father to talk to him about his marriage. His courage failed him at the last moment, and he went away after discussing some fatuous subject. The next day he again went to his father with the same resolution and again lapsed into fatuity. He went back to his room and regretted his cowardice. He would be unworthy of Malathi if he was going to be such a spineless worm. Afraid of a father! He was not a baby asking for a toy, but a full-grown adult out on serious business, very serious business. It was very doubtful if a squirming coward would be any good to Malathi as a husband.

He went back to his father, who was on the veranda reading something. Mother had gone out to see some friends; Seenu had gone to school. This was the best time to talk to Father confidentially.

Father put down the book on seeing Chandran, and pulled the spectacles from over his nose. Chandran drew a chair close to Father's easy chair.

'Have you read this book, Chandran?'

Chandran looked at it—some old novel, Dickens. 'No.' At

another time he would have added, 'I hate Dickens' laborious humour,' and involved himself in a debate. But now he merely said, 'I will try to read it later.' He did not want to throw away precious time in literary discussions.

'Father, please don't mistake me. I want to marry D.W. Krishna Iyer's daughter.'

Father put on his spectacles and looked at his son with a frown. He sat up and asked: 'Who is he?'

'Head Clerk in the Executive Engineer's office.'

'Why do you want to marry his daughter?'

'I like her.'

'Do you know the girl?'

'Yes. I have seen her often.'

'Where?'

Chandran told him.

'Have you spoken to each other?'

'No. . . .'

'Does she know you?'

'I don't know.'

Father laughed, and it cut into Chandran's soul.

Father asked: 'In that case why this girl alone and not any other?'

Chandran said: 'I like her,' and left Father's company abruptly as Father said: 'I don't know anything about these things. I must speak to your mother.'

Later Mother came into Chandran's room and asked, 'What is all this?' Chandran answered with an insolent silence.

'Who is this girl?' There was great anxiety in her voice.

Chandran told her. She was very disappointed. A Head Clerk's daughter was not what she had hoped to get for her son. 'Chandar, why won't you consider any of the dozens of girls that have been proposed to you?'

Chandran rejected this suggestion indignantly.

'But suppose those girls are richer and more beautiful?'

'I don't care. I shall marry this girl and no one else.'

'But how are you sure they are prepared to give their daughter to you?'

'They will have to.'

'Extraordinary! Do you think marriage is a child's game? We don't know anything about them, who they are, what they are, what they are worth, if the stars and the other things about the girl are all right, and above all, whether they are prepared to marry their girl at all. . . .'

'They will have to. I hear that this season she will be married because she is getting on for sixteen.'

'Sixteen!' Mother screamed. 'They can't be all right if they have kept the girl unmarried till sixteen. She must have attained puberty ages ago. They can't be all right. We have a face to keep in this town. Do you think it is all child's play?' She left the room in a temper.

In a few days this hostility had to be abandoned, because Chandran's parents could not bear for long the sight of an unhappy Chandran. For his sake they were prepared to compromise to this extent: they were prepared to consider the proposal if it came from the other side. Whatever happened they would not take the initiative in the matter; for they belonged to the bridegroom's side, and according to time-honoured practice it was the bride's people who proposed first. Anything done contrary to this would make them the laughing-stock of the community.

Chandran raved: 'To the dust-pot with your silly customs.'

But his mother replied that she at any rate belonged to a generation which was in no way worse than the present one for all its observances; and as long as she lived she would insist on respecting the old customs. Ordinary talk at home was becoming rarer every day. It was always a debate on Custom and Reason. His father usually remained quiet during these debates. One of the major mysteries in life for Chandran at this period was the question as to which side his father favoured. He did not appear to place active obstacles in Chandran's way, but he did little else. He appeared to distrust his own wisdom in these matters and to have handed the full rein to his wife. Chandran once or twice tried to sound him and gain him to his side; but he was evasive and noncommittal.

Chandran's only support and consolation at this juncture was Mohan. To his room he went every night after dinner. This visit was not entirely from an unmixed motive. While on his way he could tarry for a while before her house and gladden his heart with a sight of her under the hall-lamp as she passed from one part of the house to another. Probably she was going to bed; blessed be those pillows. Or probably she went in and read; ah, blessed books with the touch of her hands on them. He would often speculate what hour she would go to bed, what hour she would rise, and how she lay down and slept and how her bed looked. Could he not just dash into the house, hide in the passage, steal up to her bed at night, crush her in his arms, and carry her away?

If it happened to be late, and the lights in the house were put out, he would walk distractedly up and down before the house, and then go to Room 14 of the Modern Indian Lodge.

Mohan would put away whatever poem he was writing. But for him Chandran would have been shrivelled up by the heat of a hopeless love. Mohan would put away his pad, and clear a space on the carpet for Chandran.

Chandran would give him the latest bulletin from the battle front, and then pass on to a discussion of theories.

'If the girl's father were called something other than a Head Clerk, and given a hundred more to his pay, I am sure your parents would move heaven and earth to secure this alliance,' said the poet.

'Why should we be cudgelled and nose-led by our elders?' Chandran asked indignantly. 'Why can't we be allowed to arrange our lives as we please? Why can't they leave us to rise or sink on our own ideals?'

These were mighty questions; and the poet tackled them in his own way. 'Money is the greatest god in life. Father and mother and brother do not care for anything but your money. Give them money and they will leave you alone. I am just writing a few lines entitled "Moneylove". It is free verse. You must hear it. I have dedicated it to you.' Mohan picked up the pad and read:

> The parents love you, you thought.
> No, no, not you, my dear.
> They've loved nothing less for its own sake.
> They fed you and petted you and pampered you
> Because some day they hope you will bring them money;
> Much money, so much and more and still more;
> Because some day, they hope, you'll earn a
> Bride who'll bring much money, so much and
> More and still more. . . .

There were two more stanzas in the same strain. It brought the tears to Chandran's eyes. He hated his father and mother. He took this poem with him when he went home.

He gave it to his father next day. Father read through it twice and asked with a dry smile: 'Did you write this?'

'Never mind the authorship,' Chandran said.

'Do you believe what these lines say?'

'I do,' said Chandran, and did not stay there for further talk.

When he was gone Father explained the poem to Mother, who began to cry. Father calmed her and said: 'This is what he seems to feel. I don't know what to do.'

'We have promised to consider it if it is made from that side. What more can we do?'

'I don't know.'

'They seem to be thorough rogues. The marriage season has already begun. Why can't they approach us? They expect Chandran to go to them, touch their feet, and beg them for their girl.'

'They probably do not know that Chandran is available,' said Father.

'Why do you defend them? They can't be ignorant of the existence of a possible bridegroom like Chandran. That man, the girl's father, seems to be a deep man. He is playing a deep game. He is waiting for our boy to go to him, when he can get a good husband for his daughter without giving a dowry and without an expensive wedding. . . . This boy Chandra is talking nonsense. This is what we get from our children for all our troubles. . . . I am in a mood to let him do anything he likes. . . . But what more can we do? I shall drown myself in Sarayu before I allow any proposal to go from here.'

DARK ROOM

Editor's note: The only novel of Narayan which has a touch of social consciousness for its background. Savitri, a traditional Hindu wife, married to the dashing execu- tive, Ramani, puts up with many of the tantrums of her temperamental husband, but when it becomes too much for her, she takes refuge in the 'the dark room', a room not used for any purpose except to store things. But Mother going into the dark room is a big trauma for the children and an indication that something is wrong between the elders.

In the month of September the streets rang with the cries of haw- kers selling dolls— the earliest intimation of the coming Navaratri festival.

'Mother, aren't we buying some dolls this year for the festival?'

'What's the use of buying them year after year; where are we to keep them?'

'In the next house they have bought for ten rupees a pair of Rama and Sita, each image as large as a real child.'

'We have as many as we can manage. Why should we buy any more?'

'Mother, you must buy some new dolls.'

'We have already three casks full of dolls and toys.'

A day before the festival the casks were brought into the hall from an obscure storing-place in the house. Ranga had now a lot of work to do. It was an agreeable change for him from the monotony of sweeping, washing clothes, and running errands. He enjoyed this work. He expressed his gay mood by tying a preposterous turban round his head with his towel and tucking up his dhoti.

'Oh, look at Ranga's turban!' screamed Kamala.

'Hey, you look like a cow,' added Sumati.

'Do I?' Ranga bellowed like a cow, and sent the children into fits of laughter.

'Don't waste time in playing. Open the casks and take out the dolls,' said Savitri.

Ranga untied the ropes and brought out the dolls in their yel- lowing newspaper wrappings. 'Handle them carefully, they may break.' In a short while dust and sheets of old newspaper, startled cockroaches and silverfish, were all in a heap on one side of Ranga, and, on the other, all the unwrapped dolls. Most of them had been given to Savitri by her mother, and the rest bought by her at various times. There they were—dolls, images, and toys of all colours, sizes, and shapes; soldiers, guards, and fat merchants; birds, beasts, and toys; gods and demons; fruits and cooking utensils; everything of clay, metal, wood, and cloth.

Ranga in his preposterous turban, stooping into the casks and bringing out the dolls, looked like an intoxicated conjurer giving a wild performance. The children waited, breathlessly watching for the next item, and shrieked at his absurd comments: 'Ah, here is my friend the parrot. He pecks at my flesh.' He would suck the blood on his finger and vow to break the parrot's beak before the end of the festival. He would hurriedly take out and put down a merchant or a grass-seller, complaining that they were uttering terrible swear-words and that he couldn't hold them. He would pretend to put the toy foods into his mouth and munch them with great satisfaction. Or he would scream at the sight of a cobra or a tiger. It was pure drama.

Savitri squatted down and wiped the dust off the dolls, and odd memories of her childhood stirred in her. Her eyes fell on a wooden rattle with the colour coming away in flakes, with which she had played when she was just a few months old. So her mother had told her. There was a toy flute into which she had wasted her babyhood breath. Savitri felt a sudden inexplicable self-pity at the thought of herself as an infant. She next felt an intense admiration for her mother, who never let even the slightest toy be lost but preserved everything carefully, and brought it all out for the Navaratri display. Savitri had a sudden longing to be back in her mother's house. She charged herself with neglecting her mother and not writing to her for several months now. . . . How frightfully she (Savitri) and her sister used to quarrel over these dolls and their arrangements! She remembered a particular Navaratri which was completely ruined because she and her sister had scratched each other's faces and were not on speaking terms. Poor girl ! Who would have dreamt that she would grow into a bulky matron, with a doctor husband and seven children, away from everybody in Burma? That reminded her, she had not answered her letters received a month ago; positively, next Thursday she would write so as to catch the Friday's steamer.

Now Ranga had put down a rosy-cheeked, auburn-haired doll which was eloquent with memories of her father. She remembered the evening when he had awakened her and given her the cardboard box containing this doll. How she adored this cardboard box and the doll and secretly used to thrust cooked rice into its mouth and steal sugar for it ! Poor Father, so decrepit now. . . !

A crash broke this reverie. Ranga had dropped a bluish elephant, as large as an ordinary cat.

'You ass, did you fall asleep?'

'Oh, it is broken!' wailed Sumati.

'Make him buy a new one, Mother. Don't give him his pay,' suggested Kamala.

Savitri felt very unhappy over the broken elephant: it was one of a pair that her mother had got from *her* mother, and it had been given to Savitri with special admonitions, and not to her sister, because she could not be depended upon to be so careful, and Savitri's mother had been very reluctant to separate the pair. . . .

'I told you to be careful,' Savitri said, 'and yet, you ass—'

Ranga picked up the broken elephant. 'Oh, madam, only its trunk is broken,' he announced gleefully.

'What is left of an elephant when its trunk is gone?' Savitri asked mournfully.

Ranga stood examining the trunkless elephant and said: 'It looks like a buffalo now. Why not have it in the show as a buffalo, madam?'

'Fool, stop your jokes.'

'He doesn't care a bit!' Kamala said, horrified.

Ranga said to Kamala, 'Little madam, I know now how buffaloes are made.'

'How?' asked Kamala, suddenly interested.

'By breaking off the trunks of elephants,' said Ranga. Then he said, 'Allow me to take this home, madam.'

'Impossible,' said Kamala. 'Mother, don't let him take it. Tell him he must pay for it.'

'It is broken. Why do you want it?' Savitri asked.

'My little boy will tie a string round its neck, drag it about, and call it his dog. He has been worrying me to get him a dog for a long time.'

Kamala said, 'You won't get it,' and snatched the elephant from his hand.

Now all the dolls and toys were there, over five hundred of them, all in a jumble, like the creations of an eccentric God who had not yet created a world.

Babu had given definite instructions that the arrangement of the platform for the dolls was to be left entirely to him, and they were to do nothing till he returned from school. The girls were impatient.

'It is not a boy's business. This is entirely our affair. Why should we wait for him?'

Babu burst in at five o'clock and asked, looking about impatiently, 'Have you put up the platforms yet?'

'No, we are waiting for you. There is no hurry. Eat your tiffin and come,' said Savitri.

In two minutes he was ready to do his work. The girls jeered: 'Are you a girl to take a hand in the doll business? Go and play cricket. You are a man.'

'Shut up, or I will break all the dolls,' he said, at which the girls screamed. Babu hectored Ranga and sent him spinning about on errands. With about eight narrow long planks, resting on raised supports at the ends, he constructed graduated step-like platforms. He pulled out of the rolls of bedding in the house all the white bedsheets and spread them on the planks; he disturbed all the objects in the house and confiscated all the kerosene tins and stools, etc., for constructing supports for the planks. He brought in bamboo poles and built a pavilion round the platform. He cut up strips of coloured paper and pasted them round the bamboo poles and covered their nakedness. He filled the whole pavilion with resplendent hangings and decorations. He did his work with concentration, while the two girls sat down and watched him, not daring to make the slightest comment; for at the slightest word Babu barked and menaced the speaker. He gave Ranga no time to regale the company with his jokes, but kept him standing on a high table in order to execute decorations on the pavilion roof.

In a couple of hours a gorgeous setting was ready for the dolls. Babu surveyed his work from a distance and said to his mother, 'You can arrange your knick-knacks now.' He turned to his sisters and said, 'Move carefully within the pavilion. If I find you up to some mischief, tearing the decorations or disturbing the platforms, you will drive me to a desperate act.'

Savitri said to the girls, pointing to the pavilion, 'Could you have made a thing like this? You prated so much when he began the work.' Sumati was a little apologetic and appreciative, but Kamala said, 'If you had given me a little paste and paper I too could have done it. It is not a great feat.' Savitri said, 'Now lift the dolls carefully and arrange them one by one. Sumati, since you are taller than Kamala you will arrange the dolls on the first four platforms and, Kamala, you will do it on the lower four platforms. Don't break anything, and don't fight.'

In an hour a fantastic world was raised: a world inhabited by all

God's creations that the human mind had counted; creatures in all gay colours and absurd proportions and grotesque companies. There were green parrots which stood taller than the elephants beside them; there were horses of yellow and white and green colours dwarfed beside painted brinjals; there was a finger-sized Turkish soldier with not a bit of equipment missing; the fat, round-bellied merchant, wearing a coat on his bare body, squatted there, a picture of contentment, gazing at his cereals before him, unmindful of the company of a curly-tailed dog of porcelain on one side and a grimacing tiger on the other. Here and there out of the company of animals and vegetables and mortals emerged the gods—the great indigo-blue Rama, holding his mighty bow in one hand, and with his spouse, Sita, by his side, their serenity unaffected by the company about them, consisting of a lacquered wooden spoon, a very tiny celluloid doll clothed in a pink sari, a sly fox with a stolen goose in its mouth, and a balancing acrobat in leaf-green breeches; there stood the great Krishna trampling to death the demon serpent Kalinga, undistracted by the leer of a teddy-bear which could beat a drum. Mortals and immortals, animals and vegetables, gods and sly foxes, acrobats and bears, warriors and cooking utensils, were all the same here, in this fantastic universe conjured out of coloured paper, wood, and doll-maker's clay.

'It is all very well now, but the trouble will be in putting them all back carefully after nine days, in their casks. It is the most tedious work one could think of,' said Savitri.

'Mother, don't dismantle them again. Why can't we let them stay out for ever? It is always so terribly dull when the decorations are torn down and the dolls are returned to the casks.'

Next morning Babu took a look at his work and decided to improve it. It was very well as far as gum and paper could go, but the lighting was defective. All the illumination that the pavilion got was from the bulb hanging a few yards from it in the hall. He would get his friend Chandru in, and fix up a festoon of ornamental coloured bulbs under the pavilion arch; he would transform the doll pavilion into something unique in the whole of Extension.

He brought Chandru in the afternoon. Chandru was very much his senior, but Babu spent much of his time with him. Chandru was studying in the Intermediate and had a genius for electricity. He had made miniature dynamos, electric bells, and telegraph sets.

Sumati and Kamala were delighted. 'It is going to beat the pavilion in the Police Inspector's house,' they said ecstatically. Chandru worked wonders with a piece of wire and a spanner. In a short while he had created a new circuit with an independent switch. When the switch was put on, a festoon of coloured bulbs twinkled in the archway and two powerful bulbs flooded all the dolls with a bluish light.

'When you switch on in the evening, do it very carefully,' warned Chandru, and left.

It was a great triumph for Babu. He felt very proud of being responsible for the illumination. 'If you like I will ask him to come and add an electric train to the dolls. That will be wonderful,' he said.

At five o'clock the two girls worried Babu to put the lights on. He told them he knew the right time to do it and warned them not to go near the switch. 'Lighting at six,' he said.

'We will be out at six,' they protested, 'inviting people. A lot of our friends will be coming now to invite us to their houses, and we would so love to have the illuminations at once. Please.'

'Will you leave that to me or not? I know when to do it, and I want you to mind your own business now.'

Savitri said to Babu, 'Don't be so strict. You have done everything for their sake, why should you grudge them the light now?'

'All right, at five-thirty,' said Babu.

At five-thirty nearly a dozen visitors had already arrived. Everyone wore bright silks, and sat gazing at the dolls. Finding so many ladies sitting in the hall, Babu hesitated at the door, wondering how he was to reach the switch in the pavilion. He called Sumati and said, 'With the tip of your finger push that small rod to one side, to the left. You must do it very gently.'

Sumati pushed the switch gently, then less gently, and then Babu shed his shyness and dashed to the switch. He rattled it, but nothing happened. Not only were the pavilion lights not on, but the usual hall bulbs had also gone out. Babu looked at Sumati and said, 'I knew that if I let you touch it something or other would happen.' He stood contemplating the new circuit, rattled the switch once more and said that somebody had tampered with it and that he would get at that person soon. Muttering that one couldn't plumb the depth of mischief in girls, he walked out of the hall. Nobody yet realized that anything was wrong because there was good sunlight.

At about seven-thirty the conditions were different. There was no light in the house. Visitors were received in the pale light of a hurricane lantern, and the pavilion was lit by flickering oil- lamps transferred from the puja room. The atmosphere was dim and gloomy. The sisters' rage knew no limits. 'Mother, do you understand now why we did not want any boy to come and interfere in our business? As if it wouldn't have been a pretty sight without those lights. Who wanted them anyway? We never asked him to come and fix the lights.'

Babu was in utter despair. Chandru had gone to the cinema and would not be back till nearly ten. And he had no friend who knew anything about electricity.

'Send someone to the Electric office,' said Savitri.

'Shall I go?' asked Babu.

Savitri hesitated. How could she send him out all alone so late? 'Take Ranga with you.'

And protected by Ranga's company, Babu set out to the Electric office in Market Road—a distance of about two miles.

Babu stood before the entrance to the Electric office and said to someone, 'There is no light in our house in the South Extension.'

'Go in and tell it to the people you will find there.'

Babu went in and was directed to a room in which three fellows were sitting, smoking and talking. One of them asked him, 'Who are you, boy?'

'The lights are out in our house in the South Extension.'

'Put the switches on,' somebody said, and all three laughed.

Babu felt awkward, but the light had to be set right. He pleaded: 'Can't you do something? We have tried the switches.'

'Probably the fuse has gone. Have you seen if the meter fuses are all right?'

'I haven't. There is nobody in the house.'

'Then, why do you want the lights?' If the meter fuse is burnt, it is none of our concern. We will come only when the pole fuse is burnt. Go and see if the meter fuse is all right.'

When Babu reached home he found his father had already arrived. He was in a terrible temper. Ranga's absence delayed the opening of the garage door and had infuriated him. In that state he entered the house and found it dark. Now failure of the electric current was one of the things which completely upset him. He stood in the doorway and roared, 'What is this?' Savitri let the question wither without an answer. The girls did not dare to answer. 'Is everybody in this house dead?' he asked.

Savitri was angered by this, 'What a thing to say on a day like this, and at this hour! I have seen very few who will swear and curse at auspicious times as you do.'

'Then why couldn't you have opened your precious mouth and said what the matter was?'

'There is nothing the matter. You see that there is no current and that there are no lights, and that's all that's the matter.'

'Has anybody gone to the Electric office?'

'Babu has gone there.'

'Babu, Babu, a very big man to go.'

This irrational pointless cynicism enraged Savitri, but she remained silent.

Ramani passed in to undress, grumbling all the way. Standing in the dark, he cursed the whole household and all humanity. 'Ranga! Here, Ranga!' he howled in the dark.

'I told you Ranga had gone to the Electric office with Babu,' Savitri said.

'Why should everybody go to the Electric office? Is Babu to be protected like a girl? Whose arrangement is it?' He raved, 'Bring some light, somebody.'

Savitri sent the hurricane lantern along with Kamala. Kamala set the lamp on the floor while her father looked at her fixedly. 'Here, that's not the place to put the lantern. Do I want illumination for my feet? Bad training, rotten training.' He lifted the lantern and looked about for a place and said, 'Don't you know that when you bring a lantern you have to bring a piece of paper to keep under it? When will you learn all this?'

'Very well, Father,' Kamala said, much intimidated by his manner.

This submissiveness pleased Ramani. He said, 'You must be a good girl, otherwise people won't like you.' He placed the lantern on the window-sill. Kamala turned to go and took a few steps. 'Little girl, don't shuffle your feet while walking,' said Ramani.

'Hereafter I will walk properly, Father.'

He was thoroughly pleased with her. He felt he ought to bestow on her some attention—honour her with a little conversation. 'Have you been in the dark all the evening?'

'No, Father, we had current till six o'clock and then—' She hesitated.

'What happened?'

'Babu's friend put up new bulbs for the dolls, and when Babu pressed a switch something happened, and all the lights went out.'

When Babu returned from the Electric office he found his father standing in the hall and shouting. As soon as he sighted Babu he asked, 'You blackguard, who asked you to tamper with the electric lights?' Babu stood stunned. 'Don't try to escape by being silent. Are you following your mother's example?'

'No, Father.'

'Who asked you to tamper with the electric lights?'

'I didn't touch anything. I brought in Chandru. He knows all about electricity.'

His father moved towards him and twisted his ear, saying, 'How often have I asked you to keep to your books and mind your business?'

'I'll try to set it right, Father, as soon as Chandru comes home.'

'Who asked you to go near the dolls' business? Are you a girl? Tell me, are you a girl?'

This insistent question was accompanied by violent twists of the ear. Babu's body shook under the grip of his father's hot fingers. 'No, Father, I am not a woman.'

'Then why did you go near the dolls?' He twisted the other ear too. 'Will you do a thing like this again? Tell me!'

In helpless anger Babu remained silent. His father slapped him on the cheek. 'Don't beat me, Father,' he said, and Ramani gave him a few more slaps. At this point Savitri dashed forward to protect Babu. She took him aside, glaring at her husband, who said, 'Leave him alone, he doesn't need your petting.' She felt faint with anger. 'Why do you beat him?' was all that she could ask, and then she burst out crying. At the sight of her tears, Babu could not control himself any longer. He sobbed, 'I didn't know. . . I didn't know it was wrong to add those lights.'

Ramani left, remarking that he was sick of this sentimental show. He came back after a wash. 'Now to dinner. We will manage with the available lights.' Savitri squatted down, her face covered with her hands. 'I see that you are holding a stage-show. I can't stand here and watch you. Are you coming in for food or not. . . ? All right, you can please yourself.' He turned and walked to the dining-room calling, 'Has that effeminate boy eaten? Babu, come for your dinner!'

When he was gone, Savitri rose, went to the dark room next to the store, and threw herself on the floor. Later the cook tracked her down there and requested her to take her food, but she refused. The children came to her one by one and tried to coax her. She turned her face to the wall and shut her eyes.

The next morning the cook brought her a tumbler of coffee. She drank it. The cook took back the tumbler from her hand and asked nervously, 'What shall I cook?'

'Don't ask me,' she said.

'There are only a couple of potatoes. We will have to send for some vegetables and also for some mustard.'

'Do the cooking without the vegetables and the mustard or go and ask whoever is keen on having them for money. Don't come and mention them to me.'

The cook went away, his head bent in perplexity. Had anybody heard of cooking without mustard? Presently he got over his despair and began to enjoy the excitement of the situation. A part of his mind said, 'Go on, prepare the sauce and everything without mustard, and with only two potatoes, and if the master raves, tell him I waited long enough and gave sufficient notice.' Another part of him said, 'Look here, this is an opportunity provided by the gods. Show them your worth.' In the backyard Ranga was splitting firewood. The cook said to him, 'When the master and the mistress quarrel it is we that suffer.'

'Not many words passed between them last night,' Ranga said. 'All the same, the situation appears to be very serious.'

'It is no business of a wife's to butt in when the father is dealing with his son. It is a bad habit. Only a battered son will grow into a sound man.'

'My wife is also like that,' admitted Ranga. 'I have only to look at my son and she will pounce on me. Last year when I went to the village my first boy did something or other. He skinned our neighbour's son's forehead with a sharp stone, and what should a father do?'

'You will have to run up to the shop now and bring vegetables,' said the cook.

'Certainly, but listen to this now,' persisted Ranga. 'What should a father do? I merely slapped the boy's cheek and he howled as I have never heard anyone howl before, the humbug. And the wife sprang on me from somewhere and hit me on the head with a brass vessel. I have sworn to leave the children alone even if they should be going down a well. Women are terrible.'

The servant-maid who was washing the vessels under the tap looked up and said, 'Wouldn't you like to say so! What do you know of the fire in a mother's belly when her child is suffering?'

The cook said, 'Only once has my wife tried to interfere, and then I nearly broke her bones. She has learnt to leave me alone now. Women must be taught their place.' With this he dismissed the subject and turned to the immediate business on hand. 'I'm responsible for the running of the house today. I'm going to show these people what I can do. The mistress of the house said, "Do anything, don't ask me," and I could well cook a dinner that a dog wouldn't touch. But is it a proper thing to do, after having been in the house for five years? Ranga, it is eight o'clock. Master will be coming for food in about two hours. Run to the Nair's shop and buy onions for two annas, potatoes for four annas, two lemons, coriander for one pie. . . .' He knew what his master liked, and he was out to provide it. 'Tell the Nair that he will get the money by and by.'

Kamala went to her mother and asked, 'Mother, are you still angry?' Savitri did not reply.

'Father won't beat Babu again. Please don't go on lying there.' She hated to see her mother in this condition, during the Navaratri of all times. 'Mother, what sweets are we preparing for distributing in the evening?'

'We'll see,' said Savitri.

This reminder pained her. She cursed her own depression of spirits, which threatened to spoil the festival. 'I don't like these quarrels,' Kamala said, and left her. She felt indignant. Her school was closed so that they might remain in the doll-land, visit each other, and eat sweets; but Mother went on lying on the floor with her face to the wall. She traced the whole cause of the trouble to Babu, and threw furious looks at him.

Babu went about without so much as looking at the pavilion. His whole manner declared, 'This is what a man gets for helping in women's business. It is your school after all, not mine, that is closed for this silly festival. Please don't call me for anything.' He was troubled about his mother. It was he who had received the slaps, so why should she go on lying there as if a great calamity had befallen the house? Perhaps he ought not to have cried like a girl. The memory of his tears hurt him now. He loathed himself and resolved he would never cry again in his life. Before starting for school he went to the dark room and said to his mother, 'Why do you go on lying there? It was only a slight slap that he gave me after all. You make too much of it. I am going to school now.'

'Have you taken your food?' she asked.

'Yes, get up and go about your business.'

THE ENGLISH TEACHER

Editor's note: Narayan's 'love-marriage', as one used to refer to it, to Rajam lasted only six years at the end of which she died from an attack of typhoid. 'I have described this part of my experience of her sickness and death in *The English Teacher* so fully that I do not, and perhaps cannot, go over it again. More than any other book, *The English Teacher* is autobiographical in content, very little part of it being fiction. The "English Teacher" of the novel, Krishna, is a fictional character in the fictional city of Malgudi; but he goes through the same experience I had gone through, and he calls his wife Susila, and the child is Leela instead of Hema. The toll that typhoid took and the desolation that followed, with a child to look after, and the psychic adjustments, are based on my own experience.'

The next three days I was very busy. My table was placed in the front room of the new house. All my papers and books were arranged neatly. My clothes hung on a peg. The rest of the house was swept and cleaned.

My mother arrived from the village with a sack full of vessels, and helped to make up the house for me. She was stocking the store-room and the kitchen and spent most her time travelling in a *jutka* to the market and coming back with something or other. She worked far into the night, arranging and rearranging the kitchen and the store. At night she sat down with me on the veranda and talked of her housekeeping philosophy. I liked this veranda very much. We had a cool breeze here. I felt immensely satisfied with my choice of the house now. I hoped my wife too would like it. But my mother, the moment she arrived from the village, said, 'What an awful kitchen! So narrow! And the dining-room would have been better if they had added at least a yard in length that side. . . .'

'We can't have everything our way in a house built by someone else. . . .' I became rather impatient if anyone criticized this house. She understood it and said: 'I'm not saying it is a bad house. . . .' She had been used to our large, sprawling home in the village, and everything else seemed to her small and choking. I explained this fact to her and she agreed it was so: 'But do you know how hard it is to keep a huge house like ours clean? It takes me a whole lifetime to keep it tidy, but I don't grudge it. Only I want a little more co-operation. Your father is becoming rather difficult nowadays. . . .'

She explained how impatient he became when he heard the swish of a broom or the noise of scrubbing, and shouted at her to stop it all. As he was growing old, these noises got on his nerves. And so every time she wanted to clean the house, she had to wait till he went away to the fields. 'And do you know, when I delay this, how many other things get out of routine? Unless I have cleaned the house I can't go and bathe. After bathing I've to worship, and only after that can I go near the cows. . . . And if I fail to look at the cowshed for half an hour, do you know what happens?' She was completely wrapped up in her duties. Housekeeping was a grand affair for her. The essence of her existence consisted the thrills and pangs and the satisfaction that she derived in running a well-ordered household. She was unsparing and violent where she met slovenliness. 'If a woman can't take charge of a house and run it sensibly, she must be made to get into man's dress and go out in a procession. . . .' I thought of my wife and shuddered at the fate that might be awaiting her in the few weeks my mother was going to stay and help us run the house. My wife was the last daughter of the family and was greatly petted by her parents, in her own house, where she spent most of her time reading, knitting, embroidering or looking after a garden. In spite of it, after my marriage my mother kept her in the village and trained her up in housekeeping. My wife had picked up many sensible points in cooking and household economy, and her own parents were tremendously impressed with her attainments when she next visited them. They were thrilled beyond words and remarked when I went there, 'We are so happy, Susila has such a fine house for her training. Every girl on earth should be made to pass through your mother's hands. . . ' which, when I conveyed it to my mother, pleased her. She said: 'I really do not mind doing it for everyone, but there are those who neither know nor learn when taught. I feel like kicking them when I come across that type.' I know she was referring to her eldest daughter-in-law, my brother's wife, whom she detested heartily. I had half a suspicion that my eldest brother went away to seek his livelihood in Hyderabad solely for this reason, for there used to be very painful scenes at home while the first daughter-in-law was staying in our house, my mother's idiosyncrasy being what it was and the other being of a haughty disposition. She was the daughter of a retired High Court Judge, and would never allow a remark or a look from my mother to pass unchallenged, and as a result great strife existed in the household for a number of years. My mother used to declare when my elder brother was not present, 'Whatever happens, even with a ten-thousand rupee dowry, I shall never accept a girl from a High Court Judge's family again. . . .'

It had always been my great anxiety that my wife should not share this fate. My mother seemed to feel that some reference of more immediate interest was due to me and said: 'Susila is a modest girl. She is not obstinate.' I was grateful for that negative compliment. That was at the beginning of our married years. They had constant contact after that, and with every effort Susila came out better burnished than before. And then came a point when my mother declared: 'Susila has learnt how to conduct herself before guests.' At this point they separated; now they were meeting again, with Susila having a home of her own to look after, and my mother ready to teach the obedient pupil her business. It was really this which I secretly dreaded.

On the following Friday, I was pacing the little Malgudi railway station in great agitation. I had never known such suspense before. She was certain to arrive with a lot of luggage, and the little child. How was all this to be transferred from the train to the platform? And the child must not be hurt. I made a mental note, 'Must shout as soon as the train stops: "Be careful with the baby."' This seemed to my fevered imagination the all-important thing to say on arrival, as otherwise I fancied the child's head was sure to be banged against the doorway. . . . And how many infants were damaged and destroyed by careless mothers in the process of coming out of trains! Why couldn't they make these railway carriages of safer dimensions? It ought to be done in the interest of baby welfare in India. 'Mind the baby and the door.' And then the luggage! Susila was sure to bring with her a huge amount of luggage. She required four trunks for her saris alone! Women never understood the importance of travelling light. Why should they? As long as there were men to bear all the anxieties and bother and see them through their travails. It would teach them a lesson to be left to shift for themselves. Then they would know the value of economy in these matters, I wrung my hands in despair. How was she going to get out with the child and all that luggage! The train stopped for just seven minutes. I would help her down first and then throw the things out, and if there were any boxes left over they would have to be lost with the train, that was all. No one could help it. I turned to the gnarled blue-uniformed man behind me. He was known as Number Five and I had known him for several years now. Whatever had to be done on the railway platform was done with his help. I had offered him three times his usual wages to help me today. I turned to him and asked: 'Can you manage even if there is too much luggage?'

'Yes, master, no difficulty. The train stops for seven minutes.' He seemed to have a grand notion of seven minutes; a miserable flash it seemed to me. 'We unload whole wagons within that time.'

'I will tell the pointsman to stop it at the outer signal, if necessary,' he added. It was a very strength-giving statement to me. I felt relieved. But I think I lost my head once again. I believe, in this needless anxiety, I became slightly demented. Otherwise I would not have rushed at the stationmaster the moment I set eyes on him. I saw him come out of his room and move down the platform to gaze on a far-off signal post. I ran behind him, panting: 'Good morning, stationmaster!' He bestowed an official smile and moved off to the end of the platform and looked up. I felt I had a lot of doubts to clear on railway matters, and asked inanely: 'Looking at the signals?'

'Yes,' he replied, and took his eyes down, and turned to go back to his room. I asked: 'Can't they arrange to stop this train a little longer here?'

'What for? Isn't there enough trouble as it is?'

I laughed sympathetically and said: 'I said so because it may not be possible for passengers to unload all their trunks.'

'I should like to see a passenger who carried luggage that will take more than six minutes. I have been here thirty years.'

I said: 'My wife is arriving today with the infant. I thought she would require a lot of time in order to get down carefully. And then she is bound to have numerous boxes. These women, you know,' I said laughing artificially, seeking his indulgence. He was a good man and laughed with me. 'Well, sometimes it has happened that the train was held up for the convenience of a second-class passenger. Are your people travelling second?'

'I can't say,' I said. I knew well she wouldn't travel second, although I implored her in every letter to do so. She wrote rather diplomatically: 'Yes, don't be anxious, I and the baby will travel down quite safely.' I even wrote to my father-in-law, but that gentleman preserved a discreet silence on the matter. I knew by temperament he disliked the extravagance of travelling second, although he could afford it and in other ways had proved himself no miser. I felt furious at the thought of him and told the station-master: 'Some people are born niggards. . .would put up with any trouble rather than. . . .' But before I could finish my sentence a bell rang inside the station office and the stationmaster ran in, leaving me to face my travail and anguish alone. I turned and saw my porter standing away from me, borrowing a piece of tobacco from some-one. 'Here, Number Five, don't get lost.' A small crowd was gather-ing unobtrusively on the platform. I feared he might get lost at the critical moment. A bell sounded. People moved about. We heard the distant puffing and whistling. The engine appeared around the bend.

A whirling blur of faces went past me as the train shot in and stopped. People were clambering up and down. Number Five followed me about, munching his tobacco casually. 'Search on that side of the mail van.' I hurried through the crowd, peering into the compartment. I saw my father-in-law struggling to get to the door-way. I ran up to his carriage. Through numerous people getting in and out, I saw her sitting serenely in her seat with the baby lying on her lap. 'Only three minutes more!' I cried. 'Come out!' My father-in-law got down. I and Number Five fought our way up, and in a moment I was beside my wife in the compartment.

'No time to be sitting down; give me the baby,' I said. She merely smiled and said: 'I will carry the baby down. You will get these boxes. That wicker box, bring it yourself, it contains baby's bottle and milk vessels.' She picked up the child and unconcernedly moved on. She hesitated for a second at the thick of the crowd and said: 'Way please,' and they made way for her. I cried: 'Susila, mind the door and baby.' All the things I wanted to say on this occasion were muddled and gone out of mind. I looked at her apprehensive-ly till she was safely down on the platform, helped by her father. Number Five worked wonders within a split second.

I wouldn't have cared if the train had left now. The mother and child stood beside the trunks piled up on the platform. I gazed on my wife, fresh and beautiful, her hair shining, her dress without a wrinkle on it, and her face fresh, with not a sign of fatigue. She wore her usual indigo-coloured silk sari. I looked at her and whispered: 'Once again this sari, still so fond of it,' as my father-in-law went back to the compartment to give a final look round. 'When will she wake up?' I asked pointing at the child, whom I found enchanting, with her pink face and blue shirt.

'Father is coming down,' she said, hinting that I had neglected him and ought to welcome him with a little more ceremony. I obeyed her instantly, went up to my father-in- law and said: 'I am very happy, sir, you have come. . . .' He smiled and said: 'Your wife and daughter got comfortable places, they slept well.'

'Did they, how, how? I thought there was such a crowd. . . .' My wife answered: 'What if there are a lot of others in the compartment? Other people must also travel. I didn't mind it.' I knew she was indirectly supporting her father, anticipating my attacks on him for travelling third. 'I only thought you might find it difficult to put the child to sleep,' I said.

'Oh, everybody made way for us, and we got a whole berth to ourselves,' she said, demanding of me by every look and breath that I should be sufficiently grateful to her for it. I turned to him and said: 'I'm so happy you managed it so well, sir.' He was pleased. He said: 'People are ever so good when they see Susila and the baby.'

'I hope you will stop with us for at least a week,' I said, and looked at my wife for approval. But her father declined the invitation with profuse thanks. He was to be back in his town the next day and he was returning by the evening train. He said: 'There were three Bombay men, they liked Leela so much that they tried to give her a lot of biscuits. She was only too eager to accept, but I prevented. . . .'

'Biscuits are bad for the baby,' I said. We moved on. I stretched out my hand: 'Let me carry her,' I said. My wife declined: 'You don't know how to carry a baby yet. You will sprain her.' She clasped her closer, and walked off the platform.

A Victoria carriage waited for us outside. Our trunks were stuffed into it, and we squeezed ourselves in. I shared the narrow seat behind the driver with my father-in-law, leaving the other seat for mother and child. Between us were heaped all the trunks and I caught patches of her face through the gaps in the trunks. She talked incessantly about the habits of the infant, enquired about the plan of our house, and asked the names of buildings and streets that we passed.

My mother came down and welcomed her at the gate. She had decorated the threshold with a festoon of green mango leaves and the floor and doorway with white flour designs. She was standing at the doorway and as soon as we got down cried: 'Let Susila and the child stay where they are.' She had a pan of vermilion solution ready at hand and circled it before the young mother and child, before allowing them to get down from the carriage. After that she held out her arms, and the baby vanished in her embrace.

A look at my mother, her eagerness as she devoured them with her look and led them into the house, and I was moved by the extraordinary tenderness which appeared in her face. All my dread of yesterday as to how she would prove as a mother-in-law was suddenly eased.

My mother was swamped by this little daughter of mine. She found little time to talk or think of anything else. She fussed over the young mother and the child. She felt it her primary duty to keep the young mother happy and free to look after the little one. The child seemed to be their meeting point; and immediately established a great understanding and harmony between them. All day my mother compelled my wife to stay in her own room and spent her entire time in the kitchen preparing food and drink for her and the child. When the child cried at nights, my mother, sleeping in the hall, sprang up and rocked the cradle, before the young mother could be disturbed. The child still drew nourishment from its mother, and so the latter needed all the attention she could get.

My mother stayed with us the maximum time she could spare— two months—and then returned to the village.

I left the college usually at 4.30 p.m., the moment the last bell rang, and avoiding all interruptions reached home within about twenty minutes. As soon as I turned the street I caught a glimpse of Susila tinkering in her little garden in our compound, or watching our child as she toddled about picking pebbles and mud. . . . It was not in my wife's nature to be demonstrative, but I knew she waited there for me. So I said: 'I have taken only twenty minutes and already you are out to look for me!' She flushed when I said this, and covered it up with: 'I didn't come out to look for you, but just to play with the child. . . .' My daughter came up and hugged my knees, and held up her hands for my books. I gave her the books. She went up the steps and put them on the table in my room. I followed her in. I took off my coat and shirt, picked up my towel and went to the bathroom, with the child on my arm, as she pointed at the various articles about the house and explained them to me in her own terms. Most of her expressions were still monosyllables, but she made up a great deal by her vigorous gesticulations. She insisted upon watching me as I put my head under the tap. The sight of it thrilled her and she shrieked as water splashed about. I put her safely away from the spray as I bathed, but she stealthily came nearer step by step and tried to catch some of the drops between her fingers. 'Ay, child, keep off water.' At this she pretended to move off, but the moment I shut my eyes under water and opened them again, she would have come nearer and drenched a corner of her dress, which was a signal for me to turn off the water and dry myself. I rubbed myself, lifted her on my arm, went to my room, and brushed my hair. I did this as a religious duty because I felt myself to be such a contrast to them when I returned in the evening, in my sagging grey cotton suit, with grimy face, and ink-stained fingers, while the mother and daughter looked particularly radiant in the evenings, with their hair dressed and beflowered, faces elegantly powdered.

By the time I reached this stage my wife came out and said: 'Your coffee is getting cold. Won't you come in?'

'Yes, yes,' and we moved off to our little dining-room. An alcove at the end of the dining-room served for a shrine. There on a pedestal she kept a few silver images of gods, and covered them with flowers; two small lamps were lit before them every morning. I often saw her standing there with the light in her face, her eyes closed and her lips lightly moving. I was usually amused to see her thus, and often asked what exactly it was that she repeated before her gods. She never answered this question. To this day I have never learnt what magical words she uttered there with closed eyes. Even when I mildly joked about it, 'Oh! Becoming a yogi!' she never tried to defend herself, but merely treated my references with the utmost indifference. She seemed to have a deep secret life. There hung about this alcove a perpetual smell of burnt camphor and faded flowers.

I sat down on the plank facing the shrine, with the child on my lap. A little plate came up with some delicacy or titbit heaped on it—my tiffin. Susila placed this in front of me and waited to see my reaction. I looked up at her standing before me and asked: 'What is this?' She replied: 'Find out for yourself, let us see if you recognize it. . . .' As I gazed at it wondering what it might be, the child thrust her hand out for it. I put a little into her mouth while the mother protested: 'You are going to spoil her giving her whatever she wants. . . .'

'No, just a little. . . .'

'It will make her sick, she has been eating all sorts of things lately. Don't blame me if she gets sick. . . .'

'Oh, she won't, just a little won't do her any harm. . . .' As Leela held up her hands for more, her mother cried: 'No, baby, it won't do. Don't trouble Father, come away, come away,' and the little one stuck to me fast, avoiding her mother's gaze, and I put my left arm about her and said: 'Don't worry about her, I won't give her any more. . . .'

As I finished what was on the plate Susila asked: 'Do you want some more?' This was always a most embarrassing question for me. As I hesitated she asked, 'Why, is it not good?'

'It is good,' I groaned, 'but. . . .'

'But smells rather smoky, doesn't it? But for the smell it would be perfect,' she said. And I couldn't but agree with her. 'I prepared such a large quantity thinking you would like it. . . .' She went in and brought out a little more and pushed it on to my plate and I ate with relish just because she was so desperately eager to get me to appreciate her handiwork!

She gave me coffee. We left the kitchen, and sat down in the hall. The child went over to her box in a corner and rummaged its contents and threw them about and became quite absorbed in this activity. My wife sat in the doorway, leaning against the door and watching the street. We spent an hour or more, sitting there and gossiping. She listened eagerly to all the things I told her about my college, work and life. Though she hadn't met a single person who belonged to that world, she knew the names of most of my colleagues and the boys and all about them. She knew all about Brown and what pleased or displeased him. She took sides with me in all my discussions and partisanships, and hated everyone I hated and respected anyone I respected. She told me a great deal about our neighbours, their hopes and fears, and promises and qualities. This talk went on till darkness crept in, and the lights had to be switched on. At the same time the clattering at the toy box ceased. This was a signal that the child would demand attention. She came towards us whimpering and uttering vague complaints. My wife got up and went in to light the oven and cook the dinner, while I took charge of Leela and tried to keep her engaged till her food was ready.

On the first of every month, I came home with ten-rupee notes bulging in an envelope, my monthly salary, and placed it in her hand. She was my cash-keeper. And what a ruthless accountant she seemed to be. In her hands, a hundred rupees seemed to do the work of two hundred, and all through the month she was able to give me money when I asked. When I handled my finances independently, after making a few routine savings and payments, I simply paid for whatever caught my eye and paid off anyone who approached me, with the result that after the first ten days, I went about without money. Now it was in the hands of someone who seemed to understand perfectly where every rupee was going or should go, and managed them with a determined hand. She kept the cash in a little lacquer box, locked it up in her almirah, and kept a minute account of it in the last page of a diary, four years old.

We sat down at my table to draw up the monthly budget and list of provisions. She tore off a sheet of notepaper, and wrote down a complete list—from rice down to mustard. 'I have written down the precise quantity, don't change anything as you did once.' This was a reference to a slight change that I once attempted to make in her list. She had written down two seers of Bengal gram, but the National Provision Stores could not supply that quantity, and so the shopman suggested he would give half of it, and to make up the purchase, he doubled the quantity of jaggery. All done with my permission. But when I returned home with these, she saw the alterations and was completely upset. I found that there was an autocratic strain in her nature in these matters, and unsuspected depths of rage. 'Why has he made this alteration?' she had asked, her face going red. 'He didn't have enough of the other stuff,' I replied, tired and fatigued by the shopping and on the point of irritability myself. 'If he hasn't got a simple thing like Bengal gram, what sort of a shop has he?'

'Come and see it for yourself, if you like,' I replied, going into my room. She muttered: 'Why should it make you angry? I wonder!' I lay down on my canvas chair, determined to ignore her, and took out a book. She came presently into my room with a paper-screw full of sugar and said: 'This man has given underweight of sugar. He has cheated you.' I lowered the book, frowned at her and asked: 'What do you mean?'

'I fear to speak to you if you get angry,' she said.

'Who is angry?' I asked. 'What is the matter, tell me?'

'I wrote for two measures of sugar, and see this: he has billed for two measures and actually given a measure-and-a-half. I have measured it just now.' She looked at me victoriously, waiting to hear how I was going to answer this charge. I merely said: 'He wouldn't do such a thing. You must have some extraordinary measure with you at home.'

'Nothing wrong with my measure. Even your mother measured everything with it and said it was correct.' So this was a legacy from her mother-in-law. She had taught the girl even this. She had a bronze tumbler, which she always declared was a correct half measure, and she would never recognize other standards and measures. She insisted upon making all her purchases, ghee or oil or milk or salt, with the aid of this measure, and declared that all other measures, including the Government stamped ones, were incorrect, and were kept maliciously incorrect because some municipal members were businessmen! She used the same tumbler for weighing too, placing it for weight in the scale pan, declaring that the curious thing about the vessel was that by weight too it was exactly half seer, and she would challenge anyone to disprove it. All tradespeople somehow succumbed to this challenge and allowed her to have her own way. She carried this tumbler about wherever she went, and I now found that she had procured a similar one for her daughter-in-law, and had trained her in the use of it.

'Throw away that tumbler and use an honest measure,' I said. Susila merely looked at me and said: 'Please don't speak so loudly. The child is asleep,' and tried to go out of the room. I called her back and said: 'If you use an honest measure you will find others have also done so.'

'This National Provisions man is a thief,' she cried, 'the sooner you change the better.' This annoyed me very much. I had known the N.P.S. man for years and liked him. I went all the way to South Extension to patronize his shop, and I liked the man because he was fat and talkative, and Sastri the logic man always said that it was the best shop in the town. I rather prided myself on going to the shop. I liked the fat, thoughtful proprietor. I said: 'There is nothing wrong with him. He is the best shopman known. I won't change him. . . .' 'I don't know why you should be so fond of him when he is giving undermeasure and rotten stuff. . .' she replied. I was by this time very angry: 'Yes, I am fond of him because he is my second cousin,' I said with a venomous grin.

Her hatred of him was not mitigated. She said: 'You would pay cart-hire and go all the way to South Extension to be cheated by him rather than go to a nearer shop. And his rate!' She finished the rest of her sentence with a shiver. 'I don't care if he overcharges—I won't drop him,' I declared. 'Hush, remember the child is sleeping,' she said and left the room. I lay in my chair fretting for fifteen minutes and then tried to resume my study, but could read only for five minutes. I got up and went over to the store-room as she was putting away the provisions and articles in their respective tin or glass containers. I stood at the doorway and watched her. I felt a great pity for her; the more because I had not shown very great patience. I asked: 'I will return the jaggery if it is too much. Have you absolutely no use for it?' In answer she pushed before me a glass goblet and said: 'This can hold just half a *viss* of jaggery and not more; which is more than enough for our monthly use. If it is kept in any other place, ants swarm on it,' she said. I now saw the logic of her indignation, and by the time our next shopping was done, she had induced me to change over to the Co-operative Stores.

Since then every time the monthly list was drawn up she warned me: 'Don't alter anything in it.' I followed her list with strict precision, always feeling that one could never be sure what mess any small change might entail. If there were alterations to be made, I rather erred on the side of omission and went again next day after taking her suggestion. She was very proud of her list. It was precise. Every quantity was conceived with the correct idea as to how long it should last. There were over two dozen different articles to be indented and she listed them with foresight and calculation. She was immensely proud of this ability. She gave me twenty rupees or more for these purchases. I went out to the Co-operative Stores in the Market Road and returned home three hours later followed by a coolie carrying them all in paper bags and bundles, stuffed into a large basket. She always waited for them at the door with uncon-cealed enthusiasm. The moment I was at the gate she held out her hand for the bill, and hurriedly ran her eyes down the columns checking the figures and prices. 'Oh! you have got all the things, and the cost didn't go up above 22-80 total. . . slightly better than it was last month. Which item is cheaper this month?' She was in raptures over it. I loved to see her so pleased, and handed her the change to the last pie. She paid the coolie three annas; she would never alter this figure whatever happened. If any one had the hardihood to expect more she declared: 'Don't stand there and argue. Be off. Your master has offered you an anna more than you deserve. After all the market is only half a mile away!' She carried the packages to the store-room, and put each in its container, neatly labelled and ranged along a rack. She always needed my assistance to deal with rice. It was the bulkiest bag. It was my set duty on these days to drag the gunny sack along to the store, lift it and empty it into a zinc drum. I invited her displeasure if I didn't do it carefully. If any rice scattered accidentally on the floor, she said: 'I don't know when you will learn economic ways. You are so wasteful. On the quantity you throw about another family could comfortably live.'

She watched these containers as a sort of barometer, the level of their contents indicating the progress of the month. Each had to be at a particular date: and on the last date of the month—just enough for another day, when they would be replenished. She watched these with a keen eye like a technician watching an all-important meter at a power house.

All went very well as long as she was reigning supreme in the kitchen—till my mother sent an old lady from the village to cook for us and assist us.

One evening we were sitting as usual in the front veranda of the house when an old lady stood at our gate, with a small trunk under her arm, and asked: 'Is this teacher Krishnan's house?'

'Yes, who are you, come in. . . .' I opened the gate for her. She looked at me, wrinkling her eyes and said, 'Kittu . . . I have seen you as a baby and a boy. How big you have grown!' She came up to the veranda, peered closely into my wife's face and said: 'You are our daughter-in-law. I am an old friend of Kamu,' she said, referring to my mother by her maiden name. By this time Leela, who had been playing near her box, came out on hearing a new voice. At the sight of her the old lady cried: 'So this is Kamu's grandchild!' She picked her up in her arms and fondled her. Susila's heart melted at the sight of it and she said: 'Come into the house, won't you?' The old lady went in, sat under the lamp and took out of a corner of her sari a crumpled letter and gave it to me. It was from my mother: 'I am sending this letter with an old friend of mine, who was assisting me in household work when you were a baby. She then went away to live with her son. He died last year, and she has absolutely no one to support her. She came to me a few weeks ago in search of work. But I have no need for assistance nowadays. Moreover your father grows rather irritable if he sees any extra person in the house. So I have given her bus fare and sent her on to you. I have always felt that Susila needed an assistant in the house, the baby demanding all the attention she can give. My friend will cook and look after the child. And you can give her whatever salary you like.'

While the old lady kept fondling the child, sitting on the floor, I read the letter under the hall light and my wife read it over my shoulder. We looked at each other. There was consternation in her look. There were many questions which she was aching to ask me. I adjourned to my room and she followed me.

'What shall we do?' she asked, looking desperate.

'Why do you look so panicky? We will send her back if you do not want her.'

'No, no. How can that be? Your mother has sent her. We have got to have her.'

'I think it will be good to have her. All your time is now spent in the kitchen when you are not tending the baby. I don't like you to spend all your time cooking either tiffin or food.'

'But I like it. What is wrong in it?' she asked.

'You must spend some more time reading or stitching or singing. Man or woman is not born merely to cook and eat,' I said, and added: 'You have neglected your books. Have you finished *Ivanhoe*?' She had been trying to get through *Ivanhoe* for years now, and Lamb's *Tales from Shakespeare*. But she never went beyond the fiftieth page. Her library also contained a book of hymns by a Tamil saint, a few select stanzas of *Kamba Ramayana*, Palgrave's *Golden Treasury* and a leather-bound Bhagavad-Gita in Sanskrit. I knew how fond she was of books. She was always planning how she was going to devour all the books and become the member of some library. But it never became more than an ambition.

In the earlier years of our married life we often sat together with one or other of the books, in the single top-floor room in her father's house, and tried to read. The first half an hour would be wasted because of an irresponsible mood coming over her, which made her laugh at everything: even the most solemn poem would provoke her, especially such poems as were addressed by a lover. 'My true love hath my heart and I have his.' She would laugh till she became red in the face. 'Why can't each keep his own or her own heart instead of this exchange?' She then put out her hand and searched all my pockets saying: 'In case you should take away mine!'

'Hush, listen to the poem,' I said, and she would listen to me with suppressed mirth and shake her head in disapproval. And then another line that amused her very much was, 'Oh, mistress mine, where are you roaming?' She would not allow me to progress a line beyond, saying: 'I shall die of this poem some day. What is the matter with the woman, loafing all over the place except where her husband is?'

However much she might understand or not understand, she derived a curious delight in turning over the pages of a book, and the great thing was that I should sit by her side and explain. While she read the Tamil classics and Sanskrit texts without my help, she liked English to be explained by me. If I showed the slightest hesitation, she would declare: 'Perhaps you don't care to explain English unless you are paid a hundred rupees a month for it?'

But all that stopped after the child was born. When the child left her alone she had to be in the kitchen, and my argument now appealed to her. She said: 'But that will mean an extra expense. What shall we pay her?'

'About eight rupees, just what everyone pays, I think,' I said.

'Oh, too much,' she said. 'I'm sure she will waste another eight rupees' worth of things. This is an unnecessary expense,' she said. I explained: 'Very necessary and we can afford it. In addition to the provident fund, why should we send thirty-five rupees to the savings bank? I think about twenty-five rupees a month for the bank will be more than enough. Many of my friends do not save even five rupees.'

'Why do you want to follow their example? We must live within our means, and save enough.' She often declared: 'When we are old we must never trouble others for help. And remember there is a daughter, for whose marriage we must save.'

'When we bring forth some more daughters and sons. . .' I began, and she covered my mouth with her fingers. 'You men! What do you care! You would think differently if God somehow made you share the bothers of bringing forth! Where is your promise?' I often reiterated and confirmed our solemn pact that Leela should be our only child. And anything I said otherwise, even in jest, worried her very much.

With the future so much in mind she planned all our finances. She kept a watch over every rupee as it arrived, and never let it depart lightly, and as far as possible tried to end its career in the savings bank.

But now our savings were affected to the extent of at least ten rupees—as she explained, 'Six rupees, old lady's salary' (Susila stubbornly refused more than that for a year) and 'four rupees for all her waste, putting it at a minimum. . . .'

She was disconsolate over it for a long time, till I appeased her by saying: 'Oh, don't worry about it. When I get some money from examination papers I will give you the whole of it for the savings bank.'

In course of time we found that we simply couldn't do without the old lady. She cooked the food for us, tended the child, gave us the necessary courage when the child had fever or stomach-ache and we became distraught; she knew a lot of tricks about children's health, she grew very fond of the child and took her out and kept her very happy. She established herself as a benign elder at home, and for us it meant a great deal. Her devotion to the child enabled me to take my wife twice or thrice a month to a picture, on a walk along the river, or out shopping. My wife grew very fond of her and called her 'Granny', so did Leela. But Susila had a price to pay for this pleasure. She lost her supremacy over the kitchen and the store. The levels in the containers at the store went down in other ways than my wife calculated. Susila protested and fought against it for some time, but the old lady had her own way of brushing aside our objections. And Susila adjusted her own outlook in the matter. 'Didn't I bargain for a waste of four rupees a month? Well, it is not so hard, because she wastes only three rupees. . . .' Our provision bill fluctuated by only three rupees, and it was a small price to pay for the great company and service of the old lady, who lived on one meal a day, just a handful of cooked rice and buttermilk. It was a wonder how she found the energy for so much activity. My wife often sat down with her in order to induce her to eat well, but it was of no avail.

I sat in my room, at the table. It was Thursday and it was a light day for me at college—only two hours of work in the afternoon, and not much preparation for that either. *Pride and Prejudice* for a senior class, non-detailed study, which meant just reading it to the boys. And a composition class. I sat at my table as usual after morning coffee looking over the books ranged on the table and casually turning over the pages of some exercise books. 'Nothing to do. Why not write poetry? Ages since I wrote anything!' My conscience had a habit of asserting itself once in six months and reminding me that I ought to write poetry. At such moments I opened the bottom-most drawer of my table and pulled out a notebook of about five hundred pages, handsomely bound. I had spent nearly a week at a local press getting this done some years ago. Its smooth pages contained my most cherished thoughts on life and nature and humanity. In addition to shorter fragments that I wrote at various times on a miscellany of topics, it contained a long unfinished poem on an epic scale to which I added a few dozen lines whenever my conscience stirred in me. I always fancied that I was born for a poetic career and some day I hoped to take the world by storm with the publication. Some of the pieces were written in English and some in Tamil. (I hadn't yet made up my mind as to which language was to be enriched with my contributions to its literature, but the language was unimportant. The chief thing seemed to be the actual effort.) I turned over the pages looking at my previous writing. The last entry was several months ago, on nature. I felt satisfied with it but felt acute discomfort on realizing that I had hardly done anything more than that. Today I was going to make up for all lost time: I took out my pen, dipped it in ink, and sat hesitating. Everything was ready except a subject. What should I write about?

My wife had come in and was stealthily watching the pages over my shoulder. As I sat biting the end of my pen, she remarked from behind me: 'Oh, the poetry book is out: why are you staring at a blank page?' Her interruption was always welcome. I put away my book, and said: 'Sit down,' dragging a stool nearer. 'No, I'm going away. Write your poetry. I won't disturb you. You may forget what you wanted to write.' 'I have not even thought of what to write,' I said. 'Some day I want to fill all the pages of this book and then it will be published and read all over the world.' At this she turned over the leaves of the notebook briskly; and laughed: 'There seem to be over a thousand pages, and you have hardly filled the first ten.' 'The trouble is I have not enough subjects to write on,' I confessed. She drew herself up and asked: 'Let me see if you can write about me.'

'A beautiful idea,' I cried. 'Let me see you.'

I sat up very attentively and looked at her keenly and fixedly like an artist or a photographer viewing his subject. I said: 'Just move a little to your left please. Turn your head right. Look at me straight here. That's right. . . . Now I can write about you. Don't drop your lovely eyelashes so much. You make me forget my task. Ah, now, don't grin please. Very good, stay as you are and see how I write now, steady. . . .' I drew up the notebook, ran the fountain pen hurriedly over it and filled a whole page beginning:

'She was a phantom of delight
When first she gleamed upon my sight:
A lovely apparition, sent
To be a moment's ornament.'

It went on for thirty lines ending:

'And yet a spirit still, and bright
With something of an angel-light.'

I constantly paused to look at her while writing, and said: 'Perfect.
Thank you. Now listen.'

'Oh, how fast you write!' she said admiringly.

'You will also find how well I've written. Now listen,' I said, and
read as if to my class, slowly and deliberately, pausing to explain
now and then.

'I never knew you could write so well.'

'It is a pity that you should have underrated me so long; but now
you know better. Keep it up,' I said. 'And if possible don't look at
the pages, say roughly between 150 and 200, in the *Golden Treasury*.
Because someone called Wordsworth has written similar poems.'
This was an invitation for her to run in and fetch her copy of the
Golden Treasury and turn over precisely the forbidden pages. She
scoured every title and first line and at last pitched upon the
original. She read it through, and said: 'Aren't you ashamed to
copy?'

'No,' I replied. 'Mine is entirely different. He had written about
someone entirely different from my subject.'

'I wouldn't do such a thing as copying.'

'I should be ashamed to have your memory,' I said. 'You have
had the copy of the *Golden Treasury* for years now, and yet you
listened to my reading with gaping wonder! I wouldn't give you
even two out of a hundred if you were my student.' At this point
our conversation was interrupted by my old clock. It burst in upon
us all of a sudden. It purred and bleated and made so much noise
that it threw us all into confusion. Susila picked it up and tried to
stop it without success, till I snatched Taine and smothered it.

'Now, why did it do it?' she demanded. I shook my head. 'Just,
for pleasure,' I replied. She gazed on its brown face and said: 'It is
not even showing the correct time. It is showing two o'clock, four
hours ahead! Why do you keep it on your table?' I had no answer

to give. I merely said: 'It has been with me for years, poor darling!'

'I will give it away this afternoon—a man comes to buy all old things.'

'No, no, take care, don't do it. . .' I warned. She didn't answer, but merely looked at it and mumbled: 'This is not the first time. When you are away it starts bleating after I have rocked the cradle for hours and made the child sleep, and I don't know how to stop it. It won't do for our house. It is a bother. . . .'

That evening when I returned home from college the first thing I noticed was that my room looked different. My table had lost its usual quality and looked tidy, with all books dusted and neatly arranged. It looked like a savage suddenly appearing neatly trimmed and groomed. The usual corner with old newspapers and magazines piled up was clean swept. The pile was gone. So was the clock on the table. The table looked barren without it. For years it had been there. With composition books still under my arm, I searched her out. I found her in the bathroom, washing the child's hands. 'What have you done with my clock?' I asked. She looked up and asked in answer: 'How do you like your room? I have cleaned and tidied it up. What a lot of rubbish you gathered there! Hereafter on every Thursday. . . .'

'Answer first, where is the clock?' I said.

'Please wait, I will finish the child's business first and then answer.'

I stood at the bathroom doorway and grimly waited. She finished the child's business and came out bearing her on her arm. While passing me she seized the child's hand and tapped me under the chin with it and passed on without a word to her room. She later met me in my room as I sat gloomily gazing at the table.

'Why have you not had your tiffin or wash?' she asked, coming up behind and gently touching my shoulder.

'I don't want any tiffin,' I snapped.

'Why are you so angry?' she asked

'Who asked you to give away that clock?' I asked.

'I didn't give it away. That man gave me twelve annas for it—a very high price indeed.'

'Now you are a. . .' I began. I looked at the paper corner and wailed: 'You have given away those papers too! There were old answer papers there. . . .'

'Yes, I saw them,' she said. 'They were four years old. Why do you want old papers?' she asked. I was too angry to answer. 'You have no business to tamper with my things,' I said. 'I don't want any tiffin or coffee.' I picked up my coat, put it on and rushed out of the house, without answering her question: 'Where are you going?'

I went straight back to the college. I had no definite plan. There was no one in the college. I peeped into the debating hall, hoping there might be somebody there. But the evening was free from all engagements. I remembered that I hadn't had my coffee. I walked about the empty corridors of the college. I saw the servant and asked him to open our common room. I sent him to fetch me coffee and tiffin from the restaurant. I opened my locker and took out a few composition books. I sat correcting them till late at night. I heard the college clock strike nine. I then got up and retraced my way home. I went about my work with a business-like air. I took off my coat, went at great speed to the bathroom and washed. I first took a peep into my wife's room. I saw her rocking the baby in the cradle. I went into the kitchen and told the old lady: 'Have the rest dined?' The old lady answered: 'Susila waited till eight-thirty.'

I was not interested in this. Her name enraged me. I snapped: 'All right, all right, put up my leaf and serve me. I only wanted to know if the child had eaten.' This was to clear any misconception anyone might entertain that I was interested in Susila.

I ate in silence. I heard steps approaching, and told myself: 'Oh, she is coming.' I trembled with anxiety, lest she should be going away elsewhere. I caught a glimpse of her as she came into the dining-room. I bowed my head, and went on with my dinner unconcerned, though fully aware that she was standing before me, dutifully as ever, to see that I was served correctly. She moved off to the kitchen, spoke some words to the old lady, and came out, and softly moved back to her own room. I felt angry: 'Doesn't even care to wait and see me served. She doesn't care. If she cared, would she sell my clock? I must teach her a lesson.'

After dinner I was back in my room and sat down at my table. I had never been so studious at any time in my life. I took out some composition books. I noticed on a corner of my table a small paper packet. I found enclosed in it a few coins. On the paper was written in her handwriting:

Time-piece 12 annas
Old paper 1 rupee
———
Total   One rupee and twelve annas.

I felt furious at the sight of it. I took the coins and went over to her room. The light was out there. I stood in the doorway and muttered: 'Who cares for this money? I can do without it?' I flung it on her bed and returned to my room.

Later, as I sat in my room working, I heard the silent night punctuated by sobs. I went to her room and saw her lying with her face to the wall, sobbing. I was completely shaken. I didn't bargain for this. I watched her silently for a moment, and collected myself sufficiently to say: 'What is the use of crying, after committing a serious blunder?' Through her sobs, she spluttered: 'What do you care, what use it is or not? If I had known you cared more for a dilapidated clock. . . .' She didn't finish her sentence, but broke down and wept bitterly. I was baffled. I was in an anguish myself. I wanted to take her in my arms and comfort her. But there was a most forbidding pride within me. I merely said: 'If you are going to talk and behave like a normal human being, I can talk to you. I can't stand all this nonsense.'

'You go away to your room. Why do you come and abuse me at midnight?' she said.

'Stop crying, otherwise people will think a couple of lunatics are living in this house. . . .'

I went back to my room—a very determined man. I lay on a mat, trying to sleep, and spent a miserable and sleepless night.

We treated each other like strangers for the next forty-eight hours—all aloof and bitter. The child looked on this with puzzlement, but made it up by attending to her toys and going to the old lady for company. It was becoming a torture. I could stand no more of it. I had hoped Susila would try to make it up, and that I could immediately accept it. But she confined herself to her room and minded her business with great concentration and never took notice of me. I caught a glimpse of her face occasionally and found that her eyes were swollen. I felt a great pity for her, when I saw her slender neck, as she was going away from the bathroom. I blamed myself for being such a savage. But I couldn't approach her. The child would not help us either; she was too absorbed in her own activities. It came to a point when I simply could not stand any more of it. So the moment I returned home from college next evening I said to her, going to her room:

'Let us go to a picture. . . .'

'What picture?' she asked.

'*Tarzan*—at Variety Hall. You will like it very much. . . .'

'Baby?'

'The old lady will look after her. We shall be back at nine. Dress up. . . .' I was about to say, 'Look sharp,' but I checked myself and said: 'There is a lot of time. You needn't hustle yourself.'

'No, I'll be ready in ten minutes. . .' she said rising.

By the time we were coming out of the Variety Hall that night we were in such agreement and showed such tender concern for each other's views and feelings that we both wondered how we could have treated each other so cruelly. 'I thought we might buy a new clock, that's why I gave away the old one,' she said.

'You did the best thing possible,' I said. 'Even in the hostel that wretched clock worried everyone near about. I am glad you have rid me of it.'

'They make such beautiful ones nowadays,' she said.

'Yes, yes, right. We will go out and buy one tomorrow evening,' I said. When we reached home we decided that we should avoid quarrelling with each other since, as she put it, 'They say such quarrels affect a child's health.'

MR SAMPATH

Editor's note: With *Mr Sampath*, Narayan plunges into the zany, eccentric and, at the same time, true-to-life world of Malgudi which is to be the special background of his tales from now on though we have known it earlier. As always, there is a hard core of autobiography in this book. The narrator, Srinivas, is an editor even as Narayan was at this point in his life. Sampath, the printer, a character taken from real life, when he finds that he cannot any longer run his press, takes to film production, an endeavour into which he draws Srinivas, willy-nilly. Here we see what happens during the opening ceremony of the film studio.

The next important event was the opening ceremony. A special bus ran from the city to the studio on the other bank of the river. The bus was painted 'Sunrise Pictures' along its whole body, and placards were hung out on its sides: 'The Burning of Kama—Switching-on Ceremony'. It slowly perambulated along the Market Road, and anyone who carried an invitation to the function could stop it and get in.

The invitation was printed on gold-sprinkled cartridge sheets, on which was stamped a map of India, represented as a mother with a bashful maiden kneeling at her feet, offering a sprig of flowers, entitled 'Burning of Kama'. The maiden was presumably 'Sunrise Pictures'.

'Is this your idea?' Srinivas asked Sampath, who worked without food and sleep for the sake of the function. Sampath was cautious in answering: 'Why, is it not good?' Srinivas hesitated for a moment whether he should be candid or just not answer the question. He decided against expressing an opinion and asked: 'What do others say?'

'Everybody says it is so good. Somu was in raptures when he saw it. Our boys did it, you know—something patriotic: we offer our very best to the country, or something like that.'

'Your idea?' Srinivas asked. Sampath was rather reluctant to be cross-questioned, and turned the subject to the task of printing: 'What a trouble it was getting this through in time! They couldn't fool me. I sat tight and got it through.' Srinivas quietly gloated over this vision of Sampath harassed by printers. 'I've not been home at all for three nights; I sat up at the Brown Press and handled the machine myself. How I wish I'd my own press now!' He sighed a little. 'No need to worry; we are on the way to getting our big press.' He seemed distressed at the memory of printing, and Srinivas obligingly changed the subject. 'How many are you inviting?'

'Over a thousand!' Sampath said, brightening. 'It is going to be the biggest function our city has seen.'

As the bus turned into Nallappa's Grove, far off one saw the bunting flying in the air, made up of flags of all nations, including China, Scandinavia and the Netherlands. One could pick them out by referring to *Pears' Encyclopaedia*. The bunting was an odd treasure belonging to the municipal council; no one could say how they had come to gather all this medley of ensigns; but they were very obliging and lent them for all functions, private and public, unstintingly. And no gathering was complete unless it was held under the arcade of these multi-coloured banners: there were even a few ship's signals included among them.

The vast gathering was herded into studio number one, in which hundreds of wooden folding chairs were arrayed. The switching-on was fixed for 4.20, since at 4.30 an inauspicious period of the day was beginning. The district judge, who was to preside, was not to be seen. They fidgeted and waited for him and ran a dozen times to the gate. Sampath calmed Somu by pulling him along to the microphone and announcing: 'Ladies and gentlemen, the president is held up by some unexpected work, but he will be here very soon. Meanwhile, in order not to lose the auspicious hour, the switch will be put on.' He himself passed on to the camera on the tripod, and asked: 'Ready?' and pressed the switch. The lights were directed on to a board fixed on an easel on which the art department had chalked up: 'Sunrise Pictures proudly presents its maiden effort, "The Burning of Kama",' and they shot a hundred feet of it. De Mello cried, 'Cut.' He had come in a dark suit, his moustache oiled and tipped. Thus they caught the auspicious moment, although the big wicker chair meant for the president was still vacant.

A committee of astrologers had studied the conjunction of planets and fixed the day for the inauguration ceremony. There had been a regular conference for fixing the correct moment, for as Somu explained to the others: 'We cannot take risks in these matters. The planets must be beneficial to us.' And he gave three rupees and a coconut, each on a plate, for the Brahmins who had given him the date. The Brahmins officiated at the ceremony now, after deciding what the ritual should be. A couple of framed portraits of

Shiva and a saint, who was Somu's family protector, were leant against the wall, smothered under flowers. The holy men sat before them with their foreheads stamped with ash and vermilion and their backs covered with hand-spun long wraps. They each wore a rosary around the throat, and they sat reading some sacred texts. In front of them were kept trays loaded with coconut, camphor and offerings for the gods. A few minutes before the appointed moment they rose, lit the camphor, and circled the flame before the gods, sounding a bell. Then they went to the camera and stuck a string of jasmine and a dot of sandal paste on it. De Mello trembled when he saw this. They seemed to be so reckless in dealing with the camera. He felt like crying out: 'It's a Mitchel, so—please. . . . It costs Rs 40,000,' but he checked himself as he confessed later: 'In this country, sir, one doesn't know when a religious susceptibility is likely to be hurt. A mere sneeze will take you to the stake sometimes—better be on the safe side.' The priests finished with the camera and then offered him a flower, which he did not know what to do with, but vaguely pressed it to his nose and eyes, and then they gave him a pinch of vermilion and ash, which also worried him, till he saw what others did, and followed their example and rubbed it on his brow. He looked intimidated by these religious observances. It was an odd sight: De Mello in a dark suit, probably of Hollywood cut, and his forehead coloured with the religious marking. 'It's just as well,' Srinivas remarked to himself. 'They are initiating a new religion, and that camera decked with flowers is their new god, who must be propitiated.' To him it seemed no different from the propitiation of the harvest god in the field. To Somu and all these people, God, at the present moment, was a being who might give them profits or ruin them with a loss; with all their immense commitments they felt they ought to be particularly careful not to displease Him. As he was a champion of this religious sect, there was nothing odd in De Mello's submissiveness before it. Srinivas wished he had his *Banner*. What an article he could write under the heading: 'The God in the Lens.'

And these rituals were being witnessed by an audience of over five hundred with open-mouthed wonder. There was suddenly a bustle: 'The president has arrived,' and Somu ran out in great excitement to receive him. There was a stir in the audience, and people craned their necks to look at the president. Though they saw him every day, they never failed to see him as the president with renewed interest, and in this setting he was peculiarly interesting.

In strode a strong dark man, wearing coloured glasses and grinning at the assembly. 'I'm sorry,' he said loudly. 'I was held up by court work. Is it all over?' They propelled him to his wicker chair; he pulled the invitation out of his pocket, to study the items of the programme. He looked at the flower-decked camera and the Brahmins and asked: 'Is this the first scene you are going to shoot?' Sampath explained to the president and apologized, garlanded him, and gave him a bouquet. 'Why are they centring all their affection on him? Have they met here today to fuss about him or to get their film started?' Srinivas wondered. He was struck with the rather pointless manner in which things seemed to be moving. 'Subtle irrelevancies,' he told himself as he sat, unobserved on an upturned box in a corner of the studio. They presently brought the president to the microphone. He said, with the rose garland around his neck: 'Ladies and gentlemen, I know nothing about films, and court work held me up and delayed the pleasure of being here earlier. I don't usually see films—except probably once a year when my little daughter or son drag me there.' And he smiled in appreciation of this human touch. He rambled on thus for about an hour; and people looked as though they were subsiding in their seats. He went on to advise them how to make films. 'I see all around too many mythological and ancient subjects. We must throw all of them overboard. Films must educate. You must appeal to the villager and tell him how to live, how to keep his surroundings clean; why he should not fall into money-lenders' hands, and so on. The film must not only tell a story but must also convey a message to the ignorant masses. There are problems of cultivation and soil—all these you can tackle: there is nothing that you cannot include, if only you have the mind to be of service to your fellow men. They say that the film is the quickest medium of instruction; we all like to see films; let us see ones that tell us something. You have been too long concerned with demons and gods and their prowesses. I think we had better take a vow to boycott Indian films till they take up modern themes.' At this point he was gently interrupted. They had all along wished they could gag him, but it was not an easy thing to choke off a district judge, particularly when he was the president of the occasion. So Sampath and Somu popped up on either side of the judge and carried on a prolonged conversation with him in an undertone. After they withdrew, the judge said: 'I'm sorry I forgot to notice'—he fumbled in his pocket and pulled out the invitation—'what story they are starting. Now my friend Somu tells me it is an epic subject. Our epics undoubtedly are a veritable storehouse of wisdom and spirituality. They contain messages which are of eternal value and applicable to all times and climes, irrespective of age, race, or sex and so on. The thing is that they must be well done. India has a lesson to teach the rest of the world. Let us show the world a sample of our ancient culture and wisdom and civilization. Blessed as this district is by a river and jungles and mountains, with these energetic captains at the helm, I've no doubt that Malgudi will soon be the envy of the rest of India and will be called the Hollywood of India.' De Mello's voice could be heard corroborating the sentiment with a timely 'Hear! Hear!' and resounding applause rang out. The president went to his seat, but came back to the microphone to say: 'I'm sorry I forgot again. I'm asked to announce the happy news that there is going to be a dance entertainment by some talented young artists.' To the accompaniment of the studio orchestra some new recruits to the studio threw their limbs about and gave a dance programme with the studio lights focused on them. Afterwards, with the president beside the camera, and Somu and Sampath touching the switch, still photos were taken from four different angles. This was followed by a few baskets being brought in, out of which were taken paper bags stuffed with coconuts and sweets, which were distributed to all those present. Sampath went to the microphone and thanked the audience and the president for the visit.

When they were moving out, Srinivas noticed a familiar head stirring in the third row. It was his old landlord, tranformed by a faded turban, a pair of glasses over his nose, and a black alpaca coat, almost green with years. Srinivas ran up to him and accosted him. He felt so surprised that he could not contain himself. 'Oh, you are here?' The old man gave him his toothless smile. 'First time for thirty years I have come out so far—Sampath wouldn't leave me alone. He sent me a car. Where is your artist friend? I thought he would be here.'

'Ravi! He must be in the office. He doesn't usually fancy these occasions.' The old man looked about for Sampath and called to him loudly. Srinivas slipped away, somehow not wishing to be present at their meeting, feeling vaguely perhaps that Sampath might try and get a cheque out of the old man at this opportunity. Srinivas was busy putting the finishing touches to his script. He worked continuously, not budging from his seat from nine in the morning till nine in the evening. Even Ravi, who came in when he had a little leisure, hesitated at the door and turned back without uttering a word. Srinivas worked in a frenzy. He was very eager to complete his part of the work, though he had at the back of his mind a constant misgiving about the final treatment they might hatch out of it, but he ruthlessly pushed away this doubt, saying to himself: 'It is not my concern what they do with my work.'

Sampath was not to be seen for nearly a week, and then he turned up one evening, bubbling with enthusiasm. A look at him, and Srinivas decided that it would be useless to try to get on with his work. He put away his papers. Sampath began: 'She has come!'

'When?'

'Five days ago, and we have been putting her through the tests. De Mello says she is the right type for the screen. She is a fine girl.'

'Is she the same as—?' asked Srinivas, indicating the old sketch. Sampath smiled at this suggestion. He scrutinized the sketch, remarking under his breath: 'Extraordinary how two entirely unconnected people can resemble each other.' He laughed heartily, as if it were the biggest joke he had heard in his life. He seemed extraordianarily tickled by it. 'Yes, she is somewhat like this picture, but there is a lot of difference, you know. In fact, this is her first visit to this town. She has never been here before. She was born and bred in Madras.'

'Where is she at the moment?' asked Srinivas.

'I've found her a room in Modern Lodge. I could've put her up at my house if it was necessary; after all, I find that she is related to me, a sort of cousin of mine, though we never suspected it. Anyway, our problem is solved about Parvathi. She is going to do it wonderfully well. I foresee a very great future for her. We are finalizing the rest of the cast tomorrow; after that we must go into rehearsals.'

Srinivas was present at the rehearsal hall in the studio. It was a small room on the first floor, furnished with a few lounges covered with orange and black cretonne, a coir mattress spread on the floor and a large portrait of Somu decorating the wall. On the opposite wall was a chart, showing the life history of a film—starting with the story-idea and ending with the spectator in the theatre. The rehearsal was announced for eleven, and Srinivas caught an early bus and was the first to arrive. He sat there all alone, looking at the portrait of Somu and at the chart. A medley of studio sounds—voices of people, hammerings, and the tuning of musical instruments—kept coming up. Through the window he could see far-off Sarayu winding its way, glimmering in the sun, the leaves of trees on its back throwing off tiny relfections of the sun, and a blue sky beyond, and further away the tower of the municipal office, which reminded him of his *Banner*. Its whole career seemed to have been dedicated to attacking the Malgudi municipality and its unvarying incompetence. He felt a nostalgia for the whirring of the wheels of a press and the cool dampness of a galley proof. 'When am I going to see it back in print?' he asked himself. His whole work now seemed to him to have a meaning because, beyond all this, there was the promise of reviving *The Banner*. He had not yet spoken to Sampath about what he was to be paid for his work. He felt he could never speak about it. He found on his table on the second of every month a cheque for one hundred and fifty rupees, and that saw him through the month, and he was quite satisfied. How long it was to continue and how long he could expect it, or how much more, he never bothered.

His wife occasionally, waiting on him for his mood, asked him, and all that he replied was: 'You get what you need for the month?'

'Yes. But—'

'Then why do you bother about anything? You may always rest assured that we will get what we need without any difficulty. You will be happy as long as you don't expect more.'

'But, but—'

'There are no further points in this scheme of life,' he cut her short. And that was the basis on which his career and daily life progressed. 'Of course, if *The Banner* could be revived,' he reflected, 'I could breathe more freely. Now I don't know what I'm doing, whether I'm helping Sampath or Sampath is helping me—the whole position is vague and obscure. The clear-cut lines of life are visible only when I'm at my table and turning out *The Banner*.' He had now a lot of time to reflect on *The Banner*. For one thing, he decided to rescue Ravi and get him to work for *The Banner*. 'The *Banner* can justify its existence only if it saves a man like Ravi and shows the world something of his creative powers. . . .' He made a mental note of all the changes he was going to make in *The Banner*. He would print thirty-six pages of every issue; a quarter for international affairs, half for Indian politics, and a quarter for art and culture and philosophy. This was going to help him in his search for an unknown stabilizing factor in life, for an unchanging value, a knowledge of the self, a piece of knowledge which would support as on a rock the faith of Man and his peace; a knowledge of his true identity, which would bring no depression at the coming of age, nor puzzle the mind with conundrums and antitheses. 'I must have a permanent page for it,' he told himself. 'This single page will be the keystone of the whole paper—all its varied activities brought in and examined: it will give a perspective and provide an answer for many questions—a sort of crucible, in which the basic gold can be discovered. What shall I call the feature? The Crucible? Too obvious. . . .'

It was so peaceful here and the outlook so enchanting with the heat-haze quivering over the river-sand that he lost all sense of time passing, leaning back in the cane chair, which he had dragged to the window. He presently began to wish that the others would not turn up but leave him alone to think out his plans. But it seemed to him that perverse fates were always waiting around, just to spite such a wish. He heard footsteps on the stairs and presently Sampath and the new girl made their entry.

'Meet my cousin Shanti, who is going to act Parvathi,' Sampath said expansively. Srinivas rose in his seat, nodded an acknowledgment, and sat down. He saw before him a very pretty girl, of a height which you wouldn't notice either as too much or too little, a perfect figure, rosy complexion, and arched eyebrows and almond-shaped eyes—everything that should send a man, especially an artist, into hysterics. Srinivas, as he saw her, felt her enchantment growing upon him. Her feet were encased in velvet sandals, over her ankles fell the folds of her azure translucent sari, edged with gold; at her throat sparkled a tiny diamond star. She seemed to have donned her personality, part by part, with infinite care. Srinivas said to himself: 'It's all nonsense to say that she does all this only to attract men. That is a self-compliment Man concocts for himself. She spends her day doing all this to herself because she can't help it, any more than the full moon can help being round and lustrous.' He caught himself growing poetic, caught himself trying to look at a piece of her fair skin which showed below her close-fitting sheeny jacket. He pulled himself up. It seemed a familiar situation; he recollected that in the story Shiva himself was in a similar plight, before he discovered the god of the sugar-cane bow taking aim. He seemed to realize the significance of this mythological piece more than ever now. And he prayed: 'Oh, God, open your third eye and do some burning up here also.' 'Mankind has not yet learned to react to beauty properly,' he said to himself. Shanti, who had by now seated herself on a sofa with Sampath beside her, muttered something to Sampath. And Sampath said: 'My cousin says you look thoughtful.' She at once puckered her brow and blushed and threw up her hands in semi-anger, and almost beat him as she said in an undertone: 'Why do you mis-represent me? I never said any such a thing.' She shot scared glances at Srinivas, who found his composure shaken. He said: 'Don't bother. I don't mind, even if you have said it,' and at once all her confusion and indignation left her. She said with perfect calm: 'I only said that we seemed to have disturbed you while you were thinking out something, and he says—' She threw a look at Sampath. Srinivas wanted to cut short this conversation and said rather brusquely: 'I have waited here for two hours now. You said that rehearsals were at ten.'

'Apologies, Editor,' replied Sampath. 'Shall I speak the truth? The real culprit is—' He merely looked at his cousin, and she at once said apologetically: 'Am I responsible? I didn't know.'

'Well, you have taken a little over three hours dressing up, you know,' Sampath said. Srinivas noted that they seemed to have taken to each other very well. He said to the girl: 'You are his cousin, I hear?'

'I didn't know that when I replied,' she asked.

'Have you a lot of film experience?' he asked and felt that he was uttering fatuous rubbish. Before she could answer he turned to Sampath and asked: 'Have you told her the story?' And he realized that it was none of his business and that he was once again uttering a fatuity. But that fact didn't deter Sampath from building up an elaborate reply of how he had been talking to her night and day of the part she was to play, of how he was constantly impressing upon her the inner significance of the episode, and he added with warmth: 'My association with you is not in vain, Editor.' He con-stantly shot side glances to observe the effect of his speech on the lady, and Srinivas listened to him without saying a word in reply, as he told himself: 'I don't seem to be able to open my mouth without uttering nonsense.'

Presently more footsteps on the staircase, and half a dozen persons entered, followed by Somu. Somu, who came in breezily, became a little awkward at seeing the beauty, and shuffled his steps, stroked his moustache, and in various ways became confused. 'He will also find it difficult to speak anything but nonsense,' Srinivas said to himself. The visitors spread themselves around, and Somu said, pointing at a strong paunchy man: 'This is Shiva.' The paunchy man nodded agreeably as if godhead were conferred on him that instant. He had a gruff voice as he said: 'I have played the part of Shiva in over a hundred dramas and twenty films for the last twenty years. I act no other part because I'm a devotee of Shiva.'

'You must have heard of him,' Sampath added. 'V.L.G.—' Srinivas cast his mind back and made an honest attempt to recollect his name. It suddenly flashed upon him. He used to notice it on the wall of the magistrate's court at Talapur, years and years ago—'V.L.G. in. . . .' some Shiva story or other. He almost cried out as he said: 'Yes, yes, I remember it: rainbow-coloured posters!'— that colour scheme used to make his flesh creep in those days; and at the recollection of it he once again shuddered. 'Yes, it was in *Daksha Yagna,*' Shiva said, much pleased with his own reputation. 'I always do Shiva, no other part, I'm a devotee of Shiva.'

'He gets into the spirit of his role,' Sampath said. Shiva acknowledged it with a nod and repeated for the third time: 'I do no other role. I'm a devotee of Shiva. Both in work and in leisure I want to contemplate Shiva.' True to his faith his forehead was smeared with sacred ash and a line of sandal paste. Srinivas viewed him critically, remarking to himself: 'His eyes are all right, but the rest, as I visualized Shiva, is not here. He certainly was without a paunch—the sort of austerity which is the main characteristic of Shiva in the story is missing. And he should not have such loose, hanging lips, all the inconvenient, ungodly paddings of middle age are here—what a pity! Some tens and thousands of persons have probably formed their notions of a god from him for a quarter of a century.' As if in continuation of his reflections Sampath said: 'When his name is on the poster as Shiva, the public of our country simply smash the box-office.' Shiva accepted the compliment without undue modesty. He added in a gruff tone: 'So many people were troubling me, and I refused them because I wanted some rest. But when I heard about the starting of this studio I said I must do a picture here,' and Somu beamed on him gratefully. Srinivas felt inclined to ask more questions, so that he might clear the doubt at the back of his mind as to what special reason the actor had for conferring this favour on this particular studio; but he left the matter alone, one of the many doubts in life which could never be cleared. V.L.G. took out of his pocket a small casket, out of it he fished a piece of tobacco and put it in his mouth, and then proceeded to smear a bit of lime on the back of a betel leaf and stuffed it also into his mouth. He chewed with an air of satisfaction; and from his experience of tobacco-chewers, Srinivas understood that V.L.G. was not going to talk any more, but would be grateful to be left alone to enjoy his tobacco. He seemed to settle down to it quietly and definitely. Others, too, seemed to understand the position, and they left Shiva alone and turned their attention to the man next to him—a puny youth, with a big head and sunken cheeks and long hair combed back on his head. 'He is going to be Kama,' said Sampath. 'He has been doing such roles in various films.' Srinivas looked at him. He wondered if he might get up and make a scene. I'm not going to allow the story to be done by this horrible pair.' But presently another inner voice said: 'If it is not this horrible pair, some other horrible pair will do it, so why bother?' And his further reflections were cut short by the lady remarking as she looked at her tiny wristwatch: 'It's four o'clock. When do we start the rehearsal?'

'As soon as we finish coffee, which is coming now,' said Sampath. It was six-thirty when they finished their coffee, and then they unanimously decided to postpone the rehearsals, and got up to go away with relief and satisfaction.

THE FINANCIAL EXPERT

Editor's note: Margayya, the financial expert who sits under a tree and shows yokels how to borrow more and more money from the Co-operative Bank, is shooed from his spot by the new manager of the bank. He tries to conduct his business as usual from outside the compound of the bank but his heart is not really in it. He has to find other means for self-aggrandizement. This opening chapter is a splendid example of Narayan's ability to create a wholly credible character from what would have seemed, to another writer, intractable material.

From time immemorial people seemed to have been calling him 'Margayya'. No one knew, except his father and mother, who were only dimly recollected by a few cronies in his ancestral village that he had been named after the enchanting god Krishna. Everyone called him Margayya and thought that he had been called so at his naming ceremony. He himself must have forgotten his original name: he had gradually got into the habit of signing his name 'Margayya' even in legal documents. And what did it mean? It was purely derivative: 'Marga' meant 'The Way' and 'Ayya' was an honorific suffix: taken together it denoted one who showed the way. He showed the way out to those in financial trouble. And in all those villages that lay within a hundred-mile radius of Malgudi, was there anyone who could honestly declare that he was not in financial difficulties? The emergence of Margayya was an unexpected and incalculable offshoot of a co-operator's zeal. This statement will be better understood if we watch him in his setting a little more closely.

One of the proudest buildings in Malgudi was the Central Co-operative Land Mortgage Bank, which was built in the year 1914 and named after a famous Registrar of Co-operative Societies, Sir——, who had been knighted for his devotion to Co-operation after he had, in fact, lost his voice explaining Co-operative principles to peasants in the village at one end and to the officials in charge of the files at the Secretariat end. It was said that he died while serving on a Rural Indebtedness Sub-committee. After his death it was discovered that he had left all his savings for the construction of the bank. He now watched, from within a teak frame suspended on the central landing, all the comings and goings, and he was said to be responsible for occasional poltergeist phenomena, the rattling of paperweights, flying ledgers, and sounds like the brisk opening of folios, the banging of fists on a table, and so on—evidenced by successive night-watchmen. This could be easily understood, for the ghost of the Registrar had many reasons to feel sad and frustrated. All the principles of co-operation for which he had sacrificed his life were dissolving under his eyes, if he could look beyond the portals of the bank itself, right across the little stretch of lawn under the banyan tree, in whose shade Margayya sat and transacted his business. There was always a semi-circle of peasants sitting round him, and by their attitude and expression one might easily guess that they were supplicants. Margayya, though very much their junior (he was just forty-two), commanded the respect of those who sat before him. He was to them a wizard who enabled them to draw unlimited loans from the Co-operative Bank. If the purpose of the co-operative movement was the promotion of thrift and the elimination of middlemen, those two were just the objects that were defeated here under the banyan tree: Margayya didn't believe in advocating thrift: his living depended upon helping people to take loans from the bank opposite and from each other.

His tin box, a grey, discoloured, knobby affair, which was small enough to be carried under his arm, contained practically his entire equipment: a bottle of ink, a pen and a blotter, a small register whose pages carried an assortment of names and figures, and above all—the most important item—loan application forms of the co-operative bank. These last named were his greatest asset in life, and half his time was occupied in acquiring them. He had his own agency at work to provide him with these forms. When a customer came, the very first question Margayya asked was, 'Have you secured the application form?'

'No.'

'Then go into that building and bring one—try and get one or two spare forms as well.' It was not always possible to secure more than one form, for the clerks there were very strict and perverse. They had no special reason to decline to give as many forms as were required except the impulse to refuse anything that is persistently asked for. All the same, Margayya managed to gather quite a lot of forms and kept them handy. They were taken out for use on special occasions. Sometimes a villager arrived who did not have a form and who could not succeed in acquiring one by asking for it in the bank. On such occasions Margayya charged a fee for the blank form itself, and then another for filling in the relevant details.

The clerks of the bank had their own methods of worrying the villagers. A villager who wanted to know his account had to ask for it at the counter and invariably the accounts clerk snapped back, 'Where is your pass-book?' A pass-book was a thing the villager could never keep his hand on. If it was not out of sight it was certain to be out of date. This placed the villager fully at the mercy of the clerk, who would say: 'You will have to wait till I get through all the work I have now on hand. I'm not being paid to look after only your business here.' And then the peasant would have to hang about for a day or two before getting an answer to his question, which would only be after placating the clerk with an offering in cash or kind.

It was under such circumstances that Margayya's help proved invaluable. He kept more or less parallel accounts of at least fifty of the members of the bank. What its red-tape obstructed, he cleared up by his own contrivance. He carried most of the figures in his head. He had only to sight a customer (for instance Mallanna of Koppal, as it now happened to be) to say at once: 'Oh! you have come back for a new loan, I suppose. If you pay seventy-five rupees more, you can again take three hundred rupees within a week! The by-law allows a new loan when fifty per cent is paid up.'

'How can I burden myself with a further loan of three hundred, Margayya? It's unthinkable.'

Now would begin all the persuasiveness that was Margayya's stock-in-trade. He asked point blank, 'What difference is it going to make? Are you not already paying a monthly instalment of seventeen rupees eight annas? Are you or are you not?'

'Yes. . . I'm paying. God knows how much I have to—'

'I don't want all that,' Margayya said, cutting him short. 'I am not concerned with all that—how you pay or what you do. You may perhaps pledge your life or your wife's saris. It is none of my concern: all that I want to know is whether you are paying an instalment now or not.'

'Yes, master, I do pay.'

'You will continue to pay the same thing, that is all. Call me a dog if they ask you for even one anna more. You fool, don't you see the difference? You pay seventeen rupees eight annas now for nothing, but under my present plan you will pay the same seventeen rupees eight annas but with another three hundred rupees in your purse. Don't you see the difference?'

'But what's the use of three hundred rupees, master?'

'Oh! I see, you don't see a use for it. All right, don't come to me again. I have no use for nincompoops like you. You are the sort of fellow who won't—' He elaborated a bawdy joke about him and his capacity, which made the atmosphere under the tree genial all round. The other villagers sitting around laughed. But Margayya assumed a stern look, and pretended to pass on to the next question in hand. He sat poring over some papers, with his spectacles uneasily poised over his nose. Those spectacles were a recent acquisition, the first indication that he was on the wrong side of forty. He resisted them as long as he could—he hated the idea of growing old, but 'long-sight' does not wait for approval or welcome. You cannot hoodwink yourself or anyone else too long about it—the strain of holding a piece of paper at arm's length while reading stretches the nerves of the forearm and invites comments from others. Margayya's wife laughed aloud one day and asked: 'Why don't you buy a pair of glasses like other young men of your age? Otherwise you will sprain your hand.' He acted upon this advice and obtained a pair of glasses mounted in silver from the V.N. Stores in the market. He and the proprietor of the shop had been playmates once, and Margayya took the glasses on trial, and forgot to go that way again. He was accosted about it on the road occasionally by the rotund optician, who was snubbed by Margayya: 'Haven't you the elementary courtesy to know the time and place for such reminders?'

'Sorry, sorry,' the other hastened to apologize, 'I didn't intend to hurt or insult you.'

'What greater insult can a man face than this sort of thing? What will an onlooker think? I am busy from morning to night—no time even for a cup of coffee in the afternoon! All right, it doesn't matter. Will you send someone to my house? I'm not able to use those glasses either. I wanted to come and exchange them if possible, but—' it trailed off into indefiniteness, and the optician went away once again and soon ceased to bother about it. It was one of his many bad debts, and very soon he changed his commodity; gradually his show-case began to display powder-puffs, scents, chocolate bars—and the silver-rimmed glasses sat securely on Margayya's nose.

He now took off his spectacles and folded the sides as if disposing once and for all of the problem of Mallanna. He looked away at a man on his right and remarked: 'You may have to wait for a week more before I can take up your affair.'

'Brother, this is urgent, my daughter's marriage is coming off next month.'

'Your daughter's marriage! I have to find you the money for it, but the moment my service is done, you will forget me. You will not need your Margayya any more.' The other made several deprecating noises, as a protestation of his loyalty. He was a villager called Kanda who had come walking from his village fifteen miles away. He owned about twenty acres of land and a house and cattle, but all of it was tied up in mortgages—most through Margayya's advice and assistance. He was a gambler and drank heavily, and he always asked for money on the pretext of having to marry his daughters, of whom he had a good number. Margayya preferred not to know what happened to all the money, but helped him to borrow as much as he wanted. 'The only course now left is for you to take a joint-loan, but the difficulty will be to find someone as a partner.' He looked round at the gathering before him and asked, 'All of you are members of the Co-operative Society. Can't someone help a fellow-creature?' Most of them shook their heads. One of them remarked, 'How can you ask for our joint-signature? It's risky to do it even for one's own brother.'

'It's most risky between brothers,' added Margayya. 'But I'm not suggesting it for brothers now. I am only suggesting it between human beings.' They all laughed and understood that he was referring to an elder brother of his with whom he was known to be on throat-cutting terms. He prepared to deliver a speech: 'Here is a great man, you cannot find a more important man round about Somanur. He has lands, cattle, yes, he's a big man in every way. No doubt, he has certain habits; no use shutting our eyes to it; but I guarantee he will get over them. He must have a joint-loan because he needs at least five hundred rupees immediately to see him through his daughter's marriage. You know how it is with the dowry system—' Everybody made a sympathetic noise and shook their heads. 'Very bad, very bad. Why should we criticize what our ancestors have brought into existence?' someone asked.

'Why not?' another protested.

'Some people are ruined by the dowry.'

'Why do you say some people?' Margayya asked. 'Why am I here? Three daughters were born to my father. Five cart-loads of paddy came to us every half year, from the fields. We just heaped them up on the floor of the hall, we had five halls to our house, but where has it all gone? To the three daughters. By the time my father found husbands for them there was nothing left for us to eat at home!'

'But is it not said that a man who begets a son is blessed in three lives, because he gives away the greatest treasure on earth?' said someone.

'And how much more blessed is he that gives away three daughters? He is blessed no doubt, but he also becomes a bankrupt,' Margayya said.

The talk thus went on and on, round and round, always touching practical politics again at some point or other. Maragayya put his spectacles on, looked fixedly at Mallanna, and said: 'Come and sit near me.' The villager moved up. Margayya told the gathering, 'We have to talk privately.' And they all looked away and pretended not to hear although all their attention was concentrated on the whispering that now started between the two. Margayya said: 'It's going to be impossible for Kanda to get a joint-loan, but he ought to be ready to accept whatever is available. I know you can help him and help yourself—you will lose nothing. In fact, you will gain a little interest. You will clear half your present loan by paying seventy-five rupees and apply for a fresh one. Since you don't want it, give it to Kanda. He will pay you seven-and-a-half per cent. You give the four-and-a-half per cent to that father-in-law' (Margayya always referred to the Co-operative Bank with a fresh sobriquet) 'and take the three per cent yourself. He will pay back the instalments to you. I will collect and give them to you.' Mallanna took time to grasp all the intricacies of this proposition, and then asked: 'Suppose he doesn't?' Margayya looked horrified at this doubt. 'What is there to be afraid of when I am here?' At this one of the men who were supposed to be out of earshot remarked: 'Ah, what is possible in this world without mutual trust?' Margayya added, 'Listen to him. He knows the world.'

The result of all this talk was that Mallanna agreed to the proposal. Margayya grew busy filling up a loan application form with all the details of Mallanna's heritage, etc. He read it out aloud, seized hold of Mallanna's left thumb, pressed it on a small ink pad he carried in his box and pressed it again on the application form and endorsed it. He took out of the box seventy-five rupees in cash, and handed them to Mallanna with: 'Why should I trust you with this without a scrap of paper? Now credit this to your account and halve your loan; and then present that application.'

'If they refuse to take it?'

'Why should they refuse? They have got to accept it. You are a shareholder, and they have got to accept your application. It's not their grandfather's money that they are giving you but your own. By-law—' He quoted the by-law, and encouraged by it, the other got up and moved on.

It is impossible to describe more clearly than this Margayya's activity under the tree. He advanced a little loan (for interest) so that the little loan might wedge out another loan from the Co-operative Bank; which in its turn was passed on to someone in need for a higher interest. Margayya kept himself as the centre of all the complex transactions, and made all the parties concerned pay him for his services, the bank opposite him being involved in it willy-nilly. It was as strenuous a job as any other in the town and he felt that he deserved the difficult income he ground out of a couple of hundred rupees in his box, sitting there morning till evening. When the evening sun hit him on the nape of the neck he pulled down the lid of his box and locked it up, and his gathering under-stood that the financial wizard was closing his office for the day.

Margayya deposited the box under a bench in the front room of his house. His little son immediately came running out from the kitchen with a shout: 'Appa!' and gripped his hand, asking: 'What have you brought today?' Margayya hoisted him up on his shoulder: 'Well, tomorrow I will buy you a new engine, a small engine.' The child was pleased to hear it. He asked, 'How small will the engine be? Will it be so tiny?' He indicated with his thumb and first finger a minute size. 'All right,' said Margayya and put him down. This was almost a daily ritual. The boy revelled in visions of miniature articles—a tiny engine, tiny cows, tiny table, tiny everything, of the maximum size of a mustard seed. Margayya put him down and briskly removed his upper cloth and shirt, picked up a towel that was hanging from a nail on the wall, and moved to the backyard. Beyond a small clump of banana trees, which waved their huge fan-like leaves in the darkness, there was a single well of crumbling masonry, with a pulley over its cross-bar. Margayya paused for a moment to admire the starry sky. Down below at his feet the earth was damp and marshy. All the drain water of two houses flowed into the banana beds. It was a common backyard for his house and the one next door, which was his brother's. It was really a single house, but a partition wall divided it into two from the street to the backyard.

No. 14 D, Vinayak Street had been a famous landmark, for it was the earliest house to be built in that area. Margayya's father was considered a hero for settling there in a lonely place where there was supposed to be no security for life or property. Moreover it was built on the fringe of a cremation ground and often the glow of a burning pyre lit up its walls. After the death of the old man the brothers fell out, their wives fell out, and their children fell out. They could not tolerate the idea of even breathing the same air or being enclosed by the same walls. They got involved in litigation and partitioned everything that their father had left. Everything that could be cut in two with an axe or scissors or a knife was divided between them, and the other things were catalogued, numbered and then shared out. But one thing that could neither be numbered nor cut up was the backyard of the house with its single well. They could do nothing about it. It fell to Margayya's share, and he would willingly have seen his brother's family perish without water by closing it to them, but public opinion prevented the exercise of his right. People insisted that the well should remain common property, and so the dividing wall came up to it, and stopped there, the well acting as a blockade between the two brothers, but accessible from either side.

Now Margayya looked about for the small brass pot. He could not see it anywhere.

'Hey, little man!' he called out, 'where is the well-pot?' He liked to call his son out constantly. When he came home, he could not bear to be kept away from him even for a moment. He felt uneasy and irritated when the child did not answer his call. He saw the youngster stooping over the lamp, trying to thrust a piece of paper into the chimney. He watched him from the doorway. He suppressed the inclination to call him away and warn him. The child thrust a piece of paper into the lamp, and when it burned brightly he recoiled at the sudden spurt of fire. But when it blackened and burnt out he drew near the lamp again, gingerly putting his finger near the metal plate on the top. Before Margayya could stop him, he had touched it. He let out a shriek. Margayya was beside him in a moment. His shriek brought in Margayya's wife, who had gone to a neighbouring shop. She came rushing into the house with cries of 'What is it? What is it? What has happened?' Margayya felt embarrassed, like a man caught shirking a duty. He told his wife curtly, 'Why do you shout so much, as if a great calamity had befallen this household—so that your sister-in-law in the neighbourhood may think how active we are, I suppose?'

'Sister-in-law—how proud you are of your relatives!' Her further remarks could not be continued because of the howling set up by the child, whose burnt finger still remained unattended. At this the mother snatched him up from her husband's arms, and hugged him close to her, hurting him more, whereupon he shouted in a new key. Margayya tried to tear him out of his wife's arms, crying: 'Quick, get that ointment. Where is it? You can keep nothing in its place.'

'You need not shout!' the wife answered, running about and rummaging in the cupboard. She grumbled: 'You can't look after him even for a second without letting him hurt himself.'

'You need not get hysterical about it, gentle lady, I had gone for a moment to the well.'

'Everyone gets tap-water in this town. We alone—' she began attacking on a new front.

'All right, all right,' he said, curbing her, and turning his attention to the finger. 'You must never, never go near fire again, do you understand?'

'Will you buy me a little elephant tomorrow?' the child asked, his cheeks still wet with tears. By now they had discovered a little wooden crucible containing some black ointment in the cupboard, hidden behind a small basket containing loose cotton (which Margayya's wife twisted into wicks for the lamp in God's niche). She applied the ointment to the injured finger, and set the child roaring in a higher key. This time he said, 'I want a big peppermint.'

At night when the lights were put out and the sounds of Vinayak Street had quietened, Margayya said to his wife, lying on the other side of their sleeping child: 'Do you know—poor boy! I could have prevented Balu from hurting himself. I just stood there and watched. I wanted to see what he would do alone by himself.' His wife made a noise of deprecation: 'It is as I suspected. You were at the bottom of the whole trouble. I don't know. . . I don't know. . . that boy is terribly mischievous. . . and you are. . . you are. . . .' She could not find the right word for it. Her instinct was full of foreboding, and she left the sentence unfinished. After a long pause she added: 'It's impossible to manage him during the afternoons. He constantly runs out of the house into the street. I don't have a moment's peace or rest.'

'Don't get cantankerous about such a small child,' said Margayya, who disliked all these adverse remarks about his son. It seemed to him such a pity that that small bundle of man curled beside him like a tiny pillow should be so talked about. His wife retorted: 'Yes, I wish you could stay at home and look after him instead of coming in the evening and dandling him for a moment after he has exhausted all his tricks.'

'Yes, gladly, provided you agree to go out and arrange loans for all those village idiots.'

The child levied an exacting penalty on his parents the next day for the little patch of burn on his finger. He held his finger upright and would not let anyone come near him. He refused to be put into a new shirt, refused food, refused to walk, and insisted on being carried about by his mother or father. Margayya examined the hurt finger and said: 'It looks all right, there seems to be nothing wrong there.'

'Don't say so,' screamed the boy in his own childish slang. 'I'm hurt. I want a peppermint.' Margayya was engaged all the morning in nursing his finger and plying him with peppermints. His wife remarked: 'He'll be ill with peppermints before you are done with him.'

'Why don't you look after him, then?' he asked.

'I won't go to Mother,' screamed the boy. 'I will be with you.'

Margayya had some odd jobs to do while at home in the mornings. He went to the nearby Urban Stores and bought sugar or butter, he cut up the firewood into smaller sizes if his wife complained about it, or he opened his tin box and refreshed his memory by poring over the pages of his red-bound account book. But today the boy would not let him do anything except fuss over him.

The child kept Margayya at home for over an hour beyond his usual time. He could leave for the Co-operative Bank only at midday, stealing out when, oblivious of his surroundings, the little fellow's attention was engaged in splashing about a bucket of water in the backyard. When the water was exhausted he looked all round and let out such an angry shout for his father that the people on the other side of the wall remarked to each other: 'This is the worst of begetting sons late in life! They pet them and spoil them and make them little monsters.' The lady on the other side of the wall could well say this because she was the mother of ten.

Margayya looked up as a shadow fell on his notebook. He saw a uniformed servant standing before him. It was Arul Doss, the head peon of the Co-operative Bank, an old Christian who had grown up with the institution. He had wrinkles round his eyes, and a white moustache and mild eyes. Margayya looked up at him and wondered what to do—whether to treat him as a hostile visitor or as a friend. Instinctively he recoiled from anyone coming out of that building, where he knew he was being viewed as a public enemy. He hesitated for a moment, then looked up silently at the figure before him. 'Sit down, won't you, Arul Doss?' Arul Doss shot a glance over his shoulder at the office.

'He will not like it if he sees me dallying here. He, I mean the Secretary, asks you to come—' said Arul.

'Me!' Margayya could hardly believe his ears. 'The Secretary! What have I to do with your Secretary?'

'I don't know at all, but he said, "Go and tell Margayya to come here for a moment."'

On hearing this, Margayya became indignant. 'Go and tell them I an not their paid—paid—' He was about to say 'servant' but he remembered in time, even in his mental stress, that the man standing before him was literally both paid and a servant, and thought it would be injudicious to say so now. So he left off the sentence abruptly and asked: 'Do they pay me to appear before them when they want me?'

'I don't know,' said this very loyal Co-operative man. 'He told me to tell you. The Secretary is no ordinary person, you know,' he added. 'He receives a salary of over five hundred rupees a month, an amount which you and I will probably not see even after a hundred years of service.' Now Margayya's blood was stirred. Many angry memories welled up in him of all the indignities that he had suffered at the hands of his brother, who cut him off with half a house, while he himself passed for a man of means, a respectable citizen. Margayya felt that the world treated him with contempt because he had no money. People thought they could order him about. He said to Arul Doss: 'Arul Doss, I don't know about you; you can speak for yourself. But you need not speak for me. You may not see a hundred rupees even after a hundred years of service, but I think I shall do so very soon—and who knows, if your Secretary seeks any improvement of his position, he can come to me.'

Arul Doss took a few moments to understand, then swayed with laughter. Tears rolled down his cheeks. 'Well, I have been a servant in this department for twenty-nine years, but I've never heard a crazier proposal. All right, all right.' He was convulsed with laughter as he turned to go. Margayya looked at his back helplessly. He cast his eyes down and surveyed himself: perhaps he cut a ridiculous figure, with his dhoti going brown for lack of laundering and with his shirt collar frayed, and those awful silver spectacles. 'I hate these spectacles. I wish I could do without them.' But age, age—who could help long-sight? 'If I wore gold spectacles, perhaps they would take me seriously and not order me about. Who is this Secretary to call me through the peon? I won't be ridiculed. I'm at least as good as they.' He called out: 'Look here, Arul Doss.' With a beaming face, Arul Doss turned round.

'Tell your Secretary that if he is a Secretary, I'm really the proprietor of a bank, and that he can come here and meet me if he has any business—'

'Shall I repeat those very words?' Arul Doss asked, ready to burst out laughing again.

'Absolutely,' Margayya said, 'and another thing, if you find yourself thrown out of there, you can come to me for a job. I like you, you seem to be a hard-working, loyal fellow.' Further parleys were cut off because a couple of villagers came round for consultation, and started forming a semi-circle in front of Margayya. Though Arul Doss still lingered for a further joke, Margayya turned away abruptly, remarking: 'All right, you may go now.'

'Please,' said a peasant, 'be careful, sir. That Arul Doss is a bad fellow.'

'I'm also a bad fellow,' snapped Margayya.

'It's not that. They say that the Secretary just does what this fellow says. If we go in to get just one single form, he charges us two annas each time. Is that also a Government rule?' asked the peasant.

'Go away, you fools,' Margayya said. 'You are people who have no self-respect. As long as you are shareholders you are masters of the bank. They are your paid servants.'

'Ah, is that so?' asked the peasant. And the group looked up at each other with amazement. Another man, who had a long blanket wrapped round his shoulder, a big cloth turban crowning his head, and wore shorts and was bare-foot, said: 'We may be masters as you say, but who is going to obey us? If we go in, we have to do as they say. Otherwise, they won't give us money.'

'Whose money are they giving away?'asked Margayya. 'It is your own.'

'Margayya, we don't want all that. Why should we talk of other people?'

'True, true,' said one or two others approvingly.

Encouraged by this, the peasant said: 'We should not talk about others unnecessarily.' He lowered his voice and said: 'If they hear it they may—'

Margayya's blood rushed to his head: 'You get away from here,' he thundered. 'I don't want to have anything to do with people without self-respect, who don't know their importance and strength. What better words can we expect from a head weighed down by so many folds of a dirty turban?' The peasant was somewhat cowed by Margayya's manner. He mumbled: 'I don't mean to offend you, sir. If I did would I be here?'

'That's all right. No further unnecessary talk. If you have any business, tell me. Otherwise get out of here. Before dusk I have to attend to so many people. You are not the only one who has business with me.'

'I want a small loan, sir,' began the peasant. 'I want to know how much more I have to pay to clear the balance loan.'

'Why don't you go in there and ask your Arul Doss?'

'Oh, they are all very bad, unhelpful people, sir; that's why I never like to go there, but come to you first. Why do we come to you, sir, of all persons in this big city? It's because you know our joys and sorrows and our troubles, our difficulties and—'

'All right, all right,' Margayya said, cutting him short, yet greatly mollified by his manner. 'I know what you are trying to say. Don't I?' He looked round at his clients. And they shook their heads approvingly, making appropriate sounds with their tongues, in order to please him.

After all these bouts he settled down to business. He had a busy day: filling up forms, writing applications, writing even petitions unconnected with money-business for one or two clients, talking, arguing, and calculating. He was nearly hoarse by the time the sun's rays touched him on the nape of his neck, and the shadows of the banyan tree fell on the drive leading to the Co-operative Bank. He started to close his office. He put back his writing pad, neatly folded up some pieces of paper on which he had noted figures, scrutinized again the little register, counted some cash, and checked some receipts. He arranged all these back in the small tin box, laid a few sheets of loan application forms flat on top of them so as to prevent their creasing, restored to its corner the ink bottle, and laid beside it the red wooden pen. Everything in its place. He hated, more than anything else, having to fumble for his papers or stationery; and a disordered box was as hateful to him as the thought of Arul Doss. His mind was oppressed with thoughts of Arul Doss. He felt insulted and sore. What right had he or anyone to insult or browbeat him? What had he done that they themselves did not do? He would teach this Arul Doss a lesson—no matter at what cost. . . .

At this moment he heard a step approaching, and looking up saw a man, wearing a brown suit, standing before him. His hands were in his pockets, and behind him at a respectable distance stood Arul Doss. The man looked very smart, with a hat on his head; a very tidy young man who looked 'as if he had just come from Europe,' Margayya reflected. Looking at him he felt himself to be such a contrast with his brown dhoti, torn shirt, and the absurd litle tuft under the black cap. 'No wonder they treat me as they do,' he said to himself. 'Perhaps I should have exercised greater care in my speech. God knows what that Arul Doss has reported. . . . I should not have spoken. This fellow looks as if he could do anything.' Margayya looked at Arul Doss, and shuddered, noting the wicked gleam in his eye. He soon recovered his self-possession: 'I am not a baby to worry about these things. What can anybody do to me?' He resolutely fixed his gaze on the hard knobs on his box, gave its contents a final pat, and was about to draw down the lid when the other man suddenly stooped, thrust his hand inside and picked out a handful of papers, demanding: 'How did you come by these? These are our application forms!'

Margayya checked the indignation that was rising within him: 'Put them back, will you? What right have you to put your hand into my box? You look like an educated man. Don't you know that ordinary simple law?' In his indignation he lost for a moment all fear. Arul Doss came forward and said, 'Take care how you speak. He is our Secretary. He will hand you over to the police.'

'Stop your nonsense, you earthworm! Things have come to this, have they, when every earthworm pretends that it is a cobra and tries to sway its hood. . . . I will nip off your head as well as your tail, if you start any of your tricks with me. Take care. Get out of my way.'

Arul Doss was cowed. He withdrew a little, but he was not to be dismissed so easily. He began: 'He is our Secretary—'

'That's all right. It's written all over him,' yelled Margayya. 'What else can he be? He can speak for himself, can't he? You keep away, you miserable ten-rupee earner. I want none of your impertinence here. If you want an old piece of cloth, torn or used, come to me.' The Secretary seemed to watch all this with detachment. Arul Doss fretted inwardly, tried to be officious, but had to withdraw because the Secretary himself ordered him away. 'You go over there,' he said, indicating a spot far off. Arul Doss moved reluctantly away. Margayya felt triumphant, and turned his attention to the man before him. 'Secretary, you will put back that paper or I will call the police now.'

'Yes, I want to call the police myself. You are in possession of something that belongs to our office.'

'No, it belongs to the shareholders.'

'Are you a shareholder?'

'Yes, more than that—'

'Nonsense. Don't make false statements. You'll get into trouble. Reports have come to me of your activities. Here is my warning. If you are seen here again, you will find yourself in prison. Go—' He nodded to Arul Doss to come nearer, and held out to him the loan application forms. Arul Doss avidly seized them and carried them off like a trophy. The Secretary abruptly turned round and walked back to the porch of the building, where his car was waiting.

Presently Margayya bundle⁴ up his belongings and started homeward. With his box under his arm and his head bowed in thought he wandered down the Market Road. He paused for a moment at the entrance of the Regal Hair-Cutting Saloon, in whose doorway a huge looking-glass was kept. He saw to his dismay that he was still wearing his spectacles. He pulled them off quickly, folded up their sides and put them into his pocket. He didn't feel flattered at the sight of his own reflection. 'I look like a wayside barber with this little miserable box under my arm. People probably expect me to open the lid and take out soap and a brush. No wonder the Secretary feels he can treat me as he likes. If I looked like him, would he have dared to snatch the papers from my box? I can't look like him. I am destined to look like a wayside barber, and that is my fate. I'm only fit for the company of those blanket-wrapped rustics.' He was thoroughly vexed with himself and his lot.

He moved to the side of the road, as cyclists rang their bells and dodged him; *jutka* men shouted at him, and pedestrians collided against him. His mind was occupied with thoughts of his own miserableness. He felt himself shrinking. Two students emerged laughing from the Bombay Anand Bhavan, their lips red with betel leaves. They stared at Margayya. 'They are laughing at me,' he thought. 'Perhaps they want to ask me to go with them to their rooms and give them a hair-cut!' He kept glancing over his shoulder at them, and caught them turning and glancing at him too, with a grin on their faces. Somebody driving by in a car of the latest model seemed to look at him for a fleeting second and Margayya fancied that he caught a glimpse of contempt in his eyes. . . . Now at the western end of Market Road he saw the V.N.Stores, with its owner standing at the door. 'He may put his hand into my pocket and snatch the glasses or compel me to give him a shave.' He side-stepped into Kabir Lane, and, feeling ashamed of the little box that he carried under his arm, wished he could fling it away, but his sense of possession would not let him. As he passed through the narrow Kabir Lane, with small houses abutting the road, people seemed to stare at him as if to say: 'Barber, come early tomorrow morning: you must be ready here before I go for my bath.' He hurried off. He reached Vinayak Street, raced up the steps of his house and flung the box unceremoniously under the bench. His wife was washing the child on the back veranda. At the sound of his arrival the little fellow let out a yell of joy, through the towel.

'What's happened to make you come back so early?' asked Margayya's wife.

'Early! Why, can't I come home when I please? I am nobody's slave.' She had tried to tidy herself up in the evening after the day's work. 'She looks. . . .' He noticed how plebeian she looked, with her faded jacket, her patched, discoloured sari and her anaemic eyes. 'How can anyone treat me respectfully when my wife is so indifferent-looking?' His son came up and clung to his hand: 'Father, what you have brought me today?' He picked him up on his arm. 'Can't you put him into a cleaner shirt?' he asked.

'He has only four,' his wife answered. 'And he has already soiled three today. I have been telling you to buy some clothes.'

'Don't start all that now. I am in no mood for lectures.' His wife bit her lip and made a wry face. The child let out a howl for no reason whatever. She felt annoyed and said: 'He is always like this. He is all right till you come home. But the moment you step in, he won't even finish washing his face.'

'Where should I go if you don't want me to return home?'

'Nobody said such thing,' she replied sullenly. The little boy shouted, put his hand into his father's coat-pocket and pulled out his reading glasses, and insisted upon putting them over his own nose. His mother cried: 'Give those glasses back or I'll. . . .' She raised her arm, at which he started yelling so much that they could not hear each other's remarks. Margayya carried him off to a shop and bought him sweets, leaving his wife behind, fretting with rage.

In the quiet of midnight, Margayya spoke to his wife seriously: 'Do you know why we get on each other's nerves and quarrel?'

'Yes,' she said at last. 'Now let me sleep.' And turned over. Margayya stretched out his hand and shook her by the shoulder. 'Wake up. I have much to tell you.'

'Can't you wait till the morning?' she asked.

'No.' He spoke to her of the day's events. She sat up in bed. 'Who is that Secretary? What right has he to threaten you?'

'He has every right because he has more money, authority, dress, looks—above all, more money. It's money which gives people all this. Money alone is important in this world. Everything else will come to us naturally if we have money in our purse.'

She said: 'You shouldn't have been so rude to Arul Doss. You should not have said that you'd employ the Secretary. That's not the way to speak to people earning five hundred rupees a month.'

'Let him get five thousand, what do I care? I can also earn a thousand or five thousand, and then these fellows will have to look out.' Much of his self-assurance was returning in the presence of his wife. All the despair and inferiority that he had been feeling was gradually leaving him. He felt more self-confident and aggressive. He felt he could hold out his hand and grab as much of the good things of life as he wanted. He felt himself being puffed up with hope and plans and self-assurance. He said, 'Even you will learn to behave with me when I have money. Your rudeness now is understandable. For isn't there a famous saying, "He that hath not is spurned even by his wife; even the mother that bore him spurns him." It was a very wise man who said it. Well, you will see. I'll not carry about that barber's box any more, and I'll not be seen in this torn dhoti. I will become respectable like anyone else. That Secretary will have to call me "Mister" and stand up when I enter. No more torn mats and dirty, greasy saris for you. Our boy will have a cycle, he will have a suit and go to a convent in a car. And those people'(he indicated the next house) 'will have to wonder and burst their hearts with envy. He will have to come to me on his knees and wait for advice. I have finished with those villagers.'

He became like one possessed. He was agitated, as if he had made a startling discovery. He couldn't yet afford to keep away from the place where he worked. He went there as usual, but he had taken care to tidy himself up as much as possible. He wore a lace-edged dhoti which he normally kept folded in his box. It was of fine texture, but much yellowed now. He had always kept it in his box with a piece of camphor, and he now smelt like an incense-holder as he emerged from his small room, clad in this gorgeous dhoti. It had been given to him, as it now seemed a century-and-a-half ago, on the day of his wedding when he was sitting beside his wife on a flower-decked swing, surrounded by a lot of women-folk joking and singing and teasing the newly-weds, after the feast at night. He sighed at the thought of those days. How they had fussed about him and tried to satisfy his smallest request and keep him pleased in every way. How eminent he had felt then! People seemed to feel honoured when he spoke to them. He had only to turn his head even slightly for someone or other to come rushing up and inquire what his wishes were. He had thought that that would continue for ever. What a totally false view of life one acquired on one's wedding day! It reminded him of his brother. How he bargained with the bride's people over the dowry! He used to be so fond of him. His brother's face stood out prominently from among the wedding group in Margayya's memory, as he sat in the corner, beyond the sacrificial smoke, in their village home. Margayya sighed at the memory of it; they had got on quite nicely, but their wives couldn't. 'If women got on smoothly. . . .' Half the trouble in this world is due to women who cannot tolerate each other.

His wife was amused to see him so gaudily dressed. 'What's the matter?' she asked. 'Are you going to a wedding party?' 'This is the only good one I have. They will never see me in that again,' he said, indicating his discarded dhoti. 'Keep it and give it to Arul Doss. He may come for it.' He was pleased with his own venom aimed at the distant Arul Doss. This quiet pleasure pricked his veins and thrilled his body. He put on a new shirt which he had stitched two years ago but had not had the heart to wear—always reserving it for some future occasion. The child too seemed to be quite pleased to see his father in a new dress. He clapped his hands in joy and left him in peace, concentrating his attention on a piece of elephant made of lacquer-painted wood. Margayya had elaborately tied up his dhoti, with folds going up, in the dignified Poona style, instead of the Southern fashion, looked down upon by people of other provinces. He explained to his wife: 'You see, if we are treated with contempt by people it is our fault. Our style of tying dhoti and our style of dressing—it is all so silly! No wonder.' He talked like a man who had just arrived from a far-off land, he spoke with such detachment and superiority. His wife was somewhat taken aback. She treated him with the utmost consideration when she served him his frugal meal. Usually he would have to ask, 'Food ready? Food ready?' several times and then pick up his plate and sit down and wait indefinitely as she kept blowing the fire. If he said: 'Hurry up, please.' She would retort: 'With my breath gone, blowing on this wet firewood, have you the heart. . .' etc. But today she said: 'Your plate is there, food is ready.' She served him quietly, with a sort of docile agreeableness. 'I got this brinjal from the back garden,' she said. 'You didn't know I had a garden.' 'No. Nice stuff,'he murmured agreeably. Even the little fellow ate his food quietly, only once letting out a shout when he thought his mother wouldn't serve him his ghee. On that occasion he threw a handful of rice in his mother's face. She just ignored it, instead of flying at him, and the episode ended there. At the end of the meal Margayya picked up his plate as usual to wash and restore it to its corner in the kitchen. But she at once said, 'Oh, don't, I will attend to it.' He got up grandly and washed his hands, wiping them on a towel readily brought to his side by his wife. She gave him a few scented nuts and a betel leaf and saw him off at the door as he went down the street. He had opened his little box and picked up a few papers, which he carried in his hand. It looked better. He walked with the feeling that a new existence was opening before him.

His clients were somewhat surprised to see him in his new dress. He didn't squat under the tree, but remained standing.

'Why are you standing, Margayya?'

'Because I am not sitting,' Margayya replied.

'Why not?'

'Because I like to stand—that's all,' he replied.

He handed a filled-up application to someone and said: 'Give it in there, and come away.' He told another: 'Well, you will get your money today. Give me back my advance.' He carried on his business without sitting down. One of the men looked up and down and asked: 'Going to a marriage party?'

'Yes,' replied Margayya. 'Every day is a day of marriage for me. Do you think I like a change of wife each day?' He cracked his usual jokes. He placed his paper on the ledge of a wall and wrote. He had brought with him, hidden in his pocket, the little ink-bottle wrapped in paper, and his pen. As he bowed his head and wrote he muttered: 'I just want to help people to get over their money troubles. I do it as a sort of service, but let no one imagine I have no better business.'

'What else do you do, sir?' asked a very innocent man.

'Well, I have to do the same service for myself too, you see. I have to do something to earn money.'

'You get interest on all the amounts you give us.'

'Yes, yes, but that's hardly enough to pay for my snuff,' he said grandly, taking out a small box and inhaling a pinch. It sent a stinging sensation up his nostrils into his brain, and he felt his forehead throbbing with excitement. It made him feel so energetic that he felt like thumping a table and arguing. He said aggressively: 'I want to do so much for you fellows, do you know why?' They shook their heads bewildered. 'Not because of the petty interest you give me—that's nothing for me. It is because I want you all to get over your money worries and improve your lives. You must all adopt civilized ways. That's why I am trying to help you to get money from that bastard office.' He pointed at the Co-operative Bank. They all turned and looked at it. Arul Doss was seen approaching. 'He is coming,' they all said in one voice. Arul Doss approached them somewhat diffidently. His gait was halting and slow. He stopped quite far away, and pretended to look for a carriage or something on the road. Margayya thrust himself forward and watched aggressively. Arul Doss stole a glance now and then at Margayya. Margayya felt annoyed. The sting of the snuff was still fresh. He cried out: 'Arul Doss, what are you looking for? If it is for me, come along, because I am here.' Arul Doss seemed happy to seize this opportunity to approach. Margayya said: 'Mark my words, this is God-given shade under the tree; if you or your Secretary is up to any mischief, I will make you feel sorry for your—' The villagers were overawed by Margayya's manner of handling Arul Doss. Arul Doss had no doubt come spying but now he felt uncomfortable at Margayya's sallies. If Margayya had been squatting under the tree with his box, he might have had a tale to bear, but now he saw nothing wrong. He had only one worry—that of being called an earthworm again before so many people. He tried to turn and go, saying, 'I just came to see if the Secretary's car had come.'

'Has your Secretary a car?' Margayya asked patronizingly.

'Haven't you noticed that big red one?'

Margayya snapped his fingers and said: 'As if I had no better things to observe. Tell your Secretary—' He checked himself, not being sure what his tongue might utter. 'Arul Doss, if you are in need of an old dhoti or shirt, go and ask my wife. She will give it to you.' Arul Doss's face beamed with happiness.

'Oh, surely, surely,' he said. He approached nearer to Margayya and whispered. Margayya raised his hand to his face and put his head back. The other's breath smelt of onion. Margayya asked: 'Do you nibble raw onion in the morning?' Arul Doss ignored the question and whispered: 'You must not think that I myself tried to bother you yesterday. It's all that fellow's orders.' He pointed towards his office. 'He is a vicious creature! You won't think that I. . . . You can carry on here as you like, sir. Don't worry about anything.' He turned and abruptly walked back. Margayya looked after him and commented to his circle: 'That's the worst blackguard under the sun—both of them are. This fellow carries tales to him and then he comes and behaves like a great governor here. What do I care? If a man thinks that he is governor let him show off at home, not here, for I don't care for governors.'

WAITING FOR THE MAHATMA

Editor's note: This is the longest excerpt from any of Narayan's novels in this collection. *Waiting for the Mahatma* is a daring and successful attempt at introducing Gandhiji as a character in a novel and getting him to take an interest in a young couple, the girl his follower and the young man a pleasant but aimless individual. The story is really about how the young man is transformed into a person with ideals, both because of his love for the girl and because of the Mahatma's influence.

His mother, who died delivering him, and his father, who was killed in Mesopotamia, might have been figures in a legend as far as Sriram was concerned. He had, however, concrete evidence of his mother in a framed photograph which for years hung too high on the wall for him to see; when he grew tall enough to study the dim picture, he didn't feel pleased with her appearance; he wished she looked like that portrait of a European queen with apple cheeks and wavy coiffure hanging in the little shop opposite his house, where he often went to buy peppermints with the daily money given him by his granny. Of his father, at least, there were recurring reminders. On the first of every month the postman brought a brown, oblong cover, addressed to his granny. Invariably Granny wept when the envelope came to her hand. It made his childish mind wonder what could be there in that envelope to sting the tears out of her eyes. It was only years later he understood that his granny had been receiving a military pension meant for him. When the envelope came she invariably remarked: 'I don't have to spend your pension in order to maintain you. God has left us enough to live,' and took it to the fourth house in their row, which was known as the 'Fund Office' (what it meant, he never understood) and came back to say: 'There is nothing so fleeting as untethered cash. You can do what you like with it when you are old enough.'

That portrait in the opposite shop fascinated his adolescent mind. The shopman was known as Kanni, a parched, cantankerous, formidable man, who sat on his haunches all day briskly handing out goods to his customers. Until eleven at night, when he closed the shop, his hollow voice could be heard haranguing someone, or arguing, or cowing his credit-demanding clientele: 'What do you think I am! How dare you come again without cash? You think you can do me in? You are mistaken. I can swallow ten of you at the same time, remember.' The only softening influence in this shop of cigars, bidis, explosive aerated drinks, and hard words was the portrait of the lady with apple cheeks, curls falling down the brim of her coronet, and large, dark eyes. 'Those eyes look at me,' Sriram often thought. For the pleasure of returning that look, he went again and again, to buy something or other at the shop.

'Whose is that picture?' he asked once, pausing between sips of a coloured drink.

'How should I know?' Kanni said. 'It's probably some queen, probably Queen Victoria,' although he might with equal justification have claimed her to be Maria Theresa or Ann Boleyn.

'What did you pay for it?'

'Why do you want to know all that?'said Kanni, mildly irritated. If it had been any one else, he would have shouted, 'If you have finished your business, be gone. Don't stand there and ask a dozen questions.'

But Sriram occupied a unique position. He was a good customer, paid down a lot of cash every day, and deserved respect for his bank balance. He asked, 'Where did you get that picture?'

Kanni was in a jovial mood and answered, 'You know that man, the Revenue Inspector in Pillaiah Street. He owed me a lot of money. I had waited long enough, so one day I walked in and brought away this picture hanging in his room. Something at least for my dues.'

'If there is any chance,' said Sriram with timid hesitation, 'of your giving it away, tell me its price.'

'Oh, oh!' said Kanni, laughing. He was in a fine mood. 'I know you can buy up the queen herself, master zamindar. But I won't part with it. It has brought me luck. Ever since I hung the picture there, my business has multiplied tenfold.'

One evening his grandmother asked: 'Do you know what star it will be tomorrow?'

'No. How should I?' he asked, comfortably reclining on the cold cement window-sill, and watching the street. He had sat there, morning to night, ever since he could remember. When he was a year old his grandmother put him down there and showed him the various diversions passing outside: bullock-carts, horse-carriages, and the first few motor-cars of the age, honking away and rattling down the road. He would not be fed unless he was allowed to watch the goings-on of the street. She held a spoonful of rice and curd to his lips and exclaimed: 'Oh, see that great motor-car. Shall our little Ram travel in it?' And when he blinked at the mention of his name and opened his mouth, she thrust in the rice. The window became such a habit with him that when he grew up he sought no other diversion except to sit there, sometimes with a book, and watch the street. His grandmother often reproached him for it. She asked: 'Why don't you go and mix with others of your age?'

'I am quite happy where I am,' he answered briefly.

'If you left that seat, you would have many things to see and learn,' said the old lady sharply. 'Do you know at your age your father could read the almanac upside down, and could say at a moment's notice what star was reigning over which particular day?'

'He was probably a very wise man,' ventured Sriram.

'He *was* very wise. Don't say "probably"!' corrected his grandmother. 'And your grandfather, you know how clever he was! They say that the grandfather's reincarnation is in his grandson. You have the same shaped nose as he had and the same eyebrows. His fingers were also long just like yours. But there it stops. I very much wish you had not inherited any of it, but only his brain.'

'I wish you had kept a portrait of him for me to see, Granny,' Sriram said. 'Then I could have worshipped it and become just as clever as he.'

The old lady was pleased with this, and said: 'I'll teach you how you could improve yourself.' Dragging him by the hand to the little circle of light under the hall lamp, she took the brown-paper-covered almanac from under a tile of their sloping roof. Then she sat down on the floor, clamoured for her glasses till they were fetched, and forced Sriram to open the almanac and go through it to a particular page. It was full of minute, bewildering symbols in intricate columns. She pushed his face close to the page.

'What is it you are trying to do?' he pleaded pathetically.

She put her finger on a letter and asked: 'What is this?'

'*Sa.* . . .' he said.

'It means *Sadhaya*. That's your star.' She drew her finger along the line and pointed at the morrow's date. 'Tomorrow is this date, which means it's your birth star. It's going to be your twentieth birthday, although you behave as if you are half that. I am going to celebrate it. Would you like to invite any of your friends?'

'No, never,' said Sriram positively.

So all alone next day he celebrated his twentieth birthday. His guest as well as hostess was his grandmother. No one outside could have guessed what an important occasion was being celebrated in that house in Kabir Street numbered '14'. The house was over two hundred years old and looked it. It was the last house in the street, or 'The first house' as his great- grandfather used to say at the time he built it. From here one saw the backs of market buildings and heard night and day the babble of the big crowd moving on the Market Road. Next door to Sriram's house was a small printing press which groaned away all day and next to it another two-hundred-year-old house in which six noisy families lived, and beyond that was the Fund Office, where Granny kept her grandson's money. A crooked street ran in from of these houses; their closeness to the market and to a Higher Elementary Town School, the Local Fund Dispensary, and above all to the half-dozen benches around the market fountain, was said to give these houses in Kabir Street a unique value.

The houses were all alike—a large single roof sloping down to the slender rosewood pillars with carvings and brass-decorations on them, and a *pyol*, an open brick platform under the windows, on which the household slept in summer. The walls were two feet thick, the doors were made of century-old teak planks with bronze knobs, and the tiles were of burnt mud which had weathered the storms and rains of centuries. All these houses were alike; you could see end to end the slender pillars and tiles sloping down as if all of them belonged to a single house. Many changes had occurred since they were built two centuries ago. Many of them had changed hands, the original owners having been lost in the toils of litigation, some were rented out to tradesmen, such as the Sun Press, the Butter Factory, or the Fund Office, while their owners retired to villages or built themselves modern villas in Lawley Extension. But there were still one or two houses which main- tained a continuity, a link with the past. Number 14 was one such. There the family lineage began centuries ago and continued still, though reduced to just two members—Sriram and his grand-mother.

Granny had somewhere secured a yard-long sugarcane for the celebration, although it was not the season. She said: 'No birthday is truly celebrated unless and until a sugarcane is seen in the house. It's auspicious.' She strung mango leaves across the doorway, and decorated the threshold with coloured rice-powder. A neighbour passing down the road stopped to ask: 'What's the celebration? Shall we blow out the ovens in our houses and come for the feast in yours?'

'Yes, by all means. Most welcome,' said the old lady courteously, and added as if to neutralize the invitation, 'you are always wel-come.' She felt sorry at not being able to call in the neighbours, but that recluse grandson of hers had forbidden her to invite anyone. Left to herself she would have engaged pipes and drums and processions, for this particular birthday was a thing she had been planning all along, this twentieth birthday when she would hand over the Savings Pass-Book to her grandson and relinquish the trust.

It was an adventure accompanying Granny to the Fund Office, four doors off. She seemed to shrink in stature under an open sky—she who dominated the landscape under the roof of Number 14 lost her stature completely in the open. Sriram couldn't help remarking, 'You look like a baby, Granny.' Granny half-closed her eyes in the glare and whispered, 'Hush! Don't talk aloud, others may hear.'

'Hear what?'

'Whatever it may be. What happens behind one's door must be known only to the folk concerned. Others had better shut up.'

As if confirming her worst suspicion, Kanni cried breezily from his shop: 'Oh, Grandmother and her pet on an outing! A fine sight! The young gentleman is shooting up, madam!'

Sriram felt proud of this compliment; he was seized with a feeling of towering height, and he pursed his lips in a determined manner. He gripped in his right hand the brown calico-bound pass-book presented to him with a somewhat dramatic gesture by his grandmother a moment ago.

'Oh, the young *subedar* is going to the right school with the right book,' Kanni remarked. 'He must live to be as great as his father and grandfather put together.'

Granny muttered, quickening her steps, 'Don't stand and talk to that man; he will plague us with his remarks; that's why I never wanted your grandfather to sell that site opposite, but he was an obstinate man, such an obstinate man! He was also fond of this Kanni, who was then a young fellow.'

'Was Grandfather also buying plantains?'

'Not only plantains,' she muttered, with a shudder, recollecting his habit of buying cheroots in Kanni's shop. She had thought it degrading for any person to be seen smoking a cheroot. 'Like a baby sucking a candy stick!' she was wont to remark, disturbing the even tenor of their married life. She had always blamed Kanni for encouraging her husband to smoke and never got over a slight grudge on that account.

Before reaching the Fund Office they had interruptions from other neighbours who peeped out of their doorways and demanded to be told what extraordinary thing made the old lady go out in the company of her grandson. They could understand her going out all alone on the first of the month in the direction of the Fund Office—that was understandable. But what made the lady go out in the company of the young fellow, who was—an unusual sight—holding on to a bank book?

'What!' cried a lady who was a privileged friend of Granny's, 'Does it mean that this urchin is going to have an independent account?'

'He is no longer an urchin,' cried the old woman. 'He's old enough to take charge of his own affairs. How long should I look after him! I'm not immortal. Each responsibility should be shaken off as and when occasion arises to push off each responsibility.' This was a somewhat involved sentiment expressed in a round-about manner, but her friend seemed to understand it at once, and cried, coming down the steps of her house, 'How wisely you speak! The girls of these days should learn from you how to conduct themselves,' which pleased Granny so much that she stopped to whisper in her ear: 'I was only a trustee of his money. From today he will take care of his own money.'

'Wisely done, wisely done,' the other cried and asked, 'how much in all?'

'That you will never know,' said Granny and walked off. Sriram, who had gone ahead, asked: 'How is it, Granny, you stop and talk to everyone! What were you telling her?'

'Nothing,' she replied. 'You follow the same rule and you will be a happier man. Your grandfather ruined himself by talking. Anything that happened to him, good or bad, was bound to be known to everyone in the town within ten minutes; otherwise his soul felt restless.'

'Why should anything be concealed from anyone?' asked the boy.

'Because it's better so, that's all,' said the lady.

All these interruptions on the way delayed her arrival at the bank. The clock struck four as she showed her face at the counter.

'Must you be on the last second, madam?' the manager asked. 'Is there any reason why you could not come a little earlier?'

'No, none,' she said, 'except that I'm not a young creature who can frisk along.' The manager, used to her ways, got down from his high seat, opened a side door, and without a word, let her in.

Sriram was being initiated into the mysteries of banking. The bank manager opened the last page of his pass-book and said: 'What figure do you see here?' Sriram wondered for a moment if he was testing him in arithmetic, a most terrible memory of his early school days. He became wary and ventured to say: 'Thirty- eight thousand, five hundred rupees, seven annas, and six pies.'

'Quite right!' cried Granny. She appeared surprised at the intelligence he exhibited.

Sriram asked petulantly, 'What did you take me for, Granny? Did you think I would not be good enough even for this?'

'Yes,' she said quietly. 'How should I think otherwise, considering how well you have fared in your studies!'

The manager, a suave and peace-loving man, steered them out of these dangerous zones, by changing the subject: 'You see, this is your savings deposit. You may draw two hundred and fifty rupees a week, not more than that. Here is the withdrawal form. See that you don't lose it, and that nobody gets at it.'

'Why? Would it be possible for anyone else to get at my money with that form?'

'Usually not, but it's our duty to take all possible precautions in money matters,' said the manager.

Granny for some reason felt upset at Sriram's questions, 'Why do you ask so much? If the manager says, "Do this" or "Do that" it's your duty to obey, that is all.'

'I always like to know what I am doing,' said Sriram, and added, 'There's nothing wrong in that.'

Granny turned to the manager and said with pride, 'You see the present generation! They are not like us. How many years have you been seeing me here. Have you ever heard me asking why or how and why not at any time?'

The manager made indistinct noises, not wishing to displease either his old customer or the new one. He placed before the old lady a letter, tapped the bottom of the page with his finger, and said, 'May I have your signature here? It's the new authorization, and you won't be bothered to come here often as before.'

'After twenty years, relief!' Granny cried. She had the triumphant expression of one who had run hard and reached the winning post. Sriram did not fully realize what it all meant, but took it quite casually. He simply said, 'If I had been you I wouldn't have taken all this trouble to accumulate the money.'

'You are not me, and that's just as well. Don't say such things before this man who has watched and guarded your property all these years!'

Sriram wanted to test how far the magic toy put into his hands would work. He seized the pen-holder, stabbed it into the ink- well, wrote off a withdrawal for two hundred and fifty rupees, tore off the page and pushed it before the manager with an air of challenge. 'Let us see if I am really the owner of this money!'

The manager was taken aback by the speed of his activity. He smiled and said: 'But my dear fellow, you know we close at four, and cash closes at two every day. If you want cash, you must be here before two on any working day. Change the date, and you can come and collect it the first thing tomorrow. Are you sure that you want all that sum urgently for the first draw?'

'Yes, I am positive,' said Sriram. 'I would have taken more if you had permitted more than two hundred and fifty at a time.

'May I know why you need all this amount?' asked Granny.

'Is it or is it not my money?' asked Sriram.

'It is and it is not,' said Granny in a mystifying manner. 'Remember, I don't have to ask you what you do with your own funds. It's your own business. You are old enough to know what you do. I don't have to bother myself at all about it. It's purely your own business. But I want to ask you—just to know things, that is all—why you want two hundred and fifty rupees now. It's your business, I know but remember one thing. One is always better off with money unspent. It's always safe to have one's bank balance undamaged.'

'Quite right, quite right,' echoed the bank manager. 'Great

words of wisdom. I tell you, young man, come tomorrow morning,' he said, picking up the form.

Granny cried: 'Give it here,' and snatching the paper from his hand said, 'Correct it to fifty. You need only fifty rupees now and not two hundred and fifty. I'd have torn up this, but for the fact that it is your first withdrawal form and I don't want to commit any inauspicious act.'

'Ah! That's a good idea,' said the manager. 'It's better if you carry less cash about you nowadays with pick-pockets about.'

He dipped the pen in the ink and passed it to Sriram. 'Write your signature in full on all the corrections.'

Sriram obeyed, muttering, 'See! This is just what I suspected! I'm supposed to be the master of this money, but I cannot draw what I want! A nice situation!'

The manager took the form back and said: 'Come at ten-thirty tomorrow morning for your cash.'

'I hope you won't expect me to come again with my grandmother!' Sriram said with heavy cynicism.

Next day Sriram stood at Kanni's shop and ordered coloured drinks and plantains. 'How much?' he asked after he was satisfied.

'Four annas,' said Kanni.

Sriram drew from his pocket several rolls of notes, and pulled one out for Kanni. It was a veritable display of wealth. Kanni was duly impressed. He immediately became deferential.

'Have you examined your pockets to see if there may not be some small change lying somewhere there?'

'If I had small change, would I be holding this out to you?' asked Sriram grandly.

'All right, all right.'

Kanni received the amount and transferred it immediately to his cash chest. Sriram waited for change. Kanni attended to other customers.

Sriram said, 'Where is my change?'

Kanni said: 'Please wait. I have something to tell you. You see—'

An itinerant tea vendor just then came up with his stove and kettle to ask for a packet of cigarettes. And then there were four other customers. The place was crowded and Kanni's customers had to stand on the road below his platform and hold out their hands like supplicants. All the while Sriram stood gazing on the portrait of the rosy-cheeked queen who stared out at the world through the plantain bunches suspended from the ceiling. School children came in and clamoured for peppermints in bottles. Kanni served everyone like a machine.

When everybody was gone Sriram asked, 'How long do you want me to wait for my change?'

'Don't be angry, master,' Kanni said. He pulled out a long note-book, blew the dust off its cover, turned an ancient page, and pointed at a figure and asked, 'Do you see this?'

'Yes,' said Sriram, wondering why everybody was asking him to read figures these days. He read out: 'Nine rupees, twelve annas.'

'It's a debt from your grandfather which is several years old. I'm sure he'd have paid it if he had lived—but, one doesn't know when death comes: I used to get him special cheroots from Singapore, you know.'

'Why didn't you ask Granny?'

'Granny! Not I. He wouldn't have liked it at all. I knew some day you would come and pay.'

'Oh,' Sriram said generously. 'Take it, by all means,' and turned to go.

'That's a worthy grandson,' muttered Kanni. 'Now the old man's soul will rest in peace.'

'But where will the soul be waiting? Don't you think he will have been re-born somewhere?' said Sriram.

Kanni did not wish to be involved in speculations on post-mortem existence, and turned his attention to the other customers.

Before going away Sriram said, 'I can buy that picture off you whenever you can sell it, remember.'

'Surely, surely. When I wind up this shop, I will remember to give it to you, not till then: it's a talisman for me.'

'If the lady's husband turns up and demands the picture, what will you do?' Sriram asked, which made Kanni pause and reflect for a moment what his line of action should be.

Sriram walked down the street, not having any definite aim. He felt like a man with a high-powered talisman in his pocket, something that would enable him to fly or go anywhere he pleased. He thrust his fingers into his *jibba* pocket and went on twirling the notes. He wished he had asked the manager to give him new ones: he had given him what appeared to be second-hand notes: probably the Fund Office manager reserved the good notes for big men. Who was a big man anyway? Anyone was a big man. Himself not excluded. He had money, but people still seemed to think he was a little boy tied to the apron strings of his grandmother. His grandmother was very good no doubt, but she ought to leave him alone. She did not treat him as a grown-up person. It was exasperating to be treated like a kid all the time. Why wouldn't she let him draw two hundred and fifty instead of fifty, if he wanted it? It would be his business in future, and she ought to allow him to do what he pleased. Anyway it was a good thing he had only fifty to display before Kanni. If he had shown two hundred he might have claimed half of it as his grandfather's debt. Sriram was for a moment seized with the problem of life on earth: was one born and tended and brought up to the twentieth year just in order to pay off a cheroot bill? This philosophical trend he immediately checked with the thought: 'I shall probably know all this philosophy when I grow a little older, not now. . . .' He dismissed his thought with: 'I am an adult with my own money, going home just when I please. Granny can't ask me what I have been doing. . . .'

He walked round and round the Market Road, gazing on shops, and wondering if there was anything he could buy. The money in his pocket clamoured to be spent. But yet there seemed to be nothing worth buying in the shops. He halted for a moment, reflecting how hard it was to relieve oneself of one's cash. A man who wore a cotton vest and a tucked-in dhoti held up to him a canvas folding-chair,

'Going cheap, do you want it?'

Sriram examined it. This seemed to be something worth having in one's house. It had a red striped canvas seat and could be folded up. There was not a single piece of furniture at home.

'Ten rupees sir, best teakwood.'

Sriram examined it keenly, although he could not see the difference between rosewood and teak or any other wood.

'Is this real teak?' he asked.

'Guaranteed Mempi Hill teak, sir, that is why it costs ten rupees: if it were ordinary jungle wood, you could have got it for four.'

'I will give seven rupees,' said Sriram with an air of finality, looking away. He pretended to have no further interest in the transaction. The man came down to eight rupees. Sriram offered him an extra half-rupee if he would carry it to his door.

Granny opened the door and asked in surprise, 'What is this?' Sriram set up the canvas chair right in the middle of the hall and said, 'This is a present for you, Granny.'

'What! For me!' She examined the canvas and said, 'It's no use for me. This is some kind of leather, probably cow-hide, and I can't pollute myself by sitting on it. I wish you had told me before going out to buy.'

Sriram examined the seat keenly, dusted it, tapped it with his palm and said, 'This is not leather, Granny, it is only canvas.'

'What is canvas made of?' she asked.

Sriram said, 'I have no idea,' and she completed the answer with, 'Canvas is only another name for leather. I don't want it. You sleep on it if you like.'

He followed this advice to the letter. All day he lounged on this canvas seat and looked at the ceiling or read a tattered novel borrowed from the municipal library. When evening came he visited the Bombay Anand Bhavan and ordered a lot of sweets and delicacies, and washed them down with coffee. After that he picked up a *beeda* covered with coloured coconut gratings, chewed it with great contentment, and went for a stroll along the river or saw the latest Tamil film in the Regal Picture Palace.

It was an unruffled, quiet existence, which went on without a break for the next four years, the passing of time being hardly noticed in this scheme—except when one or the other of the festivals of the season turned up and his granny wanted him to bring something from the market. 'Another Dussehra!' or 'Another Deepavali! It looks as though I lighted crackers only yesterday!' he would cry surprised at the passage of time.

It was April. The summer sun shone like a ruthless arc lamp—and all the water in the well evaporated and the road-dust became bleached and weightless and flew about like flour spraying off the grinding wheels. Granny said as Sriram was starting out for the evening, 'Why don't you fetch some good jaggery for tomorrow, and some jasmine for the puja? He had planned to go towards Lawley Extension today and not to the market and he felt reluctant to oblige her. But she was insistent. She said, 'Tomorrow is New Year's Day.'

'Already another New Year!' he cried. 'It seems as though we celebrated one yesterday.'

'Whether yesterday or the day before, it's a New Year's Day. I want certain things for its celebration. If you are not going, I'll go myself. It's not for me! It's only to make some sweet stuff for you.'

Grumbling a great deal, he got up, dressed himself, and started out. When he arrived at the market he was pleased that his granny had forced him to go there.

As he approached the market fountain a pretty girl came up and stopped him.

'Your contribution?' she asked, shaking a sealed tin collection box.

Sriram's throat went dry and no sound came. He had never been spoken to by any girl before; she was slender and young, with eyes that sparkled with happiness. He wanted to ask, 'How old are you? What caste are you? Where is your horoscope? Are you free to marry me?' She looked so different from the beauty in Kanni's shop; his critical faculties were at once alert, and he realized how shallow was the other beauty, the European queen, and wondered that he had ever given her a thought. He wouldn't look at the picture again even if Kanni should give it to him free.

The girl rattled the money-box. The sound brought him back from his reverie, and he said, 'Yes, Yes'; he fumbled in his *jibba* side-pocket for loose change and brought out an eight-anna silver coin and dropped it into the slot. The girl smiled at him in return and went away, seeming to move with the lightest of steps like a dancer. Sriram had a wild hope that she would let him touch her hand, but she moved off and disappeared into the market crowd.

'What a dangerous thing for such a beauty to be about!' he thought. It was a busy hour with cycles, horse carriages and motor-cars passing down the road, and a jostling crowd was moving in and out of the arched gateway of the market. People were carrying vegetables, rolls of banana leaves and all kinds of New Year purchases. Young urchins were hanging about with baskets on their heads soliciting, 'Coolie, sir, coolie?' She had disappeared into the market like a bird gliding on wings. He felt that he wanted to sing a song for her. But she was gone. He realized he hadn't even asked what the contribution was for. He wished he hadn't given just a nickel but thrust a ten-rupee note into her collection-box (he could afford it), and that would have given her a better impression of him, and possibly have made her stand and talk to him. He should have asked her where she lived. What a fool not have held her up. He ought to have emptied all his money into her money-box. She had vanished through the market arch.

He vaguely followed this trail, hoping that he would be able to catch another glimpse of her. If ever he saw her again he would

take charge of the money-box and make the collection for her,
whatever it might be for. He looked over the crowd for a glimpse
again of the white sari, over the shoulders of the jostling crowd,
around the vegetable stalls. . . . But it was a hopeless quest, not a
chance of seeing her again. Who could she be and where did she
come from? Could it be that she was the daughter of a judge or
might she be an other-worldly creature who had come suddenly to
meet him and whom he did not know how to treat? What a fool he
was. He felt how sadly he lacked the necessary polish for such
encounters. That was why it was urged on him to go to a college
and pass his B.A. Those who went to colleges and passed their B.A.
were certainly people who knew how to conduct themselves before
girls.

He passed into the market arch in the direction she took. At the
fly-ridden jaggery shop he said tentatively: 'A lot of people are
about collecting money for all sorts of things.'

The jaggery merchant said sourly, 'Who will not collect money
if there are people to give?'

'I saw a girl jingling a money-box. Even girls have taken to it,'
Sriram said, holding his breath, hoping to hear something.

'Oh, that,' the other said, 'I too had to give some cash. We have
to. We can't refuse.'

'Who is she?' Sriram asked, unable to carry on diplomatically any
further.

The jaggery merchant threw a swift look at him which seemed
slightly sneering, and said: 'She has something to do with Mahatma
Gandhi and is collecting a fund. You know the Mahatma is coming.'

Sriram suddenly came out of an age-old somnolence, and woke
to the fact that Malgudi was about to have the honour of receiving
Mahatma Gandhi.

In that huge gathering sitting on the sands of Sarayu, awaiting the
arrival of Mahatma Gandhi, Sriram was a tiny speck. There were a
lot of volunteers clad in white khaddar moving around the dais.
The chromium stand of the microphone gleamed in the sun. Police
stood about here and there. Busybodies were going about asking
people to remain calm and silent. People obeyed them. Sriram
envied these volunteers and busybodies their importance, and
wondered if he could do anything to attain the same status. The

sands were warm, the sun was severe. The crowd sat on the ground uncomplainingly.

The river flowed, the leaves of the huge banyan and peepul trees on the banks rustled; the waiting crowd kept up a steady babble, constantly punctuated by the pop of soda-water bottles; longitudinal cucumber slices, crescent-shaped, and brushed up with the peel of a lime dipped in salt, were disappearing from the wooden tray of a vendor who was announcing in a subdued tone (as a concession to the coming of a great man), 'Cucumber for thirst, the best for thirst.' He had wound a green Turkish towel around his head as a protection from the sun.

Sriram felt parched, and looked at the tray longingly. He wished he could go up and buy a crescent. The thought of biting into its cool succulence was tantalizing. He was at a distance and if he left his seat he'd have no chance of getting back to it. He watched a lot of others giving their cash and working their teeth into the crescent. 'Waiting for the Mahatma makes one very thirsty,' he thought.

Every ten minutes someone started a canard that the great man had arrived, and it created a stir in the crowd. It became a joke, something to relieve the tedium of waiting. Any person, a microphone-fitter or a volunteer, who dared to cross the dais was greeted with laughter and booing from a hundred thousand throats. A lot of familiar characters, such as an old teacher of his and the pawnbroker in Market Road, made themselves unrecognizable by wearing white khaddar caps. They felt it was the right dress to wear on this occasion. 'That Khaddar Store off the Market Fountain must have done a roaring business in white caps today,' Sriram thought. Far off, pulled obscurely to one side was a police van with a number of men peering through the safety grill.

There was a sudden lull when Gandhi arrived on the platform and took his seat.

'That's Mahadev Desai,' someone whispered into Sriram's ears.

'Who is the man behind Gandhiji?'

'That's Mr Natesh, our Municipal Chairman.'

Someone sneered at the mention of his name. 'Some people conveniently adopt patriotism when Mahatmaji arrives.'

'Otherwise how can they have a ride in the big procession and a seat on the dais?'

Over the talk the amplifiers burst out, 'Please, please be silent.'

Mahatma Gandhi stood on the dais, with his palms brought together in a salute. A mighty cry rang out, 'Mahatma Gandhi-

ki- jai!' Then he raised his arm, and instantly a silence fell on the gathering. He clapped his hands rhythmically and said: 'I want you all to keep this up, this beating for a while.' People were half-hearted. And the voice in the amplifier boomed, 'No good. Not enough. I like to see more vigour in your arms, more rhythm, more spirit. It must be like the drum-beats of the non-violent soldiers marching on to cut the chains that bind Mother India. I want to hear the great beat. I like to see all arms upraised, and clapping. There is nothing to be ashamed of in it. I want to see unity in it. I want you all to do it with a single mind.' And at once, every man, woman, and child, raised their arms and clapped over their heads.

Sriram wondered for a moment if it would be necessary for him to add his quota to this voluminous noise. He was hesitant.

'I see some in that corner not quite willing to join us. Come on, you will be proud of this preparation.'

And Sriram felt he had been found out, and followed the lead.

Now a mighty choral chant began: *Raghupathi Raghava Raja Ram, Pathitha Pavana Seetha Ram*, to a simple tune, led by a girl at the microphone. It went on and on, and ceased when Mahatmaji began his speech. Natesh interpreted in Tamil what Gandhi said in Hindi. At the outset Mahatma Gandhi explained that he'd speak only in Hindi as a matter of principle. 'I will not address you in English. It's the language of our rulers. It has enslaved us. I very much wish I could speak to you in your own sweet language, Tamil; but alas, I am too hard-pressed for time to master it now, although I hope if God in His infinite mercy grants me the longevity due to me, that is one hundred and twenty-five years, I shall be able next time to speak to you in Tamil without troubling our friend Natesh.'

'Natesh has a knack of acquiring good certificates,' someone murmured in an aggrieved tone.

'Runs with the hare and hunts with the hounds,' said a school-master.

'He knows all of them inside out. Don't imagine the old gentleman does not know whom he is dealing with.'

'I notice two men there talking,' boomed Gandhiji's voice. 'It's not good to talk now, when perhaps the one next to you is anxious to listen. If you disturb his hearing, it is one form of *himsa.'* And at once the commentators lowered their heads and became silent. People were afraid to stir or speak.

Mahatma Gandhi said: 'I see before me a vast army. Everyone of you has certain good points and certain defects, and you must all strive to discipline yourselves before we can hope to attain freedom for our country. An army is always in training and keeps itself in good shape by regular drill and discipline. We, the citizens of this country, are all soldiers of a non-violent army, but even such an army has to practise a few things daily in order to keep itself in proper condition: we do not have to bask in the sun and cry "Left" or "Right". But we have a system of our own to follow: that's *Ram Dhun*; spinning on the *charka* and the practice of absolute Truth and Non- violence.'

At the next evening's meeting Sriram secured a nearer seat. He now understood the technique of attending these gatherings. If he hesitated and looked timid, people pushed him back and down. But if he looked like someone who owned the place, everyone stood aside to let him pass. He wore a pair of large dark glasses which gave him, he felt, an authoritative look. He strode through the crowd. The place was cut up into sectors with stockades of bamboo, so that people were penned in groups. He assumed a tone of bluster which carried him through the various obstacles and brought him to the first row right below the dais. It took him farther away from the sellers of cucumber and aerated water who operated on the fringe of the vast crowd. But there was another advantage in this place: he found himself beside the enclosure where the women were assembled. Most of them were without ornaments, knowing Gandhiji's aversion to all show and luxury. Even then they were an attractive lot, in their saris of varied colours, and Sriram sat unashamedly staring at the gathering, his favourite hobby for the moment being to speculate on what type he would prefer for a wife.

He fancied himself the centre of attraction if any woman happened to look in his direction. 'Oh, she is impressed with my glasses—takes me to be a big fellow, I suppose.' He recollected Gandhiji's suggestion on the previous day: 'All women are your sisters and mothers. Never look at them with thoughts of lust. If you are troubled by such thoughts, this is the remedy: walk with your head down, looking at the ground during the day, and with your eyes up, looking at the stars at night.' He had said this in answering a question that someone from the audience had put to him. Sriram felt uncomfortable at the recollection. 'He will probably read my thoughts.' It seemed to be a risky business sitting so near the dais.

Gandhi seemed to be a man who spotted disturbers and cross-thinkers however far away they sat. He was sure to catch him the moment he arrived on the platform, and say, 'You there! Come up and make a clean breast of it. Tell this assembly what your thoughts were. Don't look in the direction of the girls at all if you cannot control your thoughts.' Sriram resolutely looked away in another direction, where men were seated. 'A most uninteresting and boring collection of human faces; wherever I turn I see only some shopkeeper or a schoolmaster. What is the use of spending one's life looking at them?' Very soon, unconsciously, he turned again towards the women, telling himself, 'So many sisters and mothers. I wish they would let me speak to them. Of course I have no evil thoughts in my mind at the moment.'

Presently Mahatmaji ascended the platform and Sriram hastily took his eyes off the ladies and joined in the hand clapping with well-timed devotion and then in the singing of *Raghupathi Raghava Raja Ram*. After that Gandhi spoke on non-violence, and explained how it could be practised in daily life. 'It is a perfectly simple procedure provided you have faith in it. If you watch yourself you will avoid all actions, big or small, and all thoughts, however obscure, which may cause pain to another. If you are watchful, it will come to you naturally,' he said. 'When someone has wronged you or has done something which appears to you to be evil, just pray for the destruction of that evil. Cultivate an extra affection for the person and you will find that you are able to bring about a change in him. Two thousand years ago, Jesus Christ meant the same thing when he said, "Turn the other cheek."'

Thus he went on. Sometimes Sriram felt it impossible to follow his words. He could not grasp what he was saying, but he looked rapt, he tried to concentrate and understand. This was the first time he felt the need to try and follow something, the first time that he found himself at a disadvantage. Until now he had had a conviction, especially after he began to operate his own bank account, that he understood everything in life. This was the first time he was assailed by doubts of his own prowess and understanding. When Mahatmaji spoke of untouchability and caste, Sriram reflected, 'There must be a great deal in what he says. We always think we are superior people. How Granny bullies that ragged scavenger who comes to our house every day to sweep the backyard!' Granny was so orthodox that she would not let the scavenger approach nearer than ten yards, and habitually adopted a bullying tone while addressing him. Sriram also took a devilish pleasure in joining the baiting and finding fault with the scavenger's work, although he never paid the slightest attention to their comments. He simply went about his business, driving his broom vigorously and interrupting himself only to ask, 'When will master give me an old shirt he promised so long ago?'

He suddenly noticed on the dais the girl who had jingled a money-box in his face a few days ago, at the market. She was clad in a sari of khaddar, white home-spun, and he noticed how well it suited her. Before, he had felt that the wearing of khaddar was a fad, that it was apparel fit only for cranks, but now he realized it could be the loveliest of stuff. He paused for a moment to consider whether it was the wearer who was enriching the cloth or whether the material was good in itself. But he had to put off the whole problem. It was no time for abstract considerations. There she stood, like a vision beside the microphone, on the high dais, commanding the whole scene, a person who was worthy of standing beside Mahatmaji's microphone. How confidently she faced the crowd! He wished he could go about announcing, 'I know who that is beside the microphone into which Mahatmaji is speaking.' The only trouble was that if they turned and asked him, 'What is her name?' he would feel lost. It would be awkward to say, 'I don't know, she came jingling a collection-box the other day at the market. I wish I could say where she lives. I should be grateful for any information.'

At this moment applause rang out, and he joined in it. Gandhiji held up his hand to say, 'It is not enough for you to clap your hands and show your appreciation of me. I am not prepared to accept it all so easily. I want you really to make sure of a change in your hearts before you ever think of asking the British to leave the shores of India. It's all very well for you to take up the cry and create an uproar. But that's not enough. I want you to clear your hearts and minds and make certain that only love resides there, and there is no residue of bitterness for past history. Only then can you say to the British, "Please leave this country to be managed or mismanaged by us, that's purely our own business, and come back any time you like as our friend and distinguished guest, not as our rulers," and you will find John Bull packing his suitcase. But be sure you have in your heart love and not bitterness.' Sriram told himself, looking at the vision beside the microphone, 'Definitely it's not bitterness. I love her.'

'But,' Mahatmaji was saying, 'if I have the slightest suspicion that your heart is not pure or that there is bitterness there, I'd rather have the British stay on. It's the lesser of two evils.'

Sriram thought: 'Oh, revered Mahatmaji, have no doubt that my heart is pure and without bitterness. How can I have any bitterness in my heart for a creature who looks so divine?'

She was at a great height on the platform, and her features were not very clear in the afternoon sun which seemed to set her face ablaze. She might be quite dark and yet wear a temporarily fair face illumined by the sun or she might really be fair. If she were dark, without a doubt his grandmother would not approve of his marrying her. In any case it was unlikely that they would have her blessing, since she had other plans for his marriage: a brother's granddaughter brought up in Kumbum, a most horrible, countrified girl who would guard his cash. If Grandmother was so solicitous of his money she was welcome to take it all and hand it to the Kumbum girl. That would be the lesser of two evils, but he would not marry the Kumbum girl, an unsightly creature with a tight oily braid falling on her nape and dressed in a gaudy village sari, when the thing to do was to wear khadi, khadi alone was going to save the nation from ruin and get the English out of India, as that venerable saint Mahatmaji explained untiringly. He felt sad and depressed at the thought that in the twentieth century there were still people like the Kumbum girl, whom he had seen many many years ago when his uncle came down to engage a lawyer for a civil suit in the village.

Sriram wanted to go and assure the girl on the grandstand that he fully and without the slightest reservation approved of her outlook and habits. It was imperative that he should approach her and tell her that. He seized the chance at the end of the meeting.

Mahatmaji started to descend from the platform. There was a general rush forward, and a number of volunteers began pushing back the crowd, imploring people not to choke the space around the platform. Mahatmaji himself seemed to be oblivious of all the turmoil going on around him. Sriram found a gap in the cordon made by the volunteers and slipped through. The heat of the sun hit him on the nape, the huge trees on the river's edge rustled above the din of the crowd, birds were creating a furore in the branches, being unaccustomed to so much noise below. The crowd was so great that Sriram for a moment forgot where he was, which part of the town he was in, and but for the noise of the birds would not have remembered he was on the banks of Sarayu. 'If that girl can be with Mahatmaji I can also be there,' he told himself indignantly as he threaded his way through the crowd. There was a plethora of white-capped young men, volunteers who cleared a way for Mahatmaji to move in. Sriram felt that it would have been so much better if he had not made himself so conspicuously different with his half-arm shirt and *mull-* dhoti, probably products of the hated mills. He feared that any moment someone might discover him and put him out. If they challenged him and asked, 'Who are you?' he felt he wouldn't be able to answer coherently, or he might just retort, 'Who do you think you are talking to, that girl supporting the Mahatma is familiar to me. I am going to know her, but don't ask me her name. She came with a collection-box one day at the market. . . .'

But no such occasion arose. No one questioned him and he was soon mixed up with a group of people walking behind Mahatmaji in the lane made by the volunteers, as crowds lined the sides. He decided to keep going till he was stopped. If someone stopped him he could always turn round and go home. They would not kill him for it anyway. Killing! He was amused at the word: no word could be more incongruous in the vicinity of one who would not hurt even the British. One could be confident he would not let a would-be follower be slaughtered by his volunteers.

Presently Sriram found himself in such a position of vantage that he lost all fear of being taken for an intruder and walked along with a jaunty and familiar air, so that people lining the route looked on him with interest. He heard his name called, 'Sriram!' An old man who used to be his teacher years before was calling him. Even in his present situation Sriram could not easily break away from the call of a teacher: it was almost a reflex: he hesitated for a moment wondering whether he would not do well to run away without appearing to notice the call, but almost as if reading his mind, his teacher called again, 'A moment! Sriram.' He stopped to have a word with his master, an old man who had wrapped himself in a coloured shawl and looked like an apostle with a slight beard growing on his chin. He gripped Sriram's elbow eagerly and asked, 'Have you joined them?'

'Whom?'

'Them—' said the teacher, pointing.

Sriram hesitated for a moment, wondering what he should reply, and mumbled, 'I mean to. . . .'

'Very good, very good,' said the master. 'In spite of your marks I always knew that you would go far, smart fellow. You are not dull but only lazy. If you worked well you could always score first-class marks like anyone else, but you were always lazy; I remember how you stammered when asked which was the capital of England. Ho! Ho!' he laughed at the memory. Sriram became restive and wriggled in his grip.

The teacher said, 'I am proud to see you here, my boy. Join the Congress, work for the country, you will go far, God bless you. . . .'

'I am glad you think so,' said Sriram and turned to dash away.

The teacher put his face close to his and asked in a whisper, 'What will Mahatmaji do now after going in there?'

'Where?' Sriram asked, not knowing where Gandhi was going, although he was following him.

'Into his hut,' replied the teacher.

'He will probably rest,' answered Sriram, resolutely preparing to dash off. If he allowed too great a distance to develop between himself and the group they might not admit him in at all.

A little boy thrust himself forward and asked, 'Can you get me Mahatma's autograph?'

'Certainly not,' replied Sriram, gently struggling to release himself from his teacher's hold.

His teacher whispered in his ear, 'Whatever happens, don't let down our country.'

'No, sir, never, I promise,' replied Sriram, gently pushing away his old master and running after the group, which was fast disappearing from his view.

They were approaching a wicket gate made of thorns and bamboo. He saw the girl going ahead to open the gate. He sprinted forward as the crowd watched. He had an added assurance in his steps now he felt that he belonged to the Congress. The teacher had put a new idea into his head and he almost felt he was a veteran of the party. He soon joined the group and he had mustered enough pluck to step up beside the girl. It was a proud moment for him. He looked at her. She did not seem to notice his presence. He sweated all over with excitement and panted for breath, but could not make out the details of her personality, complexion or features. However, he noted with satisfaction that she was not very tall, himself being of medium height. Gandhi was saying something to her and she was nodding and smiling. He did not understand what they were saying, but he also smiled out of sympathetic respect. He wanted to look as much like them as possible, and cursed himself for the hundredth time that day for being dressed in mill cloth.

The Mahatma entered his hut. This was one of the dozen huts belonging to the city sweepers who lived on the banks of the river. It was probably the worst area in the town, and an exaggeration even to call them huts; they were just hovels, put together with rags, tin-sheets, and shreds of coconut matting, all crowded in anyhow, with scratchy fowls cackling about and children growing in the street dust. The municipal services were neither extended here nor missed, although the people living in the hovels were employed by the municipality for scavenging work in the town. They were paid ten rupees a month per head, and since they worked in families of four or five, each had a considerable income by Malgudi standards. They hardly ever lived in their huts, spending all their time around the municipal building or at the toddy shop run by the government nearby, which absorbed all their earnings. These men spent less than a tenth of their income on food or clothing, always depending upon mendicancy in their off hours for survival. Deep into the night their voices could be heard clamouring for alms, in all the semi-dark streets of Malgudi. Troublesome children were silenced at the sound of their approach. Their possessions were few; if a cow or a calf died in the city they were called in to carry off the carcass and then the colony at the river's edge brightened up, for they held a feast on the flesh of the dead animal and made money out of its hide. Reformers looked on with wrath and horror, but did little else, since as an untouchable class they lived outside the town limits, beyond Nallappa's Grove, where nobody went, and they used only a part of the river on its downward course.

This was the background to the life of the people in whose camp Gandhi had elected to stay during his visit to Malgudi. It had come as a thunderbolt to the Municipal Chairman, Mr Natesh, who had been for weeks preparing his palatial house, Neel Bagh in the aristocratic Lawley Extension, for receiving Gandhi. His arguments as to why he alone should be Mahatmaji's host seemed unassailable: 'I have spent two lakhs on the building, my garden and lawns alone have cost me twenty-five thousand rupees so far. What do you think I have done it for? I am a simple man, sir, my needs are very simple. I don't need any luxury. I can live in a hut, but the reason I have built it on this scale is so that I should be able for at least once in my lifetime to receive a great soul like Mahatmaji. This is the only house in which he can stay comfortably when he comes to this town. Let me say without appearing to be boastful that it is the biggest and the best furnished house in Malgudi, and we as the people of Malgudi have a responsibility to give him our very best, so how can we house him in any lesser place?'

The Reception Committee applauded his speech. The District Collector, who was the head of the district, and the District Superintendent of Police, who was next to him in authority, attended the meeting as 'ex-officio' members.

A dissenting voice said, 'Why not give the Circuit House for Mahatmaji?'

The Circuit House on the edge of the town was an old East India Company building standing on an acre of land, on the Trunk Road. Robert Clive was supposed to have halted there while marching to relieve the siege of Trichinopoly. The citizens of Malgudi were very proud of this building and never missed an opportunity to show it off to anyone visiting the town and it always housed the distinguished visitors who came this way. It was a matter of prestige for Governors to be put up there. Even in this remote spot they had arranged to have all their conveniences undiminished with resplendent sanitary fittings in the bathrooms. It was also known as the Glass House, by virtue of a glass-fronted bay room from which the distinguished guests could watch the wild animals that were supposed to stray near the building at night in those days.

The dissenting voice in the Reception Committee said, 'Is it the privilege of the ruling race alone to be given the Circuit House? Is our Mahatmaji unworthy of it?'

The Collector, who was the custodian of British prestige, rose to a point of order and administered a gentle reproof to the man who spoke: 'It is not good to go beyond the relevant facts at the moment: If we have considered the Circuit House as unsuitable it is because we have no time to rig it up for receiving Mr Gandhi.'

It was a point of professional honour for him to say Mr Gandhi and not *Mahatma*, and but for the fact that as the Collector he could close the entire meeting and put all the members behind bars under the Defence of India Act, many would have protested and walked out, but they held their peace and he drove home the point.

'Since Mr Gandhi's arrival has been a sudden decision, we are naturally unable to get the building ready for him; if I may say so, our Chairman's house seems to suit the purpose and we must be grateful to him for so kindly obliging us.'

'And I am arranging to move to the Glass House leaving my house for Mahatmaji's occupation.'

That seemed to decide it, and his partisans cheered loudly. It was resolved by ten votes to one that Mahatmaji should stay in Neel Bagh, and the Chairman left the meeting with a heavy, serious look. He wrote to Gandhiji's secretary, receiving a reply which he read at the next meeting: 'Mahatma Gandhi wishes that no particular trouble should be taken about his lodging, and that the matter may be conveniently left over till he is actually there.'

The council debated the meaning of the communication and finally concluded that it only meant that though the Mahatma was unwilling to be committed to anything he would not refuse to occupy Neel Bagh.

The dissenting voice said, 'How do you know that he does not mean something else?'

But he was soon overwhelmed by the gentle reprimand of the Collector. The communication was finally understood to mean, 'I know Mahatmaji's mind, he does not want to trouble anyone if it is a trouble.'

'He probably does not know that it is no trouble for us at all.'

'Quite so, quite so,' said another soothsayer. And they were all pleased at this interpretation.

A further flattering comparison was raised by someone who wanted to create a pleasant impression on the Chairman: 'Let us not forget that Mahatmaji takes up his residence at Birla House at Delhi and Calcutta; I am sure he will have no objection to staying in a palatial building like the one our Chairman has built.'

The dissenting voice said, 'Had we better not write and ask if we have understood him right, and get his confirmation?'

He was not allowed to complete his sentence but was hissed down, and the District Superintendent of Police added slowly, 'Even for security arrangements any other place would present difficulties.'

For this sentiment he received an appreciative nod from his superior, the District Collector.

When Gandhi arrived, he was ceremoniously received, all the big-wigs of Malgudi and the local gentry being introduced to him one by one by the Chairman of the municipality. The police attempted to control the crowd, which was constantly shouting, 'Mahatma Gandhi-*ki- jai*.' When the Chairman read his address of welcome at the elaborately constructed archway outside the railway station, he could hardly be heard, much to his chagrin. He had spent a whole week composing the text of the address with the help of a local journalist, adding whatever would show off either his patriotism or the eminent position Malgudi occupied in the country's life. The Collector had taken the trouble to go through the address before it was sent for printing in order to make sure that it contained no insult to the British Empire, that it did not hinder the war effort, and that it in no way betrayed military secrets. He had to censor it in several places: where the Chairman compared Malgudi to Switzerland (the Collector scored this out because he felt it might embarrass a neutral state); a reference to the hosiery trade (since the Censor felt this was a blatant advertisement for the Chairman's goods and in any case he did not want enemy planes to come looking for this institution thinking it was a camouflage for the manufacture of war material) and all those passages which hinted at the work done by Gandhiji in the political field. The picture of him as a social reformer was left intact and even enlarged; anyone who read the address would conclude that politics were the last thing that Mahatmaji was interested in. In any case, in view of the reception, the Collector might well have left the whole thing alone since cries of 'Mahatmaji-*ki-jai*' and 'Down with the Municipal Chairman' made the speech inaudible. The crowd was so noisy that Mahatmaji had to remonstrate once or twice. When he held up his hand the crowd subsided and waited to listen to him. He said quietly, 'This is sheer lack of order, which I cannot commend. Your Chairman is reading something and I am in courtesy bound to know what he is saying. You must all keep quiet. Let him proceed.'

'No,' cried the crowd. 'We want to hear Mahatmaji and not the Municipal Chairman.'

'Yes,' replied Mahatmaji. 'You will soon hear me, in about an hour on the banks of your Sarayu river. That is the programme as framed.'

'By whom?'

'Never mind by whom. It has my approval. That is how it stands. On the sands of Sarayu in about an hour. Your Chairman has agreed to let me off without a reply to his very kind address. You will have to listen to what he has to say because I very much wish to. . . .'

This quietened the mob somewhat and the Chairman continued

his reading of the address, although he looked intimidated by the exchanges. The Collector looked displeased and fidgety, feeling he ought to have taken into custody the dissenting member, who had perhaps started all this trouble in the crowd. He leaned over and whispered to the Chairman, 'Don't bother, read on leisurely. You don't have to rush through,' but the Chairman only wished to come to the end of his reading; he was anxious to be done with the address before the crowd burst out again. He did not complete his message a second too soon, as presently the crowd broke into a tremendous uproar, which forced the Police Superintendent hastily to go down and see what was the matter, an action which had to be taken with a lot of discretion since Gandhi disliked all police arrangements.

Through archways and ringing cries of 'Gandhi-*ki-jai*,' Gandhi drove in the huge Bentley which the Chairman had left at his disposal. People sat on trees and house-tops all along the way and cheered Gandhiji as he passed. The police had cordoned off various side streets that led off from the Market Road, so the passage was clear from the little Malgudi station to Lawley Extension. There were police everywhere, although the District Superintendent of Police felt that the security arrangements had not been satisfactory. All shops had been closed and all schools, and the whole town had gone into festivity on this occasion. Schoolchildren felt delighted at the thought of Gandhi. Office-goers were happy, and even banks were closed. They waited in the sun for hours, saw him pass in his Bentley, a white-clad figure, fair-skinned and radiant, with his palms pressed together in a salute.

When they entered Neel Bagh, whose massive gates were of cast iron patterned after the gates of Buckingham Palace, the Chairman, who was seated in the front seat, waited to be asked: 'Whose house is this?' But Gandhiji did not seem to notice anything. They passed through the drive with hedges trimmed, flower pots putting forth exotic blooms, and lawns stretching away on either side, and he kept his ears alert to catch any remark that Gandhiji might let fall, but still he said nothing. He was busy looking through some papers which his secretary had passed to him.

The thought that Gandhiji was actually within his gates sent a thrill of joy up and down the Chairman's spine. He had arranged everything nicely. All his own things for a few days had been sent off to the Circuit House (which the Collector had given him on condition that he limewash its walls and repaint its wooden doors and shutters). He felt a thrill at the thought of his own sacrifice. Some years before he could never have thought of forsaking his own air-conditioned suite and choosing to reside at the Circuit House, for anybody's sake. The Chairman had now surrendered his whole house to Gandhiji. No doubt it was big enough to accommodate his own family without interfering with his venerable guest and his party (a miscellaneous gathering of men and women, dressed in white khaddar, who attended on Mahatmaji in various capacities, who all looked alike and whose names he could never clearly grasp); but he did not like to stay on because it seemed impossible to live under the same roof with such a distinguished man and to take away a little from the sense of patriotic sacrifice that his action entailed. So he decided to transfer himself to the Circuit House.

He had effected a few alterations in his house, such as substituting khaddar hangings for the gaudy chintz that had adorned his doorways and windows, and had taken down the pictures of hunting gentry, vague gods and kings. He had even the temerity to remove the picture of George V's wedding and substitute pictures of Maulana Azad, Jawaharlal Nehru, Sarojini Naidu, Motilal Nehru, C.Rajagopalachari and Annie Besant. He had ordered his works manager to secure within a given time 'all the available portraits of our national leaders', a wholesale order which was satisfactorily executed; and all the other pictures were taken down and sent off to the basement room. He had also discreetly managed to get a picture of Krishna discoursing to Arjuna on Bhagavad-Gita, knowing well Gandhi's bias towards Bhagavad-Gita. He had kept on the window-sill and in a few other places a few specimens of *charka* (spinning wheels).

No film decorator sought to create atmosphere with greater deliberation. He worked all the previous night to attain this effect, and had also secured for himself a khaddar *jibba* and a white Gandhi cap, for his wife a white khaddar sari, and for his son a complete outfit in khaddar. His car drove nearly a hundred miles within the city in order to search for a white khaddar cap to fit his six- year-old son's dolicho-cephalic head, and on his shirt front he had embroidered the tricolour and a spinning wheel.

Now he hoped as he approached the main building that his wife and son would emerge in their proper make-up to meet Gandhi: he hoped his wife would have had the good sense to take away the diamond studs not only in her ears but also in their son's. He had forgotten to caution them about it. The moment the car stopped in the decorated porch of the house, the Chairman jumped down, held the door open and helped Mahatmaji to alight.

'You are most welcome to this humble abode of mine, great sire,' he said in confusion, unable to talk coherently. Mahatmaji got down from the car and looked at the house.

'Is this your house?' he asked.

'Yes, sir, by the grace of God, I built it four years ago,' the Chairman said, his throat going dry.

He led Gandhi up the veranda steps. He had placed a divan in the veranda covered with khaddar printed cloth. He seated Gandhi on it and asked his secretary in a whisper: 'May I give Mahatmaji a glassful of orange juice? The oranges are from my own estates in Mempi.' A number of visitors and a miscellaneous crowd of people were passing in and out. It seemed to the Chairman that Mahatmaji's presence had the effect of knocking down the walls of a house, and converting it into a public place—but that was the price one had to pay for having the great man there. People were squatting on the lawns and the Chairman saw helplessly that some were plucking flowers in his annual bed, which had been tended by his municipal overseers.

Gandhi turned in his direction and asked: 'What were you saying?' His secretary communicated the offer of oranges.

Gandhi said: 'Yes, most welcome. I shall be happy to look at the oranges grown in your own gardens.'

The Chairman ran excitedly about and returned bearing a large tray filled with uniform golden oranges. He was panting with the effort. He had gone so far in self-abnegation that he would not accept the services of his usual attendants. He placed the tray in front of Mahatmaji.

'My humble offering to a great man: these are from my own orchards on the Mempi Hills,' he said. 'They were plucked this morning.'

Then he asked, 'May I have the honour of giving you a glass of orange juice? You must have had a tiring day.'

The Mahatma declined, explaining that it was not his hour for taking anything. He picked up one fruit and examined it with appreciative comments, turning it slowly between his fingers. The Chairman felt as happy as if he himself were being scrutinized and approved. On the edge of the crowd, standing below on the drive, Mahatmaji noticed a little boy and beckoned to him to come nearer.

The boy hesitated. Mahatmaji said: '*Av, Av*—' in Hindi. When it made no impression on the boy, he said in the little Tamil he had picked up for this part of the country, '*Inge Va.*' Others pushed the boy forward; he came haltingly. Gandhi offered him a seat on his divan, and gave him an orange. This acted as a signal. Presently the divan was swarming with children. When the tray was empty, the Mahatma asked the Chairman: 'Have you some more?' The Chairman went in and brought a further supply in a basket; and all the children threw off their reserve, became clamorous and soon the basket was empty. 'There are some flowers and garlands in the car,' Gandhi whispered to his secretary—this had been presented to him on his arrival and all along the way by various associations. The place was fragrant with roses and jasmine. These he distributed to all the little girls he saw in the gathering. The Chairman felt chagrined at the thought that the event was developing into a children's party. After the oranges and flowers he hoped that the children would leave, but he found them still there. 'They are probably waiting for apples, now, I suppose!' he reflected bitterly.

Gandhi had completely relaxed. His secretary was telling him: 'In fifteen minutes the deputation from——will be here, and after that—' He was reading from an engagement pad.

The Chairman regretted that both the District Superintendent of Police and the Collector had turned away at his Buckingham Palace gate after escorting the procession that far as an act of official courtesy: if they were here now, they would have managed the crowd. For a moment he wondered with real anxiety whether the crowd proposed to stay there all night. But his problem was unexpectedly solved for him. Mahatmaji saw one child standing apart from the rest—a small dark fellow with a protruding belly and wearing nothing over his body except a cast-off knitted vest, adult size, full of holes, which reached down to his ankles. The boy stood aloof from the rest, on the very edge of the crowd. His face was covered with mud, his feet were dirty, he had stuck his fingers into his mouth and was watching the proceedings on the veranda keenly, his eyes bulging with wonder and desire. He had not dared to come up the steps, though attracted by the oranges. He was trying to edge his way through.

Mahatma's eyes travelled over the crowd and rested on this boy—following his gaze the Chairman was bewildered. He had a feeling of uneasiness. Mahatmaji beckoned to the young fellow. One of his men went and brought him along. The Chairman's blood boiled. Of course people must like poor people and so on, but why bring in such a dirty boy, an untouchable up the steps and make him so important? For a moment he felt a little annoyed with Mahatmaji himself, but soon suppressed it as a sinful emotion. He felt the need to detach himself sufficiently from his surroundings to watch without perturbation the happenings around him. Mahatmaji had the young urchin hoisted beside him on the divan. 'Oh, Lord, all the world's gutters are on this boy, and he is going to leave a permanent stain on that Kashmir counterpane.' The boy was making himself comfortable on the divan, having accepted the hospitality offered him by the Mahatma. He nestled close to the Mahatma, who was smoothing out his matted hair with his fingers, and was engaged in an earnest conversation with him.

The Chairman was unable to catch the trend of their talk. He stepped nearer, trying to listen with all reverence. The reward he got for it was a smile from the Mahatma himself. The boy was saying: 'My father sweeps the streets.'

'With a long broom or a short broom?' the Mahatma asked.

The boy explained, 'He has both a long broom and a short broom.' He was spitting out the seeds of an orange.

The Mahatma turned to someone and explained: 'It means that he is both a municipal sweeper and that he has scavenging work to do in private houses also. The long broom ought to be the municipal emblem.'

'Where is your father at the moment?'

'He is working at the market. He will take me home when he has finished his work.'

'And how have you managed to come here?'

'I was sitting on the road waiting for my father and I came along with the crowd. No one stopped me when I entered the gates.'

'That's a very clever boy,' Mahatmaji said. 'I'm very happy to see you. But you must not spit those pips all over the place, in fact you must never spit at all. It's very unclean to do so, and may cause others a lot of trouble. When you eat an orange, others must not notice it at all. The place must be absolutely tidy even if you have polished off six at a time.'

He laughed happily at his own quip, and then taught the boy what to do with the pips, how to hide the skin, and what to do with all the superfluous bits packed within an orange. The boy laughed with joy. All the men around watched the proceedings with respectful attention. And then Gandhi asked:

'Where do you live?'

The boy threw up his arm to indicate a far distance: 'There at the end of the river. . .'

'Will you let me come to your house?'

The boy hesitated and said, 'Not now—because, because it's so far away.'

'Don't bother about that. I've a motor-car here given to me, you see, by this very rich man. I can be there in a moment. I'll take you along in the motor-car too if you will show me your house.'

'It is not a house like this,' said the boy, 'but made of bamboo or something.'

'Is that so!' said the Mahatma. 'Then I'll like it all the more. I'll be very happy there.'

He had a brief session with a delegation which had come to see him by appointment; when it left, he dictated some notes, wrote something, and then, picking up his staff, said to the Chairman, 'Let us go to this young man's house. I'm sure you will also like it.'

'Now?' asked the Chairman in great consternation. He mumbled, 'Shall we not go there tomorrow?'

'No. I've offered to take this child home. I must not disappoint him. I'd like to see his father too, if he can be met anywhere on the way.'

Mahatmaji gave his forefinger to the young boy to clutch and allowed himself to be led down the veranda steps. The Chairman asked dolefully, 'Won't you come in and have a look round my humble home?'

'I know how it will be. It must be very grand. But would you not rather spare an old man like me the bother of walking through those vast spaces? I'm a tired old man. You are very hospitable. Anyway, come along with us to this little man's home. If I feel like it, you will let me stay there.'

The Chairman mumbled, 'I hoped—' but Gandhiji swept him aside with a smile: 'You will come along with me too. Let me invite you to come and stay with me in a hut.'

Unable to say anything more, the Chairman merely replied, 'All right, sir, I obey.'

The warmth of Mahatma's invitation made him forget his problems as a Chairman and his own responsibilities. Otherwise he would not have become oblivious of the fact that the sweepers' colony was anything but a show-piece. Not till the Collector later sought him out and arraigned him for his lapse did it occur to him what a blunder he had committed.

The Collector said, 'Have you so little sense, Chairman, that you could not have delayed Mr Gandhi's visit at least by two hours, time to give the people a chance to sweep and clean up that awful place? You know as well as I do, what it is like?' All of which the Chairman took in without a word.

He was gloating over the words spoken to him by Mahatmaji. Not till his wife later attacked him did he remember his omission in another direction. She said in a tone full of wrath, 'There I was waiting, dressed as you wanted, with the boy, and you simply went away without even calling us!'

'Why couldn't you have come out?' he asked idiotically.

'How could I, when you had said I must wait for your call?' She sobbed, 'With the great man at our house, I'd not the good fortune even to go before him. And the child—what a disappointment for him!'

When they got over their initial surprise, the authorities did everything to transform the place. All the stench mysteriously vanished; all the garbage and offal that lay about, and flesh and hide put out to sun-dry on the roofs, disappeared. All that night municipal and other employees kept working, with the aid of petrol lamps: light there was such a rarity that the children kept dancing all night around the lamps. Gandhiji noticed the hectic activity, but out of a sense of charity refrained from commenting on it. Only when it was all over did he say, 'Now one can believe that the true cleansers of the city live here.' The men of the colony tied round their heads their whitest turbans and the women wore their best saris, dragged their children to the river and scrubbed them till they yelled, and decorated their coiffures with yellow chrysanthemum flowers. The men left off fighting, did their best to keep away from the drink shops, and even the few confirmed topers had their drinks on the sly, and suppressed their impulse to beat their wives or break their household pots. The whole place looked bright with lamps and green mango leaves tied across lamp-posts and tree branches.

Gandhi occupied a hut which had a low entrance. He didn't like to oust anyone from his hut, but chose one facing the river sand, after making certain that it had been vacant, the occupant of the hut having gone elsewhere. The Chairman brought in a low divan and covered the floor with a coarse rush mat for Gandhi's visitors to sit on. Sriram lowered himself unobtrusively on the mat. Gandhi sat on his divan, and dictated to one of his secretaries. They wrote voluminously. Mahatmaji performed a number of things simultaneously. He spoke to visitors. He dictated. He wrote. He prayed. He had his sparse dinner of nuts and milk, and presently he even laid himself down on the divan and went off to sleep. It was then that someone turned off the lamp, and people walked out of the hut.

Sriram now felt that he could not continue to sit there. Although no one bothered to ask him what he was doing, he could not stay any more. When he saw the girl was preparing to leave the hut, he felt he had better get up and go; otherwise someone might say something unpleasant to him.

The girl lifted Gandhi's spinning wheel, put it away noiselessly and tip-toed out of the room. She passed without noticing him at first, but the fixed stare with which he followed her movements seemed to affect her. She went past him, but suddenly stopped and whispered; 'You will have to go now,' and Sriram sprang up and found himself outside the hut in one bound.

She said rather grimly: 'Don't you know that when Bapuji sleeps, we have to leave him?'

He felt like asking, 'Who is Bapuji?' but used his judgement for a second, understood that it must refer to the Mahatma, and not wanting to risk being chased out by the resolute girl said, 'Of course, I knew it. I was only waiting for you to come out.'

'Who are you? I don't think I have seen you before.'

This was the question he had been waiting to be asked all along, but now when it came he found himself tongue-tied. He felt so confused and muddled that she took pity on him and said, 'What is your name?'

He answered, 'Sriram.'

'What are you doing here?' she asked.

'Don't you remember me?' he said irrelevantly. 'I saw you when you came with a money-box in the market, the other day. . . .'

'Oh, I see,' she said out of politeness. 'But I might not remember you since quite a lot of people put money into my box that day. Anyway I asked you now what you are doing here?'

'Perhaps one of the volunteers,' Sriram said.

'Why "perhaps"?' she asked.

'Because I'm not yet one,' he replied.

'Anybody cannot be a volunteer,' she said. 'Don't you know that?' she asked.

'Don't I know that? I think I know that and more.'

'What more?' she asked.

'That I am not an anybody,' he replied and was amazed at his own foolhardiness in talking to the girl in that fashion; she could put him out of the camp in a moment.

'You are a somebody, I suppose?' the girl asked laughing.

'Well, you will help me to become somebody, I hope,' he said, feeling surprised at his own powers of rash and reckless speech.

She seemed a match for him, for presently she asked, with a little irritation, 'Are we going to stand here and talk the whole night?'

'Yes unless you show me where we can go.'

'I know where I ought to go,' she said. 'You see that hut there,' she pointed to a small hut four doors off Gandhi's, 'That's where all the women of this camp are quartered.'

'How many of them are there?' Sriram asked just to keep up the conversation.

She answered sharply, 'More than you see before you now,' and added, 'why are you interested?'

Sriram felt a little piqued, 'You seem to be a very ill-tempered and sharp-tongued girl. You can't answer a single question without a challenge.'

'Hush! You will wake up Bapuji standing and talking here,' she said.

'Well, if he is going to be awakened by anyone's talk, it will be yours, because no one else is doing the talking,' he replied.

'I have a right to ask you what you are doing here and report to our *Chalak* if I don't like you,' she said with a sudden tone of authority.

'Why should you not like me?' he asked.

'No one except close associates and people with appointments are allowed to enter Bapuji's presence.'

'I will tell them I am your friend and that you took me in,' he replied.

'Would you utter a falsehood?' she asked.

'Why not?'

'None except absolute truth-speakers are allowed to come into Mahatma's camp. People who come here must take an oath of absolute truth before going into Mahatma's presence.'

'I will take the vow when I become a member of the camp. Till then I will pass off something that looks like truth,' he said.

'When Mahatma hears about this he will be very pained and he will talk to you about it.'

Sriram was now genuinely scared and asked pathetically, 'What have I done that you should threaten and menace me?'

This softened her, and for the first time he noticed a little tenderness had crept into her tone.

'Do you mind moving off and waiting there? We should not be talking like this near Mahatmaji's hut. I will go to my hut and then join you there.'

She turned and disappeared; she had the lightning-like motion of a dancer, again the sort of pirouetting movement that she had adopted while carrying off other people's coins in a jingling box. She passed down the lane. He moved off slowly. He was tired of standing. He sat on a boulder at the edge of the river, kicking up the sand with his toes, and ruminating on his good fortune. He had never hoped for anything like it. It might have been a dream. This time yesterday he could not have thought he would talk on these terms to the money-box girl. He realized he had not yet asked her name. He remembered that he had felt hungry and thirsty long ago. 'I wish they would give us all something to eat in Mahatmaji's camp.' He remembered that Mahatma ate only groundnuts and dates. He looked about hoping there would be vendors of these articles. The Taluk Office gong sounded nine. He counted it deliberately, and wondered what his granny would make of his absence now. 'She will fret and report to the police, I suppose!' he reflected cynically. He wished he had asked his teacher to go and tell Granny not to expect him home till Gandhiji left the town. On second thoughts it struck him that it was just as well that he had not spoken to the teacher, who would probably have gone and spread the rumour that his interest in Gandhi was only a show and that he was really going after a girl. What was her name? Amazing how he had not yet asked her it, and the moment she came back he said, 'What is your name?'

'Bharathi,' she answered. 'Why?'

'Just to know, that's all. Have I told you my name is Sriram?'

'Yes, you have told me that more than once,' she said. 'I have heard again and again that you are Sriram.'

'You are too sharp-tongued,' he replied, 'it is a wonder they tolerate you here, where peace and kindness must be practised.'

'I am practising kindness, otherwise I should not be speaking to you at all. If I didn't want to be kind to you I wouldn't have gone in and taken my *Chalak's* permission and come right away here. We must have permission to talk to people at this hour. There is such a thing as discipline in every camp. Don't imagine that because it is Mahatmaji's camp it is without any discipline. He would be the first to tell you about it if you raised the question with him.'

'You have the same style of talk as my grandmother. She is as sharp-tongued as you are,' Sriram said pathetically.

She ignored the comparison and asked, 'What about your mother?'

'I have never seen her, my grandmother has always been father and mother to me. Why don't you meet her? You will like her, both of you speak so much alike?'

'Yes, yes,' said the girl soothingly, 'someday I will come and meet her as soon as this is all over. You see how busy I am now.'

She became tender when she found that she was talking to someone without a mother, and Sriram noticing this felt it was worthwhile being motherless and grandmother-tended. She sat on the same step, with her legs dangling in the river, leaving a gap of a couple of feet between them. The river rumbled into the dark starlit night, the leaves of the huge tree over the ancient steps rustled and sighed. Far off bullock-carts and pedestrians were fording the river at Nallappa's Grove. Distant voices came through the night. Mahatmaji's camp was asleep. It was so quiet that Sriram felt like taking the girl in his arms, but he resisted the idea. He feared that if he touched her she might push him into the river. The girl was a termagant, she would surely develop into the same type as his grandmother with that sharp tongue of hers. Her proximity pricked his blood and set it coursing.

'There is no one about. What can she do?' he reflected. 'Let her try and push me into the river, and she will know with whom she is dealing,' and the next moment he blamed himself for his own crude thoughts. 'It is not safe with the Mahatma there. He may already have read my thoughts and be coming here.' He was a Mahatma because awake or asleep he was fully aware of what was going on all round him. God alone could say what the Mahatma would do to someone who did not possess absolute purity of thought where girls were concerned. It meant hardship, no doubt, but if one was to live in this camp one had to follow the orders that emanated from the great soul. He struggled against evil thoughts and said, 'Bharati?' She looked startled at being called so familiarly and he himself felt startled by the music of her name.

'What a nice name!' he remarked.

'I am glad you like it,' she said. 'The name was given by Bapuji himself.'

'Oh, how grand!' he cried.

She added, 'You know my father died during the 1920 movement. Just when I was born. When he learnt of it Bapuji, who had come down South, made himself my godfather and named me Bharati, which means — I hope you know what.'

'Yes, Bharat is India, and Bharati is the daughter of India, I suppose.'

'Right,' she said, and he was pleased at her commendation.

'After my mother died, I was practically adopted by the local Sevak Sangh, and I have not know any other home since,' she said.

'Do you mean to say that you are all the time with these people?'

'What is wrong in it?' she asked. 'It has been my home.'

'Not that, I was only envying you. I too wish I could be with you all and do something instead of wasting my life.'

This appealed to her and she asked, 'What do you want to do?'

'The same as what you are doing. What are you doing?' he asked.

'I do whatever I am asked to do by the Sevak Sangh. Sometimes they ask me to go and teach people spinning and tell them about Mahatmaji's ideas. Sometimes they send me to villages and poor quarters. I meet them and talk to them and do a few things. I attend to Mahatmaji's needs.'

'Please let me also do something along with you,' he pleaded. 'Why don't you take me as your pupil? I want to do something good. I want to talk to poor people.'

'What will you tell them?' she asked ruthlessly.

He made some indistinct sounds. 'I will tell them whatever you ask me to tell them,' he said, and this homage to her superior intelligence pleased her.

'H'm! But why?' she asked.

He summoned all his courage and answered, 'Because I like you, and I like to be with you.'

She burst into a laugh and said, 'That won't be sufficient. . . . They. . .' she indicated a vast army of hostile folk behind her back, 'they may chase you away if you speak like that.'

He became sullen and unhappy. He rallied and said presently, 'Well, I too would willingly do something.'

'What?' she taunted him again.

He looked at her face helplessly, desperately, and asked, 'Are you making fun of me?'

'No, but I wish to understand what you are saying.'

She relented a little, presently, and said, 'I will take you to Bapu, will you come?'

He was panic-stricken. 'No, no, I can't.'

'You have been there already.'

He could give no reasonable explanation and now he realized the enormity of his rashness. He said, 'No, no, I would be at a loss to know how to talk to him, how to reply to him and what to tell him.'

'But you sat there before him like someone always known to him!' she said, 'like his best friend.'

She laughed and enjoyed teasing him.

'Somehow I did it, but I won't do it again,' he declared. 'He may find me out if I go before him again.'

Suddenly she became very serious and said, 'You will have to face Bapuji if you want to work with us.'

Sriram became speechless. His heart palpitated with excitement. He wished he could get up and run away, flee once and for all the place, be done with it, and turn his back on the whole business for ever. This was too much. The gods seemed to be out to punish him for his hardihood and presumption.

He cried, 'Bharati, tell me if I can meet you anywhere else, otherwise please let me go.' He was in a cold sweat. 'What should I say when I speak to him? I would blabber like an idiot.'

'You are already doing it,' she said, unable to restrain her laughter.

He said pathetically, 'You seem to enjoy bothering me. I am sorry I ever came here.'

'Why are you so cowardly?' she asked.

Sriram said resolutely, 'I can't talk to Mahatmaji. I wouldn't know how to conduct myself before him.'

'Just be yourself. It will be all right.'

'I wouldn't be able to answer his questions properly.'

'He is not going to examine you like an inspector of schools. You don't have to talk to him unless you have something to say. You may keep your mouth shut and he won't mind. You may just be yourself, say anything you feel like saying. He will not mind anything at all, but you will have to speak the truth if you speak at all.'

'Truth! In everything!' he looked scared.

'Yes, in everything. You may speak as bluntly as you like, and he will not take it amiss, provided it is just truth.'

Sriram looked more crushed than ever. In this dark night he seemed to have a terrific problem ahead of him. After brooding over it for a while he said, 'Bharati, tell me if I may meet you anywhere else. Otherwise let me go.'

She replied with equal resolution, 'If you wish to meet me come to Bapuji, the only place where you may see me. Of course, if you don't want to see me any more, go away.'

This placed him in a dilemma. 'Where? How?' he asked.

'Come to the door of Bapu's hut and wait for me.'

'When? Where?'

'At three a.m., tomorrow morning. I'll take you to him.'

Saying this, she jumped to her feet and ran off towards her hut.

THE GUIDE

Editor's note: The most famous of Narayan's novels. *The Guide* tells the story of Raju, who earns a living by acting as a guide to visitors to Malgudi. When an antiquarian named Marco and his beautiful dancer-wife Rosie arrive in Malgudi, Raju attaches himself to them, and only disaster can result. Rosie leaves Marco, Raju promotes her in the dancing world, and it seems the sky is the limit when he gets involved in a criminal conspiracy. Coming out of prison, he is taken to be a holy man by the simple villagers and has no option but to fulfil that role, as his rustic devotees either disbelieve the story Raju tells them about his part, or say it does not matter to them. The final chapter which is excerpted here tells about the ambiguous apotheosis of Raju with gentle irony.

Raju's narration concluded with the crowing of the cock. Velan had listened without moving a muscle, supporting his back against the ancient, stone railing along the steps. Raju felt his throat smarting with the continuous talk all night. The village had not yet wakened to life. Velan yielded himself to a big yawn, and remained silent. Raju had mentioned without a single omission every detail from his birth to his emergence from the gates of the prison. He imagined that Velan would rise with disgust and swear, 'And we took you for such a noble soul all along! If one like you does penance, it'll drive off even the little rain that we may hope for. Begone, you, before we feel tempted to throw you out. You have fooled us.'

Raju waited for these words as if for words of reprieve. He looked on Velan's silence with anxiety and suspense, as if he waited on a judge's verdict again, a second time. The judge here seemed to be one of sterner cast than the one he had encountered in the court-hall. Velan kept still—so still that Raju feared that he had fallen asleep.

Raju asked, 'Now you have heard me fully?' like a lawyer who has a misgiving that the judge has been wool-gathering.

'Yes, Swami.'

Raju was taken aback at still being addressed as 'Swami'. 'What do you think of it?'

Velan looked quite pained at having to answer such a question. 'I don't know why you tell me all this, Swami. It's very kind of you to address at such length your humble servant.'

Every respectful word that this man employed pierced Raju like a shaft. 'This man will finish me before I know where I am.'

After profound thought, the judge rose in his seat. 'I'll go back to the village to do my morning duties. I will come back later. And I'll never speak a word of what I have heard to anyone.' He dramatically thumped his chest. 'It has gone down there, and there it will remain.' With this, he made a deep obeisance, went down the steps and across the sandy river.

A wandering newspaper correspondent who had come to the village picked up the news. The government had sent a commission to inquire into the drought conditions and suggest remedies, and with it came a press correspondent. While wandering around he heard about the Swamiji, went to the temple across the river, and sent off a wire to his paper at Madras, which circulated in all the towns of India. 'Holy man's penance to end drought', said the heading, and then a brief description followed.

This was the starting point.

Public interest was roused. The newspaper office was besieged for more news. They ordered the reporter to go back. He sent a second telegram to say 'Fifth day of fast'. He described the scene: how the Swami came to the river's edge, faced its source, stood knee-deep in the water from six to eight in the morning, muttering something between his lips, his eyes shut, his palms pressed together in a salute to the gods, presumably. It had been difficult enough to find knee-deep water, but the villagers had made an artificial basin in sand and, when it didn't fill, fetched water from distant wells and filled it, so that the man had always knee-deep water to stand in. The holy man stood there for two hours, then walked up the steps slowly and lay down on a mat in the pillared hall of the temple, while his devotees kept fanning him continuously. He took notice of hardly anyone , though there was a big crowd around. He fasted totally. He lay down and shut his eyes in order that his penance might be successful. For that purpose he conserved all his energy. When he was not standing in the water, he was in deep meditation. The villagers had set aside all their normal avocations in order to be near this great soul all the time. When he slept they remained there, guarding him, and though there was a fair-sized crowd, it remained totally silent.

But each day the crowd increased. In a week there was a permanent hum pervading the place. Children shouted and played about, women came carrying baskets filled with pots, firewood, and foodstuffs, and cooked the food for their men and children. There were small curls of smoke going up all along the river-bank, on the opposite slope and on this bank also. It was studded with picnic groups, with the women's bright-coloured saris shining in the sun; men too had festive dress. Bullocks unyoked from their carts jingled their bells as they ate the straw under the trees. People swarmed around little water-holes.

Raju saw them across his pillared hall whenever he opened his eyes. He knew what that smoke meant; he knew that they were eating and enjoying themselves. He wondered what they might be eating—rice boiled with a pinch of saffron, melted ghee—and what were the vegetables? Probably none in this drought. The sight tormented him.

This was actually the fourth day of his fast. Fortunately on the first day he had concealed a little stale food, left over from the previous day, in an aluminium vessel behind a stone pillar in the innermost sanctum—some rice mixed with butter-milk, and a piece of vegetable thrown in. Fortunately, too, he was able on the first day to snatch a little privacy at the end of the day's prayer and penance, late at night. The crowd had not been so heavy then. Velan had business at home and had gone, leaving two others to attend on the Swami. The Swami had been lying on the mat in the pillared hall, with the two villagers looking on and waving a huge palmyra fan at his face. He had felt weakened by his day's fasting. He had suddenly told them, 'Sleep, if you like; I'll be back,' and he rose in a businesslike manner and passed into his inner sanctum.

'I don't have to tell the fellows where I am going or why or how long I shall be gone out of sight.' He felt indignant. He had lost all privacy. People all the time watching and staring, lynx-eyed, as if he were a thief! In the inner sanctum he briskly thrust his hand into a niche and pulled out his aluminium pot. He sat down behind the pedestal, swallowed his food in three or four large mouthfuls, making as little noise as possible. It was stale rice, dry and stiff and two days old; it tasted awful, but it appeased his hunger. He washed it down with water. He went to the backyard and rinsed his mouth noiselessly—he didn't want to smell of food when he went back to his mat.

Lying on his mat, he brooded. He felt sick of the whole thing. When the assembly was at its thickest, could he not stand up on a high pedestal and cry, 'Get out, all of you, and leave me alone, I am not the man to save you. No power on earth can save you if you are doomed. Why do you bother me with all this fasting and austerity?'

It would not help. They might enjoy it as a joke. He had his back to the wall, there was no further retreat. This realization helped him to get through the trial with a little more resignation on the second day of his penance. Once again he stood up in water, muttering with his face to the hills, and watching the picnic groups enjoying themselves all over the place. At night he left Velan for a while and sneaked in to look for leftover food in his aluminium vessel—it was really an act of desperation. He knew full well that he had finished off the vessel the previous night. Still he hoped, childishly, for a miracle. 'When they want me to perform all sorts of miracles, why not make a start with my own aluminium vessel?' he reflected caustically. He felt weak. He was enraged at the emptiness of his larder. He wondered for a moment if he could make a last desperate appeal to Velan to let him eat—and if only he minded, how he could save him! Velan ought to know, yet the fool would not stop thinking that he was a saviour. He banged down the the aluminium vessel in irritation and went back to his mat. What if the vessel did get shattered? It was not going to be of any use. What was the point of pampering an empty vessel? When he was seated, Velan asked respectfully, 'What was that noise, master?'

'An empty vessel. Have you not heard the saying, "An empty vessel makes much noise"?'

Velan permitted himself a polite laugh and declared with admiration, 'How many good sentiments and philosophies you have gathered in that head of yours, sir!'

Raju almost glared at him. This single man was responsible for his present plight. Why would he not go away and leave him alone? What a wise plan it would have been if the crocodile had got him him while he crossed the river! But that poor old thing, which had remained almost a myth, had become dehydrated. When its belly was ripped open they found in it ten thousand rupees' worth of jewellery. Did this mean that the crocodile had been in the habit of eating only women? No, a few snuffboxes and earrings of men were also found. The question of the day was: Who was entitled to all this treasure? The villagers hushed up the affair. They did not want the government to get scent of it and come round and claim it, as it did all buried treasure. They gave out that only a couple of worthless trinkets had been found inside the crocodile, although in actual fact the man who cut it open acquired a fortune. He had no problems for the rest of his life. Who permitted him to cut open the crocodile? Who could say? People didn't wait for permission under such circumstances. Thus had gone on the talk among the people about the crocodile when it was found dead.

Velan, fanning him, had fallen asleep—he had just doubled up in his seat with the fan in his hand. Raju, who lay awake, had let his mind roam and touch the depths of morbid and fantastic thought. He was now touched by the sight of this man hunched in his seat. The poor fellow was tremendously excited and straining himself in order to make this penance a success, providing the great man concerned with every comfort—except, of course, food. Why not give the poor devil a chance? Raju said to himself, instead of hankering after food which one could not get anyway. He felt enraged at the persistence of food-thoughts. With a sort of vindictive resolution he told himself, 'I'll chase away all thought of food. For the next ten days I shall eradicate all thoughts of tongue and stomach from my mind.'

This resolution gave him a peculiar strength. He developed on those lines: 'If by avoiding food I should help the trees bloom, and the grass grow, why not do it thoroughly?' For the first time in his life he was making an earnest effort; for the first time he was learning the thrill of full application, outside money and love; for the first time he was doing a thing in which he was not personally interested. He felt suddenly so enthusiastic that it gave him a new strength to go through with the ordeal. The fourth day of his fast found him quite sprightly. He went down to the river, stood facing upstream with his eyes shut, and repeated the litany. It was no more than a supplication to the heavens to send down rain and save humanity. It was set in a certain rhythmic chant, which lulled his senses and awareness, so that as he went on saying it over and over again the world around became blank. He nearly lost all sensation, except the numbness at his knees, through constant contact with cold water. Lack of food gave him a peculiar floating feeling, which he rather enjoyed, with the thought in the background, 'This enjoyment is something Velan cannot take away from me.'

The hum of humanity around was increasing. His awareness of his surroundings was gradually lessening in a sort of inverse proportion. He was not aware of it, but the world was beginning to press around. The pen of the wandering journalist had done the trick. Its repercussions were far and wide. The railways were the first to feel the pressure. They had to run special trains for the crowds that were going to Malgudi. People travelled on footboards and on the roofs of coaches. The little Malgudi station was choked with passengers. Outside, the station buses stood, the conductors crying, 'Special for Mangala leaving. Hurry up. Hurry up.' People rushed up from the station into the buses and almost sat on top of one another. Gaffur's taxi drove up and down a dozen times a day. And the crowd congregated around the river at Mangala. People sat in groups along its sand-bank, down its stones and steps, all the way up the opposite bank, wherever they could squeeze themselves in.

Never had this part of the country seen such a crowd. Shops sprang up overnight, as if by magic, on bamboo poles roofed with thatch, displaying coloured soda bottles and bunches of bananas and coconut-toffees. The Tea Propaganda Board opened a big tea-stall, and its posters, green tea plantations along the slopes of blue mountains, were pasted all around the temple wall. (People drank too much coffee and too little tea in these parts.) It had put up a tea-bar and served free tea in porcelain cups all day. The public swarmed around it like flies, and the flies swarmed on all the cups and sugar-bowls. The presence of the fly brought in the Health Department, which feared an outbreak of some epidemic in that crowded place without water. The khaki-clad health inspectors sprayed every inch of space with DDT and, with needle in hand, coaxed people to inoculate themselves against cholera, malaria, and what-not. A few youngsters just for fun bared their biceps, while a big crowd stood about and watched. There was a blank space on the rear wall of the temple where they cleaned up the ground and made a space for people to sit around and watch a film show when it grew dark. They attracted people to it by playing popular hits on the gramophone with its loudspeakers mounted on the withering treetops. Men, women, and children crowded in to watch the film shows, which were all about mosquitoes, malaria, plague, and tuberculosis, and BCG vaccination. When a huge close-up of a mosquito was shown as the cause of malaria, a peasant was over-heard saying, 'Such mosquitoes! No wonder the people get malaria in those countries. Our own mosquitoes are so tiny that they are harmless,' which depressed the lecturer on malaria so much that he remained silent for ten minutes. When he had done with health, he showed a few Government of India films about dams, river valleys, and various projects, with ministers delivering speeches. Far off, outside the periphery, a man had opened a gambling booth with a dart-board on a pole, and he had also erected a crude merry-go-round, which whined all day. Pedlars of various kinds were also threading in and out, selling balloons, reed whistles, and sweets.

A large crowd always stood around and watched the saint with profound awe. They touched the water at his feet and sprinkled it over their heads. They stood indefinitely around, until the master of ceremonies, Velan, begged them to move. 'Please go away. The Swami must have fresh air. If you have had your *darshan*, move on and let others have theirs. Don't be selfish.' And then the people moved on and enjoyed themselves in various ways.

When the Swami went in to lie on his mat in the hall, they came again to look at him and stood about until Velan once again told them to keep moving. A few were specially privileged to sit on the mat very close to the great man. One of them was the schoolmaster, who took charge of all the telegrams and letters that were pouring in from all over the country wishing the Swami success. The post-office at Mangala normally had a visiting postman who came once a week, and when a telegram came it was received at Aruna, a slightly bigger village seven miles down the river course, and was kept there until someone could be found going to Mangala. But now the little telegraph office had no rest—day and night messages poured in, just addressed, 'Swamiji', that was all. They were piling up every hour and had to be sent down by special messengers. In addition to the arriving telegrams, there were many going out. The place was swarming with press reporters, who were rushing their hour-to-hour stories to their papers all over the world. They were an aggressive lot and the little telegraph-master was scared of them. They banged on his window and cried , 'Urgent!' They held out packets and packed-up films and photographs, and ordered him to dispatch them at once. They cried, 'Urgent, urgent! If this packet does not reach my office today. . . ' and they threatened terrifying prospects and said all sorts of frightening things.

'Press. Urgent!' 'Press. Urgent!' They went on shouting till they reduced the man to a nervous wreck. He had promised his children that he would take them to see the Swamiji. The children cried, 'They are also showing an Ali Baba film, a friend told me.' But the man was given no time to fulfil his promise to his children. When the pressmen gave him respite, the keys rattled with incoming messages. He had spent a fairly peaceful life until then, and the present strain tore at his nerves. He sent off an SOS to all his official superiors whenever he found breathing space: 'Handling two hundred messages today. Want relief.'

The roads were choked with traffic, country carts, buses and cycles, jeeps and automobiles of all kinds and ages. Pedestrians in files with hampers and baskets crossed the fields like swarms of ants converging on a lump of sugar. The air rang with the music of a few who had chosen to help the Swami by sitting near him, singing devotional songs to the accompaniment of a harmonium and tabla.

The busiest man here was an American, wearing a thin bush-shirt over corduroys. He arrived in a jeep with a trailer, dusty, rugged, with a mop of tousled hair, at about one in the afternoon on the tenth day of the fast and set himself to work immediately. He had picked up an interpreter at Madras and had driven straight through, three hundred and seventy-five miles. He pushed everything aside and took charge of the scene. He looked about for only a moment, driving his jeep down to the hibiscus bush behind the temple. He jumped off and strode past everyone to the pillared hall. He went up to the recumbent Swami and brought his palms together, muttering, 'Namaste'—the Indian salute, which he had learned the moment he landed in India. He had briefed himself on all local manners. Raju looked on him with interest; the large, pink-faced arrival was a novel change in the routine.

The pink visitor stooped low to ask the schoolmaster, sitting beside the Swami, 'Can I speak to him in English?'

'Yes. He knows English.'

The man lowered himself on to the edge of the mat and with difficulty sat down on the floor, Indian fashion, crossing his legs. He bent close to the Swami to say, 'I'm James J. Malone. I'm from California. My business is production of films and TV shows. I have come to shoot this subject , take it back to our country, and show it to our people there. I have in my pocket the sanction from New Delhi for this project. May I have yours?'

Raju thought over it and serenely nodded.

'Okay. Thanks a lot. I won't disturb you—but will you let me shoot pictures of you? I wouldn't disturb you. Will it bother you if I move a few things up and fix the cable and lights?'

'No; you may do your work,' said the sage.

The man became extremely busy. He sprang to his feet, pulled the trailer into position, and started his generator. Its throbbing filled the place, overwhelming all other noises. It brought in a huge crowd of men, women, and children to watch the fun. All the other attractions in the camp became secondary. As Malone drew the cables about, a big crowd followed him. He grinned at them affably and went about his business. Velan and one or two others ran through the crowd, crying, 'Is this a fish market? Get away, all of you who have no work here!' But nobody was affected by his orders. They climbed pillars and pedestals and clung to all sorts of places to reach positions of vantage. Malone went on with his job without noticing anything. Finally, when he had the lights ready, he brought in his camera and took pictures of the people and the temple, and of the Swami from various angles and distances.

'I'm sorry, Swami, if the light is too strong.' When he had finished with the pictures, he brought in a microphone, put it near the Swami's face, and said, 'Let us chat. Okay? Tell me, how do you like it here?'

'I am only doing what I have to do; that's all. My likes and dislikes do not count.'

'How long have you been without food now?'

'Ten days.'

'Do you feel weak?'

'Yes.'

'When will you break your fast?'

'Twelfth day.'

'Do you expect to have the rains by then?'

'Why not?'

'Can fasting abolish all wars and bring world peace?'

'Yes.'

'Do you champion fasting for everyone?'

'Yes.'

'What about the caste system? Is it going?'

'Yes.'

'Will you tell us something about your early life?'

'What do you want me to say?'

'Er—for instance, have you always been a Yogi?'

'Yes; more or less.'

It was very hard for the Swami to keep up a continuous flow of talk. He felt exhausted and lay back. Velan and others looked on with concern. The schoolmaster said, 'He is fatigued.'

'Well, I guess we will let him rest for a while. I'm sorry to bother you.'

The Swami lay back with his eyes closed. A couple of doctors, deputed by the government to watch and report, went to the Swami, felt his pulse and heart. They helped him to stretch himself on the mat. A big hush fell upon the crowd. Velan plied his fan more vigorously than ever. He looked distraught and unhappy. In fact, keeping a sympathetic fast, he was now eating on alternate days, confining his diet to saltless boiled greens. He looked worn out. He said to the master, 'One more day. I don't know how he is going to bear it. I dread to think how he can pull through another day.'

Malone resigned himself to waiting. He looked at the doctor and asked, 'How do you find him?'

'Not very satisfactory; blood pressure is two hundred systolic. We suspect one of the kidneys is affected. Uremia is setting in. We are trying to give him small doses of saline and glucose. His life is valuable to the country.'

'Would you say a few words about his health?' Malone asked, thrusting his microphone forward. He was sitting on the head of a carved elephant decorating the steps to the pillared hall.

The doctors looked at each other in panic and said, 'Sorry. We are government servants—we cannot do it without permission. Our reports are released only from headquarters. We cannot give them direct. Sorry.'

'Okay. I wouldn't hurt your customs.' He looked at his watch and said, 'I guess that's all for the day.' He approached the schoolmaster and said, 'Tell me, what time does he step into the river tomorrow?'

'Six a.m.'

'Could you come over and show me the location?' The schoolmaster got up and took him along. The man said, 'Wait, wait. You'll not mind understudying him for a minute. Show me where he starts from, how he gets up, and where he steps and stands.'

The teacher hesitated, feeling too shy to understudy the sage. The man urged him on. 'Come on; be co-operative. I'll take care of it, if there is any trouble.'

The teacher started from the pedestal. 'He starts here. Now follow me.' He showed the whole route down to the river, and the spot where the Swami would stop and pray, standing in water for two hours. The crowd followed keenly every inch of this movement, and someone in the crowd was joking, 'Oh! The master is also going to do penance and starve!' And they all laughed.

Malone threw a smile at them from time to time, although he did not know what they were saying. He surveyed the place from various angles, measured the distance from the generator, shook the schoolmaster's hand, and went back to his jeep. 'See you tomorrow morning.' He drove off amidst a great roar and puffing of his engine as his jeep rattled over the pits and ditches beyond the hibiscus, until he reached the road.

The eleventh day, morning. The crowd, pouring in all night, had nearly trebled itself because it was the last day of the fast. All night one could hear voices of people and the sound of vehicles rattling over the roads and pathways. Velan and a band of his assistants formed a cordon and kept the crowd out of the pillared hall. They said, 'The Swami must have fresh air to breathe. It's the only thing he takes now. Don't choke the air. Everyone can have his *darshan* at the river, I promise. Go away now. He is resting.' It was an all-night vigil. The numerous lanterns and lamps created a criss-cross of bewildering shadows on all hedges, trees, and walls.

At five-thirty in the morning the doctors examined the Swami. They wrote and signed a bulletin saying: 'Swami's condition grave. Declines glucose and saline. Should break the fast immediately. Advise procedure.' They sent a man running to send off this telegram to their headquarters.

It was a top-priority government telegram, and it fetched a reply within an hour: 'Imperative that Swami should be saved. Persuade best to co-operate. Should not risk life. Try give glucose and saline. Persuade Swami resume fast later.'

They sat beside the Swami and read the message to him. He smiled at it. He beckoned Velan to come nearer.

The doctors appealed, 'Tell him he should save himself. Please, do your best. He is very weak.'

Velan bent close to the Swami and said, 'The doctors say—'

In answer Raju asked the man to bend nearer, and whispered, 'Help me to my feet,' and clung to his arm and lifted himself. He got up to his feet. He had to be held by Velan and another on each side. In the profoundest silence the crowd followed him down. Everyone followed at a solemn, silent pace. The eastern sky was red. Many in the camp were still sleeping. Raju could not walk but he insisted upon pulling himself along all the same. He panted with the effort. He went down the steps of the river, halting for breath on each step, and finally reached his basin of water. He stepped into it, shut his eyes, and turned towards the mountain, his lips mutter-ing the prayer. Velan and another held him each by an arm. The morning sun was out by now; a great shaft of light illuminated the surroundings. It was difficult to hold Raju on his feet, as he had a tendency to flop down. They held him as if he were a baby. Raju opened his eyes, looked about, and said, 'Velan, it's raining in the hills. I can feel it coming up under my feet, up my legs—' He sagged down.

THE MAN-EATER OF MALGUDI

Editor's note: Here Narayan gets back to the quietly tumultuous town of Malgudi and its eccentric inhabitants whose lives are violently disturbed by a rough, tough and brutal taxidermist named Vasu, who makes the docile Nataraj's printing press his home, and lives there riotously with a total lack of consideration for those around him. He comes to a violent end as might be expected. The excerpt deals with the arrival of Vasu in the quiet community.

Sastri had to go a little earlier than usual since he had to perform a puja at home. I hesitated to let him go. The three-colour labels (I prided myself on the excellence of my colour-printing) for K.J.'s aerated drinks had to be got ready. It was a very serious piece of work for me. My personal view was that the coloured ink I used on the label was far safer to drink than the dye that K.J. put into his water-filled bottles. We had already printed the basic colour on the labels and the second was to be imposed today. This was a crucial stage of the work and I wanted Sastri to stay and finish the job.

He said,'Perhaps I can stay up late tonight and finish it. Not now. Meanwhile will you. . . .' He allotted me work until he should be back at two o'clock.

I had been engrossed in a talk with the usual company. On the agenda today was Nehru's third Five-Year Plan; my friend Sen saw nothing but ruin in it for the country. 'Three hundred crores—are we counting heads or money?' His audience consisted of myself and the poet, and a client who had come to ask for quotations for a business card. The discussion was warming up, as the client was a Congressman who had gone to prison fourteen times since the day Mahatma Gandhi arrived in India from South Africa. He ignored for the time being the business that had brought him and plunged into the debate, settling himself inexorably in a corner. 'What's wrong with people is they have got into the habit of blaming everything on the Government. You think democracy means that if there is no sugar in the shops, Government is responsible. What if there is no sugar? You won't die if you do not have sugar for your morning coffee some days.' Sen disputed every word of the patriot's speech.

I listened to the debate until I noticed Sastri's silhouette beyond the curtain. Sastri, when there was any emergency, treated me as a handy-boy, and I had no alternative but to accept the role. Now my duty would be to fix the block on the machine and put the second impression on all the labels and spread them out to dry, then he would come and give the third impression and put the labels out to dry again.

He explained some of the finer points to me; 'The blocks are rather worn. You'll have to let in more ink.'

'Yes, Mr Sastri.'

He looked at me through his small silver-rimmed glasses and said firmly,'Unless the labels are second-printed and dry by three o'clock today, it's going to be impossible to deliver them tomorrow. You know what kind of a man K.J. is. . . .'

What about my lunch? Sastri did not care whether I had time for food or not—he was a tyrant when it came to printing labels, but there was no way of protesting. He would brush everything aside. As if reading my mind he explained, 'I'd not trouble you but for the fact that this *satyanarayana* puja must be performed today in my house; my children and wife will be waiting for me at the door. . . .' As it was he would have to trot all the way to Vinayak Street if his family were not to starve too long.

Wife, children. Absurd. Such encumbrances were not necessary for Sastri, I felt. They were for lesser men like me. His place was at the type-board and the treadle. He produced an incongruous, unconvincing picture as a family man. But I dared not express myself aloud. The relation of employer and employee was reversed at my press whenever there was an emergency.

I accepted the situation without any fuss. According to custom my friends would not step beyond the curtain, so I was safe to go ahead with the second impression. Sastri had fixed everything. I had only to press the pedal and push the paper on to the pad. On a pale orange ground I had now to impose a sort of violet. I grew hypnotized by the sound of the wheel and the dozen kinks that were set in motion by the pressure I put on the pedals. Whenever I paused I could hear Sen's voice, 'If Nehru is practical, let him disown the Congress. . . . Why should you undertake projects which you can't afford? Anyway, in ten years what are we going to do with all the steel?' There was a sudden lull. I wondered if they had been suddenly struck dumb. I heard the shuffling of feet. I felt suddenly relieved that the third Five-Year Plan was done with.

Now an unusual thing happened. The curtain stirred, an edge

of it lifted, and the monosyllabic poet's head peeped through. An extraordinary situation must have arisen to make him do that. His eyes bulged. 'Someone to see you,' he whispered.

'Who? What does he want?'

'I don't know.'

The whispered conversation was becoming a strain. I shook my head, winked and grimaced to indicate to the poet that I was not available. The poet, ever a dense fellow, did not understand but blinked on unintelligently. His head suddenly vanished, and a moment later a new head appeared in its place—a tanned face, large powerful eyes under thick eyebrows, a large forehead and a shock of unkempt hair, like a black halo.

My first impulse was to cry out, 'Whoever you may be, why don't you brush your hair?' The new visitor had evidently pulled aside the poet before showing himself to me. Before I could open my mouth, he asked, 'You Nataraj?' I nodded. He came forward, practically tearing aside the curtain, an act which violated the sacred traditions of my press. I said, 'Why don't you kindly take a seat in the next room? I'll be with you in a moment.' He paid no attention, but stepped forward, extending his hand. I hastily wiped my fingers on a rag, muttering, 'Sorry, discoloured, been working. . . .' He gave me a hard grip. My entire hand disappeared into his fist—he was a large man, about six feet tall. He looked quite slim, but his bull-neck and hammer-fist revealed his true stature. 'Shan't we move to the other room?' I asked again.

'Not necessary. It's all the same to me,' he said. 'You are doing something? Why don't you go on? It won't bother me.' He eyed my coloured labels. 'What are they?'

I didn't want any eyes to watch my special colour effects, and see how I achieved them. I moved to the curtain and parted it courteously for him. He followed me. I showed him to the Queen Anne chair, and sat down at my usual place, on the edge of my desk. I had now regained the feeling of being master of the situation. I adopted my best smile and asked, 'Well, what can I do for you, Mr. . . ?'

'Vasu,' he said, and added, 'I knew you didn't catch my name. You were saying something at the same time as I mentioned my name.'

I felt abashed, and covered it, I suppose, with another of those silly smiles. Then I checked myself, suddenly feeling angry with him for making me so uneasy. I asked myself, 'Nataraj, are you afraid of this muscular fellow?' and said authoritatively, 'Yes?' as much as to indicate, 'You have wasted my time sufficiently; now say quickly whatever you may want to say.'

He took from his inner pocket a wad of paper, searched for a hand-written sheet and held it out to me. 'Five hundred sheets of note-paper, the finest quality, and five hundred visiting cards.'

I spread out the sheet without a word and read, 'H. Vasu, M.A., Taxidermist'. I grew interested. My irritation left me. This was the first time I had set eyes on a taxidermist. I said, assuming a friendly tone, 'Five hundred! Are you sure you need five hundred visiting cards? Could you not print them one hundred at a time? They'd be fresh then.'

'Why do you try to advise me?' he asked pugnaciously. 'I know how many I need. I'm not printing my visiting cards in order to preserve them in a glass case.'

'All right. I can print ten thousand if you want.'

He softened at my show of aggressiveness. 'Fine, fine, that's the right spirit.'

'If you'd like to have it done on the original Heidelberg. . . ' I began.

'I don't care what you do it on. I don't even know what you are talking about.'

I understood the situation now; every other sentence was likely to prove provocative. I began to feel intrigued by the man. I didn't want to lose him. Even if I wanted to, I had no means of getting rid of him. He had sought me out and I'd have to have him until he decided to leave. I might just as well be friendly, 'Surely, whatever you like. It's my duty to ask, that's all. Some people prefer it.'

'What is it anyway?' he asked.

I explained the greatness of Heidelberg and where it was. He thought it over, and suddenly said, 'Nataraj, I trust you to do your best for me. I have come to you as a friend. ' I was surprised and flattered. He explained, 'I'm new to this place, but I heard about you within an hour of coming.' He mentioned an obscure source of information. 'Well, I never give a second thought to these things,' he said. 'When I like a man, I like him, that's all.'

I wanted to ask about taxidermy, so I asked, looking at his card, 'Taxidermist? Must be an interesting job. Where is your er. . . office or. . . . '

'I hope to make a start right here. I was in Junagadh—you know the place—and there I grew interested in the art. I came across a master there, one Suleiman. When he stuffed a lion (you know, Junagadh is a place where we have lions) he could make it look more terrifying than it would be in the jungle. His stuffings go all over the world. He was a master, and he taught me the art. After all we are civilized human beings, educated and cultured, and it is up to us to prove our superiority to nature. Science conquers nature in a new way each day; why not in creation also? That's my philosophy, sir. I challenge any man to contradict me.' He sighed at the thought of Suleiman, his master. 'He was a saint. He taught me his art sincerely.'

'Where did you get your M.A.?'

'At Madras, of course. You want to know about me?' he asked.

I wonder what he would have done if I had said, ' No, I prefer to go home and eat my food.' He would probably have held me down.

He said, 'I was educated in the Presidency College. I took my Master's degree in History, Economics and Literature.' That was in the year 1931. Then he had joined the Civil Disobedience movement against British rule, broken the laws, marched, demonstrated and ended up in jail. He went repeatedly to prison and once when he was released found himself in the streets of Nagpur. There he met a *pahelwan* at a show. 'That man could bear a half-ton stone slab on his cheek and have it split by hammer strokes; he could snap steel chains and he could hit a block of hard granite with his fist and pulverize it. I was young then, his strength appealed to me. I was prepared to become his disciple at any cost. I introduced myself to the *pahelwan*.' He remained thoughtful for a while and continued, 'I learnt everything from this master. The training was unsparing. He woke me up at three o'clock every morning and put me through exercises. And he provided me with the right diet. I had to eat a hundred almonds every morning and wash them down with half a *seer* of milk; two hours later six eggs with honey; at lunch chicken and rice; at night vegetables and fruit. Not everyone can hope to have this diet, but I was lucky in finding a man who enjoyed stuffing me like that. In six months I could understudy for him. On my first day, when I banged my fist on a century-old door of a house in Lucknow, the three-inch panel of seasoned teak splintered. My master patted me on the back with tears of joy in his eyes, "You are growing on the right lines, my boy." In a few months I could also snap chains, twist iron bars, and pulverize granite. We travelled all over the country, and gave our shows at every market fair in the villages and in the town halls in the cities, and he made a lot of money. Gradually he grew flabby and lazy, and let me do everything. They announced his name on the notices, but actually I did all the twisting and smashing of stone, iron, and what-not. When I spoke to him about it he called me an ungrateful dog and other names, and tried to push me out. I resisted... and....' Vasu laughed at the recollection of this incident. 'I knew his weak spot. I hit him there with the edge of my palm with a chopping movement ... and he fell down and squirmed on the floor. I knew he could perform no more. I left him there and walked out, and gave up the strong man's life once and for all.'

'You didn't stop to help him?' I asked.

'I helped him by leaving him there, instead of holding him upside down and rattling the teeth out of his head.'

'Oh, no,' I cried horrified.

'Why not? I was a different man now, not the boy who went to him for charity. I was stronger than he.'

'After all he taught you how to be strong—he was your guru,' I said, enjoying the thrill of provoking him.

'Damn it all!' he cried. 'He made money out of me, don't you see?'

'But he also gave you twelve eggs a day and—how much milk and almonds was it?'

He threw up his arms in vexation. 'Oh, you will never understand these things, Nataraj. You know nothing, you have not seen the world. You know only what happens in this miserable little place.'

'If you think this place miserable, why do you choose to come here?' I was nearest the inner door. I could dash away if he attempted to grab me. Familiarity was making me rash and headstrong. I enjoyed taunting him.

'You think I have come here out of admiration for this miserable city? Know this, I'm here because of Mempi forest and the jungles in those hills. I'm a taxidermist. I have to be where wild animals live.'

'And die,' I added.

He appreciated my joke and laughed. 'You are a wise guy,' he said admiringly.

'You haven't told me yet why or how you became a taxidermist,' I reminded him.

'H'm!' he said. 'Don't get too curious. Let us do business first. When are you giving me the visiting cards? Tomorrow?' He might pulverize granite, smash his guru with a slicing stroke, but where printing work was concerned I was not going to be pushed. I got up and turned the sheets of a tear-off calendar on the wall. 'You can come tomorrow and ask me. I can discuss this matter only tomorrow. My staff are out today.'

At this moment my little son Babu came running in crying

'Appa!' and halted his steps abruptly on seeing a stranger. He bit his nails, grinned, and tried to turn and run. I shot out my hand and held him. 'What is it?' I asked. He was friendly with the usual crowd at my press, but the stranger's presence somehow embarrassed him. I could guess why he had come; it was either to ask for a favour— permission to go out with his friends, or cash for peppermints—or to bring a message from his mother.

'Mother says, aren't you coming home for food? She is hungry.'

'So am I,' I said, 'and if I were Mother I wouldn't wait for Father. Understand me? Here is a gentleman with whom I am engaged on some important business. Do you know what he can do?' My tone interested Babu and he looked up expectantly.

Vasu made a weary gesture, frowned and said,'Oh, stop that, Mr Nataraj. Don't start it all again. I don't want to be introduced to anyone. Now, go away, boy,' he said authoritatively.

'He is my son. . . .' I began.

'I see that,' Vasu said indifferently, and Babu wriggled himself free and ran off.

Vasu did not come next day, but appeared again fifteen days later. He arrived in a jeep. 'You have been away a long time,' I said.

'You thought you were rid of me?' he asked, and, thumping his chest,'I never forget.'

'And I never remember,' I said. Somehow this man's presence roused in me a sort of pugnacity.

He stepped in, saw the Queen Anne chair occupied by the poet, and remarked, half-jokingly, 'That's my chair, I suppose.' The poet scrambled to his feet and moved to another seat. 'H'm that's better,' Vasu said, sitting down. He smiled patronizingly at the poet and said, 'I haven't been told who you are.'

'I'm I'm. . . a teacher in the school.'

'What do you teach?' he asked relentlessly.

'Well, history, geography, science, English—anything the boys must know.'

'H'm, an all-rounder,' Vasu said. I could see the poet squirming. He was a mild, inoffensive man who was unused to such rough contacts. But Vasu seemed to enjoy bothering him. I rushed in to his rescue. I wanted to add to his stature by saying,'He is a poet. He is nominally a teacher, but actually. . . .'

'I never read poetry; no time,'said Vasu promptly, and dismissed the man from his thoughts. He turned to me and asked,'Where are my cards?'

I had a seasoned answer for such a question. 'Where have you been this whole fortnight?'

'Away, busy.'

'So was I,' I said.

'You promised to give me the cards. . . . '

'When?' I asked.

'Next day,' he said. I told him that there had been no such promise. He raised his voice and I raised mine. He asked finally,'Are we here on business or to fight? If it's a fight, tell me. I like a fight. Can't you see, man, why I am asking for my cards?'

'Don't *you* see that we have our own business practice?'

I always adopted 'we' whenever I had to speak for the press.

'What do you mean?' he asked aggressively.

'We never choose the type and stationery for a customer. It must always be the customer's responsibility.'

'You never told me that,' he cried.

'You remember I asked you to come next day. That was my purpose. I never say anything without a purpose.'

'Why couldn't you have mentioned it the same day?'

'You have a right to ask,' I said, feeling it was time to concede him something. The poet looked scared by these exchanges. He was trying to get out, but I motioned him to stay. Why should the poor man be frightened away?

'You have not answered my question,' said Vasu. 'Why couldn't you have shown me samples of type on the first day?'

I said curtly,'Because my staff were out.'

'Oh!' he said opening his eyes wide. 'I didn't know you had a staff.'

I ignored his remark and shouted,'Sastri! Please bring those ivory card samples and also the ten-point copper-plate.' I told Vasu grandly,'Now you can indicate your preferences, and we shall try to give you the utmost satisfaction.'

Sastri, with his silver-rimmed glasses on his nose, entered, bearing a couple of blank cards and a specimen type-book. He paused for a second, studying the visitor, placed them on the table, turned and disappeared through the curtain.

'How many are employed in your press?' Vasu asked.

The man's curiosity was limitless and recognized no proprieties. I felt enraged. Was he a labour commissioner or something of the kind? I replied,'As many as I need. But, as you know, present-day labour conditions are not encouraging. However, Mr Sastri is very dependable; he has been with me for years. . . .' I handed him the cards and said,'You will have to choose. These are the best cards available.' I handed him the type-book. 'Tell me what type you like.'

That paralysed him. He turned the cards between his fingers, he turned the leaves of the type-book, and cried, 'I'm damned if I know what I want. They all look alike to me. What is the difference anyway?'

This was a triumph for me.'Vasu, printing is an intricate business. That's why we don't take responsibility in these matters.'

'Oh, please do something and print me my cards,' he cried, exasperated.

'All right,' I said. 'I'll do it for you, if you trust me.'

'I trust you as a friend, otherwise I would not have come to you.'

'Actually,' I said, 'I welcome friends rather than customers. I'm not a fellow who cares for money. If anyone comes to me for pure business, I send them over to my neighbour and they are welcome to get their work done cheaper and on a better machine—original Heidelberg.'

'Oh, stop that original Heidel,' he cried impatiently. 'I want to hear no more of it. Give me my cards. My business arrangements are waiting on that, and remember also five hundred letter- heads.'

THE VENDOR OF SWEETS

Editor's note: Jagan, a conservative and philosophical man, steeped in the teachings of Mahatma Gandhi, is a prominent vendor of sweets in the town of Malgudi. He is proud of his son Mali who has gone to the United States for higher study, but his world is shattered when Mali comes back with a foreign girl. Jagan believes at first that they are married and takes some comfort from that fact but soon realizes that it is not so. A classic story of the conflict between generations.

He had never thought that he could feel so superior about it. Now it seemed to him worth all the money and the pangs of separation. 'My son is in America,' he said to a dozen persons every day, puffing with pride on each occasion. It delayed his daily routine. On his way to the shop he had only to detect the slightest acquaintance on the road, and he would block his path, and instead of discussing weather or politics, as was his custom, would lead the talk on gently to the topic of America and of his son's presence there. After days and days of hopeless waiting, when a colourful airletter had arrived by post, he had almost felt the same joy as if Mali had come back. He hardly had the patience to read the printed instruction: 'To open, cut here', but thrust his finger in desperately and gashed the airletter until it split longitudinally, forcing him to piece it together like a jigsaw puzzle for deciphering. The message simply said, 'Arrived. New York is big. The buildings are very tall, not like ours. Thousands of motor-cars in the street. Food is difficult. I am in a hostel. Next week I go to school.' Jagan read it with pleasure, although he was somewhat disturbed at the boy's mention of 'school' rather than 'college'. It had arrived by the first post, and he sat on the hall bench and pored over it for nearly an hour, scanning every word and visualizing Mali in that enormous background. He could not keep the good news to himself. The first entrance open to him was the Truth Printing Works. Nataraj was at his desk, ever affable and welcoming visitors. The door was only half open, and when the light was blocked Nataraj looked up from his proofs and smiled, and immediately Jagan made the announcement: 'Mali has reached. . . .'

'Have you received a telegram?'

'Oh, no, he's prudent. Won't waste ten rupees when ten cents—any idea how much a cent is worth in our money?'

Nataraj made a rapid calculation. A dollar was equivalent to five rupees, seven rupees on the black market as one of his customers had told him, four rupees odd according to the government, a hundred cents to a dollar. . . . He gave up the attempt at multiplication and division and thought it best to change the subject. 'You will be getting your proofs very soon.'

'Oh, yes, I know once you take it up, you will get on with it. As you know, it's contribution and a service, and not written for profit.' After this statement, he switched over to America. 'It's a place of enormous buildings and lots of motor-cars. I hope the boy will have a room on the ground floor and not too high up.'

'Our boys are very clever,' said Nataraj, 'and can take care of themselves anywhere in the world.'

Accepting this agreeable statement, Jagan withdrew from the doorway and proceeded towards his shop. On the way he caught a glimpse of the adjournment lawyer at the turning of Kabir Lane. He clapped his hands and stopped him. He could take that liberty with him as they had been classmates at the Albert Mission more than a generation ago and had been together in the National Movement (although the lawyer elegantly avoided going to prison). The lawyer, a one-toothed man with a sprinkling of silver dust on his unshaven cheeks, smiled, exposing his bare gums. 'I've got to go home; some parties are waiting for me.'

'I won't take more than a minute,' said Jagan . 'I felt you'd be happy to know that Mali has written.'

'Have you received a telegram?'

What was the matter with everybody? Jagan felt annoyance at the tendency of people to get obsessed with telegrams.

'After all, why spend ten rupees when ten cents bring over a letter in four days?'

'Four days!' said the lawyer. 'No, no, you must be mistaken. It takes longer than that. It takes at least fifteen days.'

That was the limit. How presumptuous of the man to talk of America, while he was there to provide first-hand information! People's notions were fixed. Stupid fellows! Frogs in the well!

Ahead of him, he saw the chemist at his door, looking down at the street. He greeted Jagan warmly. 'Rather late today?' he said with a lot of friendliness.

'Yes, I know, I know,' Jagan said, approaching him eagerly

'The postman was rather late today. Well, when one has a son living so far away. . . .'

'Has he reached America safely?'

'Yes, I was somewhat anxious for two or three days! Other boys would have wasted money on a telegram, but a letter at a tenth of the cost takes only a couple of days more. He's prudent, you know.'

'What's the postage? I want to send for a free catalogue from Sears Roebuck. You know, it is an interesting book. It'll give us wonderful ideas on all sorts of things.' Jagan almost groaned when the other asked,'What's the equivalent of fifty cents, which is the postage for the catalogue?'

He passed on. None so good as the cousin, who deserved all the sweets he ate for his listening capacity: all the others in the town were obsessed with their own notions, were ignorant and resisted enlightenment on the subject of America. When he was sitting in his seat, the head cook came to ask for the day's programme. Jagan repeated the formula and then added a postscript as a favour to the cook: 'Mali has safely reached the other end, and that's a big relief to me. It's a huge country with a lot of motor-cars. Everyone has a car there.' The cook listened respectfully and turned away without comment. Jagan felt relieved that the fellow had not stopped to ask about telegrams or the equivalent of a cent.

He had to hold his soul in peace until four-thirty when the cousin arrived, passed straight in to savour, and came out of the kitchen. Jagan said with a quiet firmness, 'The boy has reached the other end safely.' He flourished a fragment of the airletter, as a special favour affording the cousin a glimpse of the letter while he had only mentioned it to others.

'Excellent news! I knew he'd be all right,' he said, smacking his lips.

'He didn't send a telegram.'

'Yes, yes why should he? Letters arrive so quickly nowadays. You must offer a couple of coconuts to Ganesha at the corner temple.'

'Surely, it goes without saying,' said Jagan as if there were a specific contract between himself and the god in the matter of his son's safety. 'It shall be done this very evening.'

'I'll buy the coconut on my way,' said the cousin, and immediately Jagan snatched up a coin from his drawer and handed it to the other.

'I feel a great burden off my head today. When someone goes on such a long pilgrimage, especially if he is flying, it's always a worry, although one doesn't talk about it.'

'I know, I know,' said the cousin. 'What does he say about himself?'

'He likes the new experience, of course. Lots of tall buildings and cars everywhere. I hope he will walk carefully in the streets. . . . He says the food is good. I'm relieved. You know it's a country of millionaires. Everyone is so rich.'

Mali proved unusually communicative from across the seas, and although at times he sounded brusque, disconnected or impersonal, he generalized a good deal about the civilization in which he found himself. The blue airmail letters grew into a file. If only Mali had taken the precaution of leaving a proper margin to his epistles, Jagan would have bound them into a neat little volume at Truth Printing; surely Nataraj would have realized its importance and obliged him with speedy execution. Jagan stuffed his *jibba* pocket with the letters, and pulled them out for choice reading of passages to all and sundry, mostly to his cousin who, as ever, remained an uncomplaining listener. Gradually his reading of the Bhagavad Gita was replaced by the blue airmail letters. From their study he formed a picture of America and was able to speak with authority on the subject of American landscape, culture and civilization. He hardly noticed to whom he spoke; anyone on the road seemed good enough. His acquaintances feared that he was afflicted with the Talking Disease.

From the minute he stepped out of his house, he scanned the landscape for a familiar face, pounced hawklike on the unwary victim and held him in thrall; he even stopped the vagrant on the culvert one day in order to describe the Grand Canyon. 'Actually, there is nothing like it anywhere in the world,' he concluded and gave him five paise for listening. It was a matter of luck for another, whether he could slip away in time or got entangled in American lore. Jagan found everyone restless when he spoke, but he rushed through his narration breathlessly. He had the feeling of having to bottle up his ideas until the blessed hour that brought his cousin in, who displayed such an enthusiasm for American information that Jagan could hardly tell him enough.

The cousin often wanted to see the letters himself, but Jagan resisted the idea: he held them in sacred trust and would not allow a third person to touch them.

Day after day, the cousin collected information on American life and manners and passed them on to his own circle of listeners. Very soon most people in Malgudi knew that fifty thousand human lives were lost in road accidents, every year, in America; and how people broke down on hearing of the death of Kennedy at street corners and crowded round anyone with a transistor radio. Jagan felt quite competent to describe, as if he had watched it himself, the route of Kennedy's motorcade on that fateful day, and he felt choked when he recounted how on that very morning, in Dallas, Kennedy had mingled in enormous crowds which grabbed and tore at his clothes and hair in sheer affection; nor did he spare his listener any detail of Oswald's death later.

The only letter Jagan rigorously suppressed was the one in which Mali had written after three years' experience of America, 'I've taken to eating beef, and I don't think I'm any the worse for it. Steak is something quite tasty and juicy. Now I want to suggest why don't you people start eating beef? It'll solve the problem of useless cattle in our country and we won't have to beg food from America. I sometimes feel ashamed when India asks for American aid. Instead of that, why not slaughter useless cows which wander in the streets and block the traffic?' Jagan felt outraged. The *shastras* defined the five deadly sins and the killing of a cow headed the list.

While he was cogitating on how to make his feelings felt on the subject and collecting quotations from the *shastras* and Gandhi's writings on the cow, to be incorporated in his letter to Mali, there came a cable one morning: 'Arriving home: another person with me.' Jagan was puzzled. What sort of a person? He had terrible misgivings and the added trouble of not being able to talk about it to the cousin, as he might spread the news of 'another person' all over the town. His worst misgivings were confirmed on an afternoon when the train dumped Mali, 'another person' and an enormous quantity of baggage onto the railway platform and puffed away. The very sight of the streamlined trunks, suitcases and corded cartons filled Jagan with uneasiness and a feeling of inferiority. The old porter at the railway station could hardly handle this quantity of baggage, although normally he would seize and carry scores of boxes and baskets without a thought. Now he had to call in the boy at the cigarette shop for assistance. Mali kept muttering without moving his head or lips much, 'Be careful, awful lot of things that might break. Have spent a fortune in air-freight.' Jagan slipped into the background, pushing his cousin to the fore to do all the talking and receiving. He was overwhelmed by the spectacle of his son, who seemed to have grown taller, broader and fairer and carried himself in long strides. He wore a dark suit, with an overcoat, an airbag, a camera, an umbrella and what-not on his person.

Jagan felt that he was following a stranger. When Mali approached him, extending his hand, he tried to shrink away and shield himself behind the cousin. When he had to speak to his son, with great difficulty he restrained himself from calling him 'sir' and employing the honorific plural.

Matters became worse when Mali indicated the girl at his side and said, ' This is Grace. We are married. Grace , my dad.' Complete confusion. Married? When were you married? You didn't tell me. Don't you have to tell your father? Who is she? Anyway she looks like a Chinese. Don't you know that one can't marry a Chinese nowadays? They have invaded our borders. . . . Or perhaps she is a Japanese. How was one to find out? Any indiscreet question might upset the gentleman with the camera. Jagan threw a panicky look at his cousin and fled on the pretext of supervising the loading of the baggage into Gaffur's taxi outside. A small gaping crowd followed them to the car murmuring, 'He's come from America.' Mali took notice of Gaffur by saying, 'Jalopy going strong?' Gaffur did not understand the word (which sounded to everyone like the *jilebi* prepared in Jagan's shop). Jagan and the cousin sat with Gaffur in the front seat, leaving the back for Grace and Mali. Gaffur said without turning his head, 'Why didn't you bring a car for me?' Jagan feared that Gaffur's familiarity might upset Mali, but the young man, fresh from democratic surroundings said, 'I wish you had told me; oh, I sold my Pontiac before coming.' Gaffur, driving the car, entered into a description of the state of the nation with reference to automobiles, how you had to wait for five years to get a Fiat, three for an Ambassador, and so forth, how no importation was allowed and how a brand-new Plymouth was seized and destroyed at the customs, all of which upset the young man, freshly come home. Mali occasionally peeped out to say, 'Nothing has changed.' Grace gazed with fascination at the streets and bazaars and cooed; 'Oh, charming! Charming! Charming!'

'Honey, live in it and see what it is like,' said Mali, on hearing which Jagan wondered whether he should address her as Honey or Grace. Time enough to settle that question. When they approached the statue, she asked, 'Who is that?' No one answered her. Jagan became tense at the approach of the house beyond the statue. When they stopped, he jumped out of the car and panted up the steps in order to open the main door. He had spent the fortnight in rigging up his house to suit his son's requirements. Under the guidance of the doctor's wife known to the cousin, he had spent a fortune in building a modern toilet and bathroom adjoining Mali's bedroom and had scrubbed and colour-washed the walls and put up new tables and chairs. Mali went straight to his room to wash and change. Gaffur and the cousin left after piling the boxes in the passage. Grace was left alone, standing uncertainly in the hall. 'Sit in that chair,' Jagan said, unable to find anything else to say. He added, 'Tell me what you want. I will get it. I do not know exactly what you will like to have.'

'Oh, how kind you are!' she said genuinely pleased with his attention. She drew a chair for him and said, 'Please be seated yourself, you must be tired.'

'Oh, no,' Jagan said. 'I am a very active man. The whole secret of human energy. . . ' he began and cut short his sentence when he noticed the bewilderment in the girl's face. 'I must really be off, you know, must go back to my shop, otherwise. . . . '

'Oh, please do go and attend to your work.'

'Make yourself comfortable,' he cried and hurried out while Mali was still in the bathroom.

THE PAINTER OF SIGNS

Editor's note: In this novel, Narayan takes a further and giant step in the direction of the contemporary world when he has a birth-control propagandist named Daisy arriving in Malgudi. Even outside her profession she is a splendid example of the liberated woman. Raman, a young sign-painter, who comes across her professionally, falls violently in love with her. She is tough with him, makes it clear that she has no time for such nonsense as love, but obviously she reciprocates his affection to an extent. Raman accompanies her on a business trip and. . . .

They realized that the village walls were unsuitable for inscribing on, and decided to leave it over for the present, confining themselves to other forms of propaganda. Daisy wanted to know if any of the rockfaces would be suitable, but Raman became evasive and suggested that they could consider any fresh investigation only after the monsoon. 'And let us hope that at least from next year they will take care of their birth-rates.'

Daisy shot a look at him as if to gauge how serious he was. Raman set his face into a grim seriousness. They were all sitting on the teacher's *pyol* ready for departure. They had spent three days in this camp and were partially satisfied with the work done. The hermit's attack still rankled in her mind. 'I fear we have to contend against that man's propaganda.'

'Let's not talk about him. He understands what goes on everywhere.'

'Why should one be afraid?' Daisy asked. 'We are all working for a cause that's of national importance. I wish I could talk to him. I am sure he would be convinced.'

'I'm telling you that he knows all that is said and done anywhere. Not necessary to go and speak to him again.'

'Oh, master you must rise above all such superstitious fears.'

'Let us talk of something else,' said the teacher, and rose to leave. They had to walk back the three or four miles to the highway and hope for a bus or a lorry to pick them up. The teacher was to escort them up to a point. His wife had packed rice, curds, vegetables, and other eatables for their lunch and dinner. She had grown attached to Daisy, and became sentimental at her departure. There were tears in her eyes, and her children stood around rather overawed by the scene of parting.

Daisy looked at them critically. 'Don't suck your thumb, take it out, otherwise you will stammer,' she said to one. To another one she said, 'Stand erect, don't slouch.' She turned to their mother and added, 'Correct posture is important. Children must be taught all this early in life.' She was a born mentor, could not leave others alone, children had better not be born, but if born, must take their thumbs out of their mouths and avoid slouching. She somehow did not have any advice to offer the elders. She just looked at them as if to say, Behave yourselves, and bade the family good-bye. Raman never took his eyes off her even for a moment, fascinated by her positive manner and talk. He smiled and muttered his thanks in the midst of this babble, addressing himself to no one in particular, and stepped out. The teacher led the way mutely. A few villagers stood aside to watch them go and murmured among themselves, 'The doctor is leaving,' almost with relief. They would not have to feel apologetic any more for being fathers and mothers.

She had many words of advice, caution, and precautions for the teacher when they reached the main road on the hill. The teacher looked intimidated by Daisy's manner. She spoke as if he'd be held responsible for any birth occurring in the village. 'We will be delayed by the onset of the monsoon, but we will definitely be here as soon as possible after that,' she said half-menacingly. Raman looked at the teacher as if wondering how this frail man was going to prevent the seven-hundred-odd men and women from ever coming together. What a task she was levying on this poor man!

They waited in the shade of a tree at the cross-roads. The teacher said, 'The bus should be here any minute.' He repeated this message every few minutes in order to keep up the morale. Daisy sat on a boulder as if it were a throne. Her imperious manner both charmed and frightened Raman. In her previous incarnation, she must have been Queen Victoria, or in a still earlier incarnation Rani Jhansi, the warrior queen of Indian history. The air throbbed with the sound of a distant bus. A family of monkeys on a fig tree a few feet away chattered, the youngest one performing trapeze acts holding on to his mother's dangling tail, while she combed the male monkey's back for lice with her finger-nails. The family looked down on the human beings assembled below. The teacher hung about uncertainly. He was showing slight signs of restlessness. Perhaps he wanted to get back home, and not wait indefinitely for refreshed, and he also noticed that Daisy looked better now.

Eventually, around four o'clock, the bullock-cart rumbled in from somewhere and the teacher jumped out of it. 'Teacher, you must be starving, we've had our lunch,' said Daisy.

'I have eaten at the village.'

It was a mat-covered wagon, drawn by a white bull with small bells around its neck which jingled when it moved. A little time was spent in arguing about the fare. The teacher said, 'I have fixed him for four rupees, and he will take you to Koppal, where you can take the bus for Malgudi town.'

The cart-driver, an old man who continuously swore at the animal, stared at his passengers while they climbed into the cart, and said, 'I always like to take in newly-weds. If it had been someone else, I'd not have accepted this trip for less than six rupees, not a paisa less. The price of hay is going up. I am not the sort of person who'll let his animals feed on roadside trees. That way you can shorten the beast's life— "beast" did I say "beast"? I don't like the word, it's a cruel and insulting word for a living creature. I smashed the eyes and nose of a fellow who called me "beast" once. Today I'm like this, but when I was young, oh, God, it looks like another *janma,* and yet it's so clear before my mind like a picture, my son was so little that he sat on my lap and held the reins and drove the bullocks himself; what a noise he'd make with his tongue, that'd make the animals gallop, I tell you. So small, just the size of the whip-handle but he could drive the bulls mad. But I didn't want him to be a driver of bulls. I wanted him to study, the teacher in our village said that he would be the most intelligent boy in the country. . . . ' The old man went on talking all through the journey, to the tune of the jingling bells.

Raman occasionally interrupted whenever he felt that the old man should give rest to his vocal cords. 'Where is that son now?'

'I don't know,' the old man said. 'He went away to the town and worked in a factory, and won't remember us any more.' Raman wanted to enquire if he was married and how many children and so forth, but he avoided the topic as he did not like to stir up Daisy. The old man, just as an encouragement to the young couple, expatiated on the virtues of married life. He said, 'I lost four wives, but never remained without one at any time. I tell you, there is no greater joy than a wife for a man. My fifth wife—'

'How many children?' Raman asked, rather involuntarily.

'Nct more than four from each—God gives us children, and who

the bus, but was afraid to say so. The company was becomin
and strained. Raman moved about aimlessly. He was getting
of watching the shimmering horizon; his aesthetic sensibi
were deadened so that he was not particularly thrilled by the
and the mountain and the valleys and gorges or the ravines—
sighed for the bustle and noise of the Ellaman Street corner, arou
the Chettiar shop. He strolled up to the fig tree to watch t
monkeys. He went back to Daisy as she sat on her throne with h
thoughts, while the teacher stood a little apart, respectfully, like
courtier. Raman watched the teacher's face; it was evident that h
had been talked to on a variety of subjects, and now a phase of
silence seemed to prevail. Raman breezily declared, 'Did you see
the monkeys on the tree?' She looked up without much interest in
the direction and looked down again, saying nothing. Raman felt
an impulse to make a humorous comment about the family matters
of monkeys, but could not pluck up enough courage to do so. He
noted that she looked rather dry and her lips looked powdery,
ashen, and as if they would crack like the ground in a sun-baked
desert. He suggested solicitously, 'A drink of water?'

'Not yet,' she said. 'We have to use it sparingly.'

'Might we not finish our lunch?'

'I'm more keen on a bus,' she said with a condescending humour,
feeling perhaps it was time to relax. Somehow today she seemed to
have decided to conduct herself in a queenly manner in the presence
of the teacher, who looked crushed and submissive; although on the
pyol of his house he had ventured to be so argumentative. Raman
thought, every person is so much a part of his background—take him
away from it and he becomes limp and featureless.

'Where is the bus we heard?'

'Must have been a lorry going down somewhere else,' replied
the teacher.

'You have no idea of the bus timings?'

'Some days they are irregular and don't come at all.'

'And so?'

He blinked as if caught in a trap. 'If the bus is delayed today—it
should have arrived by this time. A bullock-cart may be found. I'll go
down the lower road and get one from the village. They generally
avoid this road because of its gradient.' At a nod from Daisy, he slipped
down the slope, and soon disappeared around a bend. Raman again
suggested lunch. They opened one packet and ate in silence. The
second packet was for the night. A drink of water after it, and he felt

are we to say no to Him?' Luckily, Daisy was in a drowse leaning back on the mat-covered side, and Raman managed to change the topic.

At some point Daisy woke up to enquire, 'We are still on the road? What time is it?'

'Six.'

'Let us get into a bus, if one comes up.'

'No bus here,' the cart-man added. 'What's wrong with this carriage? Are you unhappy in it?' They were not. There was a layer of straw and a carpet over it—very cosy—and it had an agreeably musty smell about it. They went down the mountain road and finally reached the highway from the Mempi Hills leading to the towns in the plains, passing through a fine avenue lined with palmyra and coconut trees. The ride in the cart seemed to create an intimacy; with so little space between them, the barriers between them seemed to be falling. Daisy became more communicative. Raman realized that her communicative phase was reviving now and made the best of it. She presented a stiff, frozen personality when performing a public duty or talking to people like the teacher; once that was over, her normal charm returned, the kind of face she had presented when she opened the door for him at Number Seven, Third Cross. He loved her now unreservedly. When he stole a glance at her, his heart beat fast. He did a little introspection and said to himself, It's the same person I saw in the village, and have been seeing here and there, the tight-lipped monomaniac, but now what is it in her that is sending my heart racing? Silly. . . . But he could not help it. He wanted to go on talking to her, go on hearing her voice; but the only topics she could appreciate were birth-control, population, and allied subjects! There was no use talking to her about weather, political crises, or economic theories. She just turned a deaf ear to all other themes! No use involving her in a conversation even about music, or culture, or philosophy. She either did not care for such things, or deliberately hardened herself against them, in order, probably, not to lose her concentration. She was like a yogi with his eyes fixed on the centre of his nose, seeing nothing else in life. Didn't matter. Nothing mattered as long as she was there, and remained herself, with that aroma of some strange herb, perhaps some little hair oil—but he had never seen her grooming herself, never seen her spending any time before a mirror. But then, he reflected, how could he know what she did when she shut the door of whatever room she might happen to be in at the moment? His imagination wallowed in speculation of all that she might do in the privacy of a room, dressing or washing.

At some point, the cart-man was good enough to ask him to move back a little, to the centre of the carriage, in order to keep the balance on the axle; otherwise the cart tilted forward. It was a welcome suggestion, as it placed him nearer to her fragrant presence. He desperately wanted to establish union with her, at least verbally. He realized that the best policy would be to adopt the look of a simple-minded enquirer seeking illumination. She would definitely love to behave like a guru for such a disciple. As a first step this would be excellent. Once it was established, he could go on to the next stage. It'd not be necessary to stay on birth-control forever. He could gradually touch upon other matters, he could reveal himself in all his nakedness. Nakedness? Why did this word creep in now, he wondered. It was inevitable under the present circumstances. No one could prohibit him the use of that expression. Presently, assuming a most innocent look, he remarked, 'There are some questions about the use of certain types of contraceptives which I have never understood.'

She sat up, coming out of a torpor induced by the movement of the carriage, and asked over the din of the wheels, 'What in particular is it that you want to know about?' He didn't expect to be cross-examined thus. He mumbled, 'I always wanted to know whenever you talked about it, but I didn't wish to interrupt you.'

'That's all right. What is it you want to know?' He had now to come out with it, and mentioned some vague point, which sounded so naïve that she began to laugh. First time in many days. She laughed so loudly that the cart-man turned round, nodded his head knowingly, and turned away to face the road once again.

She said, 'I hope you know enough physiology to follow any explanation?'

Raman felt caught, he did not know whether to say yes or no. If he said yes she might begin to think ill of him, or if he said no she might take him to be a simpleton without any knowledge about the world. This was the lesser of the two evils.

'Well, how could I be expected to know so much of this subject? Of course, some amount of physiology learnt in the classroom long ago and also some general knowledge picked up here and there. But it's somewhat limited, naturally.'

'Are you so innocent?' she asked.

He wondered if he should begin a confession! How that tall college girl of his class once enticed him, when they had gone on a holiday camp, to sneak behind an abandoned shed, while others were busy. And then. . . only two other instances, mere calf-love and infructuous attempts at love-making, nothing of consequence or importance. Best not to speak of it now. She might lose trust in him. He pretended total ignorance of the entire subject; giving himself a saintly aura on the whole.

She began a preamble: 'That's the reason I feel strongly that sex-education must be given from the kindergarten stage. Otherwise so much ignorance and taboo—it's led to the present state of affairs. I hope you at least know that it's the easiest thing to produce a baby—'

'Yes, of course, but not always practical,' he said, while she went on—'The more difficult thing is to stop one from coming. This is the point which I wish to emphasize everywhere, in every nook and corner of the country, dinning it into every citizen, old and young.' She seemed all of a sudden to be getting into the spirit of public speaking, forgetting that she was cooped up in a bullock-cart with an audience of one or perhaps two, if the cart- driver was to be included. She went into great detail, without the slightest inhibition, about the course a recalcitrant sperm took and the strategy to halt its journey. She touched upon various aspects of contraception, spoke with such a zeal that Raman began to wonder what freakish experience or trauma might be responsible for this sort of unmitigated antagonism to conception. He had heard all this before, over and over again, when she addressed village audiences; but now this was a sort of command performance in this narrow closed space, all alone on the highway. It thrilled him and gave him vicarious satisfaction.

It was seven o'clock. They were planning to catch the town bus leaving Koppal at eight for Malgudi. They had been journeying for over three hours now. The cart-man suddenly pulled up crying,'Damned, accursed thing.' The bullock had stumbled and hurt its leg. The cart-man got off his seat and went up to examine the injury. The passengers also got down. The old man looked both forlorn and angry. He hit the animal on its haunches with the handle of the whip, and said,'I knew it'd do this sort of thing.'

'What has happened?'they asked anxiously.

'He has hurt himself—the fool didn't use his eyes, and has injured his leg. Should not a sensible animal use his eyes and see what's ahead, if a pit or furrow is there? The son-of- a. . . .' He made allusions to the mixed-up, ill-begotten progenitors of this creature.

He quickly unyoked the animal, took its foreleg in his hand, and examined it with tender care—for all the foul references in his speech. He was almost in tears as he said,'He can't pull any more.' He stood brooding for a moment as to what he should do.

Daisy and Raman looked rather worried. 'So what do we do?' they asked in unison.

'I'll take him to the village over there, where he will have an application of medicinal leaves. . . .'

To Raman the cart-man seemed more preoccupied with the animal's leg than with their fate. He went on elaborating about the medicament for the animal until Raman was forced to enquire,'What are we to do?'

'Stay here or come with me. I'll get another bull to go forward. I promised to take you to Koppal—I'll keep the promise, don't worry.'

'How far away is the village?'

'My nephew lives there and he will help me.'

'Good. How far away is it, I asked.'

'How do I know? I don't carry a measuring rod. I can go there, and I promise that I'll be back and take you onward. I have promised you that I'll take you to Koppal. I'll take you there. Don't worry. This place is safe, no robbers or evil spirits, and I'll be back. The place is safe. You have there a nice bed of straw with a carpet. Eat your food and sleep peacefully. I'll be back. I have travelled down this road hundreds of times in my life. . . . This place is as safe as your bedroom. Eat and sleep peacefully. I'll come back with a good yoke.' He dragged the cart under a tree and, with many suggestive hints to the newly-wed couple, was gone with his animal. The jingling of its bell came from a distance. A half moon appeared in the sky.

They became self-conscious at being left alone and looked at each other in embarrassment. This sudden isolation seemed to place a moral burden on them both. For a moment Raman welcomed the opportunity, but actually felt nervous. He had had no notion how important the old cart-driver's presence had been. They stood about rather uncertainly. A fear came over him that any move on his part was likely to be misunderstood. He said, 'A nice breeze blowing.'

'Yes,'Daisy said, without any special spirit.

He looked up heavenward and declared, 'A half moon, rather pretty isn't it?'

'Yes, it is.'

'A full moon would have been glorious, don't you think?'

'Yes,' she said, still looking in the direction in which the old man had departed—he had suddenly plunged into a bush and gone off cross-country. 'What a fellow to leave us stranded like this!'she said in a tone of slight horror.

'Oh, he will come back, can't have gone very far. Are you afraid?'

She shook her head rather contemptuously. 'It is not that. I am used to worse situations in life, but he should have told us where he was going.'

'Perhaps we could abandon this cart and walk to the nearest village. It would serve him right.' She remained silent over this solution. He said, 'Would you say that you are tired or can you walk?. . . . Let us pick up our things and leave this place.' He looked at his watch rather purposelessly, and muttered, 'Half past something or other.' She ignored his suggestion, and looked about for her usual throne in such places, could find none, flashed her torch on the ground, and, finding it clear, sat down. 'The important thing is to see that there are no reptiles around,' he commented, and followed suit, sitting a little away from her. It was hard for him to decide what distance he should keep from her; with a third person in the company he could nestle close to her as in the wagon, but now he wanted to avoid the slightest trace of a suspicious movement. He shifted and moved away and sat where it would not be too near to create a bad impression or too far if she preferred his company. After an approximate calculation, he got up again and took another seat, as if it were a game of human chess—the sort of game that the Mughal emperors played with human chessmen on marble squares in medieval times. He decided that if she moved even a hair's breadth closer to where he sat, he would take it as a signal for him to make a move, and ultimately there should be no space between them whatever. He noticed that she had now got into her non-speaking phase and he would have to respect her silence.

They sat thus for a while, and then he said abruptly,'Past eight. Let me serve your dinner.' She acquiesced. He rose and went back to the cart and took out their little hamper of food. He gave it over to her, placed before her the water bottle too, and waited for her to begin. She opened the food container, tore a banana leaf in two, heaped on one a portion of rice, and held it to him. He said, 'It is kind of you,' and ate in silence. Vague sounds of night between an awkward couple. Perhaps so in his imagination. After the food she held out to him a cup of water. We are a well-matched couple—how well she looks after me! he reflected. What would I not give to know what is passing in her mind? The crux of the problem is not now, it is what comes after the dinner.

After the rice and a drink of water, her mood seemed to improve and she became communicative. 'Quite a volume of correspondence must have piled up on my desk, and it is tackling the letters that really worries me. I don't mind any amount of field-work.'

'Don't hesitate if I can be of any help,' he said.

'Well, well, I can manage it; I have always managed these things myself. I am not cut out for desk work, I think.'

'Oh, no, I would not agree with you. Well, you are so effective when you are dealing officially—as I found out when I brought the first sign-board for your office the other day. It seems so long ago,' he said wistfully.

'Actully twelve weeks ago, not longer. . . . ' she said with precision.

He smiled uncomfortably. 'I feel as if we had known each other several *janmas,*' he said rather plaintively.

'It is imagination really,'she said. 'Do you believe in reincarnation?'

He wanted to make sure that he should have the right answer for her and asked,'Do you?'

'No,'she said bluntly.

He replied,'There are some people who believe in it, and some others who don't. Opinion is divided—'

'I am asking what you think.'

'Oh I am so busy all the time, no time to brood over such questions. Well, perhaps when I sit calmly in retirement, I shall be able to sort out these questions.' Now he said rather gallantly, 'You have been walking and straining yourself since the morning. Please climb into that carriage and sleep if you like. I will remain outside and keep a watch. The cart-man has lowered the front of the cart to that culvert so that it doesn't slope down, but keeps level.'

'You have also been quite active the whole day—must be as tired. Why don't you get in and sleep first? I will stay out and watch.'

'Oh, no,' he said, 'it is a man's duty. I will stay out, you get in.'

She said after considering the question, 'Let us see. . . . ' Briskly she went up to the cart, brought out a roll of carpet and a pillow. 'You will have to sleep under the carriage, it will be cosy, only remember not to knock your head when you rise,' and they both laughed. She added, 'Some people cannot sleep with the sky open above them. . . .'

'I am one such, how did you guess. . . ?'

She knelt down, spread the carpet for him with a sprinkling of straw under it, placed the pillow, and made his bed. Raman felt tender and grateful. He put his head into the carriage to arrange her bed reciprocally, flashed his torch in, and smoothed out the straw and the little carpet the cart-man had placed there. They washed the vessels with a little water and packed them away. 'We may at least rest until the cart-driver returns. I hope it won't be difficult to wake you up.' Raman helped her to climb into her bed, hung about a little, and crept under the carriage.

The moonlight, stars, the cool breeze—everything seemed to affect his equanimity. He lay tossing on his bed of straw, looking up longingly at the bottom of the cart. He debated within himself whether to dash up, seize her, and behave like Rudolph Valentino in *The Sheik*, which he had seen as a student. Women liked an aggressive lover—so said the novelists. He recollected piecemeal all her words of the last three weeks—those three weeks had brought them closer than anyone could hope for in three years. A secret life seemed to have developed between them. When they had travelled jogging in the bullock-cart, in the narrow space, they often rubbed shoulders and their knees touched. Once when the cart bumped rather roughly over a track, they were flung against each other. Once or twice, he thrust his arm forward and tried to touch her; she fended him off unobtrusively. His whole being was convulsed with waves of desire now. He said to himself, I adore her, but this silly tension that's rising within me must be quelled. I should, perhaps, meditate on the Third Eye of Shiva, by opening which he reduced the God of Love to ashes, and, perhaps, achieved what we nowadays call sublimation. He brooded and projected himself ahead. He would just slip in and hold her down if she resisted. And then she'd become pregnant. That'd make her run to him for support. Good thing, too. Send away Aunt to her cousin's house in the village. Daisy would live in Ellaman Street with their child— nice and normal; but if she gave birth to twins—there were many cases of twins these days—they'd probably sack her for unprofessional conduct. That'd be a good thing too. She would come to depend upon him completely and he would protect her and give her a good life. Only he'd have to run around a little more and secure more orders; that would be managed. Everything seemed to be working out well, fitting into a preordained scheme; what could be more normal than, with a man and woman lying under the stars separated by an artificial man- made barrier, smashing that barrier in order to spend the night in a proper embrace? He peeped out—twinkling stars and the half moon on the horizon about to set. He felt one was wasting one's opportunities lying on hard ground. He softly crawled out, raised himself, stood at the mouth of the wagon. He hesitated for a moment whether to call her in a soft whisper and then proceed or—it seemed irrelevant to go through all such formality; this was no time for hesitation. This was a God-given moment meant for action. Man must live for the moment and extract its essence. Every minute becomes a yesterday, and is lost forever. 'Today is tomorrow's yesterday.' He heaved himself up and slid into the wagon blindly. He saw nothing, forgot his surroundings, his only aim being to seize his prey, whatever the consequences. The future was a silly, insignificant notion and meant nothing. Everything that he felt impelled to do seemed to him perfectly justifiable. He whispered: 'Don't fear, it's only me, my sweetheart. Don't torment me,' and flung his arm around where she would be.

But she was not there. The carpet was still warm. He ran his hand up and down so as to know if she had hidden herself under a layer of straw. Only his fingers felt and picked up a piece of garment of soft material, and he seized it as if it were a booty. Where is she, while her undergarment is here? The shameless creature! Where is she gone? Eloped with someone for the night, without impediments!

His tension suddenly relaxed. He felt it absurd to be holding this thing in his fist, and put it back. He called, 'Daisy! Daisy!' He got out and ran hither and thither calling her. Began to feel worried. Or could it be she was Mohini, who tempted men and fooled them? He quietly went back to his own carpet under the cart.

In the morning he crawled out from under the carriage. The cart-man had come, and cheerily explained, 'I woke up my nephew, it took me half the night to get to him , and then the rascal would not get up. I had to bang on his door till he came out and attended to me.' He asked, 'Slept well?'

'Yes, yes.'

The cart-man forbore to look into the wagon where the lady was supposed to be asleep. After waiting for a little time: 'If the lady wakes up, I can yoke the bullock and start out.' The birds were chirping and creating a din on the branches of trees. 'Where is the lady?' he asked suddenly. Raman wondered what to say. The cart-driver added, 'Must have gone to the well. There is one near by—quite shallow; but the water is very sweet. Have you washed?'

'Presently,' Raman said with casual ease. 'After she comes,' secretly wondering if he was destined to see her again but speaking in a tone as if he were waiting at the door of a bathroom. Suppose she had stumbled into that well? 'How far away is the well?' he asked.

'Just beyond that tamarind tree, that's why I unyoked here. I thought you might have noticed it.'

'Yes, of course. She mentioned the well, but I didn't look for it yet.' He sounded like a seasoned husband who left everything to a wife's management and completely depended upon her, including the directions for a morning wash.

Raman felt light in the head, the aftermath of the upsurge of love, his eventual moral collapse (as it seemed), and the frustration of it all.

'Women observe these things first,' said the cart-man. They saw Daisy approaching from beyond the tamarind tree. She had tidied herself up at the well, and looked quite bright. A few drops of water still glistened on her forehead. She had been wiping her face with the end of her sari. As she came up, he wanted to say, I know you are wearing nothing inside. We'll now leave you to put your clothes back on your good self.

The cart-man said, 'I'll give this animal a drink of water and then we may go. . . . '

Raman did not spend much time looking at her. He followed the cart-driver, saying, 'I'll have a wash at the well.'

'If you are brisk, you can catch the bus at Koppal. At the bus-stand, there is a coffee-shop. The lady must be hungry. I'll take you there as fast as possible.'

The cart-man drove his bullock towards the well. Raman followed him mutely, leaving Daisy without a word or a glance in her direction. He was aware of the flash of her grey-coloured sari from a corner of his eye. He felt that perhaps she expected him to say something, a greeting, explanation or something, and his going off must surprise her, he thought. But he did not care how she felt. He had a rage against her for deserting him. She had committed a wrong, as it seemed to him. Was it wrong? he asked, bewildered. Who was in the wrong, actually? He couldn't be sure. If he had succeeded in his desperate aim last night, he might have ended up in prison for rape. In course of time he might have had to be greeting the twins from behind the bars. Some providence had protected him in spite of himself. At this realization, he felt lighter at heart and even vaguely grateful to the girl for taking herself away in good time and thus saving him. No more reference to this; he must forget it completely and wipe it from his memory. He was appalled at the potentialities that lay buried within him. No reference, no reference, he told himself.

In spite of this resolution, when they were again sitting in the wagon on their way to the bus-stand ten miles away, he couldn't help saying the first sentence for the day. 'Thanks for saving me.'

'Yes?' she said.

'From myself,' he added. She made no response. The jingling of the bells of the bullock were the only sound for a while. He enquired gently, 'Where were you?'

'On a branch of the tamarind tree.'

'All night?' he whispered.

'Yes, until the dawn.'

'I am sorry you should have suffered there.'

'Yes, it was not comfortable but protected from the prowling tiger.' For a minute he felt a relief that it was only a tiger that had driven her out. 'You said tiger? How big was it?'

'I heard it scratching the mat under the cart, and when it appeared at the mouth of the carriage, I managed to slip out the other end to the tree. . . .'

Raman felt it would be best to observe silence. Then he asked suddenly, 'When did you learn tree climbing?'

'We used to play Gorilla when I was young; whoever becomes a Gorilla must climb a tree and stay there. We used to play this for hours day after day, and that's been helpful. I now realize the meaning of the proverb, "When you are married to the devil, you must be prepared to climb the tamarind tree"—they must have had me in mind.'

'But you are not married,' he ventured to joke.

She was grim when she said, 'They must also have meant the company one keeps.' She looked serious. Raman remained silent.

The cart-man, without turning his head, in between two swear-words aimed at his animal asked, 'Did you have a fight?'

'Yes,' Raman said.

'What about?' he asked, looking ahead at the road.

'Oh, you know, this and that. . . .'

'I used to thrash my wife when I had drinks in me,' the cart-man said. 'But you are educated persons, and you are different.'

It turned out to be a rather grim journey homeward. After her mention of the tiger and the devil, Daisy just withdrew into herself. Raman was abashed to be sitting so close to one whom he had driven up a tamarind tree. What did she mean by this proverb? He had often heard his aunt mention it. Did she think of herself as married to him already? Or did she have any clue as to the thoughts crossing his mind? For a moment he felt happy and relieved that she was perhaps beginning to take him seriously. If so, why this silence? He threw a furtive look at her, and found her gazing at him; it was ridiculous to behave like dumb animals sitting within inches of each other. She looked frozen. Still, a few droplets of water stood along her brow like the jewels in a coronet. He said to break the awkwardness, 'You remind me of Queen Victoria.'

A reckless statement, but he had decided to be reckless.

A TIGER FOR MALGUDI

Editor's note: An unusual novel not only for Narayan but for any writer. The narrator is Raja, a circus tiger, cruelly trained and treated by his owner, who escapes one day and terrorizes the people of Malgudi, and is befriended by a holy man. This episode takes place just before he meets the holy man. He takes refuge in a school and the resulting commotion gives ample scope for Narayan's very special ability to provide gentle farce.

Meanwhile I awoke after a very good stretch of sleep and heard voices outside. I looked up and saw the headmaster cowering in the attic. I stretched myself and roared, for no particular reason except that I felt alive. The poor human being in the loft must have trembled at that moment. I wished to assure him that I was not going to hurt him. If it had been the old jungle days, I'd have gone after him; already a change was coming over me, I think. My Master's presence in the vicinity, though he had not come near me yet, must have begun to affect me. I tried to assure the headmaster by raising myself and putting up my forelegs on the wall and scratching it, and growling softly, which must have shaken the poor man so much that he seemed to lose control of his bowels and bladder. Thereupon I withdrew from the wall and curled myself under the table once again in order to reassure the poor man. . . .

Meanwhile, outside, my Master noticed Alphonse taking the Chairman aside under a tree, where they spoke in whispers. When they came back, the Chairman was a changed man. He took aside, in his turn, his committee members, and spoke to them. Thereupon they took papers out of a briefcase and signed and gave them to Alphonse. All this concerned me. I was declared a man-eater and Alphonse was given written permission to shoot. 'In the normal course,' explained the Chairman, 'I should get the sanction from Delhi, but in an emergency, I am empowered to use my discretion.' My Master suspected that Alphonse had offered a substantial bribe, as he was known to be engaged in a flourishing business exporting tiger skins.

Shekar was seen coming down the ladder with a packet of food in hand. He approached Alphonse. 'Uncle, I can't see the headmaster, I held out the idli, but he didn't take it. What shall I do now?'

'You and Ramu shall share the idli,' said Alphonse.

The boy continued, 'I peeped and couldn't see him; I called and he wouldn't answer. I heard the tiger scratching something and growling. I came away. . . . ' He looked sad and anxious, moved aside and gobbled up the tiffin hurriedly.

The crowd, which watched in silence all along, let out a moan in chorus: 'Aiyo! Never thought our beloved headmaster would come to this end. . . . ' They all looked bitterly at the assistant headmaster, whom they somehow held responsible for all the delay. The assistant headmaster probably had confused feelings, happy at the thought that after all he was getting his chance to become the headmaster, but also unhappy at the same time. He wailed the loudest at the thought of the headmaster's fate.

The commotion was at its height when Alphonse, properly armed with the permit, gave a final look to his double-barrelled gun, held it this way and that and looked through the barrel, and shouted a command: 'Your attention, everybody! Everyone must retreat at least a hundred yards before the school gate which will give you an initial advantage if the tiger should decide to chase. No one can foresee how the situation will develop. The beast when shot may smash the door and rush out, and God help anyone in its way. I'll count ten and this area must be cleared; otherwise, I won't be responsible for any calamity. Now all clear out. . . . It's an emergency. The headmaster or whatever is left of him must be saved without delay. Now clear out, everyone.' He jingled the school-key bunch which he had snatched from the assistant headmaster. 'I'm risking my life. . . . I'll push the door open and shoot the same second, normally that should be enough. . . . ' After this he let out a shout like a cattle-driver and a stampede started towards the gate, as he started counting: 'One, two, three. . . .'

He turned to the Chairman and his committee and said, as a special concession, 'You may stay back in that classroom to your left and watch through the window. I've reconnoitred that area; it'll be safe for you to stay there, and you will get a good view through the window, but make sure to bolt the door.' He said to Shekar, 'Boy, show them the room and stay there yourself with your friend, until I say "all clear". He may need two shots—the interval between the first one and the second will be crucial. Anything may happen. No one can forecast with a hundred per cent certainty.'

After all these preliminaries, and before delivering the actual assault, Alphonse sat down on the veranda step and took a flask out of his hip pocket, muttering, 'This has been a big strain, must restore my nerves first. . . .' He took a long swig out of it, while several pairs of eyes were watching him, smacked his lips, shook his head with satisfaction, picked up his gun and examined it keenly, and conducted a little rehearsal by pressing the butt against his shoulder and aiming at an imaginary tiger. He withdrew the gun and placed it at his side, took out the hip flask again, and took another long swig. He was heard to mutter, 'Hands are shaky, need steadying up.' And then he stood up with gun in hand, and rehearsed again with the butt against his shoulder. 'Still shaky. . . . Bloody dilute rum, has no strength in it, I'll deal with that fellow.' He sat down again and took another drink, and another drink, till the flask was emptied.

My Master, who had stayed back unobtrusively, came forward to ask him, 'Whom were you talking to?'

'You,' said Alphonse. 'I knew you were here. I knew you'd not go. I saw you — you obstinate devil. . . . So, I thought, I thought, what did I "thought"? I don't know. I have forgotten. No, no, if the beast comes out and swallows you, it'll serve you right. . . that's what I thought. Don't look at me like that. . . I'm not drunk. . . . It's only watery rum. . .less than ten per cent proof. . . I'll deal with that cheat yet. . .that bastard. . . .'

'Are you relaxing?' my Master asked.

'Yes, sir,' he said heartily.

And then my Master asked, 'What about the tiger?'

'What about what?'

'The tiger, the tiger in there. . . .'

'Oh, yes, the tiger, he is okay, I hope?'

'Aren't you going to shoot?'

'No,' he said emphatically. 'My hands must be steadied. I must have another drink. But my flask is empty. The son-of-a-bitch didn't fill it. I'll deal with him, don't worry. This sort of a thing. . . .'

'The headmaster, what about him?'

'I don't know. Don't ask me. Am I responsible for every son-of-a-bitch?'

'Where did you learn this rare phrase?'

'In America,' he said promptly. 'I lived there for many years.'

'Would you like to rest?'

'Of course, how did you guess? I got up at four this morning and rode fifty miles. Where is my vehicle?'

My Master gave him a gentle push, and he fell flat on the ground and passed out.

My Master must have turned on him his powers of suggestion.

Taking the key bunch from Alphonse, he went up to the headmaster's room and had just inserted the key into the lock when the Chairman, watching through the window, shouted across at the top of his voice, 'What are you trying to do? Stop!'

'I'm only trying to get the tiger out, so that the headmaster may come down confidently.'

While this was going on Shekar suddenly threw back the bolt of the classroom and rushed out, followed by his friend Ramu. Both of them came and stood over Alphonse, watching him wide-eyed. 'He is still breathing,' one said to the other.

Both of them asked my Master, 'Is Uncle dying?'

My Master said to them, 'No, he will wake up — but rather late — don't worry. He will be well again. . . .'

'Why is he like this? A nice uncle. . .' the boy asked tearfully.

'Oh, he will be all right,' said my Master. 'Don't worry about him. He has drunk something that is not good and that has put him to sleep. . . .'

'Is it toddy?' asked the boy.

'Maybe,' said my Master. 'What do you know about it?'

'There is a toddy shop near our house. . .' began the boy, and my Master listened patiently, while the boy described the scenes of drunkenness that he witnessed in the evenings. Finally the boys asked, 'How will he shoot the tiger?'

'No one is going to shoot,' said my Master. 'You will see the tiger come out and walk off with me. . . .'

'He won't eat us?'

'No, he will not hurt anyone. I'm going to open the door and bring him out.'

'The headmaster?' the boy asked anxiously.

'He must have also fallen asleep. He will also come out. . .don't worry. Would you like to come in with me and see the tiger?'

The boy hesitated and, looking back for a safe spot, said, 'No, I'll stand there and watch.'

The Chairman, who had watched this dialogue, cried from behind the window, 'What are you trying to do? You are mad.'

'Come out and be with me. You will see yourself what I plan to do.'

'Explain,' the other cried. 'I do not understand you.'

My Master turned round, walked to the window, and asked, 'Are you afraid to come out of that room?'

'What a question?' exclaimed the Chairman. 'Of course, who wouldn't be! We are in a hurry. The headmaster must have help without delay. We must act before the gunman wakes up. . . .' He spoke through the window.

'Here, I have the key. I'll unlock the door and bring the tiger out of the room. One of you take a ladder in and help the headmaster come down from the attic. That's all. . . .'

'Do you mean to say that you are going in as you are, without arms or protection?'

'Yes, that's what I'm going to do. We have no time to waste.'

The Chairman said, 'By the powers vested in me in my capacity as the Second Honorary Magistrate in this town, I give you notice that you shall not open or enter that room. My committee members will bear witness to this order. It comes into immediate force, notwithstanding the fact it's not yet in written form. . . .' He looked around at his members, who crowded near the window bars and assented in a chorus.

My Master asked when it subsided, 'Why'll you prevent me from going near the tiger?'

They were at a loss to answer: 'It's unlawful to commit suicide.'

'Maybe,' said my Master, 'but which law section says that a man should not approach a tiger? Are not circus people doing it all the time?'

'Yes,' replied the Chairman weakly. 'But that's different.'

'I can tame a tiger as well as any circus ringmaster. It's after all my life that I'm risking.'

'There is no such thing as my life or your life before the eyes of the law: in the eyes of the law all lives are equal. No one can allow you to murder yourself. . . .'

'Life or death is in no one's hands: you can't die by willing or escape death by determination. A great power has determined the number of breaths for each individual, who can neither stop them nor prolong. . . . That's why God says in the Gita, "I'm life and death, I'm the killer and the killed. . . Those enemies you see before you, O Arjuna, are already dead, whether you aim your arrows at them or not!"'

The Chairman was visibly confused and bewildered. 'In that case you will have to sign an affidavit absolving us from all responsibilities for your life or death. . . .'

'You ignoramus of an Honorary Magistrate! After all that I have said, in spite of all that urgency. . . . All right, give me a paper and tell me what to write.'

The Magistrate took out a sheet of paper from his briefcase and pushed it through the window bar. My Master sat down and wrote to the Chairman's dictation through the window, absolving anyone from any responsibility. He signed the document and returned it with the comment, 'Just to respect your magistracy, although I am convinced it's uncalled for and irrelevant, and you are exercising unnecessary authority. The more important thing for you now would be to take in your custody that gun beside Alphonse. When he wakes up, no one can guess his mood, and it's not safe to leave the gun within his reach.'

The Chairman looked at the document and said. 'Stop, wait. Tell me what is it that you have written here?'

'Only what you have dictated.'

'In a language we don't know, can't accept it. . . .'

'It's in Sanskrit, in which our scriptures are written, language of the gods. I wrote only Sanskrit although I know ten other languages including Japanese.' Without further ado, he turned round, paused for a second to satisfy himself that Alphonse was asleep, and put the key into the lock on the headmaster's room

I had felt provoked at the sound of the key turning in the lock. No one had a right to come in and bother me. I was enjoying my freedom, and the happy feeling that the whip along with the hand that held it was banished forever. No more of it; it was pleasant to brood over this good fortune. It was foolish of me to have let the whip go on so long. Next time anyone displayed the whip. . .I would know what to do. Just a pat with my paw, I realized, was sufficient to ward off any pugnacious design. What ignorance so far! Now that I knew what men were made of, I had confidence that I could save myself from them. The chair, ah, that was different. That was more paralysing than other instruments of torture. But here where I'm lying, the headmaster's room, there are chairs, much bigger and more forbidding than what Captain used to wield, but they have done nothing, they have not moved to menace or hurt me. They have stayed put. Now I've learnt much about chairs and men and the world in general. Perhaps these men were planning to trap me, cage me and force me to continue those jumping turns with the suspended lamb, shamelessly standing on my hind legs before the crowd of film-makers. If this was going to be the case, I must show them that I could be vicious and violent too. So far I had shown great concern and self-control. Thus far and no further. The evidence of my intentions should be the headmaster, who I hoped was somewhere above me, unharmed and, as I hoped, peacefully sleeping. I can't be definite. He makes no sort of sound or movement, hence I guess he must be sound asleep. I don't want to be disturbed, nor am I going to let anyone bother the headmaster. So I have a double responsibility now. Someone at the door. I held myself ready to spring forward.

The door opened quietly and my Master entered, shutting the door behind him. I dashed forward to kill the intruder, but I only hurt myself in hurling against the door. I fell back. He was not there, though a moment ago I saw him enter. I just heard him say, 'Understand that you are not a tiger, don't hurt yourself. I am your friend. . . .' How I was beginning to understand his speech is a mystery. He was exercising some strange power over me. His presence sapped all my strength. When I made one more attempt to spring up, I could not raise myself. When he touched me, I tried to hit him, but my forepaw had no strength and collapsed like a rag. When I tried to snap my jaws, again I bit only the air. He merely said, 'Leave that style out. You won't have use for such violent gestures any more. It all goes into your past.' I had to become subdued, having no alternative, while he went on talking. 'It's a natural condition of existence. Every creature is born with a potential store of violence. A child, even before learning to walk, with a pat of its chubby hands just crushes the life out of a tiny ant crawling near it. And as he grows all through life he maintains a vast store of aggressiveness, which will be subdued if he is civilized, or expended in some manner that brings retaliation. But violence cannot be everlasting. Sooner or later it has to go, if not through wisdom, definitely through decrepitude, which comes on with years, whether one wants it or not. The demon, the tormentor, or the tyrant in history, if he ever survives to experience senility, becomes helpless and dependent, lacking the strength even to swat a fly. You are now an adult, full-grown tiger, and assuming you are fifteen years old, in human terms you would be over seventy years old, and at seventy and onwards one's temper gets toned down through normal decay, and let us be grateful for it. You cannot continue your ferocity forever. You have to change. . . .'

At this point someone from the other side of the door called, 'Sir, Swamiji, are you all right?'

'Yes, I am, don't you hear me talking?'

'Whom are you talking to, sir?'

'To a friendly soul,' he said.

'Do you mean the headmaster? Is he safe?'

'Yes, he is up there, but I've not begun to talk to him yet. . .he doesn't seem to be awake yet. I'll look to him presently. But at the moment I'm discoursing to the tiger. . . .'

'Oh, oh, does it understand?'

'Why not? If you could follow what I've been saying, the tiger should understand me even better since I'm closer to his ear. . . .' I let out a roar because I was feeling uncomfortable with some change coming inside me. I was beginning to understand. Don't ask me how. My Master never explained to me the mystery or the process of his influence on me.

'Don't let him out, sir,' said the voice. 'When you open the door, please warn us first. . . .'

'Surely, if you are afraid, but let me tell you, you need not fear; he has only the appearance of a tiger, but he is not one — inside he is no different from you and me.' I felt restless and wanted to do something or at least get away from the whole situation, back to my familiar life, back to the jungle, to the bed of long grass — I sighed for the feel of the grass on my belly — to the cool of the stream beside the cave and the shade of the cave with its rugged sandy floor. I was sick of human beings; they were everywhere, every inch of the earth seemed to be swarming with humanity; ever since the unfortunate day I stepped into that village in the forest to the present moment I was being hemmed in. How grand it'd be to be back in the world of bamboo shade and monkeys and jackals! Even the supercilious leopard and the owl I would not mind; compared to human company, they were pleasant, minding their own business, in spite of occasional moods to taunt and gossip.

I rose. Master became alert. 'What do you want to do now? You want to go away, I suppose! I understand. But there is no going back to your old life, even if I open the door and let you out. You can't go far. You will hurt others or you will surely be hurt. A change is coming, you will have to start a new life, a different one. . . . Now lie down in peace, I will take you out. Let us go out together, it'll be safe. But first I must get the headmaster down from his perch. He has been there too long. Now you lie still, move away to the corner over there while I help him.'

I understood and slowly moved off to the side he indicated. Whatever its disadvantage, circus life had accustomed me to understand commands. This room was not too spacious to talk of far side and near side, but I obeyed him. I moved to the other wall and crouched there humbly. I wanted to show that I had no aggressive intentions. Now my Master ordered, 'Turn your face to the wall and do not stir in the least. If the headmaster thinks you are lifeless, so much the better. The situation is delicate, and you must do nothing to worsen it. God knows how long he has been cooped up there. . . .'

He called him loudly but there was no answer. Then he went up to the door, opened it slightly and announced, 'I want a ladder and a person to climb to the loft, wake up the headmaster, and help him to come down. Is there anyone among you willing to fetch the ladder and go up?' A subdued discussion arose and a couple of men came forward to ask, 'What about the tiger? Where is he?'

'You have all improved to the extent of not referring to him as "brute" or "beast", but I'm sorry to note that you still have no confidence in him or me. Let me assure you that this tiger will harm no one.' This had no effect on anyone. There was no response. He said, 'All right, I'll manage. . . .' He shut the door again, pulled the table into position, and put up a chair on it, then another chair and a stool, and went up step by step and reached the loft, saying to himself, 'How the headmaster reached here will remain a mystery. . . .' He grasped the edge of the loft and heaved himself up.

Presently I heard him waking the headmaster and coaxing him to climb down. I could not see his actual coming down as I had to lie facing the wall; I could only hear movements and words. My Master exerted all his power to persuade him to step down. I sensed what was happening and though curious to watch, did not turn round, as I did not want to disobey my Master. The first thing the headmaster did on coming down was to cry, 'Oh, it's still here!' and I heard some scurrying of feet, and my Master saying, 'Don't look at him, but step down; he will not attack.' The headmaster groaned and whimpered and was possibly trying to go back to the loft, at which my Master must have toppled the pile of chairs and pulled him down. I heard a thud and guessed that the poor man had landed on firm ground. I could hear him moaning, 'It is still there, it's still there, how can I?' My Master kept advising, 'What if it is still there, don't look in its direction, turn away your head, come with me. . . .' He led the headmaster as he kept protesting, a sorry spectacle, in disarray, still in the coat and turban which he had worn in the morning. My Master propelled him to the door and pushed him out saying to those outside, 'Here he is, take care of him. Not a scratch, only shock. . .' and shut the door again as a medley of comments, questions, and exclamations poured into the room.

Now he addressed me, 'Now turn round, get up, and do

whatever you like.' I stretched myself, yawned, and rose to my feet. That was all I could do. I felt grateful, but I could not make out his form clearly. There was a haze in which he seemed to exist, a haze that persisted all through our association. At no time could I be certain of his outline or features — except what I could gather from his talk. He said, 'Let us go out now. You must realize that human beings for all their bluster are timid creatures, and are likely to get into a panic when they see you. But don't look at them. This is one of the rules of yoga to steady one's mind, to look down one's nose and at nothing beyond. That's one way not to be distracted and to maintain one's peace of mind. I would ask you to keep your head bowed and cast your eyes down and make no sort of sound, whatever may be the reaction of the people we pass. We are bound to meet crowds during our passage through the town. People are likely to get excited at the sight of us, but you must notice nothing.'

This was a necessary instruction since our emergence from the room created a sensation and a stampede, in spite of the warning cry my Master had given: 'Now I am coming out with the tiger. Those who are afraid, keep away, but I assure you again that Raja will not attack anyone. He will walk past you, and you will be quite safe as if a cat passed by. Believe me, Otherwise keep out of the way. I'll give you a little time to decide.' When he opened the door, he said, 'Keep close to me.' As he stepped out of the room, I was at his heels, saw no one, but only heard suppressed, excited comments and whispers from different corners. The veranda was empty, not a soul in sight, with the exception of Alphonse lying on the top step. Without a word my Master walked on briskly. We had to brush past Alphonse. The breeze of our movement seemed to have blown on his face, and he immediately sat up, rubbed his eyes to see clearly, blinked, shook his head and muttered, 'Crazy dream!' and laid himself down and apparently went back to sleep. But he sat up again to watch us go. We had gone past him a little way when he cried, 'Hey, you bearded one, you again! Won't leave me alone even in a dream! Ah! What is this?'

'Tiger,' answered my Master.

'Is it the same or another one?' asked Alphonse.

'Same and another,' answered my Master cryptically.

'How? Oh, yes, of course,' he muttered, puzzled.

'You may touch the tiger if you like.'

'No, no! Go away.' He waved us off angrily and resumed his sleep.

TALKATIVE MAN

Editor's note: The Talkative Man, the narrator, is a local journalist who has appeared in several of Narayan's short stories earlier. Dr Rann, a *sio disant* United Nations' researcher arrives in Malgudi, and not really quite sure of what is happening, the Talkative Man offers him the run of his house. The trouble starts soon enough. Dr Rann has a great eye for the girls and matters reach a climax when his deserted wife, a powerful lady named Commandant Sarasa, also shows up in Malgudi.

I had gone as usual to post my news at the mail van when my friend the stationmaster came to see me, all excited, saying, 'There is a large woman who came by 7 Down, staying at the waiting room and won't leave, just like the other fellow, that London man who you took away—perhaps you should take away this woman too.'

'None of my business, whoever she may be,' I said.

'Not my business either,' he said. 'The waiting room is not my ancestral property to be given to every —'

Before he could complete the sentence, the subject of his complaint was approaching — a six-foot woman (as it seemed at first sight), dark-complexioned, cropped head, and in jeans and a T-shirt with bulging breasts, the first of her kind in the Malgudi area. She strode towards us, and I knew there was no escape.

'You must be the journalist?' she asked menacingly having observed me at the mail van. She took out of her handbag a press-cutting of 'Timbuctoo Man', with the photograph of Rann I had managed to get.

She flourished the press-cutting and said, 'You wrote this?'

'Yes, madam,' I said meekly.

'No one can fool me,' she said.

The diminutive stationmaster tried to shrink out of sight, simpered and stayed in the background. I felt rather intimidated by the woman's manner, but still had the hardihood to retort, 'What do you mean by it?'

'I mean,' she said undaunted, 'if you know where this so-called doctor is, you will lead me to him.'

'Why?'

'For the good reason that I am his wife — perhaps the only one wedded to him in front of the holy fire at a temple.'

I took time to assimilate the idea.

'Of his possibly several wives I was the only one regularly married and the first. You look rather stunned, sir, why?'

'Oh no,' I said clumsily. I had no other explanation. The whole picture of Rann was now assuming a different quality if this lady was to be believed. The stationmaster looked embarrassed but, held by curiosity, hovered about with the rolled flags under his arm, and behind him stood the porter. We were the only ones on the railway platform. She eyed them for some time without a word and then asked,'Stationmaster, is your work for the day over?'

'Practically — 9 Up is not due until 20 hours.'

'What's 20 hours? Now the bother of addition and subtraction,' she muttered. 'Why don't you railway people use a.m.-p.m. as normal civilized beings do?'

'Yes, madam,' he said sheepishly.

'Is that your only porter?' The porter, on being noticed by the queen, came a few paces forward.

'I've served here for thirty years, madam,' he said. The queen accepted his statement without displaying any special interest, whereupon he withdrew a few paces back, but within hearing distance. She swept her arms about and said, 'Normally, they'd have a couple of cement benches on any railway platform, but here nothing. Come on, let us go into the waiting room — anyway, there at least are a couple of chairs. Come! Come! she said beckoning me authoritatively. Sheepishly I followed her. She had a commanding manner.

The stationmaster followed discreetly at a distance. She carried two chairs out of the waiting room. 'No, no,' I persisted, 'let me —'

But she would not pay any attention to my gallant offer and said, 'You have seen him, tell me all about him.'

'I cannot say much. . . . Ours was a brief meeting. I was interested because —' she did not let me complete the sentence:

'It is more important for me to know where he is rather than anything else.'

She looked so fixedly at me that I said, 'Not in my pocket,' and tried to laugh it off. 'We met for less than fifteen minutes at our Town Hall library where he had come for a reference work and did not like to be interrupted.'

'So studious indeed! How marvellous! Good to know that he is still bookish.' And she laughed somewhat cynically. Then she became serious and said, 'All that I want to know is where is he at the moment. If you will give me a hint I'll give you any reward.'

I felt slightly upset and said righteously, 'I'm in no need of a reward. I can survive without it.' The stationmaster, who was following our dialogue from a respectable distance, added, 'He is rich, madam, come from a big Kabir Street family really.'

She said, 'Stationmaster, perhaps you would like to attend to other things?'

The stationmaster shrank out of sight, and the porter too melted away. I got up saying, 'I must go now, you must excuse me. The only novelty about him was his mentioning Timbuctoo, and as a journalist I thought it had news value. After that I lost sight of him, never asked him where he was going — that's all. He was enquiring about some long distance buses. . . .That's all madam, all that I can say is that if he is staying in this place, he cannot remain unnoticed.' I had given full rein to my imagination. 'I'd suggest you look for him at Madras or a place like that instead of wasting your time here.' And I rose, carried my chair in and said, 'Goodnight.' I felt uncomfortable in her presence with a constant dread lest I should betray myself. And so I hurried away, glancing back over my shoulder to make sure she was not following me. She stuck to her chair without a word and watched me go.

Rann was in his kimono when he opened the door, on my knocking repeatedly, with a scowl on his face. I resented his attitude: in my own house he was a visitor to whom I'd offered asylum for no clear reason. It had just been an impulse to help him, nothing more, and to rescue him from bed-bugs flourishing in the railway station waiting room. Yet he behaved as if I were a hotel steward violating the privacy of a guest.

'Why don't you hang a "Don't disturb" board on your door? I thought you might have brought a souvenir from one or the other of the hotels in your travels —'

He was taken aback. 'Why do you say that?'

'I see that you are busy—' I said cynically. He wasn't. I could see that he had been lounging on the canvas easy chair (my heirloom) which I had let him have out of idiotic kindness. Yet this man dared to shut the door and look too busy to open it. There were no papers on his table, nor a book at his side in the canvas chair or anywhere. He must have been lounging and staring at the ceiling and wool-gathering, and he chose to scowl at me—me, his saviour from bed-bugs. Soon my anger was mitigated as I anticipated the pleasure of shocking him with news I knew would puncture his flamboyance and foreign style. I simply announced, from the door, like the opening lines of a play, 'A lady to see you,' and turned round, shutting the door behind me (a piece of deliberate good manners). I went down to the backyard and shut myself in the bathroom and stayed there, although I had heard him open his door and follow me. I took my own time.

When I opened the bathroom door, he stood there, his face full of questions, and he seemed to have become a little paler and shrunk a few inches into his Japanese kimono. I had not needed a wash, but I had splashed water over my head for no better reason than to taunt him. 'Oh!' I cried with feigned surprise. Then I raced along the back courtyard to my room, while he followed me. My clothes and things were widely scattered in various rooms in different blocks of that house, and I never found at any time what I wanted, towel in one room, kerchief in another, trousers at another corner, and so forth. Now I was dripping, water running over my eyes, and wet all over — very annoying. I cried, 'Where is the damned towel?' At which Rann vanished for a minute and fetched a fresh towel from his room. I felt pleased with my show of authority, murmured a thanks indistinctly, and wiped my face and head. We were standing in the passage.

'I'll return it washed tomorrow —' I said.

'Oh, that's all right,' he said. 'No hurry.'

'So soft and strong,' I said admiringly and stretched it and held it to the light from the courtyard. I noticed an embroidered corner and spelt out 'Neville'.

'What's that?' I asked.

'Hotel in Rhodesia —it's a souvenir.' Perhaps he had stolen it.

'How long were you there?'

'Oh, quite a few times in connection with the project —'

'But they say, it's difficult for coloured people —'

'Oh, it's all exaggerated. Don't you believe it. For me, no problem, the UN passport can't stop you anywhere.'

I felt inclined to provoke further elaborations on the subject, while I knew he was dying to ask questions about the lady but feeling rather awkward about reviving the subject. I felt a sudden compassion for him — his bewilderment and awkwardness as he shrank into his fancy kimono. I asked suddenly, 'You want to ask about that lady?'

'Yes, yes,' he said meekly with a sigh, 'I don't understand it at all. Who is she?'

'The stationmaster says that he saw a photograph in her hand, looking like your good self.'

'Ah!' he cried involuntarily.

'It matches the picture in the *Telegraph*.'

'How did my photo get in anyway?'

'Newspapers have their sources, you know.'

He asked, 'What sort of a person is she?'

'Well, a long time ago I gave up staring at women and studying their worth, so I'm not able to provide a good description. Anyway, I'll dress and come to your room, please wait there.'

He was waiting impatiently in his room. I had taken my own time to look for my clothes, to groom myself before my mirror, the ornate oval in a gilded frame with a vine pattern carved on it, perhaps a wedding present for my grandmother: it was full of spots and blank areas. Now fresh from an unnecessary bath and dressed in my kurta and a laced dhoti and a neatly folded upper cloth over my shoulder, I felt ready to face the emperors of the earth. I strode into his room, where he had had the good sense to leave the door open. I had a glimpse of him fidgeting impatiently in his chair. The moment he saw me he rose and offered me the seat, and lowered himself into it only after I had sat elsewhere. Now I looked as if ready to go on with our conversation and give him a hearing.

'I told you about a lady at the railway station where I had gone to post my evening dispatch.'

I knew that Rann was dying to have a description of the lady as he sat squirming and fidgeting.

'Was she tall?' he asked, trying to draw me out.

'Could be,' I replied.

'Medium height?'

'She did not seem short,' I said, 'I could see her only from a distance.'

'How far away were you?' he asked stupidly.

I felt irritated. 'I forgot to take a measuring tape with me,' I said, and tried to laugh it off. He looked miserable and I had to ask, 'Why are you bothered?'

He said, 'Because — I don't know. You are right. Dozens come and go at the railway station, do I care?'

'Bravely said,' I remarked. 'Let us go to The Boardless. You will feel better.'

He shrank from the idea. He had, apparently, a fear of being waylaid by the woman. I persuaded him, but before coming out, he spent much time to decide how to dress for the visit. I advised, 'The Boardless is a special place, where you could go in your underwear or in royal robes, it's all the same to the crowd there. No one will question or notice.' Still, he took his time to decide and came out in a pink slack shirt and grey flannel trousers.

We walked up. I took him to my usual corner, facing the Mahishasura calendar, had another chair put up. The habitués turned round to study him for a moment and then resumed their coffee and talk. I ordered dosai and coffee, but he couldn't enjoy it; he seemed overwhelmed and self-conscious. Varma, the proprietor, said 'Hello' to him formally and looked gratified that The Boardless should be attaining an international touch with this man's visit. I briefly explained, 'He is a scholar, come on business,' avoiding Timbuctoo because of its phoney sound. I thought I should do something to integrate this stranger in our society and cure him of his kimono and carpet-slipper style and alienation, and so had persuaded him to walk along. Of course, it had not been an easy passage , people stared at us — it was inevitable.

The lady's haunting presence at the railway station somehow drove Rann closer to me. He seemed to depend on me in some obscure manner for any information I might spring on him. He looked on me, I suppose, as a possible harbinger of some good news such as that the lady had left suddenly by some train or that she had thrown herself under the midnight goods train. So he watched my movements eagerly with almost a questioning look as to if say, 'Any good news? How good is the goods train? Anything under it?' Formerly, he had always shut himself in his room and bolted the door. These days he kept a door open so that he might not lose glimpse of me; while I moved about he watched me surreptitiously from his chair, which was an excellent position for spying. My forefathers must have used that same strategic postion to keep an eye on the household, particularly the army of servants, so that no one could slip out unnoticed. Rann found this advantageous. As I passed in and out he greeted me with casual ease. 'Good day to you, T.M. Starting on your interesting rounds for the day?' Sometimes he just smiled and nodded, without obviously questioning, feeling perhaps: 'If he has anything — he is bound to tell me — not the sort to keep mum—'

On the whole, he seemed to have limbered up, and was slightly more relaxed. It suited me, too. I took advantage of his leniency and the half-open door policy to step into his room informally for a chit-chat now and then. I'd walk in and make straight for the easy chair without any preamble.

I lounged in his canvas chair comfortably. He sat in his hired chair uneasily, pretended to be looking through some papers on his desk, put them away, and got up and paced the narrow room up and down like a bear in a cage. After a pause and silence for fifteen minutes I just pronounced, 'You seem very agitated, why?'

'Oh, no. I am sorting out some problems in the paper I'm writing.'

'Very well then, let me leave you in peace. . . .'

'No, no, stay,' he said. It seemed to me that he wanted to say something but was reluctant to begin or rather unable to find an opening line.

'I do not mind relaxing and lounging here all day, but you will have to do something about it — about the lady in question,' I said.

'What do I care? Hundreds of persons come and go at a railway station.'

'Not everyone carried your photo asking questions—'

'What the hell!' he cried red in the face. I enjoyed the annoyance he displayed and added, 'Also calls herself your wife.'

'Nonsense!' he cried, and paced up and down. I had never found him in such a mood or using intemperate language. The thought of this woman seemed to unloose the bolts of his mental framework.

'What's he to Hecuba or Hecuba to him?' I asked light-mindedly.

'Does she call herself Hecuba? I know no one of that name.'

I had to explain to him that I was quoting Shakespeare.

'Ah, Shakespeare. I had almost forgotten. Long time ago, of course. Would you believe it? Once I sat down and read the Oxford edition from the title page to the last.'

'Yet, thou varlet weakenth at the mention of a perfidious female!'

'I say, this is maddening! Please do something and send her away.'

'Why? This is a free town for anyone to come and go or stay. How can I arrogate to myself any right to expel anyone! I don't think I'll see her again. . . .'

'What's she like? he enquired suddenly. I couldn't continue in a mood of levity — if she was really his wife. So I just said,'Well, an impressive personality — slightly dark, but a commanding personality, rather large build, I should say. Perhaps exaggerated by the blue jeans and T-shirt and bobbed hair. The stationmaster was quite cowed by her manner and opened the waiting room promptly when asked. . . .'

'Though he made such a fuss when I wanted it! That funny character. Did she mention her husband to him also?'

'I don't know,' I said, 'but he was the first to be shown your photograph.'

'Outrageous!' he cried. 'You have done me a disservice!'

'On the contrary I was doing you a service without being asked. Do you know the number of men who curry my favour to get their names in print?'

'You could have at least consulted me!'

'It'd be against the journalists' code. Freedom of the Press and all that. Even the PM cannot say "Yes" or "No" to a journalist when he is out to make his copy,' I said grandly.

'Photograph! How did the photo get in?'

'I can't say — you have been in so many places, anyone might have snapped you.'

After about an hour's rambling talk he begged, 'Don't betray me. You have been hospitable right from the beginning, just help me now by leaving me alone and without mentioning me to that person whoever she may be, in jeans and T-shirt. Is she Indian? I'll explain everything when the time comes. Not now. Don't ask questions.'

'After all,' I said, pitying his plight, 'she is not going to live permanently in the waiting room. She will have to leave some time. Don't be seen too much for some time,' I said encouragingly.

'I need a lot of mental peace at least till I complete my work. That's why the shelter or asylum you have given is doubly valuable. I must have no sort of distraction till I complete the writing of my book. Anyone who helps me to work in peace will be my benefactor. To me nothing is more important than the book. It's going to be a sensation when it comes out. It will shake up the philosophers of today, the outlook will have to change. It's in this respect that I value your hospitality and shelter. When I publish I'll acknowledge your help surely.'

'Ah ha, my name too will be in print. Excellent! While my profession is to get a lot of people's names in print, this is the first time it will be happening to me. Great! Do you know my name?

You have never gone beyond calling me T.M. or U.C. as those people at The Boardless do — why not we adjourn to The Boardless for refreshments, after all you have visited it only once. I'm hungry.'

He resisted the suggestion.

'Are you afraid to come out?' I asked and left it at that.

'Why should I be afraid? The world is full of evil things. I have seen all sorts of things, everywhere in this world. I'm not afraid of anything. Any airline hostess or a waitress in a restaurant might turn round and backmail you if you were foolish enough to have said "How do you do?" in a friendly tone. These are situations which develop unasked. I won't be disturbed too much by these things.'

'So, a man of experience! Come out with me and if you are accosted, draw yourself up and say, "Begone phantom wretch! I know you not."'

'You are very Shakespearean today,' he commented. I was happy to see him thawing. 'I've also as I told you read Shakespeare with genuine pleasure,' he added.

I decided to protect him from wifely intrusions.

THE WORLD OF NAGARAJ

Editor's note: Nagaraj, a well-to-do middle-aged man leads a contented life with his wife in their old family house. His ambition is to write the definite work on the sage Narada, though he never gets beyond talking about it. It is all too good to last forever, and one day Tim, the rebellious son of his older brother, decides to leave his family and come to Malgudi to live with his uncle. Nagaraj finds himself in a dilemma, his respect for his older brother and his fear of antagonizing him on the one hand, and his affection and sympathy for Tim on the other, conflict with one another.

A week passed. Sita went on grumbling about the incident, and the indignity suffered by Gopu, for which she somehow held Nagaraj responsible. She kept saying, 'You should not have left him alone.' Nagaraj thought, 'This woman will not understand my position. No use my repeating that he had asked me to wait for him. Perhaps she doesn't believe my word; she doesn't want to. All the blame on me!'

Nagaraj received a postcard from Gopu, with the message:

> I have no son. I disown him. You have misappropriated and ruined him completely. You may adopt him and assign your property to him as your successor so that you may have someone who will have the right to ignite the funeral pyre when you die. . .being as you are without an issue even after so many years of married life and I know how you have steadily worked to achieve this purpose all your life, plucking him away from me and Charu when he was only two months old.

Nagaraj was agitated when he read the card; he resolved to suppress it and not let Sita see it. But she had been the one to receive it from the postman when Nagaraj was away at the Boeing Centre. She had tears when she read it, but simply dropped it on the window-sill and did not refer to it when Nagaraj came home, leaving it to him to discover it.

Nagaraj felt choked while picturing himself on the funeral pyre with Tim as his successor applying the burning faggot, according to the rules, in order to ensure a smooth passage to heaven. He suddenly felt touched by Gopu's solicitude to send him heavenward smoothly, where probably material for Narada would be more directly accessible, or even the sage himself might material-ize and guide him. Death has its good points. But a son at the firing point was essential; after all, Gopu's suggestion for adoption might be well intentioned, though crude-sounding. Nagaraj thought he should find out more about the process of adoption. Might not be a bad idea, after all. He decided to discuss it with Sita at an ap-propriate time. He must consult the old family priest first. When-ever it might happen, he was going to ask to be sent upward in his ochre robes, which had all along prepared him for his final journey in small daily doses. . . .

He thought of Sita in this connection, widowed and forlorn after being inseparable from him for thirty or forty years, and was filled with pity for her, all alone in this vast house. But she would have Tim as her adopted son, and the harmonium-playing daughter-in-law (through adoption, of course). In any case there was not likely to be any objection or trouble, and she herself loved that horrible instrument. Saroja could tote it around the whole house, sit down anywhere she liked and release the cacophony. He would not be there to hear and suffer, unless he came back as a ghost. Would he have to haunt Kabir Street? He felt somewhat lighter and pleasant while viewing himself as a ghost, but the picture of his body on the funeral pyre, with Sita bewildered and crushed, overwhelmed him with self-pity and tears streamed down his cheeks, and he was convulsed with an involuntary sob just at the moment when Sita came up to the *pyol*. She observed his state, took his hand and suggested, 'Let us go in. People are watching; I see the engineer from the last house coming. . . . Let us go in quick.' She led him to the hall bench. They sat there for a while in silence. She said, controlling the tremor in her voice, 'You must not take it to heart. Your brother has always been somewhat rough with you, but he means no harm; he must be upset with Tim. But what can anyone do with him? I think your brother must be feeling it more keenly for Charu's sake; after all, she is the mother and wants her son. What can anyone do with Tim? He cannot be influenced. Don't bother about his postcard, he has written it in a bad mood. At Kismet Tim should have come out to see him. . . .'

For a few days a terrible gloom. Nagaraj felt it acutely. 'It is better to have loved and lost than never to have loved at all,' he kept repeating irrelevantly, another quotation sticking out in some corner of his mind. 'Where is it from?' he speculated constantly. 'Shakespeare? Of course, source of ninety per cent of the world's wealth of quotations, no — ninety-nine per cent. The balance of one per cent shared by the Bible, Koran, Bhagavad Gita, and Palgrave's *Golden Treasury*.' He felt proud that he was familiar with such literary treasures. How? He was a little confounded since he had no memory of any regular studies; whatever he remembered was from cursory, casual browsing. Mostly at the Town Hall library in the early days when he regularly visited the library, actually hanging around the place from morning till evening in the days of the benign old librarian, who allowed him a lot of freedom to pull out a volume from any shelf. More than anything, he let him rummage among book dumps left there by neighbouring families who wanted to clear the space in their homes. There in the dumps were a miscellany of publications, from outdated catalogues and law reports to world classics in tatters. Nagaraj spent much time squatting beside the dump in an antechamber, browsing. Recollecting, he felt he had gathered a jumble of literary titbits, and most of them had sunk deep in his mind and floated up at unexpected, irrelevant moments. He was filled with self-admiration, but realized that he could not have continued this practice: the old librarian retired and a hot-headed youngster took his place. Nagaraj remembered with some bitterness how brusquely he had dismissed the study of Narada. 'Also, I must say in fairness to everyone, after the Boeing Sari Centre came into being, I had no time for library visits.' He chuckled within himself as he thought of his brother Gopu, who had no doubt passed B.A.—God knows by what miracle!—but an ignoramus, boor, and writer of offensive postcards and one who had made himself ridiculous at Kismet. All that he cared for was his gobar gas plant; that was his university and library combined. He had a good memory and could mug up his textbooks and pass, that was all. Did he know a single quotation from anywhere? He chuckled again. At this moment Sita came out and noticed his elation. 'Sita, don't you agree that Gopu is an ignoramus?'

'He is a B.A.,' she said.

'So am I,' said Nagaraj.

'Why think of it now?' she asked. 'It was so long ago.'

'Wonder how he passed? Must have bribed the professors,' he said mischievously.

'Why don't you think of something else? Always obsessed with your brother. . . .'

'But do you think he remembers Shakespeare?'

'Think of something else,' she said and went in.

Nagaraj reflected, 'She is a good girl, won't make things worse by agreeing with me. Good girl, Sita. So is Charu, Gopu's wife, though somewhat haughty. Am I right? No, why should I call her haughty? Unreasonable thought. My anger with Gopu is reflected on her; unfair. One may say the worst things of him and be right, still fall short of the full description. He is like one of those *asuras* in the Puranas, headstrong and haughty and vile. But in every case they had a downfall, if not destroyed totally. Evil destroys itself, say our scriptures. How will Gopu's downfall come?' He gloated over this prospect for a while. 'Maybe some catastrophe such as a thunderbolt hitting his gobar gas plant, or through an obstinate pest attacking his farm or a poisonous seed spreading amongst his grass, laying prostrate his cattle. With his hundreds of coconut, banana, mango and guava trees gone, and his farmhouse attached for unpaid taxes, he will be thrown out, and, carrying his bags, trudge all the distance from his village on foot, a bankrupt in rags with Charu hiding at his back, and knock on my door. What could be my first word of greeting? "Who are you, stranger? Your face is familiar!" Or should I say, "Begone, you hot-headed evil man. If you repent sincerely, you may step in and Sita will give you food. . . ."'

After this day-dream he felt lighter at heart. He felt he had now got something of his own. One good deed Gopu had performed was to confound the Kismet gang and puncture the strongman. 'Going off to the bus without a word to us, not even taking back his jute bag. What did it contain?' Nagaraj felt an uncontrollable curiosity. He left his seat, softly went in, hesitated for a moment to be sure that the way was clear and that Sita was in the backyard, beyond the third court. Stepped in and shut the door of the middle room where Gopu had been staying. He found Gopu's jute bag kept in a corner. It had no lock and he quickly rummaged through its contents. He found a dhoti and a shirt and towel — only one change, apparently for another day's stay; he'd wash his daily set himself and put them out to dry. Nagaraj also found a rosary of sandalwood beads, a little well-thumbed book of morning prayers to address the sun, planets and the gods presiding therein, and all the sacred rivers, and the potent Gayatri Mantra, a little brass box containing sacred ash, and a packet of incense sticks. This was a revelation. Every morning after his bath Gopu shut himself in his room and prayed. He was not the kind to talk about it, but had a secret channel of communication with God, a private arrangement with eternity. . . .

Nagaraj was overwhelmed by this idea and felt he had blasphemed a holy person by his wild, vicious thoughts. He begged pardon of the gods who, he felt, were aware of what was going on in his mind. He noticed a diary and felt tempted to open its pages and learn more of Gopu — if his prayers had any relevance to his daily life and human relationships, if he put on a porcupine exterior to cover an inner timidity. . . . But he left the diary untouched as he had a feeling of being watched from the skies. At this moment, Sita called from outside, 'What are you doing?'

Nagaraj hurriedly packed the jute bag, shoved it in a corner and opened the door. Surprised, Sita asked, 'Why have you bolted the door?'

'I thought I might look through my notes for Narada here, quietly. . . .'

'Afraid I would come and disturb?' she said rather petulantly, and added, 'I am not so foolish. . . . But your notebooks are in the other room!'

'Yes,' Nagaraj said. 'That's why I am not looking through them now.' She could not accept his explanations and stood at the doorway staring at him. He found it disturbing and said with an apologetic grin, 'I can't deceive you. Your eyes pierce through me and see my soul. If I ever wanted to deceive you I had so many occasions, but I never tried it. You are a great wife for a man.'

She was rather amused by his rambling talk but stood firm, as if she would get the truth out of him. She said, 'After all these years, you are talking as if we were newly-weds. What is it? Come out with it?'

He confessed.

She said, 'Oh, is that all? You and your brother! It's always that. You looked as if you were stealing someone's jewellery.'

'He is a careful man, won't carry valuables in his bag,' he said.

She lost interest in his enumeration of its contents and said off-tangent, 'Why don't you bring your notebooks to this room and write here, if you must, instead of in the other room?'

He resisted the idea.

She said, 'That room in the second courtyard is full of vermin and rats. Some day you will find all your notes on Narada completely eaten up and digested by the white ants which have covered the rafters, if you look up. . . .'

'You have also mentioned rats,' Nagaraj said.

'Do you think I'm being funny? What the rats leave over in

shreds will be finished off by white ants; they help each other. . . .'

It seemed to him a good idea to move into this room for writing. He got busy at once. He strode up and down, carried a bundle of Crow-brand notebooks to the middle room table, adjusted the chair and arranged his Waterman's pen to be handy when inspiration seized him. He was satisfied when he looked around and felt that life's pendulum, which had swung erratically, was coming back to normal, which meant that in the background Narada would once again appear and lend a meaning to daily existence. Anyway, he told himself, it was all for the best. The house was now normal and quiet. No speculations about Tim. No need to watch his movements. No need to glorify and find excuses for the eau-de-cologne smell. No need to hunt for earplugs. The house had become suddenly quiet; absolute calm prevailed. Sita too looked relieved and had shed her irritations and anxieties. Above all, he was free from responsibilities and custody of Tim. He could pray in peace and write in peace, sitting in a chair and at a table. He had never had the use of this table freely at any time. He threw his mind back. In their student days Gopu usurped the table and chair and drove him to a corner, where he had to crouch over a dealwood box and do his homework. When Gopu married, he shut himself in with Charu, chasing off Nagaraj to a corner in the hall. Later Tim, and still later Tim and Saroja and her harmonium occupied the room. Nagaraj felt he had somehow been kept off that table by fate. Now, for the first time, it was within his reach. He felt it was going to be a luxury for him to be able to place his notes on a table and write sitting in a chair. He had a fresh lease of life.

Next morning, after his prayers, he went straight to the *pyol*, throwing a word of cheer in Sita's direction. He hummed a little song, much to her amusement. She said, 'You have become suddenly young.'

'I have always been so. Only you didn't notice.'

'Maybe you don't need your ochre robe for writing.'

'No need. You will be the only one to talk, and I will answer. I can talk and write at the same time. Only I can't bear the harmonium noise.'

'Oh, that, and your brother! You can't get them out of your mind. . . . Sometimes I feel I should play my harmonium again. My father spent fifty rupees a month for my tutor. I feel rather dull, I must say, without Tim and Saroja, and I dream sometimes I could resume my music. . . .'

Nagaraj felt embarrassed. He thought, 'Why are these creatures music mad? Unfortunately, my opinion will provoke them.' He never expected Sita to have musical ambitions. He was at a loss for words to continue the conversation, but told himself, 'I must immediately secure cotton-wool plugs, and depend on my ochre robe. I had thought I would not need them now.' He remained silent, and then said, 'I must begin my work tomorrow morning. Everything is ready—'

'Except the harmonium accompaniment,' she remarked with a grin.

He felt, 'She is still joking, will not take me seriously. First daughter-in-law and now the adopted mother-in-law! Women are an impediment. Ah, how could I say so? The deity of learning is Saraswathi, the goddess with a veena in one hand, and the book and other things in her four arms. I am condemning the whole race of women. Wrong, I think I am losing my head. Prolonged absence from Narada has affected my mind; I must get back to my work soon.'

He got up briskly from the *pyol* and went into his study, sat at his desk and browsed through his notes in the Crow-brand exercise book. He had filled up five books and it filled him with misgivings now. He had lost touch with the subject for some weeks, thanks to Tim's problems, and much of the notes seemed incomprehensible. He had lost touch with the origins of creation and all the darkness and gloom of Bari's book. Even after five notebooks had been filled there was no trace of the main character. Not even an ant seemed to have been created; still water, water everywhere. 'And not a drop to drink,' echoed a literary oddment from a corner of his vast store of jumbled memory. Today, re-reading his notes and his attempted composition based on them, he found that none of it made sense. He felt desperate, and cried out, 'Sita, come here!' The urgency in his voice made her anxious and she almost came down at a run from the second court, where she was leaning on a pillar and reading some magazine. 'What is it?'

Nagaraj pushed across the table a bundle of notebooks and said, 'If you need paper for lighting the oven, take these, take these away.'

She looked alarmed. Had never seen him in such a mood. She collected the books and held them to her bosom protectively. 'What has come over you?'

'They are useless. I think Bari has been foisting on me some nonsense, nothing to do with Narada.'

'Why don't you ask him really what that mysterious book is about? Ask him to read the later portions and see what comes.'

'Brilliant idea. . .I tried it but. . . .'

'Ask him to dip into the old volume here and there to see if the sage is hiding anywhere.' And both laughed at this fantastic notion. This outburst relieved his mind and he reflected, 'Sita is not as bad as I think.' And at once he repented his secret thought. He touched his cheeks as was their habit while begging pardon for a mistake when young. Observing the motion of his hand, Sita asked, 'What excuse are you praying for and to whom?'

'Ah, how sharp you are! This man is lucky to have Sita for a wife.'

She blushed at this compliment and said, 'After so many years, you are discovering me. Thank Shiva. At least now you know me. But you have not answered my question, what excuse you were seeking from whom?'

'From God for not understanding you properly. I had thought you did not like Narada.'

'Still, I don't understand your preoccupation with Narada. Everyone knows that he was a great sage — that's all. No one has bothered to want to write his life story. Why should you alone bother?'

He had no answer; he blinked unhappily. He could only say, 'But others have written. Kavu pundit has four volumes in Sanskrit on the subject, and Bari has a big tome, which is over a hundred years old.'

'So why should you take the trouble again over the same subject?'

'So that our people may also know.'

'Why do you take upon yourself this task?'

'I don't know, I have always wanted to do it, felt it my duty somehow.'

She said coldly, 'You will be happier if you overcome it. It's only a notion which has somehow got nailed in your brain. Pluck out the nail. Nothing more; get rid of it.'

He listened in silence, echoing secretly Lady Macbeth's lines,

I would, while it was smiling in my face,
Have pluck'd my nipple from his boneless gums,
And dash'd the brains out, had I sworn
As you have done to this.

'Sita's words sounded similar and had a flint-like sharpness, an inescapable logic and unambiguity, very much like Lady Macbeth's advice. She wants to remove Narada from the scene of action in a very Lady Macbeth-like manner.' His heart bled at the thought of eliminating Narada, abandoning a personality who had occupied his thoughts all his waking hours for years. Sita noted his sudden silence and preoccupation and asked, 'You look suddenly sad. Why?'

He thought, 'Everyone wants my private thoughts and demands them to be exposed. After all, I too have a right to remain silent; if I speak out, no one can bear it. Out of consideration for others, and they assume I am a fool. . . .' While these thoughts were racing along thus, she watched his face, and he just said, 'I am not. . .' and checked his sentence before 'fool'.

Sita watched his face with amusement and concluded, 'If you can't drop Narada, I've nothing to say. I only wanted to suggest you could write about God Krishna, his boyhood, childhood, and his championing of the Pandavas in the great battle. . . . The subject is everywhere, easier than Narada.'

Nagaraj shook his head, 'What I want to write is something new, not widely known or appreciated. You will realize when it comes out. . . .'

She withdrew suddenly, remembering something to do in the kitchen. Nagaraj stared after her for a while and said: 'She wants to avoid the subject, probably hates Narada. Nor will she accept these notes for fuel, which was a handsome offer on my part. . . but she picked up the notebooks and hugged them to her bosom. What does she mean? Difficult women, difficult to understand. Whatever may happen, tomorrow I will start writing again at seven a.m. The times are propitious, no harmonium to madden me.' He suddenly shouted, 'Sita, tomorrow morning at seven o'clock I am going to continue my writing, even if the heavens fall. We will have to be up at five o'clock as usual, sorry to bother you, my dear.' He added within himself, 'This is a matter in which I alone can have a voice, not you, although in other matters you are welcome to speak your mind.' After this outburst, external and internal, he felt triumphant that he had established his standing not as one married to Sita but as the author of *Narad Maharaj*, as Bari would say. It was possible that the sage might reveal himself to him in a vision. Why not? Visions do not come by one's sweating for it, but unasked, as grace for concentrated meditation. 'I'll meditate on Narada more methodically hereafter.'

He rose with a new resolve and stretched his limbs, whispering to himself, 'You must never listen to women. They will not let you do anything worthwhile, nothing more important than buying brinjals and cucumber, and mustard and rice, and caressing whenever a chance occurred. One who is out to make a mark in any walk of life will have no chance.' His thoughts continued, 'What about my mother? Who knows how she must have nagged and reduced my father to what he became: just a grabber of village produce, bullying the cultivators who brought grains in cartloads. Even otherwise what would he have done, produced more than two brothers, perhaps? Ha! Ha! Wonderful brothers. A sister between us would have made some difference; she would have acted as a buffer. But poor Father had no time, having to browbeat peasants from the village all the time and squeezing out their cash, while Mother kept providing him food hour by hour to satisfy his gluttony during the day and at night perhaps his carnal desires. . . .'

'Why am I thinking such thoughts of the poor man, who came every evening to the municipal school to take me home safely, although I wanted to play marbles in the street. How concerned he was when he took charge of my school-books and carried them home; and then did my homework. I am an ungrateful wretch, indulging in evil thoughts. Poor Father, forgive me and don't send down any punishment from your seat in heaven. Forgive me, please. There is an evil half of me which floats to the surface at unexpected moments and provokes sinful thoughts. Please quell them. If you ever meet the great sage Narada in your heavenly home, please tell him to help and guide me in my effort, tomorrow morning at seven o'clock. Sita will be up at five. When I begin again there will be no stopping — all day I am going to write. I hope Bari is not deceiving me with a bogus Narada in his obscure volume; so far no sign of even that. However, tomorrow is D-Day, as they used to say during the war.'

At this moment, he heard a van stop in front of his house, and opened the door only to let in Tim, Saroja and the van driver who carried in, during several trips to and fro, two trunks, bedding rolls, a basket, a large-sized harmonium (which was known as a 'leg harmonium' and which had a stand, the bellows to be operated by a foot pedal leaving both hands free for the player to produce the maximum noise) and a folding chair. 'Got a good price for my old instrument and I was able to get this and the chair,' she explained to Sita who had come out and was watching the arrivals speechlessly. Nagaraj was confused, though he made several sounds of welcome and moved about between the street door and the middle room excitedly, accommodating and arranging their baggage, saying something all the time, not really knowing what to say. The persistent thought in his mind was, 'If you had brought ten pounds of cotton-wool to plug my ears, it would not have sufficed, considering the monster you have brought in.'

Tim went to his room, looked around and at the table and said 'These your books?'

Nagaraj picked them up apologetically. 'White ants and rats in that room — so Sita said. . . .' He hurriedly took them to his bedroom and, unobtrusively, also his brother's jute bag. He wanted to add, 'I asked Sita to burn the notes but she clutched them to her bosom and put them back on your table. . . .' But he only said aloud, 'I have not at all been able to write these days. . . .'

'So busy?' asked the boy, sneeringly, as it seemed to Nagaraj.

'Not exactly, but I missed you. . . I am glad to see you. . . .' He could not say anything more, nor ask why Tim had come back suddenly. He thought it best to avoid the question. Meanwhile Sita and Saroja were in the kitchen talking simultaneously and non-stop. Sita seemed to be particularly happy that Tim was back. She seemed to feel, 'Now our home is back to normal.' And Tim moved about the house as if nothing had happened or changed. Nagaraj had many questions to ask, but Tim gave him no chance. He shut himself in the room. Nagaraj had not the courage to knock on his door and enquire, ask, or investigate. 'He has come back in the same manner as he left — no explanation or any elaborate discussion — not in his nature, why should one expect anything different? I'll take him as he is. If his father wants him, he is welcome to come and take him. I am only a milestone. I stay and others come and pass. I must only watch, not ask questions. Tim's life and actions are, as ever, a mystery. But God has not endowed me with a temperament to solve mysteries. I have to accept them, that's all. . . . I do not mind anything except that huge harmonium; when its bellows work, the roof will be lifted off the rafters and beams. I dread it. If I speak about it, they will both walk out again, and then Gopu will come down and badger me. I must be prepared for anything. If Tim walks out again, where will he go? Back to Kismet?'

This question was answered by Sita later that night in the privacy of their bedroom, after Tim had shut himself in with Saroja. Sita sat on the edge of Nagaraj's bed after closing the door and said in an undertone, 'Saroja said they have come to stay and are not going back to Kismet.'

'Why?'

'Because they belong to this house — and nowhere else to go.'

'Should we adopt him?' he wanted to ask but suppressed it, fearing that she might break down at the reminder of Gopu's postcard.

Sita added, 'Saroja said that Tim had a fight with the Secretary of Kismet, and described it with a lot of admiration for the way Tim waged it. She was earning fifty rupees an evening for singing and playing the harmonium for the members. It went on smoothly till they brought in the leg harmonium. The Secretary then came, while she was playing, to move her instrument to a side room, telling her to operate it there as it was too noisy and disturbed the club members who were assembled in the hall for playing cards or chatting. Tim dropped whatever he was doing at the moment, rushed up in a rage and shouted at the Secretary for insulting his wife. There was a lot of commotion while Tim pushed and slapped the Secretary. Saroja was afraid that they might call the police. . . .'

'I wish the police had come and seized the harmonium,' Nagaraj said. 'I dread that tomorrow morning it will start blaring. I can have no hope of writing any more. You could as well take the notebooks back to the old room, where at least white ants may relish my notes on Narada. . . . And another thing: don't be surprised if I wear the ochre robe when I am at home. It'll force me to remain silent and not speak out and upset the children and drive them out again. I shall also acquire a lot of cotton wool and try and pack it all in my ear so that even a thunderclap may sound like a whisper.'

III: SHORT STORIES

Editor's note: Narayan has been writing short stories from the beginning of his career. His early stories tended to be derivative and the keen student can trace the influence of such classic writers as O. Henry and Guy de Maupassant in Narayan's initial forays into this form. He also toyed with the supernatural and wrote some fiction that might be called ghost stories. Some of the stories were also purely farcical, a milieu in which Narayan excels, and dealt with the predicament of people who had bought a big metal statue or a road-roller, either because it simply seemed like a good idea at the time or because they were inexorably drawn into the transaction. Narayan's stories get longer and richer as he begins to handle the medium with a sure touch. The stories included here are all comparatively long and are representative of the casually delicate art that he brings to bear on this kind of writing. There is a hard core of personal experience that runs through all of them. Thus 'Selvi' was inspired by his wondering about the person behind a popular performer. 'Uncle' is a poignant account of the loss of innocence in a young person who suddenly comes face to face with adult values. In 'Annamalai' Narayan displays an aspect of his creativity which is not widely noticed: while without a doubt he is the laureate of the small town, he does have an instinctive understanding of rustic or village people. One sees this in *The Financial Expert* and *The Guide*. Narayan can get into the skin of the illiterate but natively cunning peasant, and 'Annamalai' is a brilliant example of his ability to do so. 'The Horse and Two Goats', again a study in the limited psychology of a peasant, is also a hilarious presentation of the conflict of cultures. 'A Breath of Lucifer', the most autobiographical of these stories, is a transmutation of a fairly unpleasant personal experience into an episode that alternates between farce and panic.

SELVI

At the end of every concert, she was mobbed by autograph hunters. They would hem in and not allow her to leave the dais. At that moment Mohan, slowly progressing towards the exit, would turn round and call her across the hall, 'Selvi, hurry up. You want to miss the train?' 'Still a lot of time,' she could have said, but she was not in the habit of contradicting him; for Mohan this was a golden chance not to be missed, to order her in public and demonstrate his authority. He would then turn to a group of admirers, waiting to escort him and Selvi, particularly Selvi, to the car, and remark in apparent jest, 'Left to herself, she'll sit there and fill all the autograph books in the world till doomsday, she has no sense of time.'

The public viewed her as a rare, ethereal entity; but he alone knew her private face. 'Not bad-looking,' he commented within himself when he first saw her, 'but needs touching up.' Her eyebrows, which flourished wildly were trimmed and arched. For her complexion, by no means fair, but just on the border line, he discovered the correct skin cream and talcum which imparted to her brow and cheeks a shade confounding classification. Mohan did not want anyone to suspect that he encouraged the use of cosmetics. He had been a follower of Mahatma Gandhi and spent several years in prison, wore only cloth spun by hand, and shunned all luxury; there could be no question of his seeking modern, artificial aids to enhance the personality of his wife. But he had discovered at some stage, certain subtle cosmetics through a contact in Singapore, an adoring fan of Selvi's, who felt only too honoured to be asked to supply them regularly, and to keep it a secret.

When Selvi came on the stage, she looked radiant, rather than dark, brown, or fair, and it left the public guessing and debating whenever the question came up, as to what colour her skin was. There was a tremendous amount of speculation on all aspects of her life and person wherever her admirers gathered, especially at a place like The Boardless, where much town-talk was exchanged over coffee at the tables reserved for the habitué. Varma, the proprietor, himself loved to overhear such conversation from his pedestal at the cash counter, especially when the subject was Selvi.

He was one of her worshippers, but from a distance, often feeling, 'Goddess Lakshmi has favoured me; I have nothing more to pray for in the line of wealth or prosperity, but I crave for the favour of the other Goddess, that is Saraswathi, who is in our midst today as Selvi the divine singer; if only she will condescend to accept a cup of coffee or sweets from my hand, how grand it would be! But alas, whenever I carry a gift for her, *he* takes it and turns me back from the porch with a formal word of thanks.' Varma was only one among the thousands who had a longing to meet Selvi. But she was kept in a fortress of invisible walls. It was as if she was fated to spend her life either in solitary confinement or fettered to her gaoler in company. She was never left alone even for a moment with anyone. She had been wedded to Mohan for over two decades and had never spoken to anyone except in his presence.

Visitors kept coming all day long for a *darshan* of Selvi but few ever reached her presence. Some were received on the ground floor, some were received on the lawns, some were encouraged to go up the staircase—but none could get a glimpse of her—but only of Mohan's secretary or the secretary's secretary. Select personalities however, were received ceremoniously in the main hall upstairs and seated on sofas. Ordinary visitors would not be offered seats, but they could occupy any bench or chair found scattered here and there and wait as long as they pleased—and go back wherever they came from.

Their home was a huge building of East India Company days, displaying arches, columns and gables, once the residence of Sir Frederick Lawley, (whose statue stood at the town-square), who had kept a retinue of forty servants to sweep and dust the six over-sized halls built on two floors, with tall doors and gothic windows, and Venetian shutters; and set on several acres of ground, five miles away from the city on the road to Mempi Hills. The place was wooded with enormous trees, particularly important was an elm (or oak or beech, no one could say) at the gate, planted by Sir F. Lawley who had brought the seedling from England, said to be the only one of its kind in India. No one would tenant the house since Sir Frederick's spirit was said to hover about the place, and many weird tales were current in Malgudi at that time. The building had been abandoned since 1947, when Britain quit India. Mohan, who at some point made a bid for it, said, 'Let me try. Gandhiji's non-violence rid the country of the British rule. I was a humble disciple of Mahatmaji and I should be able to rid the place

of at least a British ghost by the same technique!' He found money
to buy the house when Selvi received a fee for lending her voice to
a film-star, who could just move her lips to synchronize with Selvi's
singing and attained thus much glory for her performance in a film.
But thereafter Mohan definitely shut out all film offers. 'I'll establish
Selvi as a unique phenomenon on her own, not as a voice for some
fat cosmetic-dummy.'

Bit by bit, by assiduous publicity and word-of-mouth recommendation, winning the favour of every journalist and music critic
available, he had built up her image, into its present stature. Hard
work it was over the years. At the end when it bore fruit, her name
acquired a unique charm, her photograph began to appear in one
publication or another every week. She was in demand
everywhere. Mohan's office was besieged by the organizers of
musical events from all over the country. 'Leave your proposal with
my secretary, and we will inform you after finalizing our calendar
for the quarter,' he would tell one. To another, he would say, 'My
schedule is tight till 1982—if there is any cancellation we'll see what
can be done. Remind me in October of 1981, I'll give you a final
answer.' He rejected several offers for no other reason than to
preserve a rarity value for Selvi. When Mohan accepted an engagement, the applicant (more a supplicant), felt grateful, notwithstanding the exorbitant fee, half to be paid immediately in cash without
a receipt. He varied his tactics occasionally. He would specify that
all the earnings of a certain concert should go to some fashionable
social service organization carrying well-known names on its list of
patrons. He would accept no remuneration for the performance
itself, but ask for expenses in cash, which would approximate to his
normal fee. He was a financial expert who knew how to conjure up
money, and at the same time keep income tax at arm's length.
Pacing his lawns and corridors restlessly, his mind was always busy,
planning how to organize and manoeuvre men and money. Suddenly he would pause, summon his stenographer and dictate, or
pick up the phone and talk at length into it.

In addition to the actual professional matters, he kept an eye on
public relations too; he attended select, exclusive parties, invited
eminent men and women to dinner at Lawley Terrace. Among the
guests would often be found a sprinkling of international figures
too. On his walls hung group photographs of himself and Selvi in
the company of the strangest assortment of personalities, Tito,
Bulgarian, Yehudi Menuhin, John Kennedy, the Nehru family, the

Pope, Charlie Chaplin, Yogis and sportsmen and political figures, taken under various circumstances and settings.

At The Boardless there was constant speculation about Selvi's early life. Varma heard at the gossip table that Selvi had been brought up by her mother in a back row of Vinayak Mudali Street, in a small house with tiles falling off, with not enough cash at home to put the tiles back on the roof and had learnt music from her, practising with her brother and sister accompanying her on their instruments.

At this time Mohan had a photo studio on Market Road. Once Selvi's mother brought the girl to be photographed for a school magazine after she had won the first prize in a music competition. Thereafter Mohan visited them casually now and then, as a sort of well-wisher of the family, sat in the single chair their home provided, drank coffee, and generally behaved as a benign god to that family by his advice and guidance. Sometimes he would request Selvi to sing and then dramatically leave the chair and sit down on the floor cross-legged with his eyes shut, in an attitude of total absorption in her melody, to indicate that in the presence of such an inspired artist it would be blasphemous to sit high in a chair.

Day after day, he performed little services to the family and then gradually took over the management of their affairs. At The Boardless no one could relate with certainty at what point exactly he began to refer to Selvi as his wife or where, when, or how, they were married. No one would dare investigate it too closely now.

Mohan had lost no time in investing the money, earned from the film, in buying Lawley Terrace. After freshening up its walls with limewash and paints, on an auspicious day he engaged Gaffur's taxi, and took Selvi and the family to the Terrace.

While her mother, brother, and sister, looked excited at the dimension of the house as they passed through the six halls, looked up at the high ceiling, and clicked their tongues, Selvi herself showed no reaction; she went through the house as if through the corridors of a museum. Mohan was a little disappointed and asked, 'How do you like this place?' At that all she could say in answer was, 'It looks big.' At the end of the guided tour, he launched on a description and history (avoiding the hauntings) of the house. She listened, without any show of interest. Her mind seemed to be elsewhere. They were all seated on the gigantic settees of the Company days, which had come with the property, and were left behind because they could not be moved. She didn't seem to notice even the immensity of the furniture on which she was seated. As a matter of fact, as he came to realize later, in the course of their hundreds of concert tours, she was habitually oblivious of her surroundings. In any setting —mansion or five-star hotels with luxurious guest rooms and attendants; or a small town or village home with no special facilities or privacy—she looked equally indifferent or contented; washed, dressed, and was ready for the concert at the appointed time in the evening. Most days she never knew or questioned where she was to sing or what fee they were getting. Whenever he said, 'Pack and get ready,' she filled a trunk with her clothes, toiletry, and tonic pills, and was ready, not even questioning where they were going. She sat in a reserved seat in the train when she was asked to do so, and was ready to leave when Mohan warned her they would have to get off at the next stop. She was undemanding, unenquiring, uncomplaining. She seemed to seemed to exist without noticing anything or anyone, rapt in some secret melody or thoughts of her own.

In the course of a quarter century, she had become a national figure; travelled widely in and out of the country. They named her the Goddess of Melody. When her name was announced, the hall, any hall, filled up to its capacity and people fought for seats. When she appeared on the dais, the audience was thrilled as if vouchsafed a vision, and she was accorded a thundering ovation. When she settled down, gently cleared her throat, and hummed softly to assist the accompanists tune their instruments, a silence fell among the audience. Her voice possessed a versatility and reach which never failed to transport her audience. Her appeal was alike to the common, unsophisticated listener as to pundits, theorists, and musicologists, and even those who didn't care for any sort of music liked to be seen in her concerts for prestige's sake.

During a concert wherever it might be, Madras, Delhi, London, New York or Singapore, Mohan occupied as a rule the central seat in the first row of the auditorium and rivetted his gaze on the singer, leaving people to wonder whether he was lost in her spell or whether he was inspiring her by thought-transference. Though his eyes were on her, his mind would be busy doing complicated arithmetic with reference to monetary problems, and he would also watch unobtrusively for any tape-recorder that might be smuggled into the hall (he never permitted recording) and note slyly the reactions of VIPs flanking him.

He planned every concert in detail. He would sit up in the

afternoon with Selvi and suggest gently but firmly, 'Wouldn't you like to start with the Kalyani Varnam—the minor one?' And she would say, 'Yes,' never having been able to utter any other word in her life. He would continue, 'The second item had better be Thiagaraja's composition in Begada, it'll be good to have a contrasting raga,' and then his list would go on to fill up about four hours. 'Don't bother to elaborate any Pallavi for this audience, but work out briefly a little detail in the Thodi composition. Afterwards you may add any item you like, light bhajans, javalis, or folk-songs,' offering her a freedom which was worthless since the programme as devised would be tight-fitting for the duration of the concert, which, according to his rule, should never exceed four hours. 'But for my planning and guidance, she'd make a mess, which none realizes,' he often reflected.

Everyone curried Mohan's favour and goodwill in the hope that it'd lead him to the proximity of the star. Mohan did encourage a particular class to call on him and received them at the Central Hall of Lawley terrace; he would call aloud to Selvi when such a person arrived, 'Here is so and so, come!' It could be no ordinary name— only a minister, or an I.G. of police or the Managing Director of a textile mill or a newspaper editor, who in his turn would always be eager to do some favour to Mohan hoping thereby to be recognized eventually by Selvi as a special friend of the family. Selvi would come out of her chamber ten minutes after being summoned, and act her part with precision: a wonderful smile, and namaste with her palms gently pressed together, which sent a thrill down the spine of the distinguished visitor, who would generally refer to her last concert, and confess how deeply moving it had been, and how a particular raga kept ringing in his ears all that evening, long after the performance. Selvi had appropriate lines in reply to such praise, 'Of course, I feel honoured that my little effort has pleased a person of your calibre,' while Mohan would interpose with a joke or a personal remark. He didn't want any visitor, however important, to hold her attention, but would draw it to himself at the right moment. At the end Mohan would feel gratified that his tutored lines, gestures, and expressions were perfectly delivered by Selvi. He would congratulate himself on shaping her up so successfully into a celebrity. 'But for my effort, she'd still be another version of her mother and brother, typical Vinayak Mudali Street products and nothing beyond that. I am glad I've been able to train her so well.' In order that she might quickly get out of the contamination of Vinayak Mudali Street, he gently, unobtrusively, began to isolate her from her mother, brother and sister. At the beginning a car would be sent to fetch them, once a week; but as Selvi's public engagements increased, her mother and others were gradually allowed to fade out of her life. Selvi tried once or twice to speak to Mohan about her mother, but he looked annoyed and said,'They must be all right. I'll arrange to get them—but where is the time for it? When we are able to spend at least three days at home, we will get them here.' Such a break was rare—generally they came home by train or car and left again within twenty-four hours. On occasions when they did have the time, and if she timidly mentioned her mother, he would almost snap, 'I know, I know, I'll send Mani to Vinayak Street—but some other time. We have asked the Governor to lunch tomorrow and they will expect you to sing, informally of course, for just thirty minutes.' 'The day after that?' Selvi would put in hesitantly, and he would ignore her and move off to make a telephone call. Selvi understood, and resigned herself to it, and never again mentioned her mother. 'If my own mother can't see me. . . !' she thought again and again, in secret anguish, having none to whom she could speak out her feelings.

Mohan noticing that she didn't bother him about her mother any more, felt happy that she had got over the obsession. 'That's the right way. Only a baby would bother about its mother.' He congratulated himself again on the way he was handling her.

Months and years passed thus. Selvi did not keep any reckoning of it, but went through her career liike an automaton switching on and off her music as ordered.

They were in Calcutta for a series of concerts, when news of her mother's death reached her. When she heard it, she refused to come out of her room in the hotel and wanted all her engagements cancelled. Mohan, who went into her room to coax her, swiftly withdrew when he noticed her tear-drenched face and dishevelled hair. All through the train journey back , she kept looking out of the window and never spoke a word, although Mohan did his best to engage her in talk. He was puzzled by her mood. Although she was generally not talkative, she would at least listen to whatever was said to her and intersperse with an occasional monosyllabic comment. Now for a stretch of thirty-six hours journey she never spoke a word, nor looked in his direction. When they reached home, he immediately arranged to take her down to Vinayak Mudali Street, and accompanied her himself to honour the dead officially, feeling certain that his gesture would be appreciated by Selvi. Both the big car and Mohan in his whitest handspun clothes seemed ill-fitting in those surroundings. His car blocked half the street in which Selvi's mother had lived. Her sister, who had married and had children in Singapore, could not arrive, her brother's whereabouts were unknown. A neighbour dropped in to explain the circumstances of the old lady's death and how they had to take charge of the body and so forth. Mohan tried to cut short his narration and send him away since it was unusual to let a non-descript to go along and talk to Selvi directly. But she said to Mohan, 'You may go back to the Terrace if you like. I'm staying here.' Mohan had not expected her to talk to him in that manner. He felt confused and muttered, 'By all means. . . I'll send back the car. . . . When do you want it?'

'Never. . . I'm staying here as I did before. . . .'

'How can you? In this street!' She ignored his objection, and said, 'My mother was my guru, here she taught me music, lived and died. . . . I'll also live and die here: what was good for her is good for me too. . . .'

He had never known her to be so truculent or voluble. She had been for years so mild and complaisant that he never thought she could act or speak beyond what she was taught. He lingered, waited for a while hoping for a change of her mood. Meanwhile the neighbour was going on with his narration, omitting no detail of the old lady's last moments and the problems that arose in connection with the performance of the final obsequies, 'I did not know where to reach you, but finally we carried her across the river and I lit the pyre with my own hands and dissolved the ashes in the Sarayu. After all I've known her as a boy, and you remember how I used to call her "Auntie" and sit up and listen when you were practising. . . . Oh! not these days of course, I can't afford to buy a ticket, or get anywhere near the hall where you sing.'

Mohan watched in consternation. He had never known her to go beyond the script written by him. She had never spoken to anyone or stayed in company after receiving his signal to terminate the interview and withdraw. Today it didn't work. She ignored his signal, and the man from Vinayak neighbourhood went on in a frenzy of re-living the funeral; he felt triumphant to have been of help on a unique occasion.

After waiting impatiently, Mohan rose to go: 'Anything you want to be sent down?' 'Nothing,' she replied. He saw that she had worn an old sari, and had no make-up or jewellery, having left it all behind at the Terrace.

'I need nothing. . . . '

'How will you manage?' She didn't answer. He asked weakly, 'You have the concert series at Bhopal, shall I tell them to change the dates?' First time he was consulting her on such problems.

'Do what you like,' she simply said.

What do you mean by it?' No answer.

He stepped out and drove away; the car had attracted a crowd, which now turned its attention to Selvi. They came forward to stare at her—a rare luxury for most, the citadel having been impregnable all these years, she had been only a hearsay and a myth to most people. Someone said, 'Why did you not come to your mother's help? She was asking for you!' Selvi broke down and was convulsed with sobs.

Three days later Mohan came again to announce: 'On the 30th you have to receive an Honorary Degree at the Delhi University. . . . ' She just shook her head negatively. 'The Prime Minister will be presiding over the function.'

When pressed, she just said, 'Please leave me out of all this, leave me alone, I want to be alone hereafter. I can't bear the sight of anyone. . . . '

'Just this one engagement. Do what you like after that. Otherwise it will be most compromising. Only one day at Delhi, we will get back immediately—also you signed the gramophone contract for recording next month. . . . ' She didn't reply. Her look suggested that it was not her concern. 'You'll be landing me in trouble, at least, the present commitments. . . . ' It was difficult to carry on negotiations with a crowd watching and following every word of their talk. He wished he could have some privacy with her, but this was a one-roomed house, where everybody came and stood about or sat down anywhere. If he could get her alone, he would either coax her or wring her neck. He felt helpless and desperate, and suddenly turned round and left. But he came again a week later. But it proved no better. She neither welcomed him nor asked him to leave. He suggested to her to come up to the car, this time he had brought his small car. She declined his invitation. 'After all that woman was old enough to die,' he reflected. 'This fool is ruining her life. . . . ' He allowed four more weeks for the mourning period and visited her again, but found a big gathering in her house overflowing into the street. She sat at the back of the little hall, holding up her thambura and was singing to the audience as if it were an auditorium. A violinist and a drummer had volunteered to play the accompaniments. 'She is frittering away her art,' he thought. She said, 'Come sit down.' He sat in a corner, listened for a while, and slipped away unobtrusively. Again and again, he visited her and found at all hours of the day, people around her, waiting for her music. News about her free music sessions spread, people thronged there in cars, bicycles and on foot. Varma of The Boardless brought a gift box of sweets wrapped in gilt paper, and handed it to Selvi silently and went away, having realized his ambition to approach his Goddess with an offering. Selvi never spoke unnecessarily. She remained brooding and withdrawn all day, not noticing or minding anyone coming in or going out.

Mohan thought he might be able to find her alone at least at night. At eleven o'clock one night he left his car in Market Raod and walked to Vinayak Mudali Street. He called in softly through the door of Selvi's house: 'My dear. it's me, I've to talk to you urgently. Please open the door, please,' appealing desperately through the darkened house. Selvi opened a window shutter, just a crack and said firmly, 'Go away, it's not proper to come here at this hour. . . .' Mohan turned back with a lump in his throat swearing half-aloud, 'Ungrateful wretch. . . .'

A HORSE AND TWO GOATS

Of the seven hundred thousand villages dotting the map of India, in which the majority of India's five hundred million live, flourish, and die, Kritam was probably the tiniest, indicated on the district survey map by a microscopic dot, the map being meant more for the revenue official out to collect tax than for the guidance of the motorist, who in any case could not hope to reach it since it sprawled far from the highway at the end of a rough track furrowed up by the iron-hooped wheels of bullock-carts. But its size did not prevent its giving itself the grandiose name Kritam, which meant in Tamil 'coronet' or 'crown' on the brow of this subcontinent. The village consisted of less than thirty houses, only one of them built with brick and cement. Painted a brilliant yellow and blue all over with gorgeous carvings of gods and gargoyles on its balustrade, it was known as the Big House. The other houses, distributed in four streets, were generally of bamboo thatch, straw mud, and other unspecified material. Muni's was the last house in the fourth street, beyond which stretched the fields. In his prosperous days Muni had owned a flock of forty sheep and goats and sallied forth every morning driving the flock to the highway a couple of miles away. There he would sit on the pedestal of a clay statue of a horse while his cattle grazed around. He carried a crook at the end of a bamboo pole and snapped foliage from the avenue trees to feed his flock; he also gathered faggots and dry sticks, bundled them, and carried them home for fuel at sunset.

His wife lit the domestic fire at dawn, boiled water in a mud pot, threw into it a handful of millet flour, added salt, and gave him his first nourishment for the day. When he started out, she would put in his hand a packed lunch, once again the same millet cooked into a little ball, which he could swallow with a raw onion at midday. She was old, but he was older and needed all the attention she could give him in order to be kept alive.

His fortunes had declined gradually, unnoticed. From a flock of forty which he drove into a pen at night, his stock had now come down to two goats, which were not worth the rent of a half-rupee a month the Big House charged for the use of the pen in their backyard. And so the two goats were tethered to the trunk of a drumstick tree which grew in front of his hut and from which occasionally Muni could shake down drumsticks. This morning he got six. He carried them in with a sense of triumph. Although no one could say precisely who owned the tree, it was his because he lived in its shadow.

She said, 'If you were content with the drumstick leaves alone, I could boil and salt some for you.'

'Oh, I am tired of eating those leaves. I have a craving to chew the drumstick out of sauce, I tell you.'

'You have only four teeth in your jaw, but your craving is for big things. All right, get the stuff for the sauce, and I will prepare it for you. After all, next year you may not be alive to ask for anything. But first get me all the stuff, including a measure of rice or millet, and I will satisfy your unholy craving. Our store is empty today. Dhaal, chilli, curry leaves, mustard, coriander, gingili oil, and one large potato. Go out and get all this.' He repeated the list after her in order not to miss any item and walked off to the shop in the third street.

He sat on an upturned packing case below the platform of the shop. The shopman paid no attention to him. Muni kept clearing his throat, coughing, and sneezing until the shopman could not stand it any more and demanded, 'What ails you? You will fly off that seat into the gutter if you sneeze so hard, young man.' Muni laughed inordinately, in order to please the shopman, at being called 'young man'. The shopman softened and said, 'You have enough of the imp inside to keep a second wife busy, but for the fact the old lady is still alive.' Muni laughed appropriately again at this joke. It completely won the shopman over; he liked his sense of humour to be appreciated. Muni engaged his attention in local gossip for a few minutes, which always ended with a reference to the postman's wife who had eloped to the city some months before.

The shopman felt most pleased to hear the worst of the postman, who had cheated him. Being an intinerant postman, he returned home to Kritam only once in ten days and every time managed to slip away again without passing the shop in the third street. By thus humouring the shopman, Muni could always ask for one or two items of food, promising repayment later. Some days the shopman was in a good mood and gave in, and sometimes he would lose his temper suddenly and bark at Muni for daring to ask for credit. This was such a day, and Muni could not progress beyond two items listed as essential components. The shopman was also displaying a remarkable memory for old facts and figures and took out an oblong ledger to support his observations. Muni felt impelled to rise and flee. But his self-respect kept him in his seat and made him listen to the worst things about himself. The shopman concluded, 'If you could find five rupees and a quarter, you will have paid off an ancient debt and then could apply for admission to *swarga*. How much have you got now?'

'I will pay you everything on the first of the next month.'

'As always, and whom do you except to rob by then?'

Muni felt caught and mumbled, 'My daughter has sent word that she will be sending me money.'

'Have you a daughter?' sneered the shopman. 'And she is sending you money! For what purpose, may I know?'

'Birthday, fiftieth birthday,' said Muni quietly.

'Birthday! How old are you?'

Muni repeated weakly, not being sure of it himself, 'Fifty.' He always calculated his age from the time of the great famine when he stood as high as the parapet around the village well, but who could calculate such things accurately nowadays with so many famines occurring? The shopman felt encouraged when other customers stood around to watch and comment. Muni thought helplessly, 'My poverty is exposed to everybody. But what can I do?'

'More likely you are seventy,' said the shopman. 'You also forget that you mentioned a birthday five weeks ago when you wanted castor oil for your holy bath.'

'Bath! Who can dream of a bath when you have to scratch the tank- bed for a bowl of water? We would all be parched and dead but for the Big House, where they let us take a pot of water from their well.' After this Muni unobtrusively rose and moved off.

He told his wife, 'That scoundrel would not give me anything. So go out and sell the drumsticks for what they are worth.'

He flung himself down in a corner to recoup from the fatigue of his visit to the shop. His wife said, 'You are getting no sauce today, nor anything else. I can't find anything to give you to eat. Fast till the evening. It'll do you good. Take the goats and be gone now,' she cried and added, 'don't come back before the sun is down.' He knew that if he obeyed her she would somehow conjure up some food for him in the evening. Only he must be careful not to argue and irritate her. Her temper was undependable in the morning but improved by evening time. She was sure to go out and work—grind corn in the Big House, sweep or scrub somewhere, and earn enough to buy foodstuff and keep a dinner ready for him in the evening.

Unleashing the goats from the drumstick tree, Muni started out, driving them ahead and uttering weird cries from time to time in order to urge them on. He passed through the village with his head bowed in thought. He did not want to look at anyone or be accosted. A couple of cronies lounging in the temple corridor hailed him, but he ignored their call. They had known him in the days of affluence when he lorded over a flock of fleecy sheep, not the miserable gawky goats that he had today. Of course he also used to have a few goats for those who fancied them, but real wealth lay in sheep; they bred fast and people came and bought the fleece in the shearing season; and then that famous butcher from the town came over on the weekly market days bringing him betel leaves, tobacco, and often enough some bhang, which they smoked in a hut in the coconut grove, undisturbed by wives and well-wishers. After a smoke one felt light and elated and inclined to forgive everyone including that brother-in-law of his who had once tried to set fire to his home. But all this seemed like the memories of a previous birth. Some pestilence afflicted his cattle (he could of course guess who had laid his animals under a curse), and even the friendly butcher would not touch one at half the price. . . and now here he was, left with the two scraggly creatures. He wished someone would rid him of their company too. The shopman had said that he was seventy. At seventy, one only waited to be summoned by God. When he was dead what would his wife do? They had lived in each other's company since they were children. He was told on their day of wedding that he was ten years old and she was eight. During the wedding ceremony they had had to recite their respective ages and names. He had thrashed her only a few times in their career, and later she had the upper hand. Progeny, none. Perhaps large progeny would have brought him the blessing of the gods. Fertility brought merit. People with fourteen sons were always so prosperous and at peace with the world and themselves. He recollected the thrill he had felt when he mentioned a daughter to that shopman; although it was not believed, what if he did not have a daughter?—his cousin in the next village had many daughters, and any one of them was as good as his; he was fond of them all and would buy them sweets if he could afford it. Still, everyone in the village whispered behind their backs that Muni and his wife were a barren couple. He avoided looking at anyone; they all professed to be so high up and everyone else in the village had more money than he 'I am the poorest fellow in our caste and no wonder that they spurn me, but I won't look at them either,' and so he passed on with his eyes downcast along the edge of the street, and people left him also very much alone, commenting only to the extent, 'Ah, there he goes with his two goats; if he slits their throats, he may have more peace of mind.' 'What has he to worry about anyway? They live on nothing and have none to worry about.' Thus people commented when he passed through the village. Only on the outskirts did he lift his head and look up. He urged and bullied the goats until they meandered along to the foot of the horse statue on the edge of the village. He sat on its pedestal for the rest of the day. The advantage of this was that he could watch the highway and see the lorries and buses pass through to the hills, and it gave him a sense of belonging to a large world. The pedestal of the statue was broad enough for him to move around as the sun travelled up and westward; or he could also crouch under the belly of the horse, for shade.

The horse was nearly life-size, moulded out of clay, baked, burnt, and brightly coloured, and reared its head proudly, prancing its forelegs in the air and flourishing its tail in a loop; beside the horse stood a warrior with scythe-like moustachios, bulging eyes, and aquiline nose. The old image-makers believed in indicating a man of strength by bulging out his eyes and sharpening his moustache tips, and also decorated the man's chest with beads which looked today like blobs of mud through the ravages of sun and wind and rain (when it came), but Muni would insist that he had known the beads to sparkle like the nine gems at one time in his life. The horse itself was said to have been as white as a dhobi-washed sheet, and had had on its back a cover of pure brocade of red and black lace, matching the multi-coloured sash around the waist of the warrior. But none in the village remembered the splendour as no one noticed its existence. Even Muni, who spent all his waking hours at its foot, never bothered to look up. It was untouched even by the young vandals of the village who gashed tree trunks with knives and tried to topple off milestones and inscribed lewd designs on all the village at one time, when this spot bordered the village; but when the highway was laid through (or perhaps when the tank and wells dried up completely here) the village moved a couple of miles inland.

Muni sat at the foot of the statue, watching his two goats graze in the arid soil among the cactus and lantana bushes. He looked at the sun; it had tilted westward no doubt, but it was not the time yet to go back home; if he went too early his wife would have no food for him. Also he must give her time cool off her temper and feel sympathetic, and then she would scrounge and manage to get some food. He watched the mountain road for a time signal. When the green bus appeared around the bend he could leave, and his wife would feel pleased that he had let the goats feed long enough.

He noticed now a new sort of vehicle coming down at full speed. It looked like both a motor-car and a bus. He used to be intrigued by the novelty of such spectacles, but of late work was going on at the source of the river on the mountain and an assortment of people and traffic went past him, and he took it all casually and described to his wife, later in the day, everything he saw. Today, while he observed the yellow vehicle coming down, he was wondering how to describe it later to his wife when it sputtered and stopped in front of him. A red-faced foreigner, who had been driving it, got down and went round it, stooping, looking, and poking under the vehicle; then he straightened himself up, looked at the dash-board, stared in Muni's direction, and approached him. 'Excuse me, is there a gas station nearby, or do I have to wait until another car comes—' He suddenly looked up at the clay horse and cried, 'Marvellous,' without completing his sentence. Muni felt he should get up and run away, and cursed his age. He could not readily put his limbs into action; some years ago he could outrun a cheetah, as happened once when he went to the forest to cut fuel and it was then that two of his sheep were mauled—a sign that bad times were coming. Though he tried, he could not easily extricate himself from his seat, and then there was also the problem of the goats. He could not leave them behind.

The red-faced man wore khaki clothes—evidently a policeman or a soldier. Muni said to himself, 'He will chase or shoot if I start running. Some dogs chase only those who run—oh, Shiva protect me. I don't know why this man should be after me.' Meanwhile the foreigner cried, 'Marvellous!' again, nodding his head. He paced around the statue with his eyes fixed on it. Muni sat frozen for a while, and then fidgeted and tried to edge away. Now the other man suddenly pressed his palms together in a salute, smiled, and said, 'Namaste! How do you do?'

At which Muni spoke the only English expression he had learnt, 'Yes, no.' Having exhausted his English vocabulary, he started in

Tamil: 'My name is Muni. These two goats are mine, and no one can gainsay it—though our village is full of slanderers these days who will not hesitate to say that what belongs to a man doesn't belong to him.' He rolled his eyes and shuddered at the thought of evil-minded men and women peopling his village.

The foreigner faithfully looked in the direction indicated by Muni's fingers, gazed for a while at the two goats and the rock, and with a puzzled expression took out his silver cigarette case and lit a cigarette. Suddenly remembering the courtesies of the season, he asked, 'Do you smoke?' Muni answered, 'Yes, no.' Whereupon the red-faced man took a cigarette and gave it to Muni, who received it with surprise, having had no offer of a smoke from anyone for years now. Those days when he smoked bhang were gone with his sheep and the large-hearted butcher. Nowadays he was not able to find even matches, let alone bhang. (His wife went across and borrowed a fire at dawn from a neighbour.) He had always wanted to smoke a cigarette; only once did the shopman give him one on credit, and he remembered how good it had tasted. The other flicked the lighter open and offered a light to Muni. Muni felt so confused about how to act that he blew on it and put it out . The other, puzzled but undaunted, flourished his lighter, presented it again, and lit Muni's cigarette. Muni drew a deep puff and started coughing; it was racking, no doubt, but extremely pleasant. When his cough subsided he wiped his eyes and took stock of the situation, understanding that the other man was not an Inquisitor of any kind. Yet, in order to make sure, he remained wary. No need to run away from a man who gave him such a potent smoke. His head was reeling from the effect of one of those strong American cigarettes made with roasted tobacco. The man said, 'I come from New York,' took out a wallet from his hip pocket, and presented his card.

Muni shrank away from the card. Perhaps he was trying to present a warrant and arrest him. Beware of khaki, one part of his mind warned. Take all the cigarettes or bhang or whatever is offered, but don't get caught. Beware of khaki. He wished he weren't seventy as the shopman had said. At seventy one didn't run, but surrendered to whatever came. He could only ward off trouble by talk. So he went on, all in the chaste Tamil for which Kritam was famous. (Even the worst detractors could not deny that the famous poetess Avvaiyar was born in this area, although no one could say whether it was in Kritam or Kuppam, the adjoining village.) Out of this heritage the Tamil language gushed through

Muni in an unimpeded flow. He said, 'Before God, sir, Bhagwan, who sees everything, I tell you, sir, that we know nothing of the case. If the murder was committed, whoever did it will not escape. Bhagwan is all-seeing. Don't ask me about it. I know nothing.' A body had been found mutilated and thrown under a tamarind tree at the border between Kritam and Kuppam a few weeks before, giving rise to much gossip and speculation. Muni added an explanation. 'Anything is possible there. People over there will stop at nothing.' The foreigner nodded his head and listened courteously though he understood nothing.

'I am sure you know when this horse was made,' said the red man and smiled ingratiatingly.

Muni reacted to the relaxed atmosphere by smiling himself, and pleaded, 'Please go away , sir, I know nothing. I promise we will hold him for you if we see any bad character around, and we will bury him up to his neck in a coconut pit if he tries to escape; but our village has always had a clean record. Must definitely be the other village.'

Now the red man implored, 'Please, please, I will speak slowly, please try to understand me. Can't you understand even a simple word of English? Everyone in this country seems to know English. I have gotten along with English everywhere in this country, but you don't speak it. Have you any religious or spiritual scruples against English speech?'

Muni made some indistinct sounds in his throat and shook his head. Encouraged, the other went on to explain at length, uttering each syllable with care and deliberation. Presently he sidled over and took a seat beside the old man, explaining, 'You see, last August, we probably had the hottest summer in history, and I was working in shirt-sleeves in my office on the fortieth floor of the Empire State Building. We had a power failure one day, you know, and there I was stuck for four hours, no elevator, no air conditioning. All the way in the train I kept thinking, and the minute I reached home in Connecticut, I told my wife Ruth, "We will visit India this winter, it's time to look at other civilizations."Next day she called the travel agent first thing and told him to fix it, and so here I am. Ruth came with me but is staying back at Srinagar, and I am the one doing the rounds and joining her later.'

Muni looked reflective at the end of this long oration and said, rather feebly, 'Yes, no,' as a concession to the other's language, and went on in Tamil, 'When I was this high'—he indicated a foot high—'I had heard my uncle say. . . .'

No one can tell what he was planning to say, as the other interrupted him at this stage to ask, 'Boy, what is the secret of your teeth? How old are you?'

The old man forgot what he had started to say and remarked, 'Sometimes we too lose our cattle. Jackals or cheetahs may sometimes carry them off, but sometimes it is just theft from over in the next village, and then we will know who has done it. Our priest at the temple can see in the camphor flame the face of the thief, and when he is caught. . . .' He gestured with his hands a perfect mincing of meat.

The American watched his hands intently and said, 'I know what you mean. Chop something? Maybe I am holding you up and you want to chop wood? Where is your axe? Hand it to me and show me what to chop. I do enjoy it, you know, just a hobby. We get a lot of driftwood along the backwater near my house, and on Sundays I do nothing but chop wood for the fireplace. I really feel different when I watch the fire in the fireplace, although it may take all the sections of the *Sunday New York Times* to get a fire started.' And he smiled at this reference.

Muni felt totally confused but decided the best thing would be to make an attempt to get away from this place. He tried to edge out, saying, 'Must go home,' and turned to go. The other seized his shoulder and said desperately, 'Is there no one, absolutely no one here, to translate for me?' He looked up and down the road, which was deserted in this hot afternoon; a sudden gust of wind churned up the dust and dead leaves on the roadside into a ghostly column and propelled it towards the mountain road. The stranger almost pinioned Muni's back to the statue and asked, 'Isn't this statue yours? Why don't you sell it to me?'

The old man now understood the reference to the horse, thought for a second, and said in his own language, 'I was an urchin this high when I heard my grandfather explain this horse and warrior, and my grandfather himself was this high when he heard his grandfather, whose grandfather. . . .'

The other man interrupted him. 'I don't want to seem to have stopped here for nothing. I will offer you a good price for this,' he said, indicating the horse. He had concluded without the least doubt that Muni owned this mud horse. Perhaps he guessed by the way he sat on its pedestal, like other souvenir-sellers in this country presiding over their wares.

Muni followed the man's eyes and pointing fingers and dimly understood the subject matter and, feeling relieved that the theme of the mutilated body had been abandoned at least for the time being, said again, enthusiastically, 'I was this high when my grandfather told me about this horse and the warrior, and my grandfather was this high when he himself. . .' and he was getting into a deeper bog of reminiscence each time he tried to indicate the antiquity of the statue.

The Tamil that Muni spoke was stimulating even as pure sound, and the foreigner listened with fascination. 'I wish I had my tape-recorder here,' he said, assuming the pleasantest expression. 'Your language sounds wonderful. I get a kick out of every word you utter, here'—he indicated his ears—'but you don't have to waste your breath in sales talk. I appreciate the article. You don't have to explain its points.'

'I never went to a school, in those days only Brahmins went to schools, but we had to go out and work in the fields morning till night, from sowing to harvest time. . . and when Pongal came and we had cut the harvest, my father allowed me to go out and play with others at the tank, and so I don't know the Parangi language you speak, even little fellows in your country probably speak the Parangi language, but here only learned men and officers know it. We had a postman in our village who could speak to you boldly in your language, but his wife ran away with someone and he does not speak to anyone at all nowadays. Who would if a wife did what she did? Women must be watched; otherwise they will sell themselves and the home.' And he laughed at his own quip.

The foreigner laughed heartily, took out another cigarette, and offered it to Muni, who now smoked with ease, deciding to stay on if the fellow was going to be so good as to keep up his cigarette supply. The American now stood up on the pedestal in the attitude of a demonstrative lecturer and said, running his finger along some of the carved decorations around the horse's neck, speaking slowly and uttering his words syllable by syllable, 'I could give a sales talk for this better than anyone else. . . . This is a marvellous combination of yellow and indigo, though faded now. . . . How do you people of this country achieve these flaming colours?'

Muni, now assured that the subject was still the horse and not the dead body, said, 'This is our guardian, it means death to our adversaries. At the end of Kali Yuga, this world and all other worlds will be destroyed, and the Redeemer will come in the shape of a horse called "Kalki"; this horse will come to life and gallop and trample down all bad men.' As he spoke of bad men the figures of his shopman and his brother-in-law assumed concrete forms in his mind, and he revelled for a moment in the predicament of the fellow under the horse's hoof: served him right for trying to set fire to his home. . . .

While he was brooding on this pleasant vision, the foreigner utilized the pause to say, 'I assure you that this will have the best home in the U.S.A. I'll push away the book-case, you know I love books and am a member of five book clubs, and the choice and bonus volumes mount up to a pile really in our living-room, as high as this horse itself. But they'll have to go. Ruth may disapprove, but I will convince her. The T.V. may have to be shifted too. We can't have everything in the living-room. Ruth will probably say what about when we have a party? I'm going to keep him right in the middle of the room. I don't see how that can interfere with the party—we'll stand around him and have our drinks.'

Muni continued his description of the end of the world. 'Our pundit discoursed at the temple once how the oceans are going to close over the earth in a huge wave and swallow us—this horse will grow bigger than the biggest wave and carry on its back only the good people and kick into the floods the evil ones—plenty of them about—' he said reflectively. 'Do you know when it is going to happen?' he asked.

The foreigner now understood by the tone of the other that a question was being asked and said, 'How am I transporting it? I can push the seat back and make room in the rear. That van can take in an elephant'—waving precisely at the back of the seat.

Muni was still hovering on visions of avatars and said again, 'I never missed our pundit's discourses at the temple in those days during every bright half of the month although he'd go on all night, and he told us that Vishnu is the highest god. Whenever evil men trouble us, he comes down to save us. He has come many times. The first time he incarnated as a great fish, and lifted the scriptures on his back when the floods and sea waves. . . .'

'I am not a millionaire, but a modest businessman. My trade is coffee.'

Amidst all this wilderness of obscure sound Muni caught the word 'coffee' and said, 'If you want to drink "kapi" drive further up, in the next town, they have Friday market, and there they open "kapi-otels"—so I learn from passers-by. Don't think I wander about. I go nowhere and look for nothing.' His thoughts went back to the avatars. 'The first avatar was in the shape of a little fish in a bowl of water, but every hour it grew bigger and bigger and became in the end a huge whale which the seas could not contain, and on the back of the whale the holy books were supported, saved and carried.' Once he had launched on the first avatar, it was inevitable that he should go on to the next, a wild boar on whose tusks the earth was lifted when a vicious conqueror of the earth carried it off and hid it at the bottom of the sea. After, describing this avatar Muni concluded, 'God will always save us whenever we are troubled by evil beings. When we were young we staged at full moon the story of the avatars. That's how I know the stories; we played them all night until the sun rose, and sometimes the European Collector would come to watch, bringing his own chair. I had a good voice and so they always taught me songs and gave me the women's roles. I was always Goddess Lakshmi, and they dressed me in a brocade sari, loaned from the Big House. . . .'

The foreigner said, 'I repeat I am not a millionaire. Ours is a modest business; after all, we can't afford to buy more than sixty minutes of T.V. time in a month, which works out to two minutes a day, that's all, although in the course of time we'll maybe sponsor a one-hour show regularly if our sales continue to go up. . . .'

Muni was intoxicated by the memory of his theatrical days and was about to explain how he had painted his face and worn a wig and diamond earrings when the visitor, feeling that he had spent too much time already, said, 'Tell me, will you accept a hundred rupees or not for the horse? I'd love to take the whiskered soldier also but no space for him this year. I'll have to cancel my air ticket and take a boat home, I suppose. Ruth can go by air if she likes, but I will go with the horse and keep him in my cabin all the way if necessary.' And he smiled at the picture of himself voyaging across the seas hugging this horse. He added, 'I will have to pad it with straw so that it doesn't break. . . .'

'When we played *Ramayana*, they dressed me as Sita,' added Muni. 'A teacher came and taught us the songs for the drama and we gave him fifty rupees. He incarnated himself as Rama, and He alone could destroy Ravana, the demon with ten heads who shook all the worlds; do you know the story of *Ramayana*?'

'I have my station wagon as you see. I can push the seat back and take the horse in if you will just lend me a hand with it.'

'Do you know *Mahabharata*? Krishna was the eighth avatar of

Vishnu, incarnated to help the Five Brothers regain their kingdom. When Krishna was a baby he danced on the thousand-hooded giant serpent and trampled it to death; and then he suckled the breasts of the demoness and left them flat as a disc though when she came to him her bosoms were large, like mounds of earth on the banks of a dug up canal.' He indicated two mounds with his hands. The stranger was completely mystified by the gesture. For the first time he said, 'I really wonder what you are saying because your answer is crucial. We have come to the point when we should be ready to talk business.'

'When the tenth avatar comes, do you know where you and I will be?' asked the old man.

'Lend me a hand and I can lift off the horse from its pedestal after picking out the cement at the joints. We can do anything if we have a basis of understanding.'

At this stage the mutual mystification was complete, and there was no need even to carry on a guessing game at the meaning of words. The old man chattered away in a spirit of balancing off the credits and debits of conversational exchange, and said in order to be on the credit side, 'Oh, honourable one, I hope God has blessed you with numerous progeny. I say this because you seem to be a good man, willing to stay beside an old man and talk to him, while all day I have none to talk to except when somebody stops by to ask for a piece of tobacco. But I seldom have it, tobacco is not what it used to be at one time, and I have given up chewing. I cannot afford it nowadays.' Noting the other's interest in his speech, Muni felt encouraged to ask, 'How many children have you?' with appropriate gestures with his hands. Realizing that a question was being asked, the red man replied, 'I said a hundred,' which encouraged Muni to go into details. 'How many of your children are boys and how many girls? Where are they? Is your daughter married? Is it difficult to find a son-in- law in your country also?'

In answer to these questions the red man dashed his hand into his pocket and brought forth his wallet in order to take immediate advantage of the bearish trend in the market. He flourished a hundred-rupee currency note and said, 'Well, this is what I meant.'

The old man now realized that some financial element was entering their talk. He peered closely at the currency note, the like of which he had never seen in his life; he knew the five and ten by their colours although always in other people's hands, while his own earning at any time was in coppers and nickels. What was this man flourishing the note for? Perhaps asking for change. He laughed to himself at the notion of anyone coming to him for changing a thousand—or ten-thousand rupee-note. He said with a grin, 'Ask our village headman, who is also a moneylender; he can change even a lakh of rupees in gold sovereigns if you prefer it that way; he thinks nobody knows, but dig the floor of his puja room and your head will reel at the sight of the hoard. The man disguises himself in rags just to mislead the public. Talk to the headman yourself because he goes mad at the sight of me. Someone took away his pumpkins with the creeper and he, for some reason, thinks it was me and my goats. . . that's why I never let my goats be seen anywhere near the farms.' His eyes travelled to his goats nosing about, attempting to wrest nutrition from minute greenery peeping out of rock and dry earth.

The foreigner followed his look and decided that it would be a sound policy to show an interest in the old man's pets. He went up casually to them and stroked their backs with every show of courteous attention. Now the truth dawned on the old man. He understood that the red man was actually making an offer for the goats. He had reared them up in the hope of selling them some day and, with the capital, opening a small shop on this very spot. Sitting here, watching towards the hills, he had often dreamt how he would put up a thatched roof here, spread a gunny sack out on the ground, and display on it fried nuts, coloured sweets, and green coconut for the thirsty and famished wayfarers on the highway, which was sometimes very busy. The animals were not prize ones for a cattle show, but he had spent his occasional savings to provide them some fancy diet now and then, and they did not look too bad. While he was reflecting thus, the red man shook his hand and left on his palm one hundred rupees in tens now, suddenly realizing that this was what the old man was asking. 'It is all for you or you may share it if you have a partner.'

The old man pointed at the station wagon and asked, 'Are you carrying them off in that?'

'Yes, of course,' said the other, understanding the transportation part of it.

The old man said, 'This will be their first ride in a motor-car. Carry them off after I get out of sight, otherwise they will never follow you, but only me even if I am travelling on the path to Yama Loka.' He laughed at his own joke, brought his palms together in a salute, turned round and went off, and was soon out of sight beyond a clump of thicket.

The red man looked at the goats grazing peacefully. Perched on the pedestal of the horse, as the westerly sun touched off the ancient faded colours of the statue with a fresh splendour, he ruminated, 'He must be gone to fetch some help, I suppose!' and settled down to wait. When a truck came downhill, he stopped it and got the help of a couple of men to detach the horse from its pedestal and place it in his station wagon. He gave them five rupees each, and for a further payment they siphoned off gas from the truck, and helped him to start his engine.

Muni hurried homeward with the cash securely tucked away at his waist in his dhoti. He shut the street door and stole up softly to his wife as she squatted before the lit oven wondering if by a miracle food would drop from the sky. Muni displayed his fortune for the day. She snatched the notes from him, counted them by the glow of the fire, and cried, 'One hundred rupees! How did you come by it? Have you been stealing?'

'I have sold our goats to a red-faced man. He was absolutely crazy to have them, gave me all this money and carried them off in his motor-car!'

Hardly had these words left his lips when they heard bleating outside. She opened the door and saw the two goats at her door. 'Here they are!' she said. 'What's the meaning of all this?'

He muttered a great curse and seized one of the goats by its ears and shouted, 'Where is that man? Don't you know you are his? Why did you come back?' The goat only wriggled in his grip. He asked the same question of the other too. The goat shook itself off. His wife glared at him and declared, 'If you have thieved, the police will come tonight and break your bones. Don't involve me. I will go away to my parents. . . .'

ANNAMALAI

The mail brought me only a postcard, with the message in Tamil crammed on the back of it in minute calligraphy. I was curious about it only for a minute—the handwriting, style of address, the black ink, and above all the ceremonial flourish of the language were well known to me. I had deciphered and read out to Annamalai on an average one letter every month for a decade- and-a-half when he was my gardener, watchman, and general custodian of me and my property at the New Extension. Now the letter began:

> At the Divine Presence of my old master, do I place with
> hesitancy this slight epistle for consideration. It's placed at
> the lotus feet of the great soul who gave me food and shelter
> and money in my lifetime, and for whose welfare I pray to
> the Almighty every hour of my waking life. God bless you,
> sir. By your grace and the grace of gods in the firmament
> above, I am in excellent health and spirits, and my kith and
> kin, namely, my younger brother Amavasai and my
> daughter, son-in-law, and the two grandchildren and my
> sister who lives four doors from me, and my maternal uncle
> and his children, who tend the coconut grove, are all well.
> This year the gods have been kind and have sent us the rains
> to nourish our lands, gardens and orchards. Our tanks have
> been full, and we work hard. . . .

I was indeed happy to have such a good report of fertility and joy from one who had nothing but problems as far as I could remember. But my happiness was shortlived. All the rosy picture lasted about ten closely packed lines, followed by an abrupt transition. I realized all this excellence of reporting was just a formality, following a polite code of epistle-writing and not to be taken literally in part or in whole, for the letter abruptly started off in an opposite direction and tone:

> My purpose in addressing your honoured self just today is
> to inform you that I am in sore need of money. The crops
> have failed this year and I am without food or money. My

health is poor. I am weak, decrepit, and in bed, and need money for food and medicine. My kith and kin are not able to support me, my brother Amavasai is a godly man but he is very poor and is burdened with a family of nine children and two wives, and so I beg you to treat this letter as if it were a telegram and send me money immediately. . . .

He did not specify the amount but left it to my good sense, and whatever could be spared seemed welcome. The letter bore his name at the bottom, but I knew he could not sign; he always affixed his signature in the form of a thumb impression whenever he had to deal with any legal document. I should certainly have been glad to send a pension, not once but regularly, in return for all his years of service. But how could I be sure that he had written the letter? I knew that he could neither read nor write, and how could I make sure that the author of the letters was not his brother Amavasai, that father of nine and husband of two, who might have hit upon an excellent scheme to draw a pension in the name of a dead brother? How could I make sure that Annamalai was still alive? His last words to me before he retired were a grand description of his own funeral, which he anticipated with considerable thrill.

I looked at the postmark to make sure that at least the card had originated correctly. But the post-office seal was just a dark smudge as usual. Even if it weren't so, even if the name of his village had been clearly set forth it would not have made any difference. I was never sure at any time of the name of his village, although as I have already said I had written the address for him scores of times in a decade-and-a-half. He would stand behind my chair after placing the postcard to be addressed on the desk. Every time I would say, 'Now recite the address properly.'

'All right, sir,' he would say, while I waited with the pen poised over the postcard. 'My brother's name is Amavasai, and it must be given to his hand.'

'That I know very well, next tell me the address precisely this time.' Because I had never got it right at any time.

He said something that sounded like 'Mara Konam' which always puzzled me. In Tamil it meant either 'wooden angle' or 'cross angle' depending on whether you stressed the first word or the second of that phonetic assemblage. With the pen ready, if I said, 'Repeat it,' he would help me by uttering slowly and deliberately the name—but a new one this time, sounding something like 'Peramanallur'.

'What is it, where is it?' I asked desperately.

'My village, sir,' he replied with a glow of pride—once again leaving me to brood over a likely meaning. Making allowance for wrong utterance you could translate it as 'Paerumai Nallur' meaning 'town of pride and goodness' or with a change of syllables, 'town of fatness and goodness'. Attempting to grope my way through all this verbal wilderness, if I said, 'Repeat it,' he generally came out with a brand-new sound. With a touch of homesickness in his tone and with an air of making a concession to someone lacking understanding, he would say, 'Write clearly NUMTHOD POST,' leaving me again to wrestle with phonetics to derive a meaning. No use, as this seemed to be an example of absolute sound with no sense, no scope for an interpretation however differently you tried to distribute the syllables and stresses or whether you attempted a translation or speculated on its meaning in Tamil, Telugu, Kannada or any of the fourteen languages listed in the Indian Constitution. While I sat brooding over all this verbiage flung at me, Annamalai waited silently with an air of supreme tolerance, only suggesting gently, 'Write in English. . . .'

'Why in English?'

'If it could be in Tamil I would have asked that chap who writes the card to write the address also; because it must be in English I have to trouble you'—a piece of logic that sounded intricate.

I persisted. 'Why not in Tamil?'

'Letters will not reach in Tamil; what our schoolmaster has often told us. When my uncle died they wrote a letter and addressed it in Tamil to his son in Conjeevaram and the man never turned up for the funeral. We all joined and buried the uncle after waiting for two days, and the son came one year later and asked, "Where is my father? I want to ask for money."' And Annamalai laughed at the recollection of this episode. Realizing that I had better not inquire too much, I solved the problem by writing briskly one under another everything as I heard it. And he would conclusively ask before picking up the card, 'Have you written via Katpadi?'

All this business would take its own time. While the space for address on the postcard was getting filled up I secretly fretted lest any line should be crowded out, but I always managed it somehow with the edge of my pen-point. The whole thing took almost an hour each time, but Annamalai never sent a card home more than once a month. He often remarked, 'No doubt, sir, that the people at home would enjoy receiving letters, but if I wrote a card to everyone who expected it, I would be a bankrupt. When I become a bankrupt will there be one soul among all my relatives who will offer a handful of rice even if I starve to death?' And so he kept his communications within practical limits, although they provided a vital link for him with his village home.

'How does one get to your village?' I asked.

'Buy a railway ticket, that's how,' he answered, feeling happy that he could talk of home. 'If you get into the Passenger at night paying two hundred and ten annas, you will get to Trichy in the morning. Another train leaves Trichy at eleven, and for seven rupees and four annas, it used to be only five fourteen before, you can reach Villipuram. One must be awake all night, otherwise the train will take you on and once they demanded two rupees extra for going further because I had slept over. I begged and pleaded and they let me go, but I had to buy another ticket next morning to get back to Katpadi. You can sleep on the station platform until midday. The bus arrives at midday and for twelve annas it will carry you further. After the bus you may hire a *jutka* or a bullock-cart for six annas and then on foot you reach home before dark; if it gets late bandits may waylay and beat us. Don't walk too long; if you leave in the afternoon you may reach Marakonam before sunset. But a card reaches there for just nine paise, isn't it wonderful?' he asked.

Once I asked, 'Why do you have the address written before the message?'

'So that I may be sure that the fellow who writes for me does not write to his own relations on my card. Otherwise how can I know?' This seemed to be a good way of ensuring that the postcard was not misused. It indicated a rather strange relationship, as he often spoke warmly of that unseen man who always wrote his messages on postcards, but perhaps a few intelligent reservations in accepting a friendship improve human relations. I often questioned him about his friend.

'He has also the same name as myself,' he said.

I asked, 'What name?'

He bowed his head and mumbled, 'My...my own name....' Name was a matter of delicacy, something not to be bandied about unnecessarily, a point of view which had not occurred to me at all until one day he spoke to me about a sign-board on the gate announcing my name. He told me point blank when I went down to the garden, 'Take away the name-board from that gate, if you will forgive my saying so.'

'Why?'

'All sorts of people read your name aloud while passing down the road. It is not good. Often urchins and tots just learning to spell shout your name and run off when I try to catch them. The other day some women also read your name and laughed to themselves. Why should they? I do not like it at all.' What a different world was his where a name was to be concealed rather than blazoned forth in print, ether waves, and celluloid!

'Where should I hang that board now that I have it?'

He just said, 'Why not inside the house, among the pictures in the hall?'

'People who want to find me should know where I live.'

'Everyone ought to know,' he said, 'otherwise why should they come so far?'

Digging the garden he was at his best. We carried on some of our choicest dialogues when his hands were wielding the pickaxe. He dug and kept digging for its own sake all day. While at work he always tied a red bandanna over his head, knotted above his ear in pirate fashion. Wearing a pair of khaki shorts, his bare back roasted to an ebonite shade by the sun, he attained a spontaneous camouflage in a background of mud and greenery; when he stood ankle-deep in slush at the bed of a banana seedling, he was indistinguishable from his surroundings. On stone, slope, and pit, he moved jauntily, with ease, but indoors he shuffled and scratched the cement floor with his feet, his joints creaked and rumbled as he carried himself upstairs. He never felt easy in the presence of walls and books and papers; he looked frightened and self-conscious, tried to mute his steps and his voice when entering my study. He came in only when he had a postcard to address. While I sat at my desk he would stand behind my chair, suppressing even his normal breath lest it should disturb my work, but he could not help the little rumbles and sighs emanating from his throat whenever he attempted to remain still. If I did not notice his presence soon enough, he would look in the direction of the gate and let out a drover's cry, 'Hai, hai!' at a shattering pitch and go on to explain, 'Again those cows, sir. Someday they are going to shatter the gate and swallow our lawn and flowers so laboriously tended by this old fellow. Many strangers passing our gate stop to exclaim, "See those red flowers, how well they have come up! All of it that old fellow's work, at his age!"'

Annamalai might have other misgivings about himself, but he had had no doubt whatever of his stature as a horticulturist. A combination of circumstances helped him to cherish his notions. I did nothing to check him. My compound was a quarter acre in extent and offered him unlimited scope for experimentations. I had been living in Vinayak Street until the owner of a lorry service moved into the neighbourhood. He was a relative of the municipal Chairman and so enjoyed the freedom of the city. His lorries rattled up and down all day, and at night they were parked on the roadside and hammered and drilled so as to be made ready for loading in the morning. No one else in my street seemed to notice the nuisance. No use in protesting and complaining as the relative of a municipal Chairman would be beyond reproach. I decided to flee since it was impossible to read or write in that street; it dawned on me that the place was not meant for my kind any more. I began to look about. I liked the lot shown by a broker in the New Extension layout who also arranged the sale of my ancient house in Vinayak Street to the same lorry-owner. I moved off with my books and writing within six months of making up my mind. A slight upland stretching away to the mountain road; a swell of ground ahead on my left and the railway line passing through a cutting, punctuated with a red gate, was my new setting. Someone had built a small cottage with a room on top and two rooms downstairs, and it was adequate for my purpose, which was to read and write in peace.

On the day I planned to move I requested my neighbour the lorry-owner to lend me a lorry for transporting myself to my new home. He gladly gave me his lorry; the satisfaction was mutual as he could go on with all the repairs and hammerings all night without a word of protest from anyone, and I for my part should look forward to the sound of only birds and breeze in my new home. So I loaded all my books and trunks onto an open truck, with four loaders perched on them. I took my seat beside the driver and bade good-bye to Vinayak Street. No one to sigh over my departure, since gradually, unnoticed, I had become the sole representative of our clan in that street, especially after the death of my uncle.

When we arrived at New Extension the loaders briskly lifted the articles off the lorry and dumped them in the hall. One of them lagged behind while the rest went back to the lorry and shouted, 'Hey, Annamalai, are you coming or not?' He ignored their call, and they made the driver hoot the horn.

I said to the man, 'They seem to want you. . . .'

His brief reply was, 'Let them.' He was trying to help me put things in order. 'Do you want this to be carried upstairs?' he asked, pointing at my table. The lorry hooted outside belligerently. He was enraged at the display of bad manners, went to the doorway, looked at them, and said, waving his arms, 'Be off if you want, don't stand there and make donkey noise.'

'How will you come back?'

'Is that your business?' he said. 'Go away if you like, don't let that donkey noise trouble this gentleman.'

I was touched by his solicitude, and looked up from the books I was retrieving from the packing cases, and noticed him for the first time. He was a thick-set, heavy-jowled man with a clean-shaven head covered with a turban, a pair of khaki shorts over heavy bow legs, and long arms reaching down to his knees; he had thick fingers, a broad nose, and enormous teeth stained red with betel juice and tobacco permanently pouched in at his cheek. There was something fierce as well as soft about him at the same time.

'They seem to have left,' I remarked as the sound of the lorry receded.

'Let them,' he said, 'I don't care.'

'How will you go back?' I asked.

'Why should I?' he said. 'Your things are all scattered in a jumble here, and they don't have the sense to stop and help. You may have no idea, sir, what they have become nowadays.'

Thus he entered my service and stayed on. He helped me to move my trunks and books and arrange them properly. Later he followed me about faithfully when I went round to inspect the garden. Whoever had owned the house before me had not bothered about the garden. It had a kind of battlement wall to mark off the backyard, and the rest was encircled with hedges of various types. Whenever I paused to examine any plant closely, Annamalai also stood by earnestly. If I asked, 'What is this?' 'This?' he said, stooping close to it, 'this is a *poon chedi* (flowering plant),' and after a second look at it declared what I myself was able to observe, 'yellow flowers.' I learnt in course of time that his classifications were extremely simple. If he liked a plant he called it '*poon chedi*' and allowed it to flourish. If it appeared suspicious, thorny, or awry in any manner he just declared, 'This is a *poondu* (weed),' and, before I had a chance to observe, would pull it off and throw it over the wall with a curse.

'Why do you curse that poor thing?'

'It is an evil plant, sir.'

'What kind of evil?'

'Oh, of several kinds. Little children who go near it will have stomach-ache.'

'There are no children for miles around.'

'What if? It can send out its poison on the air. . . .'

A sort of basement room was available, and I asked Annamalai, 'Can you live in this?'

'I can live even without this,' he said, and explained, 'I am not afraid of devils, spirits, or anything. I can live anywhere. Did I have a room when I lived in those forests?' He flourished his arm in some vague direction. 'That lorry-keeper is a rascal, sir; please forgive my talking like this in the presence of a gentleman. He is a rascal. He carried me one day in his lorry to a forest on the hill and would never let me get away from there. He had signed a contract to collect manure from those forests, and wanted someone to stay there, dig the manure, and heap it in the lorries.'

'What kind of manure?'

'Dropping of birds and dung of tigers and other wild animals and dead leaves, in deep layers everywhere, and he gave me a rupee-and-a-half a day to stay there and dig up and load the lorry when it came. I lit a fire and boiled rice and ate it, and stayed under the trees, heaped the leaves around and lit them up to scare away the tigers roaring at night.'

'Why did you choose this life just for one rupee and eight annas a day?' I asked.

He stood brooding for a few moments and replied, 'I don't know. I was sitting in a train going somewhere to seek a job. I didn't have a ticket. A fellow got in and demanded, "Where is your ticket?" I searched for it here and there and said, "Some son-of-a-bitch has stolen my ticket." But he understood and said, "We will find out who that son-of-a-bitch is. Get off the train first." And they took me out of the train with the bundle of clothes I carried. After the train left we were alone, and he said, "How much have you?" I had nothing, and he asked, "Do you want to earn one rupee and eight annas a day?" I begged him to give me work. He led me to a lorry waiting outside the railway station, handed me a spade and pick-axe, and said, "Go on in that lorry, and the driver will tell you what to do." The lorry put me down late next day on the mountain. All night I had to keep awake and keep a fire going, otherwise sometimes even elephants came up.'

'Weren't you terrified?'

'They would run away when they saw the fire, and sometimes I chanted aloud wise sayings and philosophies until they withdrew. . . leaving a lot of dung around, just what that man required. . . and he sold it to the coffee estates and made his money. . . . When I wanted to come home they would not let me, and so I stayed on. Last week when they came I was down with the shivering fever, but the lorry driver, a good man, allowed me to climb on the lorry and escape from the forest. I will never go back there, sir, that lorry man holds my wages and asserts that he has given it all as rice and potato all these months. . . . I don't know, someday you must reckon it all up for me and help me. . . .'

He left early on the following morning to fetch his baggage. He asked for an advance of five rupees, but I hesitated. I had not known him for more than twenty-four hours. I told him, 'I don't have change just at this moment.'

He smiled at me, showing his red-tinted teeth. 'You do not trust me, I see. How can you? The world is full of rogues who will do just what you fear. You must be careful with your cash, sir. If you don't protect your cash and wife. . . .' I did not hear him fully as he went downstairs muttering his comment. I was busy setting up my desk as I wished to start my work without any more delay. I heard the gate open, producing a single clear note on its hinges (which I later kept purposely without oiling as that particular sound served as a doorbell). I peeped from my western window and saw him go down the road. I thought he was going away for good, not to return to a man who would not trust him with five rupees! I felt sorry for not giving him money; at least a rupee. I saw him go up the swell of ground and disappear down the slope. He was going by a short cut to the city across the level- crossing gate.

I went back to my desk, cursing my suspiciousness. Here was one who had volunteered to help and I had shown so little grace. That whole day he was away. Next afternoon the gate latch clicked, and the gate hummed its single clear note as it moved on its hinges, and there he was, carrying a big tin trunk on his head, and a gunny sack piled on top of it. I went to welcome him. By the time I had gone down he had passed round the house and was lowering the trunk at the door of the basement room.

He would stand below my window and announce to the air, 'Sir,

I am off for a moment. I have to talk to the *mali* in the other house,' and move off without waiting for my reply. Sometimes if I heard him I said, as a matter of principle, 'Why do you have to go and bother him about our problems now?'

He would look crestfallen and reply, 'If I must not go, I won't go, if you order so.'

How could I or anyone order Annamalai? It was unthinkable, and so to evade such a drastic step I said, 'You know everything, what does he know more than you?'

He would shake his head at this heresy. 'Don't talk so, sir. If you don't want me to go, I won't go, that is all. You think I want to take off the time to gossip and loaf?'

A difficult question to answer, and I said, 'No, no, if it is important, of course. . . .'

And he moved off, muttering, 'They pay him a hundred rupees a month not for nothing. . .and I want to make this compound so good that people passing should say "Ah" when they peep through the gate. . .that is all, am I asking to be paid also a hundred rupees, like that *mali*?' He moved off, talking all the way; talking was an activity performed for its own sake and needed no listener for Annamalai. An hour later he returned clutching a drooping sapling (looking more like a shot-down bird) in his hand, held it aloft under my window and said, 'Only if we go and ask will people give us plants; otherwise why should they be interested?'

'What is it?' I asked dutifully, and his answer I knew even before he uttered it: 'Flower plant.'

Sometimes he displayed a handful of seeds tied to the end of his dhoti in a small bundle. Again I asked, 'What is it?'

'Very rare seeds, no one has seen such a thing in this extension. If you think I am lying. . . .' He would then ask, 'Where are these to be planted?'

I would point out to a corner of the compound and say, 'Don't you think we need some good covering there? All that portion looks bare. . . .' Even as I spoke I would feel the futility of my suggestion, it was just a constitutional procedure and nothing more. He might follow my instructions or his own inclination, no one could guess what he might do. He would dig up the earth earnestly at some corner and create a new bed of his own pattern, poke his forefinger into the soft earth and push the seed or the seedling in. Every morning he would stoop over it to observe minutely how it progressed. If he found a sprouting seed or any sign of life in the seedling, he watered it twice a day, but if it showed no response to his living touch, he looked outraged. 'This should have come up so well, but it is the Evil Eye that scorches our plants. . . . I know what to do now.' He dipped his finger in a solution of white lime and drew grotesque and strange emblems on a broken mud pot and mounted it up prominently on a stick so that those that entered our gate should first see the grotesque painting rather than the plants. He explained, 'When people say, "Ah, how good this garden looks!" they speak with envy and then it burns up the plants, but when they see the picture there, they will be filled with revulsion and our flowers will flourish. That is all.'

He made his own addition to the garden each day, planting wherever he fancied, and soon I found that I could have no say in the matter. I realized that he treated me with tolerant respect rather than trust, and so I let him have his own way. Our plants grew anyhow and anywhere and generally prospered although the only attention that Annamalai gave them was an ungrudging supply of water out of a hundred-foot hose-pipe, which he turned on every leaf of every plant until it was doused and drowned. He also flung at their roots from time to time every kind of garbage and litter and called it manuring. By such assiduous efforts he created a generous, massive vegetation as a setting for my home. We had many rose plants whose nomenclature we never learnt, which had developed into leafy menacing entanglements, clawing passers- by; canna grew to gigantic heights, jasmine into wild undergrowth with the blooms maliciously out of reach although they threw their scent into the night. Dahlias pushed themselves above ground after every monsoon, presented their blooms, and wilted and disappeared, but regenerated themselves again at the next season. No one could guess who planted them originally, but nature was responsible for their periodic appearance, although Annamalai took the credit for it unreservedly. Occasionally I protested when tacoma hedges bordering the compound developed into green ramparts, shutting off the view in every direction. Annamalai, a prince of courtesy at certain moments, would not immediately contradict me but look long and critically at the object of my protest. 'Don't think of them now, I will deal with them.'

'When?' I asked.

'As soon as we have the rains,' he would say.

'Why should it be so late?'

'Because a plant cut in summer will die at the roots.'

'You know how it is with rains these days, we never have them.'

This would make him gaze skyward and remark, 'How can we blame the rains when people are so evil-minded?'

'What evil?'

'Should they sell rice at one rupee a measure? Is it just? How can poor people live?'

When the rains did come eventually it would be no use reminding of his promise to trim the hedges, for he would definitely declare, 'When the rain stops, of course, for if a plant is trimmed in rain, it rots. If you want the hedge to be removed completely, tell me, I will do it in a few minutes, but you must not blame me later if every passer-by in the street stares and watches the inside of the house all the time. . . .'

But suddenly one day, irrespective of his theories, he would arm himself with a scythe and hack blindly whatever came within his reach, not only the hedge I wanted trimmed but also a lot of others I preferred to keep. When I protested against this depredation, he just said, 'The more we cut the better they will grow, sir.' At the end of this activity, all the plants, having lost their outlines, looked battered and stood up like lean ghosts, with the ground littered green all over. At the next stage he swept up the clippings, bundled them neatly, and carried them off to his friend, namesake, and letter-writer, living in the Bamboo Bazaar, who had his cows to feed; in return for Annamalai's generosity, he kept his penmanship ever at Annamalai's service.

His gardening activities ceased late in the evening. He laid away his implements in a corner of his basement room, laboriously coiled up the hose, and locked it away, muttering, 'This is my very life; otherwise how can an old fellow feed his plants and earn a good name? If some devil steals this I am undone, and you will never see me again.' So much lay behind his habit of rolling up the rubber hose, and I fancied that he slept in its coils as an added safety. After putting it away he took off his red bandanna, turned on the tap, and splashed enormous quantities of water over himself, blowing his nose, clearing his throat, and grooming himself noisily; he washed his feet, rubbing his heels on a granite slab until they shone red; now his bandanna would be employed as a towel; wiping himself dry, he disappeared into the basement and came out later wearing a shirt and a white dhoti. This was his off hour, when he visited the gate shop at the level-crossing in order to replenish his stock of tobacco and gossip with friends seated on a teak log. The railway gatekeeper who owned the shop (although for reasons of policy he gave out that it belonged to his brother-in-law) was a man of information and read out a summary of the day's news to this gathering out of a local news-sheet published by the man who owned the Truth Printing Press and who reduced the day's radio broadcasts and the contents of other newspapers into tiny paragraphs on a single sheet of paper, infringing every form of copyright. He brought out his edition in the evening for two paise, perhaps the cheapest newspaper in the world. Annamalai paid close attention to the reading and thus participated in contemporary history. When he returned home I could spot him half a mile away from my window as his red bandanna came into view over the crest of a slope. If he found me near at hand, he passed to me the news of the day. That was how I first heard of John Kennedy's assassination. I had not tuned the radio the whole day, being absorbed in some studies. I was standing at the gate when he returned home, and I asked casually, 'What is your news today?' and he answered without stopping, 'News? I don't go hunting for it, but I overheard that the chief ruler of America was killed today. They said something like *Kannady* (which means glass in Tamil); could any man give himself such a name?'

When I realized the import of his casual reference, I said, 'Look, was it Kennedy?'

'No, they said *Kannady*, and someone shot him with a gun and killed him, and probably they have already cremated him.' When I tried to get more news, he brushed me off with, 'Don't think I go after gossip, I only tell you what approaches my ears. . .and they were all talking. . . .'

'Who?' I asked.

'I don't know who they are. Why should I ask for names? They all sit and talk, having nothing else to do.'

He would come into my study bearing a postcard in hand and announcing, 'A letter for you. The postman gave it.' Actually it would be a letter for him, which he'd never know until told, when he would suddenly become tense and take a step nearer in order to absorb all the details.

'What does he say?' he would ask irritably. His only correspondent was his brother Amavasai, and he hated to hear from him. Torn between curiosity and revulsion, he would wait for me to finish reading the postcard to myself first. 'What does that fellow have to say to me?' he would ask in a tone of disgust and add, 'as if I could not survive without such a brother!'

I'd read aloud the postcard, which always began formally with a ceremonial flourish: 'To my Godly brother and protector, this insignificant younger brother Amavasai submits as follows. At this moment we are all flourishing and we also pray for our divine elder brother's welfare in one breath.' All this preamble would occupy half the space on the back of the card, to be abruptly followed by mundane matters. 'The boundary stone on the north side of our land was tampered with last night. We know who did it.'

Pushing the tobacco on his tongue out of the way in order to speak without impediment, Annamalai would demand, 'If you really know who, why don't you crack his skull? Are you bereft of all sense? Tell me that first,' and glare angrily at the postcard in my hand.

I'd read the following line by way of an explanation: 'But they don't care.'

'They don't? Why not?' The next few lines would agitate him most, but I had to read them out. 'Unless you come and deal with them personally, they will never be afraid. If you keep away, nothing will improve. You are away and do not care for your kith and kin and are indifferent to our welfare or suffering. You did not care to attend even my daughter's naming ceremony. This is not how the head of a family should behave.'

The rest of the letter generally turned out to be a regular charge-sheet, but concluded ceremoniously, mentioning again lotus feet and divinity. If I said, in order to divert his mind, 'Your brother writes well,' he would suddenly grin, very pleased at the compliment, and remark, 'He to write! Oh, oh, he is a lout. That letter is written by our schoolmaster. We generally tell him our thoughts and he will write. A gifted man.' He would prepare to go downstairs, remarking, 'Those fellows in my village are illiterate louts. Do you think my brother could talk to a telephone?' One of his urban triumphs was that he could handle the telephone. In distinguishing the mouthpiece from the earpiece, he displayed the pride of an astronaut strolling in space. He felt an intimacy with the instrument, and whenever it rang he'd run up to announce, 'Telepoon, *sami*,' even if I happened to be near it. When I came home at night he'd always run forward to declare while opening the gate, 'There was a telepoon—someone asked if you were in. . . .'

'Who was it?'

'Who? How could I know? He didn't show his face!'

'Didn't you ask his name?'

'No, what should I do with his name?'

One morning he waited at my bedroom to tell me, 'At five o'clock there was a telepoon. You were sleeping, and so I asked, "Who are you?" He said, "Trunk, trunk," and I told him, "Go away, don't trouble us. No trunk of baggage here. Master is sleeping."' To this day I have no idea where the trunk call was from. When I tried to explain to him what a 'trunk call' (long-distance call) was he kept saying, 'When you are sleeping, that fellow asks for a trunk! Why should we care?' I gave up.

The only way to exist in harmony with Annamalai was to take him as he was; to improve or enlighten him would only exhaust the reformer and disrupt nature's design. At first he used to light a fire in the basement itself, his fuel consisting of leaves and all sorts of odds and ends swept up from the garden, which created an enormous pall of smoke and blackened the walls; also there was the danger of his setting fire to himself in that room without a chimney. I admonished him one day and suggested that he use charcoal. He said, 'Impossible! Food cooked over charcoal shortens one's life, sir. Hereafter I will not cook inside the house at all.' Next day he set up three bricks under the pomegranate tree, placed a mud pot over them, and raised a roaring fire. He boiled water and cooked rice, dhaal, onion, tomato, and created a stew whose fragrance rose heavenward and in its passage enticed me to peep over the terrace and imbibe it.

When the monsoon set in I felt anxious as to how he was going to manage, but somehow even when the skies darkened and the rains fell, between two bouts he raised and kept up the fire under the pomegranate shade. When it poured incessantly he held a corrugated iron sheet over the fire and managed, never bothering to shield his own head. He ate at night, and preserved the remnant, and on the following day from time to time quietly dipped his fingers into the pot and ate a mouthful, facing the wall and shielding his aluminium plate from any Evil Eye that might happen to peep in at his door.

There was not a stronger person in the neighbourhood. When he stalked about during his hours of watch, tapping the ground with a metal rod and challenging in a stentorian voice, he created an air of utter intimidation, like a mastiff. God knows we might have needed a mastiff definitely in the early days, but not now. Annamalai did not seem to realize that such aggressive watch was no longer necessary. He did not seem to have noticed the transition of my surroundings from a lonely outpost (where I had often watched thieves break open a trunk and examine their booty by torchlight in a ditch a hundred yards from my bedroom window) into a populous colony, nor did he take note of the coming of the industrial estate beyond my house. If any person passing my gate dallied a minute, particularly at night after he had had his supper and the stars were out, Annamalai would challenge him to explain his presence. People passing my gate quickened their pace as a general policy. Occasionally he softened when someone asked for flowers for worship. If he saw me noticing the transaction, he would shout in rage, 'Go away. What do you think you are? Do flowers come up by themselves? Here is the old fellow giving his life to tending them, and you think. . .' and charge threateningly towards the would-be worshipper; but if I remained indoors and watched through the window I could see him give a handful of flowers to the person at the gate, muting his steps and tone and glancing over his shoulder to make sure that I was not watching.

Annamalai was believed to earn money by selling my flowers, according to a lady living next door to me, who had constituted herself his implacable enemy. According to Annamalai, whenever I was away on tour she demanded of him the banana leaves grown in my garden, for her guests to dine on, and his steady refusal had angered her. Whenever I passed their compound wall she would whisper, 'You are trusting that fellow too much, he is always talking to the people at the gate and always carrying on some transaction.' A crisis of the first order developed once when she charged him with the theft of her fowls. She reared poultry, which often invaded my compound through a gap in the fence, and every afternoon Annamalai would be chasing them out with stones and war cries. When I was away for weeks on end, according to the lady, every other day she missed a bird when she counted them at night. She explained how Annamalai dazed the fowl by throwing a wet towel over its head, and carried it off to the shop at the level-crossing, where his accomplices sold or cooked it.

Once feathers were found scattered around Annamalai's habitat when it was raided by a watchman of the municipal sewage farm who wore a khaki coat and pretended to be a policeman. Annamalai was duly frightened and upset. Returning home from a tour one afternoon, I found Annamalai standing on a foot- high block of stone, in order to be heard better next door, and haranguing, 'You set the police on me, do you, because you have lost a fowl? So what? What have I to do with it? If it strays into my compound I'll twist its neck, no doubt, but don't imagine that I will thieve like a cheap rascal. Why go about fowl- thieving? I care two straws for your police. They come to us for baksheesh in our village; foolish people will not know that. I am a respectable farmer with an acre of land in the village. I grow rice. Amavasai looks after it and writes to me. I receive letters by post. If I am a fowl-thief, what are those that call me so? Anyway, what do you think you are? Whom do you dare to talk to?' In this strain he spoke for about half an hour, addressing the air and the sky, but the direction of his remarks could not be mistaken. Every day at the same hour he delivered his harangue, soon after he had eaten his midday food, chewed tobacco, and tied the red bandanna securely over his ears.

Sometimes he added much autobiographical detail. Although it was beamed in the direction of the lady next door, I gathered a great deal of information in bits and pieces which enabled me to understand his earlier life. Mounted on his block of stone, he said, 'I was this high when I left home. A man who has the stuff to leave home when he is only ten won't be the sort to steal fowl. My father had said, "You are a thief. . . ." That night I slipped out of the house and walked. . . . I sat in a train going towards Madras. . . . They threw me out, but I got into the next train, and although they thrashed me and threw me out again and again, I reached Madras without a ticket. I am that kind, madam, not a fowl-thief, worked as a coolie and lived in the verandas of big buildings. I am an independent man, madam, I don't stand nonsense from others, even if it is my father. One day someone called me and put me on the deck of a steamer and sent me to a tea garden in Ceylon, where I was until the fever got me. Do you think your son will have the courage to face such things?'

At the same hour day after day I listened and could piece together his life. 'When I came back home I was rid of the shivering fever. I gave my father a hundred rupees and told him that a thief would not bring him a hundred rupees. I hated my village, with all those ignorant folk. My father knew I was planning to run away once again. One day all of them held me down, decorated the house, and married me to a girl. I and Amavasai went to the fields and ploughed and weeded. My wife cooked my food. After my daughter appeared I left home and went away to Penang. I worked in the rubber estates, earned money, and sent money home. That is all they care for at home—as long as you send money they don't care where you are or what you do. All that they want is money, money. I was happy in the rubber plantations. When the Japanese came they cut off everybody's head or broke their skulls with their guns, and they made us dig pits to bury the dead and also ourselves in the end. I escaped and was taken to Madras in a boat with a lot of others. At home I found my daughter grown up, but my wife was dead. It seems she had fever every day and was dead and gone. My son-in-law is in a government job in the town. I am not a fowl-thief. . . . My granddaughter goes to a school every day carrying a bag of books, with her anklets jingling and flowers in her hair. . . . I had brought the jewellery for her from Malaya.' Whatever the contents of his narrative, he always concluded, 'I am not a rascal. If I were a fowl-thief. . .would a government officer be my son-in-law?'

I told him, 'No one is listening. Why do you address the wall?'

'They are crouching behind it, not missing a word anyway,' he said. 'If she is a great person, let her be, what do I care? How dare she say that I stole her fowl? What do I want their fowl for? Let them keep them under their bed. I don't care. But if any creature ever strays here I'll wring its neck, that is certain.'

'And what will you do with it?'

'I don't care what. Why should I watch what happens to a headless fowl?'

The postcard that most upset him was the one which said, after the usual preamble, 'The black sheep has delivered a lamb, which is also black, but the shepherd is claiming it: every day he comes and creates a scene. We have locked up the lamb, but he threatens to break open the door and take away the lamb. He stands in the street and abuses us every day, and curses our family; such curses are not good for us.' Annamalai interrupted the letter to demand, 'Afraid of curses! Haven't you speech enough to out-curse him?' Another postcard three days later said, 'They came yesterday and carried off the black sheep, the mother, when we were away in the fields.'

'Oh, the. . . .' He checked the unholy expression that welled up from the bottom of his heart. 'I know how it must have happened. They must have kept the mother tied up in the backyard while locking up the lamb. What use would that be?' He looked at me questioningly.

I felt I must ask at this point, 'Whose sheep was it?'

'The shepherd's, of course, but he borrowed ten rupees and left me the sheep as a pledge. Give me my ten rupees and take away the sheep, that is all. How can you claim the lamb? A lamb that is born under our roof is ours.' This was an intricate legal point, I think the only one of its kind in the world, impossible for anyone to give a verdict on or quote precedents, as it concerned a unique kind of mortgage which multiplied in custody. 'I have a set of senseless dummies managing my affairs; it is people like my brother who made me want to run away from home.'

This proved a lucky break for the lady next door as the following afternoon Annamalai left to seek the company of the level-crossing gateman and other well-wishers in order to evolve a strategy to confound the erring shepherd in their village. As days passed he began to look more and more serene. I sensed that some solution had been found. He explained that someone who had arrived from the village brought the report that one night they had found the black sheep being driven off by the butcher, whereupon they waylaid him and carried it back to the bleating lamb at home. Now both the sheep and the lamb were securely locked up, while his brother and the family slept outside on the *pyol* of the house. I couldn't imagine how long they could continue this arrangement, but Annamalai said, 'Give me back my ten rupees and take away the sheep.'

'What happens to the lamb?'

'It is ours, of course. The sheep was barren until it came to our house; that shepherd boy did not pledge a pregnant sheep.'

It was the tailor incident that ended our association. The postcard from home said, 'The tailor has sold his machine to another tailor and has decamped. Things are bound to happen when you sit so far away from your kith and kin. You are allowing all your affairs to be spoilt.' Annamalai held his temples between his hands and shut his eyes, unable to stand the shock of this revelation. I asked no questions, he said nothing more and left me, and I saw him go up the slope towards the level-crossing. Later I watched him from my window as he dug at a banana root; he paused and stood frozen in a tableau with his pickaxe stuck in the ground, arms akimbo, staring at the mud at his feet. I knew at that moment that he was brooding over his domestic affairs. I went down, gently approached him, pretended to look at the banana root, but actually was dying of curiosity to know more about the tailor story. I asked some casual horticultural questions and when he started to reply I asked, 'Why are tailors becoming troublesome, unpunctual, and always stealing bits of cloth?'

My anti-tailor sentiment softened him, and he said, 'Tailor or carpenter or whoever he may be, what do I care, I am not afraid of them. I don't care for them.'

'Who is the tailor your brother mentions in his letter?'

'Oh, that! A fellow called Ranga in our village, worthless fellow, got kicked out everywhere,' and there the narrative for the day ended because of some interruption.

I got him to talk about the tailor a couple of days later. 'People didn't like him, but he was a good tailor. . .could stitch kerchief, drawers, banian, and even women's jackets. . .but the fellow had no machine and none of his relations would help him. No one would lend him money. I got a money-order from Ceylon one day for a hundred rupees—some money I had left behind. When the postman brought the money-order, this tailor also came along with him, at the same moment. How could he have known? After the postman left, he asked, "Can't you give me a hundred rupees? I can buy a machine." I asked him, "How did you know that I was receiving a hundred rupees, who told you?" and I slapped his face, spat at him for prying into my affairs. The fellow wept. I was, after all, his elder, and so I felt sorry and said, "Stop that. If you howl like that I will thrash you." Then all our village elders assembled and heard both of us, and ordered that I should lend my hundred rupees to him.'

I failed to understand how anyone could order him thus. I asked naïvely, 'Why should they have told you and what have they to do with it?'

He thought for a while and answered, 'That is how we do it, when the elders assemble and order us. . . .'

'But you didn't call the assembly?'

'I didn't, but they came and saw us, when the tailor was crying out that I had hurt him. They then wrote a bond on government paper with a stamp and made him sign it; the man who sold the paper was also there, and we gave him two rupees for writing the document.'

Later I got a picture of this transaction little by little. The tailor purchased a sewing machine with the loan from Annamalai. Annamalai's brother accommodated the tailor and the machine on the *pyol* of his house; the tailor renewed the bond from time to time, paid the interest regularly and also a daily rent for occupying the *pyol*. This was a sort of gold-edged security, and Annamalai preserved the bond in the safety of a tin box in my cellar. When the time for its renewal came each year, he undertook a trip to the village and came back after a month with a fresh signature on the bond, attested by the village headman. But now the entire basis of their financial relationship was shaken. The original tailor had decamped, and the new tailor did not recognize his indebtedness, although he sat on the *pyol* of their house and stitched away without speaking to anyone.

'You never asked for your hundred rupees back?' I asked.

'Why should I?' he asked, surprised at my question. 'As long as he was paying the interest, and renewing his signature. He might have been up to some mischief if I didn't go in person; that is why I went there every time.' After all the narration, Annamalai asked, 'What shall I do now? The rascal has decamped.'

'But where is the machine?'

'Still there. The new tailor stitches everybody's clothes in our house but won't speak to us, nor does he go away from the machine. He sleeps under it every night.'

'Why don't you throw him out?'

Annamalai thought for a while and said, 'He will not speak to us and he will not pay us the rent, saying when pressed that he paid all the rent to the first tailor along with the price of the machine. . . . Could it be possible? Is it so in the letter you read?'

Very soon another postcard came. It started with the respected preamble, all right, but ended rather abruptly with the words, 'We have nowhere to sleep, the tailor will not move. Inside the house the sheep and the lamb are locked. As the elder of our family, tell us where we should sleep. My wives threaten to go away to their parents' houses. I am sleeping with all the children in the street. Our own house has no place for us. If you keep so far away from your kith and kin, such things are bound to happen. We suffer and you don't care.'

At this point Annamalai indulged in loud thinking. 'Nothing new, these women are always running off to their parents. . .if you sneeze or cough it is enough to make them threaten that they will go away. Unlucky fellow, that brother of mine. He has no guts to say, "All right, begone, you *moodhevi*", he is afraid of them.'

'Why can't they throw out the tailor and lock up the machine along with the sheep? Then they could all sleep on the *pyol*. . . .'

'I think he is the son of our wrestler—that new tailor, and you know my brother is made of straw although he has produced nine children.' He considered the situation in silence for a while and said, 'It is also good in a way. As long as he is not thrown out, the machine is also there. . . . God is helping us by keeping him there within our hold. If my brother has no place to sleep in, let him remain awake.'

For the next three days I sensed that much confabulation was going on, as I saw the red bandanna go up the crest more often than usual. His adviser at the Bamboo Bazaar and the well-wishers at the gate shop must have attacked the core of the problem and discovered a solution. When he returned from the gate shop one evening he announced point-blank, 'I must go to my village.'

'Yes, why so suddenly?'

'The bond must be changed, renewed in the new tailor's name. You must let me go.'

'When?'

'When. . .? Whenever you think I should go.'

'I don't think you should go at all. I can't let you go now. I am planning to visit Rameswaram on a pilgrimage.'

'Yes, it is a holy place, good to visit,' he said patronizingly. 'You will acquire a lot of merit. After you come back I will go.' So we parted on the best of terms that day. As if nothing had been spoken on the subject till now, he came up again next day, stood behind my chair, and said without any preamble, 'I must go.'

'Yes, after I return from my pilgrimage.'

He turned round and went down half way, but came up again to ask, 'When are you going?'

His constant questioning put me on edge; anyway I suppressed my annoyance and replied calmly, 'I am waiting for some others to join me, perhaps in ten days.'

He seemed satisfied with the answer and shuffled down. That night when I returned home he met me at the gate. Hardly had I stepped in when he said, 'I will be back in ten days; let me go tomorrow. I will be back in ten days and I will guard the house when you are away on pilgrimage. . . .'

'Should we settle all questions standing in the street? Can't you wait until I am in?'

He didn't answer but shut the gate and went away to his room. I felt bad all that night. While I changed my clothes, ate, and read or wrote, there was an uneasiness at the back of my mind at the memory of my sharp speech. I had sounded too severe. I went down to his backyard first thing in the morning, earlier than usual. He sat under the tap with the water turned full blast on his head, and then went dripping to his basement room. He stuck a flower on a picture of God on his wall, lit an incense stick, stuck a flower over his ear, put holy ash on his forehead, knotted the bandanna over his ear, and, dressed in his shorts, emerged ready for the day, but there was no friendliness in his eyes. I spent the time pretending to examine the mango blooms, made some appreciative remarks about the state of the garden, and suddenly said, 'You want to be away for only ten days?'

'Yes, yes,' he replied eagerly, his mood softening. 'I must renew the bond, or gather people to throw out that interloper and seize his machine. . .even if it means bloodshed. Someone has to lose his life in this business. I will come back in ten days.'

It sounded to me a too ambitious programme to be completed in ten days. 'Are you sure that you want only ten days off?' I asked kindly.

'It may be a day more or less, but I promise to be back on the day I promise. Once I come back I won't go for two years, even then I won't go unless. . . . I will leave the next renewal in my brother's hands.'

I found myself irritated again and said, 'I cannot let you go now,' in a tone of extreme firmness, at which he came nearer and pleaded with his palms pressed together, 'Please, I must renew the bond now; otherwise, if it is delayed, I will lose everything, and the people in my village will laugh at me.'

'Get me the bond, I will have a look at it,' I said with authority.

I could hear him open his black trunk. He came in bearing a swath of cloth, unwound it with tender care, and took out of its folds a document on parchment paper. I looked through it. The bond was worth a hundred rupees, and whoever had drafted it made no mention of a tailor or his machine. It was just a note promising repayment of a hundred rupees with interest from time to time, stuck with numerous stamps, dates, thumb impressions, and signatures. I really could not see how it was going to help him. I read it out to him and commented, with my fingers drumming effectively on the document, 'Where is any mention of your tailor or his machine?'

'Surely there is the name Ranga on it?'

'But there is no mention of a tailor. For all it says, Ranga could be a scavenger.'

Annamalai looked panic-stricken. He put his eyes close to the document and, jabbing it with his finger, asked, 'What does it say here?'

I read it word by word again. He looked forlorn. I said, 'I will give you a hundred rupees and don't bother about the bond. What does it cost you to reach your village?'

He made loud calculations and said, 'About ten rupees by passenger from . . . .'

'Coming back, ten rupees. You have been going there for years now and you have already spent more than the principal in railway fare alone to get the bond renewed.'

'But he pays interest,' he said.

'Give me the bond. I will pay the amount and you stay on.' I felt desolate at the thought of his going away. At various times I went out on journeys short and long. Each time I just abandoned the house and returned home weeks and months later to find even a scrap of paper in the wastebasket preserved with care. Now I felt desolate.

He brushed aside my economic arguments. 'You won't know these things. I can always go to a court as long as the bond is there. . . .'

'And involve yourself in further expenses? It will be cheaper to burn that bond of yours.' He gave me up as a dense, impossible man whose economic notions were too elementary.

Next day and next again and again, I heard his steps on the stairs. 'I will come back in ten days.'

I said, 'All right, all right, you have too many transactions and you have no peace of mind to do your duty here, and you don't care what happens to me. I have to change my plans for your sake, I suppose?'

All this was lost on him, it was gibberish as far as he was concerned. I was obsessed with flimsy, impalpable things while the solid, four-square realities of the earth were really sheep and tailors and bonds. He stared at me pityingly for a moment as at an uncomprehending fool, turned, and went downstairs. The next few days I found him sulking. He answered me sharply whenever I spoke to him. He never watered the plants. He ignored the lady next door. More than all, he did not light the fire, as was his custom, in the shade of the pomegranate shrub. He had taken off the red bandanna and hooded an old blanket over his head as he sat in a corner of the basement room, in a state of mourning. When I went out or came in, he emerged from the basement and opened the gate dutifully. But no word passed between us. Once I tried to draw him into a conversation by asking breezily, 'Did you hear that they are opening a new store over there?'

'I go nowhere and seek no company. Why should you think I go about, gossiping about shops and things? None of my business.'

Another day I asked, 'Did anyone telephone?'

'Wouldn't I mention it if there had been telepoon?' he replied, glaring at me, and withdrew mumbling, 'If you have no trust in me, send me away. Why should I lie that there was no telepoon if there was one? I am not a rascal. I am also a respectable farmer; send me away.' He looked like someone else under his grey hood; his angry eyes peered at me with hostility. It seemed as if he had propped himself up with an effort all these years but now was suddenly falling to pieces.

A week later one morning I heard a sound at the gate, noticed him standing outside, his tin trunk and a gunny sack stuffed with odds and ends on the ground at his feet. He wore a dark coat which he had preserved for occasions, a white dhoti, and a neat turban on his head. He was nearly unrecognizable in this garb. He said, 'I am going by the eight o'clock train today. Here is the key of the basement room.' He then threw open the lid of his trunk and said, 'See if I have stolen anything of yours, but that lady calls me a fowl-thief. I am not a rascal.'

'Why do you have to go away like this? Is this how you should leave after fifteen years of service?' I asked.

He merely said, 'I am not well. I don't want to die in this house and bring it a bad name. Let me go home and die. There they will put new clothes and a fresh garland on my corpse and carry it in a procession along all the streets of our village with a band. Whereas if I am dead in that basement room while you are away, I will rot there till the municipal scavengers cart me away with the garbage heap. Let me not bring this house an evil reputation. I will go home and die. All the garden tools are in that room. Count them if you like. I am not a thief.' He waited for me to inspect his trunk.

I said, 'Shut it, I don't have to search your trunk.' He hoisted it on his head and placed over it the gunny bundle and was starting off.

'Wait,' I said.

'Why?' he asked without stopping, without turning.

'I want to give you—' I began, and dashed in to fetch some money. When I returned with ten rupees, he was gone.

UNCLE

I am the monarch of all I survey, being the sole occupant of this rambling ancient house in Vinayak Street. I am five-ten, too huge for the easy chair on which I am reclining now. But I remember the time when I could hardly reach the arm of this easy chair. I remember the same chair at the same spot in the hall, with some ancient portrait hanging on a nail over it, with my uncle comfortably lounging and tormenting me by pushing his glittering snuff-box just out of my reach. While trying to reach for it I tumbled down again and again; he emitted a loud guffaw each time I lost my balance and sprawled on the floor. I felt frightened by his loud laughter and whined and cried. At that moment my aunt would swoop down on me and carry me off to the kitchen, set me down in a corner, and place before me a little basin filled with water, which I splashed about. I needed no further attention except a replenishment of water from time to time. I also watched with wonderment the smoke curling up from the oven when the lady puffed her cheeks and blew on the fire through a hollow bamboo pipe. The spell would suddenly be broken when she picked me up again, with a bowl of rice in her hand, and carried me off to the street door. She would carefully seat me on the *pyol* of the house, my back supported against the slender pillars, and try to feed me. If I averted my head she gripped my neck as in a vise and forced the rice between my lips. If I howled in protest she utilized the chance to thrust more rice into my open mouth. If I spat it out she would point at a passer-by and say, 'See that demon, he will carry you off. He is on the lookout for babies who won't eat.' At that stage I must have faced the risk of dying of over rather than under feeding. Later in the day she would place a dish of eatables before me and watch me deal with it. When I turned the dish over on the floor and messed up the contents, Uncle and Aunt drew each other's attention to this marvellous spectacle and nearly danced around me in joy. In those days my uncle, though portly as ever, possessed greater agility, I believe.

My uncle stayed at home all day. I was too young to consider what he did for a living. The question never occurred to me until I was old enough to sit on a school bench and discuss life's problems with a class fellow. I was studying in the first year at Albert Mission School. Our teacher had written on the blackboard a set of words such as Man, Dog, Cat, Mat, Taj, and Joy, and had asked us to copy them down on our slates and take them to him for correction and punishment if necessary. I had copied four of the six terms and had earned the teacher's approbation. The boy in the next seat had also done well. Our duties for the hour were over, and that left us free to talk, in subdued whispers, though.

'What is your father's name?' he asked.

'I don't know. I call him Uncle.'

'Is he rich?' the boy asked.

'I don't know,' I replied. 'They make plenty of sweets at home.'

'Where does he work?' asked the boy, and the first thing I did when I went home, even before flinging off my books and schoolbag, was to ask loudly, 'Uncle, where is your office?'

He replied, 'Up above,' pointing heavenward, and I looked up.

'Are you rich?' was my second question.

My aunt emerged from the kitchen and dragged me in, saying,'Come, I have some very lovely things for you to eat.'

I felt confused and asked my aunt, 'Why won't Uncle. . .?'She merely covered my mouth with her palm and warned, 'Don't talk of all that.'

'Why?'I asked.

'Uncle doesn't like to be asked questions.'

'I will not ask hereafter,' I said and added, 'only that Suresh, he is a bad boy and he said. . . .'

'Hush,' she said.

My world was circumscribed by the boundaries of our house in Vinayak Street, and peopled by Uncle and Aunt mainly. I had no existence separately from my uncle. I clung to him all through the day. Mornings in the garden at the backyard, afternoons inside, and all evening on the front *pyol* of the house squatting beside him. When he prayed or meditated at midday I sat in front of him watching his face and imitating him. When he saw me mutter imaginary prayers with my eyes shut, he became ecstatic and cried aloud to my aunt in the kitchen, 'See this fellow, how well he prays! We must teach him some slokas. No doubt whatever, he is going to be a saint someday. What do you think?' When he prostrated to the gods in the puja room I too threw myself on the floor, encouraged by the compliments showered on me. He would stand staring at me until Aunt reminded him that his lunch was ready. When he sat down to eat I nestled close to him, pressing my elbow on his lap. Aunt would say, 'Move off, little man. Let Uncle eat in peace,' but he always countermanded her and said, 'Stay, stay.' After lunch he chewed betel leaves and areca nut, moved on to his bedroom, and stretched himself on his rosewood bench, with a small pillow under his head. Just when he fell into a doze I demanded, 'Tell me a story,' butting him with my elbow.

He pleaded, 'Let us both sleep. We may have wonderful dreams. After that I will tell you a story.'

'What dreams?' I would persist.

'Shut your eyes and don't talk, and you will get nice dreams.' And while I gave his advice a trial, he closed his eyes.

All too brief a trial. I cried, 'No, I don't see any dream yet. Tell me a story, Uncle.' He patted my head and murmured, 'Once upon a time. . .' with such a hypnotic effect that within a few minutes I fell asleep.

Sometimes I sought a change from the stories and involved him in a game. The bench on which he tried to sleep would be a mountain top, the slight gap between its edge and the wall a gorge with a valley below. I would crawl under the bench, lie on my back, and command, 'Now throw,' having first heaped at his side a variety of articles such as a flashlight without battery, a ping-pong bat, a sandalwood incense holder, a leather wallet, a coat hanger, empty bottles, a tiny stuffed cow, and several other items out of a treasure chest I possessed. And over went the most cherished objects—the more fragile the better for the game, for, in the cool semi-dark world under the bench and by the rules of the game, the possibility of a total annihilation of objects would be perfectly in order.

Ten days after first broaching the subject Suresh cornered me again when we were let off for an hour in the absence of our geography master. We were playing marbles. Suresh suddenly said,'My father knows your uncle.'

I felt uneasy. But I had not learnt the need for circumspection and asked anxiously, 'What does he say about him?'

'Your uncle came from another country, a far-off place. . . .'

'Oh, good, so?' I cried with happiness, feeling relieved that after all some good points about my uncle were emerging

Suresh said, 'But he impersonated.'

'What is "impersonate"?' I asked.

He said, 'Something not so good. My mother and father were talking, and I heard them use the word.'

The moment I came home from school and flung off my bag my aunt dragged me to the well in the backyard and forced me to wash my hands and feet, although I squirmed and protested vehemently. Next I sat on the arm of my uncle's easy chair with a plate filled with delicacies, ever available under that roof, and ate under the watchful eye of my uncle. Nothing delighted him more than to eat or watch someone eat. 'What is the news in your school today?' he would ask.

'Know what happened, Uncle?' I swallowed a mouthful and took time to suppress the word 'impersonate', which kept welling up from the depths of my being, and invent a story. 'A bad boy from the Third B—big fellow—jabbed me with his elbow. . . .'

'Did he? Were you hurt?'

'Oh, no, he came charging but I stepped aside and he banged his head against the wall, and it was covered with blood, and they carried him to the hospital.' My uncle uttered many cries of joy at the fate overtaking my adversary and induced me to develop the details, which always sounded gory.

When they let me go I bounced off to the street, where a gang awaited my arrival. We played marbles or kicked a rubber ball about with war cries and shouts, blissfully unaware of the passers-by and the traffic, until the street end melted into a blaze of luminous dust with the sun gone. We played until my uncle appeared at our doorway and announced, 'Time to turn in,' when we dispersed unceremoniously and noisily. Once again my aunt would want to give my hands and feet a scrubbing. 'How many times!' I protested. 'Won't I catch a cold at this rate?'

She just said, 'You have all the road dust on you now. Come on.' After dousing me she smeared sacred ash on my forehead and made me sit with my uncle in the back veranda of the house and recite holy verse. After which I picked up my school-books and, under my uncle's supervision, read my lessons, both the tutor and the taught feeling exhausted at the end of it. By eight-thirty I would be fed and put to sleep in a corner of the hall, at the junction of the two walls where I felt most secure.

On Fridays we visited the little shrine at the end of our street. Rather an exciting outing for me, as we passed along brilliantly lit shops displaying banana bunches, coloured drinks, bottled pepper-

mints, and red and yellow paper kites, every item seeming to
pulsate with an inner glow.

They both rose at five in the morning and moved about softly so as
not to disturb me. The first thing in the day, my uncle drew water
from the well for the family, and then watered the plants in the
garden. I woke to the sound of the pulley creaking over the well
and joined my uncle in the garden. In the morning light he looked
like a magician. One asked for nothing more in life than to be up at
that hour and watch brilliant eddying columns of water coming
through little channels dug along the ground. The hydraulic engineering for the garden was my uncle's own. He had raised the
ground beside the well to form a basin, and when he tipped a
cauldron of water over it, the column ran down the slope and
passed through to the plants according to his dictates. He controlled
the supply of water at various stages with a little trowel in hand,
with which he scooped up the mud and opened or blocked the
water course. I floated little bits of straw or leaves, or picked up ants
and helped them have a free swim along the current. Sometimes
without my uncle's knowledge I scooped off the mud bank with
my hands and diverted the water elsewhere.

I revelled in this world of mud, greens, slush, and water, forgetting for the moment such things as homework and teachers. When
the sun came over the walls of the house behind our garden, my
uncle ended his operations, poured a great quantity of water over
himself, and went in dripping, in search of a towel. When I tried to
follow him in, my aunt brought out a bucket of hot water and gave
me a bath beside the well. Soon I found myself in the puja room
murmuring prayers.

A perpetual smell of incense and flowers hung about the puja
room, which was actually an alcove in the kitchen where pictures
of gods hung on the walls. I loved the pictures; the great god
Krishna poised on the hood of a giant serpent; Vishnu, blue-
coloured, seated on the back of Garuda, the divine eagle, gliding in
space and watching us. As I watched the pictures my mind went
off into fantastic speculations while my tongue recited holy verse.
'Was the eagle a sort of aeroplane for Vishnu? Lakshmi stands on
lotus! How can anyone stand on a lotus flower without crushing
it?' From the fireplace would come my aunt's voice, 'I don't hear
you pray.' I would suppress my speculations and recite aloud,

addressing the elephant-faced god, '*Gajananam bhutaganadi sevitam...*' for three minutes in Sanskrit. I always wanted to ask for its meaning, but if I paused my aunt would shout over the hissing of the frying pan (which, incidentally, was generating an enormously appetizing fragrance), 'Why have you stopped?' Now I would turn to the picture of Saraswati, the goddess of learning, as she sat on a rock with her peacock beside a cool shrubbery, and wonder at her ability to play the veena with one hand while turning the rosary with the other, still leaving two hands free, perhaps to pat the peacock. I would raise my voice and say, '*Saraswati namastubhyam*,' which meant 'O goddess of learning, I bow to you,' or some such thing. I secretly added a personal request to this prayer. 'May you help me get through my school hours without being mauled by my teachers or other boys, may I get through this day unscathed.' Although my normal day at school was peaceful, I always approached it at the beginning of each day with dread. My teacher was unshaven and looked villainous. He frequently inhaled a pinch of snuff in the class and spoke in a grating voice, the snuff having ravaged his vocal cords, and he flourished a short, stubby cane menacingly at the whole class every now and then. I had never seen him attack anyone, but his gestures were frightening, and I sat on my bench shuddering lest he should turn in my direction and notice me.

My life was precisely organized by my uncle, and I had little time to waste. When I emerged from the puja I had to go straight to the kitchen and drink off a glass of milk. This would be an occasion for my aunt to comment on my dress or voice. She would suddenly bring her face close to mine and examine my eyes. 'What are you looking for?' I would ask, rearing my head, but she held it firmly between her palms and inspected until she was satisfied that there was no patch of dirt or swelling under my eyes. 'Oh, I was mistaken, nothing,' she would say with relief. 'Anyway, you have grown darker. You must not roast yourself in the sun so much. Why should they make you do all that drill in the sun?'

Next I passed into the jurisdiction of my uncle, who sat leaning against a pillar in the hall with eyes shut in meditation. He said, emerging from his trance, 'Boy, gather all your lessons for the day and put them in your bag. Have you sharpened your pencil? Cleaned your slate? Do you need anything?' In spite of my firm statement that I needed nothing, he came over, seized my school bag, peered into it, and probed its bottom with his fingers. It was surprising how lightly he could abandon his prayers, but he was perhaps an adept who could resume them at will, as his day was mostly divided between munching and meditation. He held up to the light a slate pencil in order to judge whether it could be used for just another day. He would sharpen its point on the stone floor, commenting, 'You must hold it here and write, and don't bite the end; this can be used for a week more.' It was painful to write with such a short stub; my thumb and forefinger became sore, and further, if my teacher noticed it he twisted my ear and snatched away the stub and made me stand on the bench as a punishment. I could not mention these problems explicitly, as I feared that my uncle might don his shirt and offer to visit my school in order to investigate. I had a secret anxiety lest he should ever appear in our school, as I thought that the boys might stand around and make fun of his girth. And so I had to manage with the stub as ordained. When he felt satisfied that I had used the pencil wisely, he would open his wooden cupboard, take out a lacquered casket with a dragon on its lid, and out of it a small cardboard box, and again from it a little package containing long slate pencils. He would take out a brand-new one and hesitate; guessing his intention, I would jump up and snatch it from his hand crying, 'Don't break it, I want it full-length.' Sometimes he gave it whole, sometimes he broke it into two saying, 'Half is long enough.' He then looked through my books page by page, and packed them securely back into the bag. He said from time to time, 'Little man, if you don't read your lessons properly you will never count for anything in life and no one will respect you. Do you understand?' 'Yes, Uncle,' I said though not very clear in my mind as to what 'respect' meant.

One evening I came home announcing, 'They are going to photograph us in our school.' My uncle, who had been lounging in the easy chair, sprang to his feet and asked, 'Who? Who is going to photograph you?'

'My teacher's brother has a friend who has a camera and he is going to photograph us.'

'Only you or others also?'

'Our class alone, not even the B section will be allowed, although they asked to be photographed too.'

Uncle's face lit up with joy. He called Aunt and said, 'Did you hear, this young man is going to be photographed tomorrow. Dress him properly.'

Next day my uncle spent a lot of time selecting clothes for me, and my aunt gave a double rub to my face and groomed me. My uncle followed me about uttering several pieces of advice before letting me out. 'You must never scowl even if the sun hits you in the eyes. You must try to look pleasant. You know in those days only girls waiting to be married used to have their photos taken. Nowadays everyone is being photographed.'

When I came home from school that evening he asked anxiously, 'How did it go off?'

I flung away the school bag to its corner and said, 'No, nothing happened. He didn't come.'

'Who?'

'Our teacher's brother's friend,' I said. 'It seems his camera has broken down or something like that, and so—no photo.'

My uncle's face fell. Both of them had been waiting at the door to see me return triumphantly from the photographer. He murmured sympathetically, 'Don't worry about it, we will find another photographer; only I thought you should not have taken out the blue shirt until Deepavali—never mind; we will buy you a new one for the festival.'

My aunt said, 'We could fold the shirt neatly and put it away until Deepavali. He has not soiled it.'

'I sat very quietly today lest the clothes should be spoilt,' I said, which was a fact. I had refused to play with my friends for fear that my shirt get crumpled. This blue shirt was of a special kind; my uncle had bought the cloth from a street hawker, who assured him that the fabric was foreign and could not normally be acquired except through smugglers operating in certain coastal villages. Uncle bought three yards of the blue cloth after a whole afternoon's haggling, and planned to stitch shirts for me and himself. He had sent for an old Muslim tailor who had the original Singer sewing machine set up on the *pyol* of a house in Kabir Lane. He behaved extremely deferentially before my uncle and would not be seated even on the floor. My uncle relaxed in his easy chair and my aunt stood at the kitchen doorway and both discussed with the tailor various matters relating to persons, times, and places which sounded remote and incomprehensible to me. He kept addressing my uncle as his saviour at the end of every sentence, and salaamed him. When the time came to take measurements my uncle stood very erect and muttered numerous instructions as to the length, cut, and number and kind (unbreakable, tin) of buttons that he favoured, and so forth. 'Note the measurements down properly,' he said sternly several times, 'lest you should forget and make a mistake; it is a rare kind of cloth, not obtainable in our country; can't afford to take chances with it, remember.'

The tailor in answer avowed again his indebtedness to my uncle. 'On the road that day if you had not—' he began.

My uncle looked embarrassed and cut him short with, 'Don't go on with all those grandmother's stories now. The past is past, remember.'

'How can I help it, sir? Every morning I and my children think of you and pray for your welfare. When they gave me up for dead with vultures circling above and passed on, you stopped by and revived me, sir, although you had this baby in your arms. . .and you gave me the strength to walk a thousand miles over mountain passes. . . .'

My uncle said curtly, 'Why don't you take the measurements?'

'I obey,' said the tailor immediately, and proceeded to measure me. He was not only deferential but also patronizing in his tone. 'Stand up, little master, otherwise you will blame this old man for any mistake that may occur. See how your venerable uncle stands erect at his age!'

He completed the measurements, noted them on a very small roll of paper, probably the torn-off margin of a newspaper, with a stubby pencil which he always carried over his ear, and departed after accepting all the advice given as they kept saying, 'Remember he is a growing boy, make allowance for that; don't want him to feel suffocated in his new shirt after the first wash. . . .'

The tailor left after uttering the only word of protest, 'If master had bought just a quarter yard more. . . .'

'Not at all necessary,' said my uncle. 'I know how much is needed, seeing that you are going to give me short arms, and no collar is wanted. . . .' The shirts came back stitched in due course and were laid away in the big trunk.

Next evening I came home gleefully announcing, 'We were photographed today.'

'Indeed!' cried my uncle. 'How stupid of them when you were not ready for it!'

'Does it mean that you are going to look like this in the photo?'

asked my aunt.

'It will not do justice to you,' said my uncle. 'They should have given us at least half an hour's notice, and then you could have. . . .'

'Our teacher suddenly said, "Come out, all of you, and stand in a line under the tree." We marched out. A man came with a small camera, lined up all the tall boys first and all the short ones in the second line with our teacher in the centre; and then he cried, "Stand steady, don't move," and it was over. Our teacher has promised to give a photo to whoever brings two rupees from home.'

'Two rupees!' repeated my uncle aghast.

Aunt said, 'Never mind, it is the child's first photo.'

'I thought the class would be let off after the photo, but we were marched back for geography lessons.'

My uncle thrust two rupees into my pocket before I left for school next day, cautioning me, 'Take it carefully to your teacher.' He sounded anxious lest I should drop the money or get robbed on the way. He stood on the front step and watched me go. I turned around a couple of times to assure him, 'Don't fear. I will be careful,' dreading lest he should suddenly don his shirt and decide to escort me.

For two weeks there was no sign of the photo. My uncle got quite agitated and asked every day, 'What did your teacher say?' I had to invent an answer each time as I did not have the courage to confront my teacher on the subject. And so I generally said, 'The photographer has been very ill. But tomorrow positively we are getting it.'

Ultimately the photo did arrive and we were given our copies at the end of the day. As I reached home I shouted from the street, 'Photo!' which brought my uncle down the steps of the house. He followed me anxiously about while I took my own time to fish out the photograph from my school bag. 'Such a small one!' my uncle cried on seeing it.

'His camera also was small!' I said.

They carried the print to a corner where a beam of sunlight streamed in through the red pane of a ventilator and observed it closely. Uncle put his spectacles on, but my aunt had to wait for her turn since they managed with a single pair between them. 'Why can't we go out, it is brighter out there, and I won't need glasses?' she suggested.

'No,' he replied firmly. 'Inquisitive fellows all around—fellows ready to peer through the wall if they could, to learn what is happening here,' said Uncle, passing on his spectacles and com-

menting, 'our boy has the brightest face in the group, but they have
made him look so dark!'

I pointed out my enemies to them: 'This is Suresh—always trying
to kill me if I am not careful. This boy also is a bad fellow.' My aunt's
eyes met mine significantly at the mention of Suresh, who looked
florid by the red light of the ventilator. 'This is our teacher. He will
not hesitate to skin alive anyone who is found talking in his class.
The man who took the photo is his brother's friend. Own brother,
not cousin. Suresh asked if he was a cousin, and it made my teacher
so wild!'

My uncle counted the heads and cried, 'Fifty? Two rupees each
and they have collected their one hundred rupees! Not even a
mount for the photo! They are robbing us in your schools
nowadays!'

Next day when I was leaving for school my uncle said, 'Come
home early. We will go out to the market. Have you any important
lessons?'

'No, none,' I said with conviction. 'I will come home for lunch
and stay on.'

'Do you wish to come with us?' he asked, aiming his question in
the direction of his wife in the kitchen. My aunt, with her years of
experience behind her, flung back the responsibility of a decision
on him, shouting from the fireplace, 'Do you want me to go with
you?' The man was cornered now and answered, 'Not if you have
things to mind at home. . . .'

'Of course, I have asked that servant woman to come and pound
the paddy today. If we miss her today she will not come again.' She
trailed off indecisively. This was a diplomatic game which, in spite
of my age of innocence, I understood very well, and so I broke in,
'Let Aunt come another day, Uncle. She will want a carriage to be
brought and all that trouble,' which was a fact; whenever she
wanted to go out she would send me running to the street corner
to fetch a *jutka,* and it was not always an easy job. Some days you
found six *jutkas* waiting for fares under the margosa shade at the
street corner, some days you couldn't find even one at a busy hour;
sometimes the *jutka* drivers who knew me would tease and not take
me seriously or pass disparaging remarks about my uncle, referring
to him as 'that Rangoon man' or mention incidents which I could
not comprehend, and generally mumble and smirk among themselves at my expense.

My uncle added, 'Quite right. We can walk to the market.'

'Yes, by all means,' said my aunt, much to everyone's relief.

We sallied out at three o'clock in the afternoon, having finished our tiffin and coffee. The main job for the day was to mount and frame the photograph. Uncle carried it in his hand delicately, enclosed in an old envelope, as if it were fragile and likely to perish at a finger's pressure. As we went down the street a neighbour standing at his door hailed us and demanded, 'Where are you taking the young fellow?' He was an engineer who worked in some distant projects on the hills, coming home once in a while and then again disappearing from our society. He was a particular friend of my uncle as they occasionally gathered for a game of cards in my house. He asked, 'I am here for a few days, can't we have a session some time?'

'Of course, of course,' said my uncle without much fervour, 'I will let you know,' and moved on.

'Won't Aunt get angry?' I asked, remembering the arguments they had had after every card session. The card players would have been sitting around in the middle of the hall, demanding coffee and edibles, and playing far into the night. My aunt would complain after the company had dispersed, 'Sitting there with your friends, you lock me up in the kitchen all day! What madness seizes you people when you touch a pack of cards, I wonder!' Worn out by her attacks, my uncle began to avoid his friends, the company gradually dwindled and disappeared. But it did not prevent them from dreaming about cards or luxuriating in visions of a grand session. Somewhere my uncle was supposed to have lost a lot of money through the card games, and my aunt was very definite that he should never go near cards again, although he kept saying, 'We play only Twenty-eight, and not Rummy, after all, Twenty-eight. . . .'

'Twenty-eight or Forty-eight, it's all the same to me,' said my aunt. 'Fifty thousand rupees just scattered like waste-paper, that is all! Sheer madness!' She was rather emphatic. My uncle, not being a quarrelsome sort, just accepted meekly whatever she said, and evidently benefited by her advice.

As we walked on I asked many questions. This was my opportunity to clear my doubts and learn about new things in life. I asked, 'Why does not Aunt like playing cards? So many nice people gather in our house and it is so interesting!'

He answered, 'It is very expensive, my boy, some people have lost all their fortune and become beggars. Gambling is bad. Don't you know how Nala lost his kingdom?' And he began to narrate the ancient story of Nala. Cyclists passed, a herd of cattle returned from the grazing fields beyond the river, some very young school-children emerged from the town primary school, the sun scorching us all. But my uncle noticed nothing while he unfolded to me the fate of Nala, holding me by the wrist lest I should be run over or gored by the cattle. I shrank behind him when we passed my school. I had skipped three classes in the afternoon and did not wish to be seen by my teachers or classmates. We could hear the voices from within the classrooms. Presently the bell for the three-thirty recess would sound and the boys would rush out to drink water at the tap or to make water on the roadside or swarm around the groundnut seller at the school gate. The headmaster was likely to prowl about to prevent the boys from fouling the road. It would be disaster for me to be seen by anyone now. Nor did I wish my uncle to get any ideas while passing the gate—such as stopping to have a word with my teacher. I quickened my steps and tried to divert his mind to other matters by suddenly saying, 'Why did Nala lose?'

Before answering he paused for a moment to ask, 'Is that noise all from your school? Why do they make all that row? Glad we don't live next door to your school!' Not wanting him to dwell too much on school matters, I trotted ahead of him, hoping to set the pace for him. But he remarked, 'Do you have to caper like that? No, my boy, I could have given you a beating five years ago, but today I am deliberately slowing my pace.' I paused for him to catch up with me. We had crossed the danger zone, gone past the school.

I asked innocently as we resumed our march, 'What game did Nala play? Did he play cards?'

'Oh, no,' Uncle said, 'I am sure he would have, if they had invented playing cards in those days. He played dice.' He went on to explain the game to me and continued the story. 'The fellow played with his brother, but malevolent gods had got into the dice and affected his chances, and he lost his kingdom and everything except his wife and had to march out of the capital like a mendicant wearing only a loincloth.'

We turned to our right and took a short cut through Kabir Street and were on Market Road. Not a busy hour, as the high school boys were still not let off. Several donkeys stood about the fountain statuesquely. When the boys emerged from the high school, I imagined, they would shout and frighten the donkeys, provoke them in various ways until they ran helter-skelter, confusing the evening traffic. Street dogs dozing on the edge of the road would join the fray and give them a chase, and there would be a hullabaloo. I missed all this imagined spectacle and told my uncle, 'We should have come a little later.'

'Why?' asked my uncle and added, 'You wish that you had attended your classes after all?'

'Oh, no,' I said, and blurted out, 'we could have seen the donkeys jump about.' Even without this spectacle, Market Road thrilled me, every inch, so full of life, movement, and activity. A candy peddler was crying his wares, sounding a bell. This man often established himself at our school gate, drawing out and pinching off portions of a pink, elastic, gluey sweet, stuck in a coil around a bamboo shaft. My mouth watered at the sight of it. I pleaded, 'Uncle, please get me a bit of it!'

He suddenly looked serious and said, 'No, no, it is dangerous to eat such stuff. You may catch cholera.'

I said with bravado, 'Not likely. He comes to our school every day, and all boys eat it, and also our drawing master. No one has suffered from cholera yet.'

All that he said was, 'I will get you something nicer to eat. Wait.' As we passed a sweetmeat shop he said, 'This is Jagan's shop. No harm in eating here. He makes things out of pure ghee.' He stopped by a resplendently arrayed sweetmeat shop and bought a packet for me.

I swiftly unpacked it and asked out of courtesy, 'Uncle, you want some?' and when he shook his head I ate it, and threw away the wrapper high up and watched it gently float down on Market Road until Uncle pulled me up, saying, 'Look in front and walk.'

The frame-maker's name was Jayraj. He had hoisted a signboard which was rather pompously worded 'Photographers & Photo-framers,' stretching the entire width of the outer wall of the market. Why he chose to display himself in the plural no one could say, since no one ever saw anyone except Mr Jayraj in the proprietor's seat in the inner sanctum. Although there was always a goodly company on the long bench sticking out from his threshold, they were all his friends, well-wishers, customers, and general listeners as Jayraj held forth on his social and personal philosophy all day. Now he gestured to us to be seated on the bench while he went on gently hammering tacks onto the sides of a frame covered with a cardboard. Presently he looked up and greeted my uncle, 'Doctor, where have you been all these days?'

I was surprised at my uncle being addressed as a doctor. Immediately I looked up and asked, 'Uncle, are you a doctor?' He merely rumpled my hair and did not answer.

Jayraj took this occasion to look at me and say, 'Brought this young man along, who is he?'

My uncle simply said, 'He is my boy, our child at home.'

'Oh, I know, yes of course, now grown up so!'

My uncle looked slightly awkward and changed the subject. He held out my photograph and asked with affected cheer, 'Oh, here is this young man's photo which must be framed. Will you do it?'

'Of course, anything for you, sir.' He looked at the photo with disgust. I thought he might fling the picture into the gutter that flowed copiously below the steps of his shop. His brow was furrowed, he pursed his lips, blinked his eyes, placed a straight finger across the picture, shook his head dolefully, and said, 'This is how people cheat schoolboys nowadays. Underdevelop and overexpose or underexpose and overdevelop. This is what they do.'

My uncle added fuel to the fire by saying, 'Not even a mount for the two rupees he charged!'

Jayraj put away the photograph and said, 'Well, mounting and framing is my duty, even if you bring the photo of a donkey's rear.' While he paused for breath my uncle tried to say something, but Jayraj didn't give him a chance. He said, 'Here I am in the heart of the city ready to serve our townfolk. Why can't people make use of me instead of some tenth-rate camera- meddler? I am open twenty-four hours of the day in the service of humanity. I even sleep here when there is work to do, and no factory act applies to me. I can't demand overtime or bonus, but my satisfaction lies in serving humanity.' He pointed at his camera, a hooded apparatus on a tripod in a corner. 'There it is, always ready. If somebody summons me I respond immediately, no matter what the subject is—a wedding, a corpse, prostitute, a minister of state, or a cat on a wall—it's all the same to me. My business is to photograph, and let me tell you straight away that my charges are more than moderate. I don't believe in doing cheap work. I photographed Mahatma Gandhi when he was here. I was summoned to Madras whenever Nehru was on a visit. Dr Radhakrishnan, Tagore, Birla, I could give you a big list of people who were pleased with my work and wrote out testimonials spontaneously. I have locked them in the safe at home. Any day you will be welcome to visit my humble home and peruse them if you like. I don't mind losing all my gold, but not the testimonials from the brilliant sons of our motherland. I want my children and their children to cherish them and say some day, "We come of a line who served the brilliant sons of Mother India, and here are the tokens."'

While this preamble was going on, his hands were busy giving the finishing touches to a wedding group; he was smoothing off the ripples of glue on the back of the picture. He squatted on his heels on the floor with a little work-bench in front of him. He held the wedding group at arm's length and said, 'Not my business, so many committing the folly every week, the government looking on, while people howl about the population problem, but why can't they ban all marriages for ten years?' He packed the framed picture in an old newspaper, tied a string around it, and put it away. Now my turn. He picked up my photograph, studied it again, and remarked, 'Fifty heads to be compressed on a postcard. Maybe they are only little men, but still. . . . Unless you look through a magnifying glass you will never know who is who.' He then asked my uncle, 'Will you leave the colour of the mount, frame, and style entirely to me or have you any ideas?'

My uncle was bewildered by this question and said, 'I want it to look nice, that is all. I want it to look,' he repeated, 'particularly nice.'

'I don't doubt it,' said Jayraj, who never liked the other person to end a conversation. 'Well, for the tone of this print there are certain shades of wooden frames and mounts suitable, and some not suitable. If you prefer something unsuitable according to me it'll still be done. I will wrap it up, present it to you, and collect my bill; but let me assure you that my heart will not be in it. Anyway, it is up to you,' he said challengingly. My uncle seemed bewildered by all this philosophy and remained silent. He looked apprehensive and wanted to know quickly the worst. The man had placed my photograph on his desk, weighting it down with a steel measuring scale. We awaited his next move. Meanwhile more people came and took their seats on the bench, like men at a dentist's parlour. Jayraj did not bother to notice his visitors, nor did he notice the crowd passing through the market gateway, shoppers, hawkers, beggars, dogs and stray cattle and coolies with baskets on their heads, all kinds of men and women, jostling, shouting, laughing, cursing, and moving as in a mass trance; they might have been able to pass in and out more easily but for Jayraj's bench sticking across the market entrance.

A very bald man came and gingerly sat down on the bench,

announcing, 'The trustee has sent me.' It made no impression on Jayraj, who had picked up a length of framing rod and was sawing it off noisily.

My uncle asked suddenly, 'When will you give it?'

Before Jayraj could muster an answer the bald man said for the fourth time, 'The trustee has sent me. . . .'

Jayraj chose this moment to tell some other young man leaning on a bicycle, 'Tomorrow at one o'clock.' The young man jumped on his bicycle and rode away.

The bald man began again, 'The trustee. . . .'

Jayraj looked at my uncle and said, 'It all depends when you want it.'

The bald man said, 'The trustee. . . is going away to Tirupathi tomorrow. . .and wants. . . .'

Jayraj completed his sentence for him, 'Wants me along. Tell him I have no time for a pilgrimage.'

'No, no, he wants the picture.'

'Where is the hurry? Let him come back from Tirupathi.'

The other looked nonplussed.

Meanwhile a woman who sold betel leaves in the market came up with a basket at her hip and asked, 'When should I bring the baby?'

'Whenever the midwife advises,' replied Jayraj. She blushed and threw the end of her sari over her face and laughed. 'Tomorrow evening at three o'clock. Dress him in his best. Put on him all the jewellery you can, and come early. If you come late the sunlight will be gone and there will be no photo. Be sure to bring two rupees with you. No credit, and then you give me the balance when I give you the photo in a frame.'

'Ah, can't you trust me so much, sir?'

'No argument, that is my system, that is all. If I want the betel leaves in your basket I pay for it at once, so also for what I do.' She went away laughing, and Jayraj said, addressing no one in particular, 'She has a child every ten months. Mother is constant, but not the father.' His assembly laughed at this quip. 'Not my business to question the parentage. I take the picture and frame it when ordered to do so and that is all.'

My uncle asked all of a sudden, 'Will you be able to frame and give me the photograph now?'

'No,' said Jayraj promptly, 'unless you expect me to stay on and work until midnight.'

'Why not? You said you could.'

'Yes, sir,' he replied. 'I said so and I will say so again, if you command me. Will you wait and take it?'

My uncle was flabbergasted. He said, 'No, I cannot. I have to go to the temple,' and he brooded over his inescapable routine of prayers, meditation, dinner, and sleep.

'It's five o'clock now. Your work will take two hours—the paste must dry. We must give the paste its time to dry. But before I can take up your work, you see that man on your side, whose scalp is shining today but once upon a time who had a shock of hair like a coir doormat,' and he nodded in the direction of the bald man who was still waiting for a reply for the trustee. Jayraj continued his theme of bald pate: 'About ten years ago one morning I noticed when he came to frame a calendar portrait of Brahma the Creator that he was growing thin on top; fortunately for us we cannot know the top of our own heads; and I did not tell him so that he might not feel discouraged about his matrimonial future; no one can question why or wherefore of baldness; it is much like life and death. God gives us the hair and takes it away when obviously it is needed elsewhere, that is all.'

Every word that Jayraj uttered pleased the bald man, who remarked at the end of it, 'Don't forget that I save on hair oil!' And he bowed his head to exhibit his shining top, at which I roared with laughter, Jayraj laughed out of courtesy, and my uncle smiled patronizingly, and into this pleasant and well-softened atmosphere the bald man pushed in a word about the business which had brought him there. 'The trustee. . .' he began, and Jayraj repeated, 'Oh, trustee, school trustee, temple trustee, hospital trustee, let him be anything; I have no use for trustees, and so why keep harping on them?'

The bald man sprang to his feet, approached the edge of the inner sanctum, leant forward almost in supplication, and prayed, 'Please, please, don't send me back empty-handed; he will be upset, thinking that I have been loafing about.'

Now Jayraj looked properly concerned and said, 'He would think so, would he? All right, he shall have it even if I have to forgo sleep tonight. No more sleep, no more rest, until the trustee is pacified. That settles it.' He said finally, looking at my uncle, 'Yours immediately after the trustee's even if it means all night vigil.'

My uncle repeated, 'All night! I may not be able to stay long.'

'You don't have to,' said Jayraj. 'Please be gone, sir, and that is not going to affect my programme or promise. Trust me. You are determined to hang this young person's group picture on your wall tonight, perhaps the most auspicious date in your calendar! Yes, sir. Each unto himself is my philosophy. Tonight it shall be done. I usually charge three rupees for this size, Doctor; does it seem exorbitant to you?'

I felt startled when this man again addressed my uncle as 'Doctor'. My uncle considered the offer and said meekly, 'The print itself costs only two rupees.'

'In that case I will leave it to your sense of justice. Do you assume that frame and mount are in any sense inferior to the photo?'

Everyone on the bench looked concerned and nodded apprecia-tively at the progress of this dialogue (like the chorus in a Greek play) and my uncle said, 'All right, three.' He peeped out at the municipal clock tower. 'It is past five, you won't take it up before seven?'

Jayraj said, 'Never before eight.'

'I have to be going. How will it reach me?'

Jayraj said, 'I'll knock on your door tonight and deliver it. Maybe you could leave the charges, amounting to three rupees. Don't mistake me for asking for money in advance. You see that room,' he indicated an antechamber, 'it is full of pictures of gods, demons, and humans, framed in glass, ordered by people who never turned up again, and in those days I never knew how to ask for payment. If a picture is not claimed immediately I keep it for twenty years in that room. That's the law here. Anyway I don't want to keep your picture for twenty years. I will bring it to you tonight. . . or. . . .' A sudden idea struck him. 'Why don't you leave this little fellow behind? He will collect the picture, and I will see that he comes home to you safely tonight.'

An impossible idea it seemed at first. My uncle shook his head and said, 'Oh, not possible. How can he stay here?'

'Trust me, have you no trust in me? Anyway at the end of the day I will deliver him and the photo at your door.'

'If you are coming our way, why do you want this boy to be left here?'

'To be frank, in order to make sure that I keep my promise and don't yield to any sudden impulse to shut my shop and run home.'

'Until midnight?'

'Oh, no, I was joking. Much earlier, much earlier.'

'What will he do for food? He is used to his supper at eight.'

Jayraj pointed to a restaurant across the street and said, 'I will nourish him properly. I love to have children around.'

My uncle looked at me and asked, 'Will you stay?'

I was thrilled. Jayraj was going to give me heavenly things to eat, and I could watch the procession of people and vehicles on Market Road. I pleaded, 'Uncle, don't be afraid.' I recollected all the dare-devilry of young men in the adventure stories I had heard. I wanted to have the pride of some achievement today. I pleaded with my uncle, 'Please leave me and go. I will come home later.'

Jayraj looked up and said, 'Don't worry about him,' and held out his hand. My uncle took out his purse and counted out three rupees on Jayraj's palm saying, 'I have never left him alone before.'

Jayraj said, 'Our boys must learn to get on by themselves. We must become a strong nation.'

After my uncle left, Jayraj pushed away my photo on to the floor and took in its place on the desk a group photo of the trustee's. He kept gazing on it and said, 'Not a very good photo. That Pictograph man again! So proud of his electronic flash! He claims he commands sunlight at his finger-tips, but when he throws it on to the faces of a group before the camera, what do they do? They shut their eyes or open them wide as if they saw a ghost. For all the garland on his chest and all his pomposity, the man at the centre and all others in the group look to me like monkeys surprised on a mango tree. . . .' The bald head kept swaying in approval. Jayraj constantly looked up from his work to make sure that the fellow was listening. I sat between them. Jayraj abruptly ordered, 'Child, move over, let that man come nearer.' I obeyed instantly.

This was my first day out, exciting and frightening at the same time. The world looked entirely different—the crowd at the market, which had seemed so entertaining before, was now terrifying. I feared that I might be engulfed and swept off, and never see my home again. As twilight came on and the street lamps were lit, I grew apprehensive. Somehow I felt I could not trust Jayraj. I stole a look at him. He looked forbidding. He wore a pair of glasses with think lenses through which his eyeballs bulged, lending him a ghoulish look; unshaven chin and grey mottled hair covering his forehead; khaki shirt and a blood- red dhoti, a frightening combina-tion. All his smiles and friendly talk before my uncle was a show to entice me. He seemed to have his own sinister plans to deal with me once I was left at his mercy. He had become cold and aloof. Otherwise, why should he have asked me to yield my place to the bald man? The moment my uncle's back was turned this man's manner had changed; he looked grim and ignored me. Where was the nourishment he had promised? I was afraid to ask. I kept looking at the restaurant across the road in the hope that he might follow my gaze and take the hint, but his hands were sawing, hammering, pasting, and smoothing while his tongue wagged uninterruptedly. Having promised me nourishment, this man was not giving it a thought. Suppose I reminded him? But I lacked the courage to speak to him. With unappeased hunger on one side, my mind was also as busy as to how to retrieve my photo from this horrible man and find my way home. I had not noticed the landmarks while coming. There were so many lanes ending on Market Road. I was not sure which one of them would lead me to Kabir Street, and from Kabir Street should I go up or down? A well stood right in the middle of that street, and beside it the striped wall of an abandoned temple in which the tailor was supposed to live. One went past it and came through onto Vinayak Street somehow. Vinayak Street seemed such a distant dream to me now. Once some gracious god could put me down there, at either end, I could always find my way home. I was beginning to feel lost.

Jayraj paused for a moment to look at me and say, 'When I promise a time for delivery, I keep it.' Analysing his statement, I found no hint of anything to eat. 'When I promise a time. . . etc.' What of the promise of food? What did 'delivery' mean? Did it include eating? It was a worrying situation for me. I could not understand whether he implied that after delivering his picture to the bald man he would summon the restaurant-keeper and order a feast, or did he simply mean that in due course he would nail my photo on four sides with wood and glass and then say, 'That is all, now get out.' When I tried to declare, 'I am very hungry, are you doing anything about it? A promise is sacred and inescapable,' I found my voice croaking, creaking, and the words in such a jumble and mumble that it only attracted the other's attention and conveyed nothing. He looked up and asked,'Did you speak?'

He looked fierce under the kerosene 'power-light' hanging from the ceiling, and the huge shadow of its tin reflector left half the shop in darkness. I had no doubt that he enticed people in there, murdered them in cold blood, and stored their bodies in the anteroom. I remembered his mysterious references to the room, and my uncle had understood. The wonder was that Uncle should listen to all that and yet leave me behind. Of course, if it came to it, I could hit him with the little rod on the work-bench and run away. This was a testing time, and Uncle perhaps wanted to try me out; hadn't they agreed that little boys should become tough? If he asked me in I should take care not to cross the threshold—but if he ordered food, but kept it as a bait far inside and then said, 'Come in here and eat'—perhaps then I should make a dash for the food, hit him with the steel rod, and run—tactics to be accomplished at lightning speed. Perhaps my uncle expected me to perform such deeds, and would admire my pluck. Hit Jayraj on the head and run and munch while running. While my mind was busy working out the details of my retreat, I noticed that the man had risen to his feet and was rummaging among old paper and cardboard, stacked in the back room. When he stood up he looked lanky and tall, with long legs and long limbs as if he had uncoiled himself. Rather snake-like, I thought.

For a moment I was seized with panic at the prospect of combatting him. The bald man had edged closer and closer and had now actually stepped into the workshop, anticipating some excitement, the light from the power-lamp imparting a blinding lustre to his bald pate. Jayraj cried from the back room, 'Impossible to get at what one wants in this cursed place, must set apart a day for cleaning up. . . . Ah, here it is.' And he brought out a portrait in a grey mount, took it close to the light, and said, 'Come nearer, the print is rather faded.' They examined it with their heads abutting each other. I looked away. I realized that while they were brewing their nefarious plan I should remain alert but without giving them any sign of noticing. 'This is the man; at one time the richest doctor in Burma. . . .' I caught these words. Occasionally from time to time I turned my head just to look at them and caught them glancing at me and turning away. I too looked away, sharpening my ears not to miss a single word; somehow I was beginning to feel that their talk had something to do with me. Jayraj's loud and guffawing tone was all gone, he was now talking in a sinister undertone. 'Ten doctors employed under him. But this fellow was only a *chokra*; he sterilized needles and wrapped up powders and medicine bottles and cleansed the syringe; actually he must have started as this man's (tapping the photo) personal bootboy. When the Japanese bombed Rangoon, these people trekked back to our country, leaving behind their palatial home and several cars and everything, but still they managed to carry with them jewellery and much gold, and a bank account in Madras, and above all also a fifteen-day- old baby in arms. The doctor took ill and died on the way. There were rumours that he was pushed off a cliff by so-and-so. The lady reached India half dead, lingered for a year, and died. The baby was all right, so was the *chokra*, all through the expedition. The *chokra*, becoming all in all, took charge of all the cash and gold and bank accounts after reaching this country, impersonating the doctor. That poor woman, the doctor's wife, need not have died, but this fellow kept her a prisoner in the house and gave her some injections and finished her. The cremation was a double-quick affair across the river.'

The bald man now moved back to my side, Jayraj had resumed his seat and was working on a frame. I still kept fixedly looking away, feeling desperate at the prospect before me—a total darkness had now fallen on the city, and there was the hopelessness of getting any refreshment.

They continued their talk in conspiratorial tones all through. The bald man asked some question. Jayraj replied, 'Who could say? I didn't know much about them. I think that the fat woman must also have been there all the time and a party to it. I learnt a lot from a servant maid who brought this picture for framing one day. I told her to call for it next day. She never came. So far no sign of anyone claiming it.'

'The same fellow who sat here a little while ago!' said the bald man in astonishment.

Jayraj lowered his voice and muttered, 'When I called him "Doctor"—you must have seen his face!' and then they carried on their talk for a long while, which was all inaudible to me. I kept glancing at them and feeling their eyes on me all the time. Finally the tap-tap of the hammer ceased and he said, 'All right, this is finished. Let the glue dry a bit. Anyway it must be said to his credit: he tended the child and brought him up—only God knows the full truth.' He suddenly called me, held out to me the photograph salvaged from the dark chamber, and asked, 'Do you wish to take this home? I can give it to you free.' And they both stared at my face and the photo while he held it out. I had a momentary curiosity to look at the face of the man who had been the subject of their talk. The photo was very faded, I could glimpse only a moustache and little else; the man was in European clothes—if what they said was true, this was my father. I looked at their faces and noticed the sneering, leering expressions on them. I flung the photo back, got up without a word, and began to run.

I raced down Market Road, not aware of the direction I was taking. I heard the man shout after me, 'Come, come, I will frame yours and give it to you, and then take you home.' The bald man's squeaky voice added something to support his friend, but I ran. I bumped into people coming to the market and was cursed. 'Have you no eyes, these boys nowadays!' I feared Jayraj might shout, 'Catch him, don't let him get away.' Presently I slowed down my pace. I had no sense of direction but presently noticed Jagan's sweet-mart on my right-hand-side this time and knew that I was going back the way I had come. My head was drumming with Jayraj's speech. It was agonizing to picture my uncle cheating, murdering, and lying. The reference to my father and mother touched me less; they were remote, unconvincing figures.

Blundering and groping along, I reached the end of Market Road. People looked at me curiously. I did not want to betray that this was my first outing alone, and so sauntered along, tried to look casual, whistled and hummed aloud, '*Raghupati Raghava Raja Ram.*' The street lighting imperceptibly dimmed and grew sparser as I reached the foot of Lawley Statue. The Lawley Extension homes were tucked far back into their respective compounds, no way of knocking on their doors for any help; nor could I approach the boys leaning on their bicycles and chatting; they were senior boys who might make fun of me or beat me. A vagrant lay stretched full length on a side away from others; he looked wild and dreadful, but he kept looking at me while others would not even notice my presence. I shrank away at the foot of this terrible statue, hoping that it would not suddenly start moving and march over me. The vagrant held out his hand and said, 'Give me a coin, I will buy something to eat.'

I turned my shirt pocket inside out to prove my statement, 'I have no money, not a paisa, and I am also hungry.'

'Go home then,' he ordered.

'I want to, but where is Vinayak Street?'

It was a grave risk betraying myself in this manner; if he realized that I was a lost soul he might abduct and sell me upcountry as a slave. 'I will go with you and show the way, will you tell your mother to give me a little rice for my trouble?'

Mother! Mother! My mind fell into a confusion. . .of that woman who died at Uncle's hand. . . . I had all along felt my aunt was my mother. 'I have only an aunt, no mother,' I said.

'Aunts don't like me, and so go by yourself. Go back half the way you came, count three streets and turn on your left, if you know which is your left hand, and then turn right and you will be in Kabir Street. . . .'

'Oh, I know Kabir Street, and the well,' I said with relief.

'Get onto it then, and take the turning beyond the well for Vinayak Street, don't wander all over the town like this. Boys like you must stay at home and read your lessons.'

'Yes, sir,' I said respectfully, feeling intimidated. 'Once I am back I promise to read my lessons.'

The directions that he gave helped me. I came through and found myself at the disused well in Kabir Street. When I reached Vinayak Street I felt triumphant. In that feeling of relief even Jayraj's words ceased to rankle in my mind. The dogs in our street set up a stormy reception for me. At that hour the street was deserted, and the only guardians were the mongrels that roamed up and down in packs. They barked viciously at first but soon recognized me. Escorted by the friendly dogs, wagging their tails and wetting the lamp-posts in their delight at meeting me, I reached my house. My uncle and aunt were on the front doorstep and flung at me a jumble of inquiries. 'Your uncle wanted to start out again and look for you,' my aunt said.

Uncle lifted me practically half in the air in the sheer joy of our reunion, and asked, 'Where is the framer? He promised to leave you here. It is past ten o'clock now.'

Before I could answer my aunt said, 'I told you not to trust such persons.'

'Where is your photograph?'

I had not thought of an answer for that. What could I say? I only burst into tears and wept at the memory of all the confusion in my mind. Safer to weep than to speak. If I spoke I feared I might blunder into mentioning the other photo out of the darkroom.

My aunt immediately swept me in, remarking sorrowfully, 'Must be very, very hungry, poor child.'

I sobbed, 'He didn't give me anything to eat.'

All night I lay tossing in my bed. I kicked my feet against the wall and groaned, and woke up with a start from a medley of nightmares composed of the day's experience. My uncle was snoring peacefully in his room: I could see him through the open door. I sat up and watched him. He had impersonated a doctor, but it didn't seem to be a very serious charge, as I had always thought that all doctors with their rubber tubes and medical smell were play-acting all the time. Imprisoning and poisoning my mother—Mother? My aunt was my mother as far as I could see, and she was quite alive and sound. There wasn't even a faded photo of that mother as there was of my father. The photographer had said something about money and jewellery. I was indifferent to both. My uncle gave me all the money I needed, never refusing me anything at any time. Jewellery—those glittering pieces—one had better not bother about. You could not buy candy with gold, could you? To think that the refugees from Rangoon should have carried such tinsel all the way! In my own way I was analysing and examining the charges against my uncle and found them flimsy, although the picture of him emanating out of dark whispers and furtive glances, in the background of a half-lit back room, was shocking.

I needed some clarifications very urgently. My aunt, sleeping on her mat at the edge of the open courtyard, stirred. I made sure that Uncle's snores were continuing, softly rose from my bed, and went over to her side. I sat on the edge of her mat and looked at her. She had observed my restlessness and asked, 'Why haven't you slept yet?'

I whispered, 'Aunt, are you awake? I want to tell you something.'

She encouraged me to speak. I gave her an account of Jayraj's narrative. She merely said, 'Forget it. Never mention it to your uncle.'

'Why?'

'Don't ask questions. Go back to your bed and sleep.'

I could do nothing more. I took the advice. The next day Jayraj managed to deliver the framed photo through someone who passed this way. My uncle examined it inch by inch by the light from the courtyard, and declared, 'Wonderful, good work, worth three rupees, surely.' He fumbled about with a hammer and nail looking for the right place, and hung it finally over his easy chair, right below the big portrait of his ancestor on the wall.

I acted on my aunt's advice and never asked any question. As I grew up and met more people, I heard oblique references to my uncle here and there, but I ignored whatever I heard. Only once did I try to strangle a classmate at the college hostel in Madras who had gossiped about my uncle. Stirred by such information, sometimes I thought of him as a monster and I felt like pricking and deflating him the next time I met him. But when I saw him on the railway platform, waiting to receive me, the joy in his perspiring face moved me, and I never questioned him in any manner. After seeing me through the Albert Mission High School he had maintained me at a college in Madras; he wrote a postcard at least once a week, and celebrated my arrival during a vacation with continuous feasting at home. He had probably gambled away a lot more money than he had spent on me. It didn't matter. Nothing ever mattered. He never denied me anything. Again and again I was prompted to ask the question, 'What am I worth? What about my parents?' but I rigorously suppressed it. Thus I maintained the delicate fabric of our relationship till the very end of his life. After his death, I examined his records—not a shade of correspondence or account to show my connection with Burma, except the lacquered casket with a dragon on it. He had bequeathed the house and all his possessions and a small annuity in the bank to me and left my aunt in my care.

A BREATH OF LUCIFER

Prologue

Nature has so designed us that we are compelled to spend at least eight hours out of twenty-four with eyes shut in sleep or in an attempt to sleep. It is a compensatory arrangement, perhaps, for the strain the visual faculty undergoes during our waking hours, owing to the glut of images impinging upon it morning till night. One who seeks serenity should, I suppose, voluntarily restrict one's range of vision. For it is mostly through the eye that the mind is strained or disturbed. Man sees more than what is necessary or good for him. If one does not control one's vision, nature will do it for one sooner or later.

Unnoticed, little by little, my right eye had been growing dimmer in the course of a year or two. I felt annoyed by the presence of a smudge of oil on the lens of my spectacles, which I pulled out and wiped with a handkerchief every other minute. When I tried to read, the smudge appeared on the first line and travelled down line by line, and it also touched up the faces of friends and foes alike whenever I happened to examine a photograph. As I raised my eyes the blot also lifted itself upward. It grew in circumference. I couldn't watch a movie without noticing an unseemly mole on the star's much prized face. No amount of cleaning of my spectacle lens was any use.

My eye doctor, after a darkroom test, pronounced that the spot was not on my spectacle lens but in the God-given lens of the eye itself, which was losing its transparency. He recorded it for my comfort on a piece of paper as 'Lentil Opacity,' to be remedied by means of a simple operation in due course.

Everyone speaks of the simplicity of the operation. It's simple in the sense that it is painless, accomplished without bloodshed. But to the surgeon it is a delicate and responsible task, demanding the utmost concentration of his powers at his finger-tips, which will have to hover with the lightness of a butterfly over the patient's eye while detaching a tiny opalescent piece from its surface.

After the operation, total immobility in a state of total black-out for nearly a week, with both eyes sealed up with a bandage; not even the faintest ray of light may pass this barrier. The visual world is shut off. At first I dreaded the prospect. It seemed an inhuman condition of existence. But actually it turned out to be a novel experience. To observe nothing. To be oblivious of the traffic beneath my window, and of the variety of noise- makers passing up and down. I only hear the sound of the traffic but feel no irritation. Perhaps such irritations are caused as much by the sight of the irritant as by its decibel value. When you have no chance of observing the traffic, you cease to bother about it. A soundproof room may not be the only way to attain tranquillity—a bandage over one's eyes may achieve the same result. I never notice the weather, another source of despair, dismay, disappointment, or ecstasy for everyone at all times. I never know whether it is cloudy or sunny outside my window; when it rains I relish the patter of raindrops and the coolness without being aware of the slush and mess of a rain-sodden landscape. I am blissfully free alike from elation as from fury or despair. The joy stimulated by one experience could be as fatiguing as the despair caused by another. I hear words and accept them without any reservation as I am unaware of the accompanying facial expression or gesture which normally modulates the spoken word. In this state, in which one accepts the word absolutely, human relationships become suddenly simplified. For this same reason, I think the yogis of yore advocated as a first step (and a final step also) in any technique of self-development the unwavering concentration of one's eyes on the tip of one's nose. Mahatma Gandhi himself advised a youth whose heart was constantly agitated by the sight of women to walk with his eyes fixed on his toe, or on the stars above.

When the outside world is screened off thus, one's vision turns immediately inward. In the depths of one's being (according to the terms of philosophers and mystics) or in the folds of one's brain (according to physiologists or psychologists) there is a memory-spot for every faculty. 'Music when soft voices die, vibrates in the memory,' said Shelley. One can recollect the fragrance of a bygone flower or a perfume, the softness of a touch. Similarly there is a visual memory too, which revives in all its sharpness under some extraordinary stimulus. The visual memory brings forth not only something seen and cherished but also wished for. My interests, let me confess, broadly speaking, are archaeological and geological. All my life I have been excessively fond of rocks, monuments, and ancient sculptures. I can never pass by a rock formation indifferently, nor an old temple or a monument. So I now watch through my bandaged eyes night and day breath-taking cornices, pillars, and carvings, countless numbers of them, as on a slow moving platform, as if one were present at the stone-cluttered yard of a superhuman sculptor. Sometimes I see a goddess enthroned on a lotus seat in a corner, and not far from her is a formless slab smoothed out by time, but faint etchings, possibly edicts of some ancient emperor, are still visible on it. A closer scrutiny reveals that this whole setting is not actually a corner—there is no corner, no direction, east, west, south, or north; it is a spot without our familiar spatial relationships.

Strangely, my visual memory does not present to me any white walls or bright ceilings. Every surface is grey and ancient, as if centuries of the burning of lamps have left congealed layers of holy oil on every surface. Sometimes I am enmeshed in a jumble of chariot wheels, crowns without heads, maces, and fragments of a dilapidated throne; suddenly this jumble sorts itself out and forms into a single regal figure standing on its feet, spanning the ground and sky. Presently all this melts out of view. The floor is strewn with sawn-off timber, and a lot of grim metallic artifacts, perhaps the left-overs of an ancient torture chamber. A fantastic contrast occurs presently—an endless billowing stretch of tarpaulin or canvas envelops the whole landscape, such enormous billows that I wonder how I can take a step forward without getting enmeshed in them. Now I find myself in a corridor of an ageless cave-temple. Although I am supposed to remain in the dark I find a subdued, serene light illuminating every object and corner softly for me, a light that throws no shadow. Nothing looks fearsome or unpleasant. Everything is in harmony with everything else and has a pleasant quality all its own. Even an occasional specimen of fauna, a tiger in shape but with the face of an angel—it is not clear what creature is represented—smoothly glides past me, throwing a friendly smile at me.

Reality is of the moment and where we are. The immediate present possesses a convincing solid quality; all else is mere recollection or anticipation. This room with the bed on which I lie day and night is very real to me, with all the spectacle that passes before me; other things seem remote and dream-like. The present rhythm of my life is set by a routine from morning at six (as I guess from the hawkers' voices in the street), when I summon my attendant [*], till the night, when I am put to bed with the announcement by the

---

[*] Whose company and conversation have inspired me to write the accompanying story.

same attendant, 'Light is shut off, sir,' punctuated by the arrivals and departures of the doctors' team and visitors who bring me news of the unreal world in which they live. Within the confines of this existence I feel snug and contented. Its routines are of the utmost importance to me. I am so much at home within it that I suspect I shall feel a regret when it ends.

R.K. Narayan
March 1969

Sam was only a voice to me, a rich, reverberating baritone. His whispers themselves possessed a solid, rumbling quality. I often speculated, judging from his voice, what he might look like: the possessor of such a voice could be statuesque, with curls falling on his nape, Roman nose, long legs able to cover the distance from my bed to the bathroom in three strides although to me it seemed an endless journey. I asked him on the very first day, 'What do you look like?'

'How can I say? Several years since I looked at a mirror!'

'Why so?'

'The women at home do not give us a chance, that is all. I have even to shave without a mirror.' He added, 'Except once when I came up against a large looking-glass at a tailor's and cried out absent-mindedly, "Ah, Errol Flynn in town!"'

'You admired Errol Flynn?'

'Who wouldn't? As Robin Hood, unforgettable; I saw the picture fifty times.'

'What do you look like?'

He paused and answered, 'Next week this time you will see for yourself; be patient till the bandages are taken off. . . .'

Sam had taken charge of my bodily self the moment I was wheeled out of the operation theatre at the Malgudi Eye Clinic in New Extension with my eyes padded, bandaged, and sealed. I was to remain blindfolded for nearly a week in bed. During this confinement Sam was engaged for eight rupees a day to act as my eyes.

He was supposed to be a trained 'male nurse', a term which he abhorred, convinced that nursing was a man's job and that the female in the profession was an impostor. He assumed a defiant and challenging pose whenever the sister at the nursing home came into my room. When she left he always had a remark to make, 'Let this lady take charge of a skull-injury case; I will bet the patient will never see his home again.'

Sam had not started life as a male nurse, if one might judge from his references. He constantly alluded to military matters, commands, campaigns, fatigue duties, and parades. What he actually did in the army was never clear to me. Perhaps if I could have watched his facial expressions and gestures I might have understood or interpreted his words differently, but in my unseeing state I had to accept literally whatever I heard. He often spoke of a colonel who had discovered his talent and encouraged and trained him in nursing. That happened somewhere on the Burma border, Indo-China, or somewhere, when their company was cut off and the medical units completely destroyed. The colonel had to manage with a small band of survivors, the most active among them being Sam, who repaired and rehabilitated the wounded and helped them return home almost intact when the war ended. Which war was it? Where was it fought? Against whom? I could never get an answer to those questions. He always spoke of 'the enemy', but I never understood who it was since Sam's fluency could not be interrupted for a clarification. I had to accept what I heard without question. Before they parted, the colonel composed a certificate which helped Sam in his career. 'I have framed it and hung it in my house beside Jesus,' he said.

At various theatres of war (again, which war I could never know) his services were in demand, mainly in surgical cases. Sam was not much interested in the physician's job. He had mostly been a surgeon's man. He only spoke of incidents where he had to hold up the guts of someone until the surgeon arrived, of necks half severed, arms amputated, and all aspects of human disjointedness and pain handled without hesitancy or failure. He asserted, 'My two hands and ten fingers are at the disposal of anyone who needs them in war or peace.'

'What do you earn out of such service?' I asked.

He replied, 'Sometimes ten rupees a day, five, two, or nothing. I have eight children, my wife, and two sisters and a niece depending on me, and all of them have to be fed, clothed, sent to schools, and provided with books and medicines. We somehow carry on. God gives me enough. The greater thing for me is the relief that I am able to give anyone in pain. . . . Oh, no, do not get up so fast. Not good for you. Don't try to swat that mosquito buzzing at your ear. You may jam your eye. I am here to deal with that mosquito. Hands down, don't put up your hand near your eyes.' He constantly admonished me, ever anxious lest I should by some careless act suffer a setback.

He slept in my room, on a mat a few feet away from my bed. He said that he woke up at five in the morning, but it could be any time since I had no means of verifying his claim by a watch or by observing the light on the walls. Night and day and all days of the week were the same to me. Sam explained that although he woke up early he lay still, without making the slightest noise, until I stirred in bed and called,'Sam!'

'Good morning, sir,' he answered with alacrity and added, 'don't get up yet,' Presently he came over and tucked up the mosquito net with scrupulous care. 'Don't get up yet,' he ordered and moved off. I could hear him open the bathroom door. Then I noticed his steps move farther off as he went in to make sure that the window shutters were secure and would not fly open and hit me in the face when I got in and fumbled about. After clearing all possible impediments in my way, he came back and said, 'Righto, sir, now that place is yours, you may go in safely. Get up slowly. Where is the hurry? Now edge out of your bed, the floor is only four inches below your feet. Slide down gently, hold my hand, here it is. . . . ' Holding both my hands in his, he walked backward and led me triumphantly to the bathroom, remarking along the way,'The ground is level and plain, walk fearlessly. . . . '

With all the assurance that he attempted to give me, the covering over my eyes subjected me to strange tricks of vision and made me nervous at every step. I had a feeling of passing through geological formations, chasms, and canyons or billowing mounds of cotton wool, tarpaulin, or heaps of smithy junk or an endless array of baffle walls one beside another. I had to move with caution. When we reached the threshold of the bathroom he gave me precise directions: 'Now move up a little to your left. Raise your right foot, and there you are. Now you do anything here. Only don't step back. Turn on your heel, if you must. That will be fine.' Presently, when I called, he re-entered the bathroom with a ready compliment on his lips: 'Ah, how careful and clean! I wish some people supposed to be endowed with full vision could leave a W.C. as tidy! Often, after they have been in, the place will be fit to be burnt down! However, my business in life is not to complain but to serve.' He then propelled me to the washbasin and handed me the toothbrush. 'Do not brush so fast. May not be good for your eyes. Now stop. I will wash the brush. Here is the water for rinsing. Ready to go back?'

'Yes, Sam!'

He turned me round and led me back towards my bed. 'You want to sit on your bed or in the chair?' he asked at the end of our expedition. While I took time to decide, he suggested, 'Why not the chair? You have been in bed all night. Sometimes I had to mind the casualties until the stretcher-bearers arrived, and I always said to the boys, "Lying in bed makes a man sick, sit up, sit up as long as you can hold yourselves together." While we had no sofas in the jungle, I made them sit and feel comfortable on anything, even on a snake-hole once, after flattening the top.'

'Where did it happen? Did you say Burma?' I asked as he guided me to the cane chair beside the window.

He at once became cautious. 'Burma? Did I say Burma? If I mentioned Burma I must have meant it and not the desert—'

'Which campaign was it?'

'Campaign? Oh, so many. I may not remember. Anyway it was a campaign and we were there. Suppose I fetch you my diary tomorrow? You can look through it when your eyes are all right again, and you will find in it all the answers.'

'Oh! that will be very nice indeed.'

'The colonel gave me such a fat, leather-bound diary, which cost him a hundred rupees in England, before he left, saying, "Sam, put your thoughts into it and all that you see and do, and some day your children will read the pages and feel proud of you." How could I tell the colonel that I could not write or read too well? My father stopped my education when I was that high, and he devoted more time to teach me how to know good toddy from bad.'

'Oh, you drink?' I asked.

'Not now. The colonel whipped me once when he saw me drunk, and I vowed I'd never touch it again,' he added as an afterthought while he poured coffee for me from the Thermos flask (which he filled by dashing out to a coffee house in the neighbourhood; it was amazing with what speed he executed these exits and entrances, although to reach the coffee house he had to run down a flight of steps, past a veranda on the ground floor, through a gate beyond a drive, and down the street; I didn't understand how he managed it all as he was always present when I called him, and had my coffee ready when I wanted it). He handed me the cup with great care, guiding my finger around the handle with precision. While I sipped the coffee I could hear him move around the bed, tidying it up. 'When the doctor comes he must find everything neat. Otherwise

he will think that a donkey has been in attendance in this ward.'
He swept and dusted. He took away the coffee cup, washed it at
the sink and put it away, and kept the toilet flush hissing and
roaring by repeated pulling of the chain. Thus he set the stage for
the doctor's arrival. When the sound of the wheels of the bondage-
trolley was heard far off, he helped me back to my bed and stationed
himself at the door. When footsteps approached, the baritone
greeted: 'Good morning, Doctor sir.'

The doctor asked, 'How is he today?'

'Slept well. Relished his food. No temperature. Conditions normal, Doctor sir.' I felt the doctor's touch on my brow as he untied
the bandage, affording me for a tenth of a second, a blurred view
of assorted faces over me; he examined my eye, applied drops,
bandaged again, and left. Sam followed him out as an act of courtesy and came back to say, 'Doctor is satisfied with your progress. I
am happy it is so.'

Occasionally I thumbed a little transistor radio, hoping for some
music, but turned it off the moment a certain shrill voice came on
the air rendering 'film hits'; but I always found the tune continuing
in a sort of hum for a minute or two after the radio was put away.
Unable to judge the direction of the voice or its source, I used to feel
puzzled at first. When I understood, I asked, 'Sam, do you sing?'

The humming ceased. 'I lost practice long ago,' he said, and
added, 'when I was at Don Bosco's, the bishop used to encourage
me. I sang in the church choir, and also played the harmonium at
concerts. We had our dramatic troupe too and I played Lucifer.
With my eyebrows painted and turned up, and with a fork at my
tail, the bishop often said that never a better Lucifer was seen
anywhere; and the public appreciated my performance. In our
story the king was a good man, but I had to get inside him and
poison his nature. The princess was also pure but I had to spoil her
heart and make her commit sins.' He chuckled at the memory of
those days.

He disliked the nurse who came on alternate days to give me a
sponge bath. Sam never approved of the idea. He said, 'Why can't
I do it? I have bathed typhoid patients running one hundred and
seven degrees—'

'Oh, yes, of course.' I had to pacify him. 'But this is different, a
very special training is necessary for handling an eye patient.'

When the nurse arrived with hot water and towels he would
linger on until she said unceremoniously, 'Out you go, I am in a

hurry.' He left reluctantly. She bolted the door, seated me in a chair, helped me off with my clothes, and ran a steaming towel over my body, talking all the time of herself, her ambition in life to visit her brother in East Africa, of her three children in school, and so forth.

When she left I asked Sam, 'What does she look like?'

'Looks like herself all right. Why do you want to bother about her? Leave her alone. I know her kind very well.'

'Is she pretty?' I asked persistently, and added, 'at any rate I can swear that her voice is sweet and her touch silken.'

'Oh! Oh!' he cried. 'Take care!'

'Even the faint garlic flavour in her breath is very pleasant, although normally I hate garlic.'

'These are not women you should encourage,' he said. 'Before you know where you are, things will have happened. When I played Lucifer, Marie, who took the part of the king's daughter, made constant attempts to entice me whenever she got a chance. I resisted her stoutly, of course; but once when our troupe was camping out, I found that she had crept into my bed at night. I tried to push her off, but she whispered a threat that she would yell at the top of her voice that I had abducted her. What could I do with such a one!' There was a pause, and he added, 'Even after we returned home from the camp she pursued me, until one day my wife saw what was happening and gashed her face with her finger-nails. That taught the slut a lesson.'

'Where is Marie these days?' I asked.

He said, 'Oh! she is married to a fellow who sells raffle tickets, but I ignore her whenever I see her at the market gate helping her husband.'

When the sound of my car was heard outside, he ran to the window to announce, 'Yes, sir, they have come.' This would be the evening visit from my family, who brought me supper. Sam would cry from the window, 'Your brother is there and that good lady his wife also. Your daughter is there and her little son. Oh! what a genius he is going to be! I can see it in him now. Yes, yes, they will be here in a minute now. Let me keep the door open.' He arranged the chairs. Voices outside my door, Sam's voice overwhelming the rest with 'Good evening, madame. Good evening, sir. Oh! You little man! Come to see your grandfather! Come, come nearer and say hello to him. You must not shy away from him.' Addressing me, he would say, 'He is terrified of your beard, sir,' and, turning back to the boy, 'He will be all right when the bandage is taken off. Then he is going to have a shave and a nice bath, not the sponge bath he is now having, and then you will see how grand your grandfather can be!' He then gave the visitors an up-to-the-minute account of the state of my recovery. He would also throw in a faint complaint. 'He is not very cooperative. Lifts his hands to his eyes constantly, and will not listen to my advice not to exert.' His listeners would comment on this, which would provoke a further comment in the great baritone, the babble maddening to one not able to watch faces and sort out the speakers, until I implored, 'Sam, you can retire for a while and leave us. I will call you later'—thus giving me a chance to have a word with my visitors. I had to assume that he took my advice and departed. At least I did not hear him again until they were ready to leave, when he said, 'Please do not fail to bring the washed clothes tomorrow. Also, the doctor has asked him to eat fruits. If you could find apples—' He carried to the car the vessels brought by them and saw them off.

After their departure he would come and say, 'Your brother, sir, looks a mighty officer. No one can fool him, very strict he must be, and I dare not talk to him. Your daughter is devoted to you, no wonder, if she was motherless and brought up by you. That grandson! Watch my words, some day he is going to be like Nehru. He has that bearing now. Do you know what he said when I took him out for a walk? "If my grandfather does not get well soon I will shoot you."' And he laughed at the memory of that pugnacious remark.

We anticipated with the greatest thrill the day on which the bandages would be taken off my eyes. On the eve of the memorable day Sam said, 'If you don't mind, I will arrange a small celebration. This is very much like New Year Eve. You must sanction a small budget for the ceremony, about ten rupees will do. With your permission—' He put his hand in and extracted the purse from under my pillow. He asked for an hour off and left. When he returned I heard him place bottles on the table.

'What have you there?' I asked.

'Soft drinks, orange, Coca-Cola, this also happens to be my birthday. I have bought cake and candles, my humble contribution for this grand evening.' He was silent and busy for a while and then began a running commentary: 'I'm now cutting the cake, blowing out the candles—'

'How many?'

'I couldn't get more than a dozen, the nearby shop did not have more.'

'Are you only twelve years old?'

He laughed, handed me a glass. 'Coca-Cola, to your health. May you open your eyes on a happy bright world—'

'And also on your face!' I said. He kept filling my glass and toasting to the health of all humanity. I could hear him gulp down his drink again and again. 'What are you drinking?'

'Orange or Coca-Cola, of course.'

'What is the smell?'

'Oh, that smell! Someone broke the spirit lamp in the next ward.'

'I heard them leave this evening!'

'Yes, yes, but just before they left they broke the lamp. I assured them, "Don't worry, I'll clean up." That's the smell on my hands. After all, we must help each other—' Presently he distributed the cake and burst into a song or two: *'He's a jolly good fellow,'* and then, *'The more we are together—'* in a stentorian voice. I could also hear his feet tapping away a dance.

After a while I felt tired and said, 'Sam, give me supper. I feel sleepy.'

After the first spell of sleep I awoke in the middle of the night and called, 'Sam.'

'Yes, sir,' he said with alacrity.

'Will you lead me to the bathroom?'

'Yes, sir.' The next moment he was at my bed, saying, 'Sit up, edge forward, two inches down to your feet; now left, right, left, march, left, right, right turn.' Normally, whenever I described the fantastic things that floated before my bandaged eyes he would reply, 'No, no, no wall, nor a pillar. No junk either, trust me and walk on—' But today when I said, 'You know why I have to walk so slowly?'

'I know, I know,' he said, 'I won't blame you. The place is cluttered.'

'I see an immense pillar in my way,' I said.

'With carvings,' he added. 'Those lovers again. These two figures! I see them. She is pouting her lips, and he is trying to chew them off, with his arm under her thigh. A sinful spectacle, that's why I gave up looking at sculptures!'

I tried to laugh it off and said, 'The bathroom.'

'The bathroom, the bathroom, that is the problem. . . .' He paused and then said all of a sudden, 'The place is on fire.'

'What do you mean on fire?'

'I know my fire when I see one. I was Lucifer once. When I came on stage with fire in my nostrils, children screamed in the auditorium and women fainted. Lucifer has been breathing around. Let us go.' He took me by my hand and hurried me out in some direction.

On the veranda I felt the cold air of the night in my face and asked, 'Are we going out—?'

He would not let me finish my sentence. 'This is no place for us. Hurry up. I have a responsibility. I cannot let you perish in the fire.'

This was the first time I had taken a step outside the bedroom, and I really felt frightened and cried, 'Oh! I feel we are on the edge of a chasm or a cavern, I can't walk.' And he said, 'Softly, softly. Do not make all that noise. I see the tiger's tail sticking out of the cave.'

'Are you joking?'

He didn't answer but gripped my shoulder and led me on. I did not know where we were going. At the stairhead he commanded, 'Halt, we are descending, now your right foot down, there, there, good, now bring the left one, only twenty steps to go.' When I had managed it without stumbling, he complimented me on my smartness.

Now a cold wind blew in my face, and I shivered. I asked, 'Are we inside or outside?' I heard the rustle of tree leaves. I felt the gravel under my bare feet. He did not bother to answer my question. I was taken through a maze of garden paths, and steps. I felt bewildered and exhausted. I suddenly stopped dead in my tracks and demanded, 'Where are you taking me?' Again he did not answer. I said, 'Had we better not go back to my bed?'

He remained silent for a while to consider my proposal and agreed, 'That might be a good idea, but dangerous. They have mined the whole area. Don't touch anything you see, stay here, don't move, I will be back.' He moved off. I was seized with panic when I heard his voice recede. I heard him sing *'He's a jolly good fellow, He's a jolly good fellow,'* followed by *'Has she got lovely cheeks? Yes, she has lovely cheeks,'* which was reassuring as it meant that he was still somewhere around.

I called out, 'Sam.'

He answered from afar, 'Coming, but don't get up yet.'

'Sam, Sam,' I pleaded, 'let me get back to my bed. Is it really on fire?'

He answered, 'Oh, no, who has been putting ideas into your head? I will take you back to your bed, but please give me time to find the way back. There has been foul play and our retreat is cut off, but please stay still and no one will spot you.' His voice still sounded far off.

I pleaded desperately, 'Come nearer.' I had a feeling of being poised over a void. I heard his approaching steps.

'Yes, sir, what is your command?'

'Why have you brought me here?' I asked.

He whispered, 'Marie, she had promised to come, should be here any minute.' He suddenly cried out, 'Marie, where are you?' and mumbled, 'she came into your room last night and the night before, almost every night. Did she disturb you? No. She is such a quiet sort, you would never have known. She came in when I put out the light, and left at sunrise. You are a good officer, have her if you like.'

I could not help remarking, 'Didn't your wife drive her away?'

Promptly came his reply: 'None of her business. How dare she interfere in my affairs? If she tries. . . . ' He could not complete the sentence, the thought of his wife having infuriated him. He said, 'That woman is no good. All my troubles are due to her.'

I pleaded, 'Sam, take me to my bed.'

'Yes, sir,' he said with alacrity, took my hand, and led me a few steps and said, 'Here is your bed,' and gave me a gentle push down until I sank at my knee and sat on the ground. The stones pricked me, but that seemed better than standing on my feet. He said, 'Well, blanket at your feet. Call out "Sam", I am really not far, not really sleeping. . . . Good night, good night, I generally pray and then sleep, no, I won't really sleep. "Sam", one word will do, one word will do . . . will do. . . . ' I heard him snore, he was sound asleep somewhere in the enormous void. I resigned myself to my fate. I put out my hand and realized that I was beside a bush, and I only hoped that some poisonous insect would not sting me. I was seized with all sorts of fears.

The night was spent thus. I must have fallen into a drowse, awakened at dawn by the bird-noises around. A woman took my hand and said, 'Why are you here?'

'Marie?' I asked.

'No, I sweep and clean your room every morning, before the others come.'

I only said, 'Lead me to my bed.'

She did not waste time on questions. After an endless journey she said, 'Here is your bed, sir, lie down.'

I suffered a setback, and the unbandaging was postponed. The doctor struggled and helped me out of a variety of ailments produced by shock and exposure. A fortnight later the bandages were taken off, but I never saw Sam again. Only a postcard addressed to the clinic several days later:

I wish you a speedy recovery. I do not know what happened that night. Some foul play, somewhere. That rogue who brought me the Coca-Cola must have drugged the drink. I will deal with him yet. I pray that you get well. After you go home, if you please, send me a money-order for Rs 48. I am charging you for only six days and not for the last day. I wish I could meet you, but my colonel has summoned me to Madras to attend on a leg amputation—Sam.

IV: ESSAYS

Editor's note: Let Narayan speak for himself. Making a case for the subjective or personal essay, as he calls it, he has said that it was enjoyable 'because it had the writer's likes, dislikes, and his observations, always with a special flavour of humour, sympathy, aversion, style, charm, and even oddity.' He got into the business of writing such essays, because he 'had to. . . . I had to write to meet a deadline every Thursday in order to fill half a column for the Sunday issue of the *Hindu*. I had rashly undertaken this task not (to be honest) for artistic reasons, but to earn a regular income. Three of my novels had already been published but they had brought me recognition rather than income. I had approached the editor of the *Hindu* for help, and he had immediately accepted my proposal for a weekly piece. I had not the ghost of an idea what I was going to do. As he had left me to do anything I wanted within my column I started writing, trusting to luck; somehow I managed to fill the column for nearly twenty years without a break.' What we can add to this rather bland statement is that his ability in this regard not unexpectedly developed and matured until he was writing long and extended pieces, improvised not for a Thursday but carefully planned and worked out. The selection here includes some of his best efforts in this genre, reflecting both his sense of humour and his ability to go to the root of the matter.

A WRITER'S NIGHTMARE

A few nights ago I had a nightmare. I had become a citizen of a strange country called Xanadu. The Government all of a sudden announced the appointment of an officer called the controller of stories. All the writers in the country sent up a memorandum to their representative in Parliament, and he asked at the new session of the house: 'May we know why there is a new department called the controller of stories?'

From the Government benches came the answer: 'Through an error in our Government printing section five tons of forms intended for the controller of *stores* were printed controller of *stories*, an unwanted "i" having crept into the text. Consequently the Government was obliged to find a use for all this printed stuff.'

'What sort of use?' asked the member.

'Since the stationery was inadvertently ready a department of stories was started.'

'Was a new incumbent entertained for the post of controller of stories and, if so, will the Honourable Minister quote the public service commission circular in this regard; what is the cost of this post and where are you going to get the money for it and under what head is it going to be charged and who will be the deciding authority and will you place on the table a copy of the auditor-general's remark in this regard?' went on the Parliament member, trying to get the Minister into an entanglement of linked-up questions. The Minister was familiar with such tactics and curtly replied, 'The answer to A is in the negative, B the Government is watching the situation, C the question does not arise, D see B, E, it will not be in public interest to answer the question at present. . . . ' He spoke so fast, without a pause, that the questioner got derailed and lost track of his own questions. Undaunted, he asked again, 'Will the Honourable Minister explain if this is in keeping with the Government's recent economy drive?'

'The answer is in the affirmative.'

'Will he kindly explain himself?'

'Yes. In the first place we have managed to utilize a vast quantity of printed paper. Anyone who is familiar with the world shortage in paper will appreciate this move, and in the second place there is no extra expenditure involved in starting this department since the controller of stores will be *ex officio* controller of stories and will generally conduct the affairs of this department, for after all stories are also stores in a manner of speaking.'

'May we know the why and how and what-about-what and wherefore of this department?'

'I am glad to have an opportunity to speak on this issue. The Government is becoming increasingly aware of the importance of stories in our national life. Since this is a welfare state the Government is obliged to keep a watch over all the activities that affect our citizens. It has come to our notice recently that sufficient attention is not being paid by the authors in this country to the subject of story. The Government has observed that next to rice and water, stories are the most-demanded stuff in daily life. . . . Every moment someone or other is always asking for a story. It may be a child asking his teacher or a novel-reader his author or a magazine-buyer his editor or a film producer who has spent lakhs and lakhs and has every equipment ready except a story, and of course all our radio stations and theatres, too, demand stories. The demand is far in excess of supply, and may I add even where a story is seen it turns out to be deplorably bad stuff? The Government has made up its mind that they will not tolerate bad stories any more.'

At this point the question-master interrupted with, 'May we know what is meant by bad stories? Will the Honourable Minister quote instances?'

'No. I cannot mention any specific bad stories at this juncture, since that would lead to the suspicion that invidious distinctions are being made, but I would like to point out that bad stories are stories that are not good, and our honourable friend must be satisfied with it for the moment.'

'May we know how this department is to function?' asked the member.

'Presently, the controller of stories will undertake the formation of a body called the Central Story Bureau which will immediately go into the business of formation of a Chief Story Officer for each state.'

'May we know what it will have to do with the story writers in the country?'

'Every story writer must fill up Form A, obtain a local treasury certificate for ten rupees, and forward both to the Central Story Bureau (general branch), and he will receive an endorsement entitling him to call himself a registered story writer. Thereafter, whenever he has an inspiration for a story, long or short, he will have to send a synopsis of it in quadruplicate to the C.S. Bureau (technical branch), and obtain its approval before proceeding to expand the work further.'

'Why should it be in quadruplicate?'

'For facilitating procedure. The Central Story Bureau (technical branch) will consist of four directorates, one each for plot, character, atmosphere and climax and each section will examine the proposed story in respect of its own jurisdiction and may suggest emendations and improvements in respect of the story before issuing a final authorization certificate to the author which must be prominently displayed in his study. Any author, who attempts to write a story without proper authorization will be fined five hundred rupees and imprisoned for a period not exceeding eighteen months. . . . The Government has every desire to avoid these extreme measures, its sole aim being improvement of national culture and we have every hope that all this will bring about a revolution in story writing within the next ten years. Incidentally I wish to inform the house that we are presently inaugurating a national story week which will see the birth of a write-better- stories movement all over the country. . . .' He concluded, 'All this is in the nature of an effort on the part of the Government for improving the standard of story writing in this country. We shall watch the results, and let me say,' here he raised his voice, 'let me warn all bad story writers that I shall not hesitate to smash their ink bottles. We don't want bad stories in this country in any form. We shall watch the situation and see how it develops, and if writers fail to show any improvement, which we shall be in a position to judge from the quarterly reports submitted by the regional story officer, I have no hesitation in saying that we, on this side of the house, will take to story writing ourselves. . . .'

And, at this stage, I woke up.

THE RELUCTANT GURU

When I accepted an invitation to become a Visiting Professor at a certain mid-Western University, I had had no clear notion as to what it meant. I asked myself again and again what does a Visiting Professor do. I also asked several of my friends in the academic world the same question. No one could give me a concrete or a convincing answer and so I contented myself with the thought that a Visiting Professor just visits and professes and if he happens to be in the special category of 'D.V.P.' (Distinguished Visiting Professor) he also tries to maintain and flourish his distinguishing qualities. Well, all that seemed to suit me excellently.

I had plunged into the role after warning my sponsors in the initial stages of our correspondence that I was a mere novice in academic matters and that it'd be up to them to see that I did not make a fool of myself on their campus. So, on the first morning, I reported myself at the English Department of the University. The Chairman of the Department who had arranged my visit was a distinguished scholar and critic, who, among other things, had also made a detailed, deep study of my writing.

I asked him what I should do now and he kept asking in his turn what I would like to do, the only definite engagement for the day he was aware of being that I was to be photographed at two o'clock. I sat brooding.

'Yesterday this time, Bangalore. . . Bombay. . . Rome. . . . London. . . New York. . . or was it the day before? Time gets lost in space.' I was still jet-dazed after thirty-six hours in the air.

He called up his secretary and told her, 'Here is Narayan. Please give him a room where he can feel comfortable, meet people or read or write as he may like. Please also find out if any of the English classes want him, and schedule his visits.' So on the first day I had nothing much to do except pose outside the building for a photographer against the signpost announcing 'English Dept'.

Most of the days following, I was left free to walk, think, or read and generally live as I pleased.

The secretary busied herself and ultimately produced a timetable for me. She would telephone me in my room to say, '11.35 tomorrow, Professor——'s class at——hall——'

'Where is it?' I would ask, slightly worried how to locate it in this vast sprawling campus and reach it in time, punctuality being my nightmare.

'It's on 52nd and anyway you don't bother about it. A car will come to fetch you.' She arranged it all with precision and forethought, not demanding more than a couple of hours a week of my time in the coming weeks.

On stepping into my very first class I felt startled, as it consisted of elderly women, each one holding a copy of *The Guide* in her hand.

I was pleased no doubt at finding my book in so many hands, but I also felt uneasy. If they cross-examined me on my book, I should feel lost; they had the advantage over me of being up-to-date with the details of my story. I stiffened into a defensive attitude, and became wary, as I took my seat.

I was also struck with their enthusiasm—elderly women who doubtless had their families, homes, children and grandchildren (one member was eighty-six years old) to mind, but who still found the time to take a seat in a classroom and study English literature, which was how my book was classified.

I sat wondering where to begin and what to say. But luckily for me their regular professor who had fetched me, eased the situation with an introductory speech, and straightaway invited the members of the class to ask questions. This is always a good method as it gives an audience something to do instead of sitting back, passively watching the speaker's predicament. One member asked as usual whether I had based my novel on some actual experience or if it was pure fiction. A familiar question, which I generally answer evasively, since I myself do not know; and also I don't see how it should make any difference to the reader. Next question was if the town Malgudi (the setting of my novels) was imaginary or real. I played the ball back by asking what was the difference between the two. Next I was asked if India was full of saints, and whether the hero of *The Guide*, who is mistaken for a saint, and later compelled to become one, was typical, and if my novel itself was 'typical' of India (Typical—did it imply that my readers expect the majority of the 550 million citizens of India [as it was over a decade ago] to go through a phase similar to the one portrayed in my novel?) I had to repeat here, and later, everywhere that a novel is about an individual living his life in a world imagined by the author, performing a set of actions (up to a limit) contrived by the author. But to take a work of fiction as a sociological study or a social document could be very misleading. My novel *The Guide* was not about the saints or the pseudo-saints of India, but about a particular person. I do not think that my explanation carried any conviction as they continued to ask in every class, outside the class, at the quadrangle, the University centre, the roadside or anywhere, the same question. Added to this the city newspaper took a special interest in my visit and featured me and my work. A reporter interviewed me, and tried to elicit my views of life after death, which happened to be the theme of my novel *The English Teacher* (known in the U.S. as *Grateful to Life and Death*). I was asked if I believed in death. I was asked if I thought it possible to communicate with spirits. I was asked if I had seen a ghost, if I was prone to mystic experience. I answered the questions candidly, emphasizing the fact that I wrote fiction. When the interview appeared in the paper I found it charmingly written but over-emphasizing my mystic aspect! This led to a very complex situation for me during the rest of my sojourn on that campus. More and more people began to ask, 'Do you believe in mysticism?' 'Can anyone practise yoga?' 'What are the steps to a mystic state?' The words—mysticism, metaphysics, philosophy, yoga and ghost contacts—all came to be mixed up. At first it was amusing but day after day when I found people on the campus looking on me with awe and wonder, perhaps saying to themselves, 'There goes the man who holds the key to a mystic life!' I began to despair how I could ever rise to that sublime level. Apart from the students, I realized that even some of the staff members were affected by this notion. A senior professor of the English Department approached me once to ask if I would meet her students. I agreed, since that was the purpose of my sojourn on the campus. Nearer the time of the actual engagement, I met her again to work out the details. 'What am I expected to do in your class?' I asked.

She replied promptly, 'My students want to hear you on Indian mysticism.'

I told her point blank, 'I know nothing about it.'

'That shouldn't matter at all,' she said.

'Of course it matters a great deal to me. When I go to a class I should like to speak on a subject which I know or at least have a pretence of knowing. I do not wish to parade my ignorance in a classroom.'

She seemed to think that it was an extraordinary piece of diffidence on my part and said encouragingly, 'Please, half an hour will be enough. You can tell them anything you like about mysticism, just for thirty minutes.'

'Not even for half a minute. Why did you commit me to this engagement?'

Her answer was startling. 'Because they have demanded it. They want you to talk on Indian mysticism.'

Two points emerged from this conversation:

(1) The word 'demand' arising from the students' side as to what was to be taught. (2) Mysticism.

These were the real pivotal points on which the entire academic situation seemed to revolve. I heard later that the students' representatives met the faculty members in order to specify what they wished to be taught in the classrooms. They wanted to brighten up (and also broaden) English literary studies, with a lot of interesting, though not relevant, additions to their reading lists. This was the basis of their demand for Indian mysticism from me. I had a chance to observe how some teachers were trying to rise to the occasion. I knew a couple of young men from India, doing their post-graduate course in English, also holding assistantships, who spoke on a different theme each day to their students. One day it'd be Fitzgerald's translation of *Omar Khayyam,* another day Ramakrishna, or Vivekananda, a third day on yoga or the theory of incarnation, a fourth day on Buddhism, and on the fifth back to English literature. It was amazing with what agility they managed all this, while the seniors pored over 'black literature' and tried to include it in their talks, discussions and seminars. In all this process there was an apparent widening of knowledge, but it actually produced shallowness. I could not help wondering if all this show of adaptability and resilience on the part of the teacher was not creating an amorphous, diffuse academic climate and if they were not becoming responsible for creating a set of hollow minds, echoing the mere sound of book titles, and regarding themselves as being versatile. Finally I questioned them, how in such a world of hotchpotch studies any examination could be conducted. I realized immediately that I was sounding hopelessly antiquated, as promptly came the reply that the examinee could frame his own questions and write the answers. I did not know if this was a universal practice or only peculiar to this University. Or if this particular Indian lecturer was joking about it. In any case, I found that these two young men were extremely popular. One of them grew a tiny beard and the other left untended his nape-draping tresses, and both looked and sounded so convincing as versatile semi-(demi)-mystics that they were keenly sought after by their students. Their weekends were crowded with social activities, in addition to a regular schedule of dating. I asked, 'What is dating? How far does one go?'

'It depends, anything from sitting around eating and drinking to making love,' came the reply.

I asked, 'What of the responsibilities after dating?'

They replied, 'None. I and my friend have decided not to go steady under any circumstances, but marry only in India after we get back.' I visited their apartment and found it bare, with a few rolls of mat on the floor; and books all over the place. I suppose there was an aroma of incense. One of them constantly said, 'I am much interested in yoga and am teaching my boys yoga.'

I asked him, 'Have you studied Patanjali's *Yoga Sutra?*'

He looked a little bewildered and said, 'Not yet but I will. . . . ' He finally said, 'What does it matter what I read or teach? Whatever book I may recommend they will read only Vatsyayana's *Kama-Sutra*. The campus book store can hardly keep up with the demand, boys and girls devour this book and seem to know nothing else about India, nor care.'

Whether through *Kama-Sutra* or mysticism, India is very much in everybody's thoughts, particularly among the American youth. And this was not a passing phase or a mere affectation. I realized presently that there was much validity in this search and I met many young men here and there, invited them to my room, and answered their questions about India. I give here a composite report of my talk to various persons at different times:

Young friend (I said), perhaps you think that all Indians are spiritually preoccupied. We aren't, we have a large background of religion and plenty of inner resources, but normally we also have to be performing ordinary tasks, such as working, earning, living and breeding. In your view, perhaps, you think that in an Indian street, you can see bearded men floating about in a state of levitation. Far from it. We have traffic, crowds, shops, pimps, pickpockets, policemen and what-not as in any other country. We have our own students' agitations—but they are for different causes, sometimes political, sometimes personal and sometimes academic, and sometimes inexplicable. Your opposite number in our country would not be wearing beads and beards and untouched long hair as you do (how smartly your Barbers' Association withdrew a rather rash resolution to increase the rate for a haircut—from 2.50 to 3 dollars!), but tight pants and coloured shirts and 'Beatles' crop-cut. The

Indian student would not normally bother about eternity, but about his immediate employment prospects after graduation. You have to realize that unemployment among the educated classes is a grim reality in our country; and a young person has to overcome this deficiency before aspiring for the luxuries of a mystic state. Of course, you are fed up with affluence, gadgets, mobility and organization, and he is fed up with poverty, manual labour, stagnation and disorganization. Your search is for a 'guru' who can promise you instant mystic elation; whereas your counterpart looks for a Foundation Grant. The young person in my country would sooner learn how to organize a business or manufacture an atom bomb or an automobile than how to stand on one's head.

As a matter of fact, if you question him, you will find that our young man has not given any serious thought to yoga and such subjects. Perhaps at a later date he may take to it when his more materialistic problems are over and when he begins to note that it's quite the fashion in your part of the world. At the moment the trend appears to be that he is coming in your direction, and you are going in his. So, logically speaking, in course of time, you may have to come to India for technology and the Indian will have to come to your country for spiritual research.

The belief in my spiritual adeptness was a factor that could not be easily shaken. I felt myself in the same situation as Raju, the hero of my *Guide* who was mistaken for a saint and began to wonder at some point himself if a sudden effulgence had begun to show in his face. I found myself in a similar situation. My telephone rang at five o'clock one morning and I scrambled out of my bed. The man at the other end announced himself as a scientist, a research scholar, and said, 'Do you know what has happened today? The Chairman of our department summoned us and announced that he was not going to renew our assistantships next term, which may mean that I cut short my stay and return to India. Do you know if this will happen?' I could not understand what he was saying or why. I even wondered if I might be listening to a telephone in a dream!

'How should I know,' I asked and added, 'but my immediate curiosity is to know why you have thought fit to call me at this hour?'

He answered, ' Don't you get up at four for your meditations? I thought that at this hour, you'd be in a state of mind to know the future.'

Evidently this scientist had caught the general trend in the atmosphere. While I could appreciate an average American's notion that every Indian was a mystic, I was rather shocked in this instance, since I expected an Indian himself to know better. But here was this young man from India convinced that I was an astrologer and mystic combined. He dogged my steps. Although he gave up calling me at dawn, he followed me about with requests to impart to him the secrets of my attainments, to show him the way, to tell him whether he was destined to get his doctorate, whether his wife's impending confinement (in India) would be safely gone through and so on and so forth. Actually, after lunch one afternoon, he took me aside to ask, 'What should I do to get a glimpse of Goddess Kali? Will she appear before me?' in the tone of one who was trying to know the T.V. channel on which a particular show would be coming. When I denied any knowledge of it myself, he just looked pained, but he also looked determined to get at me ultimately when he would gather in both hands all the secrets of meditation, astrology, and spiritual powers that I now kept away from him, for reasons best known to a 'guru' of my stature.

MISGUIDED 'GUIDE'

The letter came by airmail from Los Angeles. 'I am a producer and actor from Bombay,' it read, ' I don't know if my name is familiar to you.'

He was too modest. Millions of young men copied his screen image, walking as he did, slinging a folded coat over the shoulder carelessly, buffing up a lock of hair over the right temple, and assuming that the total effect would make the girls sigh with hopeless longing. My young nephews at home were thrilled at the sight of the handwriting of Dev Anand.

The letter went on to say; 'I was in London and came across your novel *The Guide*. I am anxious to make it into a film. I can promise you that I will keep to the spirit and quality of your writing. My plans are to make both a Hindi and an English film of this story.' He explained how he had arranged with an American film producer for collaboration. He also described how he had flown from London to New York in search of me, since someone had told him I lived there, and then across the whole continent before he could discover my address. He was ready to come to Mysore if I should indicate the slightest willingness to consider his proposal.

I cabled him an invitation, already catching the fever of hurry characteristic of the film world. He flew from Los Angeles to Bombay to Bangalore, and motored down a hundred miles without losing a moment.

A small crowd of autograph-hunters had gathered at the gate of my house in Yadava Giri. He expertly eluded the inquisitive crowd, and we were soon closeted in the dining-room, breakfasting on idli, dosai, and other South Indian delicacies, my nephews attending on the star in a state of elation. The talk was all about *The Guide* and its cinematic merits. Within an hour we had become so friendly that he could ask without embarrassment, 'What price will you demand for your story?' The cheque-book was out and the pen poised over it. I had the impression that if I had suggested that the entire face of the cheque be covered with closely knit figures, he would have obliged me. But I hemmed and hawed, suggested a slight advance, and told him to go ahead. I was sure that if the picture turned out to be a success he would share with me the glory and the profits. 'Oh, certainly,' he affirmed, 'if the picture, by God's grace, turns out to be a success, we will be on top of the world, and the sky will be the limit!'

The following months were filled with a sense of importance: Long Distance Calls, Urgent Telegrams, Express Letters, sudden arrivals and departures by plane and car. I received constant summonses to be present here or there. 'PLEASE COME TO DELHI. SUIT RESERVED AT IMPERIAL HOTEL. URGENTLY NEED YOUR PRESENCE.'

Locking away my novel-in-progress, I fly to Delhi. There is the press conference, with introductions, speeches and overflowing conviviality. The American director explains the unique nature of their present effort: for the first time in the history of Indian movie-making, they are going to bring out a hundred-per-cent- Indian story, with a hundred-per-cent-Indian cast, and a hundred- per-cent-Indian setting, for an international audience. And mark this: actually in colour-and-wide-screen-first-time-in-the- history-of-this-country.

A distinguished group of Americans, headed by the Nobel Prize winner, Pearl Buck, would produce the film. Again and again I heard the phrase: 'Sky is the limit', and the repeated assurances: 'We will make the picture just as Narayan has written it, with his co-operation at every stage.' Reporters pressed me for a statement. It was impossible to say anything but the pleasantest things in such an atmosphere of overwhelming optimism and good fellowship.

Soon we were assembled in Mysore. They wanted to see the exact spots which had inspired me to write *The Guide*. Could I show them the locations? A photographer, and some others whose business with us I never quite understood, were in the party. We started out in two cars. The American director, Tad Danielewski, explained that he would direct the English version first. He kept discussing with me the finer points of my novel. 'I guess your hero is a man of impulsive plans? Self-made, given to daydreaming?' he would ask, and add, before I could muster an answer, 'am I not right?' Of course he had to be right. Once or twice when I attempted to mitigate his impressions, he brushed aside my comments and went on with his own explanation as to what I must have had in mind when I created such-and-such a character.

I began to realize that monologue is the privilege of the film-maker, and that it was futile to try butting in with my own observations. But for some obscure reason, they seemed to need my presence, though not my voice. I must be seen and not heard.

We drove about 300 miles that day, during the course of which I showed them the river steps and a little shrine overshadowed by a banyan on the banks of Kaveri, which was the actual spot around which I wrote *The Guide*. As I had thought, nothing more needed to be done than put the actors there and start the camera. They uttered little cries of joy at finding a 'set' so readily available. In the summer, when the river dried up, they could shoot the drought scenes with equal ease. Then I took them to the tiny town of Nanjangud, with its little streets, its shops selling sweets and toys and ribbons, and a pilgrim crowd bathing in the holy waters of the Kabini, which flowed through the town. The crowd was colourful and lively around the temple, and in a few weeks it would increase a hundredfold when people from the surrounding villages arrived to participate in the annual festival—the sort of crowd described in the last pages of my novel. If the film-makers made a note of the date and sent down a cameraman at that time, they could secure the last scene of my novel in an authentic manner and absolutely free of cost.

The producer at once passed an order to his assistant to arrange for an outdoor unit to arrive here at the right time. Then we all posed at the portals of the ancient temple, with arms encircling each other's necks and smiling. This was but the first of innumerable similar scenes in which I found myself posing with the starry folk, crushed in the friendliest embrace.

From Nanjangud we drove up mountains and the forests and photographed our radiant smiles against every possible background. It was a fatiguing business on the whole, but the American director claimed that it was nothing to what he was used to. He generally went 5,000 miles in search of locations, exposing hundreds of rolls of film on the way.

After inspecting jungles, mountains, village streets, hamlets and huts, we reached the base of Gopalaswami Hill in the afternoon, and drove up the five-mile mud track; the cars had to be pushed up the steep hill after encroaching vegetation had been cleared from the path. This was a part of the forest country where at any bend of the road one could anticipate a tiger or a herd of elephants; but, luckily for us, they were out of view today.

At the summit I showed them the original of the 'Peak House' in my novel, a bungalow built fifty years ago, with glassed-in verandas affording a view of wildlife at night, and a 2,000-foot drop to a valley beyond. A hundred yards off, a foot-track wound through the undergrowth, leading on to an ancient temple whose walls were crumbling and whose immense timber doors moved on rusty hinges with a groan. Once again I felt that here everything was ready-made for the film. They could shoot in the bright sunlight, and for the indoor scenes they assured me that it would be a simple matter to haul up a generator and lights.

Sitting under a banyan tree and consuming sandwiches and lemonade, we discussed and settled the practical aspects of the expedition: where to locate the base camp and where the advance units consisting of engineers, mechanics, and truck drivers, in charge of the generator and lights. All through the journey back the talk involved schedules and arrangements for shooting the scenes in this part of the country. I was impressed with the ease they displayed in accepting such mighty logistical tasks. Film executives, it seemed to me, could solve mankind's problems on a global scale with the casual confidence of demi-gods, if only they could take time off their illusory pursuits and notice the serious aspects of existence.

Then came total silence, for many weeks. Finally I discovered that they were busy searching for their locations in Northern India.

This was a shock. I had never visualized my story in that part of India, where costumes, human types and details of daily life are different. They had settled upon Jaipur and Udaipur in Rajaputana, a thousand miles away from my location for the story.

Our next meeting was in Bombay, and I wasted no time in speaking of this problem. 'My story takes place in South India, in Malgudi, an imaginary town known to thousands of my readers all over the world,' I explained. 'It is South India in costume, tone and contents. Although the whole country is one, there are diversities, and one has to be faithful in delineating them. You have to stick to my geography and sociology. Although it is a world of fiction there are certain inner veracities.'

One of them replied: 'We feel it a privilege to be doing your story.' This sounded irrelevant as an answer to my statement.

We were sitting under a gaudy umbrella beside a blue swimming pool on Juhu beach, where the American party was housed in princely suites in a modern hotel. It was hard to believe that we were in India. Most of our discussions took place somewhat amphibiously, on the edge of the swimming pool, in which the director spent a great deal of his time.

This particular discussion was interrupted as a bulky European tourist in swimming briefs fell off the diving plank, hit the bottom and had to be hauled out and rendered first aid. After the atmosphere had cleared, I resumed my speech. They listened with a mixture of respect and condescension, evidently willing to make allowances for an author's whims.

'Please remember,' one of them tried to explain, 'that we are shooting, for the first time in India, in wide screen and Eastman Colour, and we must shoot where there is spectacle. Hence Jaipur.'

'In that case,' I had to ask, 'why all that strenuous motoring near my home? Why my story at all, if what you need is a picturesque spectacle?'

I was taken aback when their reply came! 'How do you know that Malgudi is where you think it is?'

Somewhat bewildered, I said, with what I hoped was proper humility, 'I suppose I know because I have imagined it, created it and have been writing novel after novel set in the area for the last thirty years.'

'We are out to expand the notion of Malgudi,' one of them explained. 'Malgudi will be where we place it, in Kashmir, Rajasthan, Bombay, Delhi, even Ceylon.'

I could not share the flexibility of their outlook or the expanse of their vision. It seemed to me that for their purpose a focal point was unnecessary. They appeared to be striving to achieve mere optical effects.

I recalled a talk with Satyajit Ray, the great director, some years earlier, when I met him in Calcutta. He expressed his admiration for *The Guide* but also his doubts as to whether he could ever capture the tone and atmosphere of its background. He had said, 'Its roots are so deep in the soil of your part of our country that I doubt if I could do justice to your book, being unfamiliar with its milieu. . . .' Such misgivings did not bother the American director. I noticed that though he was visiting India for the first time, he never paused to ask what was what in this bewildering country.

Finally he solved the whole problem by declaring, 'Why should we mention where the story takes place? We will avoid the name "Malgudi."' Thereafter the director not only avoided the word Malgudi but fell foul of anyone who uttered that sound.

My brother, an artist who has illustrated my stories for twenty-five years, tried to expound his view. At a dinner in his home in

Bombay, he mentioned the forbidden word to the director. Malgudi, he explained, meant a little town, not so picturesque as Jaipur, of a neutral shade, with characters wearing dhoti and *jibba* when they were not bare bodied. The Guide himself was a man of charm, creating history and archaeology out of thin air for his clients, and to provide him with solid, concrete monuments to talk about would go against the grain of the tale. The director listened and firmly said, 'There is no Malgudi, and that is all there is to it.'

But my brother persisted. I became concerned that the controversy threatened to spoil our dinner. The director replied, in a sad tone, that they could as well have planned a picture for black and white and narrow screen if all one wanted was what he contemptuously termed a 'Festival Film', while he was planning a million-dollar spectacle to open simultaneously in 2,000 theatres in America. I was getting used to arguments everyday over details. My story is about a dancer in a small town, an exponent of the strictly classical tradition of South Indian Bharat Natyam. The film-makers felt this was inadequate. They therefore engaged an expensive, popular dance director with a troupe of a hundred or more dancers, and converted my heroine's performances into an extravaganza in delirious, fruity colours and costumes. Their dancer was constantly travelling hither and thither in an Air India Boeing no matter how short the distance to be covered. The moviegoer, too, I began to realize, would be whisked all over India. Although he would see none of the countryside in which the novel was set, he would see the latest U.S. Embassy building in New Delhi, Parliament House, the Ashoka Hotel, the Lake Palace, Elephanta Caves and what-not. Unity of place seemed an unknown concept for a film-maker. (Later Mrs Indira Gandhi, whom I met after she had seen a special showing of the film, asked, 'Why should they have dragged the story all over as if it were a travelogue, instead of containing themselves to the simple background of your book?' She added as an afterthought, and in what seemed to me an understatement: 'Perhaps they have other considerations.')

The co-operation of many persons was needed in the course of the film-making, and anyone whose help was requested had to be given a copy of *The Guide*. Thus there occurred a shortage, and an inevitable black market, in copies of the book. A production executive searched the bookshops in Bombay, and cornered all the available copies at any price. He could usually be seen going about like a scholar with a bundle of books under his arm. I was also intrigued by the intense study and pencil-marking that the director was making on his copy of the book; it was as if he were studying it for a doctoral thesis. Not until I had a chance to read his 'treatment' did I understand what all his pencilling meant: he had been marking off passages and portions that were to be avoided in the film.

When the script came, I read through it with mixed feelings. The director answered my complaints with, 'I have only exteriorized what you have expressed. It is all in your book.'

'In which part of my book?' I would ask without any hope of an answer.

Or he would say, 'I could give you two hundred reasons why this change should be so,' I did not feel up to hearing them all. If I still proved truculent he would explain away, 'This is only a first draft. We could make any change you want in the final screenplay.'

The screenplay was finally presented to me with a great flourish and expression of fraternal sentiments at a hotel in Bangalore. But I learned at this time that they had already started shooting and had even completed a number of scenes. Whenever I expressed my views, the answer would be either, 'Oh, it will be rectified in the editing,' or, 'We will deal with it when we decide about the re-takes. But please wait until we have chance to see the rushes.' By now a bewildering number of hands were behind the scenes, at laboratories, workshops, carpentries, editing rooms and so forth. It was impossible to keep track of what was going on, or get hold of anyone with a final say. Soon I trained myself to give up all attempts to connect the film with the book of which I happened to be the author.

But I was not sufficiently braced for the shock that came the day when the director insisted upon the production of two tigers to fight and destroy each other over a spotted deer. He wished to establish the destructive animality of two men clashing over one woman: my heroine's husband and lover fighting over her. The director intended a tiger fight to portray depths of symbolism. It struck me as obvious. Moreover it was not in the story. But he asserted that it was; evidently I had intended the scene without realizing it.

The Indian producer, who was financing the project, groaned at the thought of the tigers. He begged me privately, 'Please do something about it. We have no time for tigers; and it will cost hell of a lot to hire them, just for a passing fancy.' I spoke to the director again, but he was insistent. No tiger, no film, and two tigers or none.

Scouts were sent out through the length and breadth of India to explore the tiger possibilities. They returned to report that only one tiger was available. It belonged to a circus and the circus owner would under no circumstance consent to have the tiger injured or killed. The director decreed, 'I want the beast to die, otherwise the scene will have no meaning.' They finally found a man in Madras, living in the heart of the city with a full-grown Bengal tiger which he occasionally lent for jungle pictures, after sewing its lips and pulling out its claws.

The director examined a photograph of the tiger, in order to satisfy himself that they were not trying to palm off a pi-dog in tiger clothing, and signed it up. Since a second tiger was not available, he had to settle for its fighting a leopard. It was an easier matter to find a deer for the sacrifice. What they termed a 'second unit' was dispatched to Madras to shoot the sequence. Ten days later the unit returned , looking forlorn.

The tiger had shrunk at the sight of the leopard, and the leopard had shown no inclination to maul the deer, whose cries of fright had been so heart-rending that they had paralysed the technicians. By prodding, kicking and irritating the animals, they had succeeded in producing a spectacle gory enough to make them retch. 'The deer was actually lifted and fed into the jaws of the other two,' said an assistant cameraman. (This shot passes on the screen, in the finished film, in the winking of an eye as a bloody smudge, to the accompaniment of a lot of wild uproar.)

Presently another crisis developed. The director wanted the hero to kiss the heroine, who of course rejected the suggestion as unbecoming an Indian woman. The director was distraught. The hero, for his part, was willing to obey the director, but he was helpless, since kissing is a co-operative effort. The American director realized that it is against Indian custom to kiss in public; but he insisted that the public in his country would boo if they missed the kiss. I am told that the heroine replied: 'There is enough kissing in your country at all times and places, off and on the screen, and your public, I am sure, will flock to a picture where, for a change, no kissing is shown.' She stood firm. Finally, the required situation was apparently faked by tricky editing.

Next: trouble at the governmental level. A representation was made to the Ministry dealing with films, by an influential group, that *The Guide* glorified adultery, and hence was not fit to be presented as a film, since it might degrade Indian womanhood. The dancer in my story, to hear their arguments, has no justification for preferring Raju the Guide to her legally-wedded husband. The Ministry summoned the movie principals to Delhi and asked them to explain how they proposed to meet the situation. They promised to revise the film script to the Ministry's satisfaction.

In my story the dancer's husband is a preoccupied archaeologist who has no time or inclination for marital life and is not interested in her artistic aspirations. Raju the Guide exploits the situation and weans her away from her husband. That is all there is to it—in my story. But now a justification had to be found for adultery.

So the archaeological husband was converted into a drunkard and womanizer who kicks out his wife when he discovers that another man has watched her dance in her room and has spoken encouragingly to her. I knew nothing about this drastic change of my characters until I saw the 'rushes' some months later. This was the point at which I lamented most over my naïveté: the contract that I had signed in blind faith, in the intoxication of cheques, bonhomie, and back-slapping, empowered them to do whatever they pleased with my story, and I had no recourse.

Near the end of the project I made another discovery: the extent to which movie producers will go to publicize a film. The excessive affability to pressmen, the entertaining of V.I.P.s, the button-holing of ministers and officials in authority, the extravagant advertising campaigns, seem to me to drain off money, energy and ingenuity that might be reserved for the creation of an honest and sensible product.

On one occasion Lord Mountbatten was passing through India, and someone was seized with the sudden idea that he could help make a success of the picture. A banquet was held at Raj Bhavan in his honour, and the Governor of Bombay, Mrs Vijayalakshmi Pandit, was kind enough to invite us to it. I was home in Mysore as Operation Mountbatten was launched, so telegrams and long-distance telephone calls poured in on me to urge me to come to Bombay at once. I flew in just in time to dress and reach Raj Bhavan. It was red-carpeted, crowded and gorgeous. When dinner was over, leaving the guests aside, our hostess managed to isolate his Lordship and the *'Guide'* makers on a side veranda of this noble building. His Lordship sat on a sofa surrounded by us; close to him sat Pearl Buck, who was one of the producers and who, by virtue of her seniority and standing, was to speak for us. As she opened the theme with a brief explanation of the epoch-making effort that was being made in India in colour and wide-screen, with a hundred-per-cent-Indian cast, story and background, his Lordship displayed no special emotion. Then came the practical demand: in order that this grand, stupendous achievement might bear fruit, would Lord Mountbatten influence Queen Elizabeth to preside at the world premiere of the film in London in due course?

Lord Mountbatten responded promptly, 'I don't think it is possible. Anyway what is the story?'

There was dead silence for a moment, as each looked at the other wondering who was to begin. I was fully aware that they ruled me out; they feared that I might take 80,000 words to narrate the story, as I had in the book. The obvious alternative was Pearl Buck, who was supposed to have written the screenplay.

Time was running out and his Lordship had others to talk to. Pearl Buck began, 'It is the story of a man called Raju. He was a tourist guide. . . . '

'Where does it take place?'

I wanted to shout, 'Malgudi, of course.' But they were explaining, 'We have taken the story through many interesting locations— Jaipur, Udaipur.'

'Let me hear the story.'

'Raju was a guide,' began Pearl Buck again.

'In Jaipur?' asked His Lordship.

'Well, no. Anyway he did not remain a guide because when Rosie came. . . . '

'Who is Rosie?'

'A dancer. . . but she changed her name when she became a. . . a. . . dancer. . . . '

'But the guide? What happened to him?'

'I am coming to it. Rosie's husband. . . . '

'Rosie is the dancer?'

'Yes, of course. . . . ' Pearl Buck struggled on, but I was in no mood to extricate her.

Within several minutes Lord Mountbatten said, 'Most interesting.' His deep bass voice was a delight to the ear, but it also had a ring of finality and discouraged further talk. 'Elizabeth's appointments are complicated these days. Anyway her private secretary Lord——must know more about it than I do. I am rather out of touch now. Anyway, perhaps I could ask Philip.' He summoned an aide and said, 'William, please remind me when we get to London. . . . ' Our producers went home feeling that a definite step had been taken to establish the film in proper quarters. As for myself, I was not so sure.

Elaborate efforts were made to shoot the last scene of the story, in which the saint fasts on the dry river's edge, in hopes of bringing rain, and a huge crowd turns up to witness the spectacle. For this scene the director selected a site at a village called Okhla, outside Delhi on the bank of the Jamuna river, which was dry and provided enormous stretches of sand. He had, of course, ruled out the spot we had visited near Mysore, explaining that two coconut trees were visible a mile away on the horizon and might spoil the appearance of unrelieved desert which he wanted. Thirty truckloads of property, carpenters, lumber, painters, artisans and art department personnel arrived at Okhla to erect a two-dimensional temple beside a dry river, at a cost of 80,000 rupees. As the director kept demanding, 'I must have 100,000 people for a helicopter shot,' I thought of the cost: five rupees per head for extras, while both the festival crowd at Nanjangud and the little temple on the river would cost nothing.

The crowd had been mobilized, the sets readied and lights mounted, and all other preparations completed for shooting the scene next morning when, at midnight, news was brought to the chiefs relaxing at the Ashoka Hotel that the Jamuna was rising dangerously as a result of unexpected rains in Simla. All hands were mobilized and they rushed desperately to the location to save the equipment. Wading in knee-deep water, they salvaged a few things. But I believe the two-dimensional temple was carried off in the floods.

Like a colony of ants laboriously building up again, the carpenters and artisans rebuilt, this time at a place in western India called Limdi, which was reputed to have an annual rainfall of a few droplets. Within one week the last scene was completed, the hero collapsing in harrowing fashion as a result of his penance. The director and technicians paid off the huge crowd and packed up their cameras and sound equipment, and were just leaving the scene when a storm broke—an unknown phenomenon in that part of the country—uprooting and tearing off everything that stood. Those who had lingered had to make their exit with dispatch.

This seemed to me an appropriate conclusion for my story, which, after all, was concerned with the subject of rain, and in which Nature, rather than film-makers, acted in consonance with the subject. I remembered that years ago when I was in New York City on my way to sign the contract, before writing *The Guide*, a sudden downpour caught me on Madison Avenue and I entered the Viking Press offices dripping wet. I still treasure a letter from Keith Jennison, who was then my editor. 'Somehow I will always, from now on,' he wrote, 'associate the rainiest days in New York with you. The afternoon we officially became your publishers was wet enough to have made me feel like a fish ever since.'

WHEN INDIA WAS A COLONY

A sudden outbreak of Anglo-India has occurred in the cinema world, involving million-dollar budgets and movement of actors and equipment on a global scale—a minor, modern version of such historic globe-trotters as Hannibal, Alexander, Napoleon and heaven knows who else, who moved their hordes and elaborate engines of destruction across continents. Their Indian-oriented counterpart today carries an elaborate load of equipment of a different type—to set up his camp in a strange land, to create illusions of his own choice.

Sir Richard Attenborough's South Africa (of *Gandhi*) was in Poona, David Lean's Chandrapore (of *A Passage to India,* which has recently completed filming) was located in Bangalore, Ootacamund and in Kashmir. First *Gandhi,* now *A Passage to India,* and, in between, *The Far Pavilions, Heat and Dust, Kim* and what-not. It's a trend and a phenomenon.

Anglo-India apparently has a market, while a purely Indian subject has none, perhaps too drab for a commercial film-maker. India is interesting only in relation to the 'Anglo' part of it, although that relevance lasted less than 200 years in the timeless history of India.

I suspect that a film-maker values, rather childishly, the glamour of the feudal trappings of the British Raj, with Indians in the background as liveried menials or for comic relief. In Attenborough's *Gandhi,* Indians are usually shown in a mass, while the few Europeans—Viceroys, Governors and Generals—are clear-cut individuals, in full regalia wherever it is warranted. Indian personalities, such as Prime Minister Nehru, the Congress party leader Vallabhbhai Patel and Maulana Azad, the Muslim nationalist, lack substance; even Mohammad Ali Jinnah, the founder of Pakistan, is presented slightly, and not as a dynamic man. Other Indian leaders who were associates of Gandhi and who suffered and sacrificed along with him and were responsible for major decisions are left out.

This inadequacy must be a result of bewilderment, to put it mildly. The Indian character was puzzling and the Englishman suppressed his curiosity as bad manners. Incidentally, he was like the American who came later under different circumstances but chose to live like Indians, tasted Indian food, wore Indian dress and tried to understand everything about Indian life.

The Englishman preferred to leave the Indian alone, carrying his home on his back like a snail. He was content to isolate himself as a ruler, keeper of law and order and collector of revenue, leaving Indians alone to their religion and ancient activities. He maintained his distance from the native all through. Indeed, the theme of E.M. Forster's *A Passage to India* was that an unbridgeable racial chasm existed between colonial India and imperial England.

I had a few occasions to meet Forster, whenever I visited London. I enjoyed those visits to Cambridge. We would spend about an hour talking of books, Indian writing and Indian affairs in general. His interest in India was deep and abiding. My second novel, *The Bachelor of Arts*, was launched some years before with his blessing, and owed its survival to his brief comment printed on the jacket. Since then, he had kept in touch with my writing. He would always ask: 'What next?' Once, when I mentioned my next one, a book of mythology, *Gods, Demons and Others*, he paused for a moment and genially asked, 'Who is left out?'

Forster would offer me tea in his room and escort me halfway down to the station. When he visited London, he would send me a note and spend a little time with me before catching his train at King's Cross. When he inscribed a copy of *A Passage to India*, he was apologetic that he could lay hand only on a paperback, at a second-hand bookshop, and gave it with the remark, 'You will find it amusing. But don't read too much into it. . . .'

I had heard a rumour in New York that David Selznick or someone had offered $250,000 for a movie option on *A Passage to India*, but that Forster had rejected it. When I asked him about it, he just said, 'I am not interested.' When I questioned him further, he said, rather petulantly, 'No more of it. Let us talk of other things.' He was, however, happy with the stage adaptation of his novel by Santha Rama Rau, who had worked in close consultation with him all through.

How did a little island so far away maintain its authority over another country many times its size? It used to be said by political orators of those days that the British Isles could be drowned out of sight if every Indian spat simultaneously in that direction. It was a David-Goliath ratio, and Britain maintained its authority for nearly two centuries. How was the feat achieved? Through a masterly organization, which utilized Indians themselves to run the bureaucratic and military machinery. Very much like the *Kheddah* operations in Mysore forests, where wild elephants are hemmed in and driven into stockades by trained ones, and then pushed and pummelled until they realize the advantages of remaining loyal and useful, in order to earn their ration of sugarcane and rice. Take this as a symbol of the British rule in India.

The Indian branch of the army was well-trained and disciplined, and could be trusted to carry out imperial orders. So was the civil service. Instead of taking the trouble to understand India and deal directly with the public, Britain transmuted Indians themselves into Brown Sahibs. After a period of training at Oxford and Cambridge, first-class men were recruited for the Indian Civil Service. They turned out to be excellent administrators. They were also educated to carry about them an air of superiority at all times and were expected to keep other Indians at a distance.

I had a close relative in the I.C.S. who could not be seen or spoken to even by members of his family living under the same roof, except by appointment. He had organized his life in a perfect colonial pattern, with a turbaned butler knocking on his door with tea in the morning; black tie and dinner jacket while dining with other I.C.S. men, even if the table were laid in a desert; dropping of visiting cards in 'Not at Home' boxes brought by servants when they formally called on each other. At home, when he joined the family gathering, he occupied a chair like a president, laughed and joked in a measured way; the utmost familiarity he could display was to correct other people's English pronunciation in an effort to promote Oxford style.

The I.C.S. manual was his Bible that warned him against being too familiar with anyone. He was advised how many mangoes he could accept out of a basket that a favour-seeker proffered; how far away he should hold himself when a garland was brought to be slipped over his neck. It was a matter of propriety for an average visitor to leave his vehicle at the gate and walk down the drive; only men of certain status could come in their cars and alight at the portico.

The I.C.S. was made up of well-paid men, above corruption, efficient and proud to maintain the traditions of the service but it dehumanized the man, especially during the national struggle for independence. These men proved ruthless in dealing with agitators, and may well be said to have out-Heroded Herod. Under such circumstances, they were viewed as a monstrous creation of the British. An elder statesman once defined the I.C.S as being neither Indian nor civil nor service. When Nehru became the Prime Minister, he weeded out many of them.

Nomination to high offices, conferment of the King's or Queen's birthday honours in which titles were announced from knighthood to Rai Sahib (the lowest in the list) that could be prefixed to names; such men also enjoyed privileges and precedence in the seating arrangements during public functions and official parties. This system brought into existence a large body of Indians who avidly pursued titles and exhibited loyalty to the Government, ever hoping to be promoted to the next grade in the coming year.

There were also instances of rejection of titles as a patriotic gesture. The Bengali poet Rabindranath Tagore returned the knighthood after the 1919 Jallianwalla Bagh massacre (General Dyer ordered troops to fire on a crowd of Indians assembled for a political meeting in a narrow, enclosed space, expertly presented in Attenborough's *Gandhi*).

The British managed to create a solid core of Anglophiles who were so brainwashed that they would harangue and argue that India would be in chaos if the British left, and would congratulate Churchill on his calling Mahatma Gandhi 'half-naked fakir' (although Gandhi himself commented, 'I am glad my friend Churchill recognizes my nakedness, but I feel I am not naked enough').

The map of India was multicoloured; red patches for British India and the yellow ones for the independent states under the rule of maharajahs and nawabs. At the head of a British province was a governor, a chosen man from Britain, one who was not expected to display any special brilliance, but possessed enough wit to keep his territory in peace, get on with the local population in general, report to the viceroy in Delhi and carry out his orders. He in turn took his orders from London. The secretary of state for India was at the apex, with the British Parliament at his back.

The governor of a province lived like a sultan with undreamt of luxury. He was loaded with the trappings of authority and housed in a mansion set in a vast parkland. During summer, he moved with his entire retinue and the secretariat to a hill station and there lived in a style so well described by Kipling. His Excellency generally divided his time between horse racing and polo, golf and swimming.

He presided over elegant public functions, such as flower shows and school prize-distributions. The Governor (and, of course, his family) lived a life of quiet splendour and came in contact with only the upper classes of society and never noticed poverty or squalor. His geographical outlook was limited to government-house vistas, parade routes, and whatever he could glimpse of the landscape from his saloon while travelling in a special train. Most of the Governors were generally kept above want and were believed to be incorruptible, although a couple of names were associated with dark tales of expecting, under the roses in a garland, gold sovereigns or currency notes; of engaging themselves in titillating encounters with society butterflies and so forth, all unverifiable, of course, but whispered about in the bazaar.

A province was divided into districts. At the head of a district was a collector (until the late 1930s, always a British I.C.S. man) and under him the Indian subcollector in the subdivisions, who would be responsible for the collection of revenue in the villages.

The native states, more that 500 in number, existed earlier as so many principalities ruled by hereditary princes, all independent of each other at one time. Through intricate historical processes, wars and mutual rivalries that offered ready opportunities for the British to intervene, they were brought, in course of time, under the sovereignty of Delhi, and had to pay subsidies. As long as the subsidy was regularly paid and subversive activities were suppressed, the ruler of a state was left alone to pursue his life of pleasure and court intrigue. In order to keep an eye on the maharajah, there was a resident representing the crown, living in the cantonment area (also known as 'civil lines', as in *A Passage to India*).

Every capital had a cantonment, which was better town-planned and more comfortable than the downtown districts sprawling around the maharajah's palace. A cantonment had barracks with soldiers under a commandant to help the Government in any possible emergency. The resident was a puppeteer behind the throne. He and his European community formed a special class living in the cantonment and enjoying exclusive privileges. It would be the maharajah's duty to guarantee from time to time enough tigers and wildlife for his white masters when they desired to hunt. Especially when the viceroy visited the state. His Highness must make sure that the honoured guest could pose for photographs with at least one tiger stretched under his feet.

Before this point could be reached, preparations would be made weeks ahead—spotting the quarry, building platforms on trees for the huntsmen to remain in safety while aiming at the tiger, which would follow the scent of a bleating goat tethered near a waterhole. After a ride on an elephant through the jungle, His Excellency would sit up on a *machan* with his party, with their guns at the ready. It was a foregone conclusion that the viceroy could never miss. However, in the darkness one can never say whose shot kills. But the credit always goes to the honoured guest, although back at home he might not hurt a fly. It would be whispered sometimes that a captive tiger driven crazy by beaters' drums and torches, and famished, and half-dead, already might well have collapsed at the very sound of a rifle shot; thereupon news would be relayed that the V.I.P. had bagged one or more tigers that were terrorizing the countryside.

The banquet that concluded the visit of the viceroy lent a touch of comic opera—the solemnity, the stiff formality and the steel-frame gradation in the seating plan were inflexible. When pudding was to be served the band in attendance should always strike up 'Roast Beef of Old England'.

I live in Mysore, once a native state, where the annual nine-day celebration called Navaratari was a season of festivity in the palace. At this time, the maharajah sat in the evenings on his ancient throne in the durbar hall. Invitees would sit cross-legged and barefoot on the throne and resume their seats. On a certain day, a European reception would be held, when the resident would arrive in state with several European guests. The timing of the resident's arrival was fixed with precision to a split second, so that he would enter the hall neither before nor after the maharajah, but at the same time with him, when the guns fired the salute.

On this occasion, the throne would quietly have been moved out of sight as it was too sacred and no one could go before it with shoes on. But Europeans could not be told to remove their shoes and so a silver chair would be substituted for the maharajah with a footstool, and a parallel silver chair provided at its side for the resident, also with footstool, whose imperial status would thus be preserved and protected. In that situation, when the European guests bowed before the maharajah, it was shared by the resident.

It was of the utmost importance to preserve British superiority under any circumstance. In the railways, they had reserved carriages for 'Europeans Only', in which no Indian would dare to step. Certain shops in the cantonment catered exclusively to Europeans; memsahibs could buy groceries without feeling contaminated by the stares of Indians. Theatre entrances and seats were marked 'Europeans Only'. Exclusiveness was important and inevitable. One noticed it even in hospitals, where European wards and Indian wards were segregated.

In 1924, there was a public outcry against this system. A young student needed urgent medical help and would not be admitted to the General Hospital, Madras, because there was a vacancy only in the European ward and none in the Indian ward. The young man died. Following this, there was a furore in the Madras Legislative Assembly. Satyamurthy, one of the boldest among Indian patriots, whose forthright comments and questions confounded the British rulers and their Indian friends, said:

'Then, sir, the last sentence is: "On the day in question, there were five vacant Indian beds and seven cases were admitted." Now, we are all told that we ought not to be racial in this country: We ought to rise above racial prejudice and that we ought to be cosmopolitan. I try my best to be like that, but my best at times fails when I am reminded that in my own country, in our own Indian hospitals maintained by the Indian tax-payer's money and run, above all, by an Indian minister, there should be beds which should be called "non-Indian" beds. Why, in the name of common sense, why?

'Have you ever heard, Mr President, of any country in the world except ours where beds are being maintained for patients on racial considerations? Do you find in England beds for Indians in those English hospitals specially maintained at the expense of the taxpayer? Do you know what it means, Mr President? You may go in mortal illness to the General Hospital—I trust you will not'— laughter—'but if you had to go, although all the available European beds be vacant, you will not be taken in because you are an Indian, whereas a fifth-rate European without a name can be admitted and given a European bed because he has the European blood. Can flesh and blood stand this? Is it right? I should like to know from the Honorable Minister,' continued Satyamurthy, 'why he maintains in this country at the expense of the tax-payer this racial distinction in hospitals? It seems to me that the time has arrived when we must speak up against this. . . .

There used to be heard a traditional rumour that in the days of the East India Company the thumbs of weavers of Dacca muslin (the finest fabric in the world) were cut off in order to prevent competition with textiles from Manchester and Lancashire. This may sound bizarre but the story has persisted for decades. The British were essentially merchants and India was primarily a market. The British temperament seemed to have been market-oriented—even in the 1930 s and 1940 s. An adviser and secretary to the maharajah whom I shall name Sir Charles Blimp (with apologies to the cartoonist David Low) promptly sabotaged a proposal for starting an automobile factory in Bangalore when land, machinery, capital and management were ready. He 'strongly' advised the young maharajah not to approve the proposal and said,'Indians lack experience and cannot run an automobile factory successfully.'

All the while, he looked benignly on the maharajah's monthly import of a new Daimler, Austin or Rolls-Royce, with special fittings for his garage, which was already crowded with cars, like the showroom of an automobile dealer. This 'adviser' to the young maharajah was a beefy, red-faced giant before whom any Indian looked puny and felt overwhelmed when he raised his arm as if to strike and issued commands. The man believed that that would be the only practical way to handle Indians. He drove his staff of 'writers' (clerical staff) to slave for him round the clock, cooped them up in a shed under a hot tin roof at the farthest end of his spacious compound, summoned them through a buzzer every ten minutes to the main building where he was settled under a fan with, perhaps, Lady Blimp 'doing fruits'. They never swerved even by a second from their ritual eating, while his clerks found it difficult to break off for lunch, as he would invariably growl, 'Why are you fellows always hungry?' Poverty and want were normally unnoticed by this gentleman.

Poverty, however, was in the province of the missionary who lived among the lowliest and the lost. Although conversion was his main aim, he established hospitals and schools and in many ways raised the standard of living and outlook of the poorer classes. Before reaching that stage, the missionary went through much travail. He viewed Indians as heathens to be saved by loud preaching.

The street-corner assembly was a routine entertainment for us in our boyhood at Madras. A preacher would arrive with harmonium and drum and, facing heavy odds and violent opposition, begin a tirade against Indian gods. A crowd would gather around and gradually music and speech would be drowned in catcalls, howls and yelling, and the audience would not rest till the preacher was chased off. It was a sort of martyrdom and he could have saved his skin and got a hearing but for a naïve notion that he should denigrate our gods as a preparation for proposing the glory of Jesus.

Even in the classroom, this was a routine procedure. I studied in a mission school and the daily Scripture class proved a torment. Our Scripture master, though a native, was so devout a convert that he would spend the first ten minutes calling Krishna a lecher and thief full of devilry. How could one ever pray to him while Jesus was waiting there to save us? His voice quavered at the thought of his God. Once, incensed by his remarks, I put the question,'If Jesus were a real God, why did he not kill the bad men?' which made the teacher so angry that he screamed, 'Stand up on the bench, you idiot.'

The school textbooks were all British manufactured at one time, compiled by Englishmen, published by British firms and shipped to India on P. and O. steamers. From a child's primer with 'A was an apple' or 'Baa, Baa, Black Sheep' to college physics by Dexter and Garlick, algebra by Ross and logarithm tables compiled by Clark, not a single Indian name was on any book either as author or publisher. Indian history was written by British historians—extremely well documented and researched, but not always impartial. History had to serve its purpose: Everything was made subservient to the glory of the Union Jack. Latter-day Indian scholars presented a contrary picture. The Black Hole of Calcutta never existed. Various Muslim rulers who invaded and proselytized with fire and sword were proved to have protected and endowed Hindu temples. When I mentioned this aspect to a distinguished British historian some years ago in London, he brushed aside my observation with: 'I'm sorry, Indians are without a sense of history. Indians are temperamentally non-historical.'

We had professors from English universities to teach literature, which I always feel was a blessing. But the professor's contact was strictly limited to the classroom. When he left the class, he rushed back to his citadel of professor's quarters and the English club where no Indian was admitted except a bearer to serve drinks. Our British principal never encouraged political activities or strikes, which were a regular feature in our days, whenever Gandhi or Nehru gave the call or were arrested.

The hardiest among the British settlers was the planter who, born and bred in his little village in England, was somehow attracted to India, not to a city and its comforts but to a deserted virgin soil on a remote mountain tract where he struggled and built up, little by little, a plantation and raised coffee, tea and cardamom, which remain our national assets even today. He was firmly settled on his land, loved his work, now and then visiting a neighbour fifty miles away or a country club hundred miles off. He loved his isolation, he loved the hill folk working on his plantation, learned their language and their habits and became a native in all but name.

V. TRAVEL

Editor's note: Travel writing comprises only a small portion of Narayan's consid-erable output, but it has a distinction of its own since the storyteller's art is evident everywhere in it. Narayan wrote two books about the old Mysore State, one called simply *Mysore* which is no longer available, and *The Emerald Route* (1977) which describes the present Karnataka State. While both books can be safely used as travel guides, the informational part is not their most important aspect. Narayan sees scenes and records characters with the sure sensitivity of the imaginative writer, describing natural sights lyrically, telling the relevant anecdote, and dramatizing his encounters with people. 'Sringeri' included here is a good example of the way he mixes different elements to present a total picture of a place. *My Dateless Diary* is an account of his first visit to the United States in 1956-57. As he says himself, 'It is not a book of information on America, nor is it a study of American culture. It is mainly autobiographical. . . .' What it really is is a record of the first encounter of a mature writer with a different culture, his sensitive responses to scenes, events and people. The book contains enough material for any number of Narayan short stories.

SRINGERI

About twelve centuries ago Sankara was born at Kaladi (near Cochin) of parents who had been childless for long. They had been praying night and day for an issue. In answer to their prayer Shiva appeared in the guise of an old man, in a dream, and asked, 'Do you want numerous children who live a hundred years but who are dullards and evil-doers or only one son who is exceptionally gifted but who will live with you for only a short time?' The mother rejected mere quantity. Sankara was born, with only sixteen years as his allotted span of life. In his fifth year he learnt the *Gayatri* and underwent spiritual and other disciplines; in his eighth year he mastered all the *Shastras*, Puranas, Vedas, Vedanta, and *Sutras*. And a little later he renounced the world and donned the ochre robe.

The rest of his life is the record of a great teacher. Through his writings, debates and talks, he spread far and wide his *advaita* philosophy—a doctrine which says that all that exists is a particle of a great soul and merges in the end in that soul. 'His was the task of ending the nightmare of separateness,' says one of his commentators.

After travelling extensively he came to Sringeri. Sringeri had already been sanctified by the presence of great sages like Vasishta, Viswamitra, Vibhandaka, Kasyapa, and others, who had their ashrams in its forests and performed *tapas*. A look at this place will make us understand why it was so favoured, a place surrounded with green hilltops and immense forests, and watered by the river Tunga, which is considered to be more sacred than any other river in the world. If Ganga springs from Vishnu's feet, Tunga springs from his face, and the gods are said to bathe in it.

Before making up his mind to settle here Sankaracharya stood on the right bank of the river and looked about. This spot is now marked by a little shrine. He had in his hand the golden image of Sharada or Saraswathi, the Goddess of Knowledge and Culture, for whom he was going to build a temple, which was to be the central power-house, so to speak, of his philosophy and the institution which was born of it. At his feet Tunga flowed, its water turned silvery by the rays of the midday sun. As he stood observing the surroundings Sankaracharya beheld a sight on the opposite bank which thrilled him and made him realize that he had come to the end of his journey. A cobra spread its hood and held it like an umbrella over a frog, protecting it from the heat of the sun. 'This is the place!' Sankaracharya said on seeing it. 'Here is harmony, an absence of hatred even among creatures which are natural enemies.' Even today on the river step a tiny niche made of a couple of stones marks the spot where this phenomenon was seen. The niche is filled with mud and sand but a slight excavation with fingers will reveal the cobra and the frog carved on a stone.

Sankaracharya crossed the river. This village was henceforth to be of vital importance to humanity, its significance to last beyond the reckoning of time. Hence he first proceeded to build four guardian temples in the surroundings hillocks, which were to protect the place from all possible dangers, diseases and evils. On the eastern hillock he built a temple for Kalabhairava, on the western hillock for Anjaneya, on the southern hillock for Durgi, and on the northern for Kali. Even today worship is being performed thrice a day in these temples. The people of Sringeri have strong faith in the protection that these guardians afford. I had a surprising instance of it from the person who was acting as my guide and who was a vaccinator. During our walk he casually mentioned that there were a few cases of typhoid in the town. When I asked him what measures they were taking to combat it he said, 'We are quite confident that none of these cases will turn fatal. My daughter too had an attack of it and a relapse, and its only effect has been the loss of hair. As long as we have these,' he pointed at the temples on the hillocks, 'we have nothing to fear. In summer we have a few cases of small-pox too. But there is nothing to worry or fear. This place is protected. If any of the cases turns fatal it will be due to extraordinary *karma* and nothing can be done about it.' I admired his grand faith; all the same I could not help pressing upon him the need for giving widespread anti-typhoid injections. He at once made a note of it. Though this incident is trivial it indicated to me a certain resilience and breadth of mind and an absence of bigotry which seem to me the very essence of the culture Sankaracharya fostered. My vaccinator friend could very well have denounced my suggestion as mere human vanity and lectured to me on the power of faith; but he did not do it, and I believe, could not do it.

There is a repose and tranquillity in the air. The river flows softly. Strolling along its edge I notice a group of young men with an elderly companion in their midst. They are all bathing in the river and washing their clothes and are at the same time listening to the lecture their elderly companion is giving them and answering the questions he is putting to them. When they get up to go, muttering their lessons, I follow them through the narrow passage between the consecrated tombs of ancient saints behind Vidyasankara temple.

I follow them into a large hall where groups of students are squatting in shady corners, quietly chanting their lessons and memorizing. A few elderly persons, wrapped in shawls, move about on noiseless feet, absorbed in their own discussion. The place has a monastic quietness.

In the upper storey there is a library containing over four thousand manuscripts and books, neatly classified, labelled and arranged in glass shelves. In an adjoining room some persons are sitting before huge heaps of manuscripts and books; they are at their task of selecting, rejecting, and classifying the vast literary store of manuscripts and books that has accumulated in the *math* from time immemorial. They have been at this task for five years and are likely to go on for a couple of years more.

In the central courtyard there is a shrine, fittingly enough, of Sankaracharya. For this is a college run by the *math*, providing a course of studies which extends over ten years; and here young men are being trained for a religious life. It has about eighty pupils with eight or ten masters, each one an authority in some branch of Sanskrit learning. Forty of the pupils are being looked after by the *math* itself. Once a year the pupils are examined and the passed candidates are led by their masters across the river to the presence of the chief guru, the apostolic head who lives in a house on the opposite bank of the river. He is a man of deep learning and austerity, whose hours are occupied with meditation, prayer, worship and studies. He tests the boys himself, and to those who pass the test he distributes clothes and money gifts.

There is a sannyasi sweeping the temple of Anjaneya and decorating the image with flowers, completely absorbed in his work, and completely indifferent to those passing him. To my enquiry my guide answers: 'He is one of the four or five sannyasis here. He speaks to no one. He came here some years ago and has been here since. We don't know where he has come from. He spends most of his time in yoga: occasionally when he is free he sweeps the temples. Since he is here he is our guest.' I observe two sannyasis sitting on the river step with closed eyes. Their purpose is also unknown. One of them, it was vaguely understood, came all the way from some place in northern India in order to discuss certain questions with the chief guru and have certain doubts cleared. After coming he never met the guru, but just stayed on, dividing his time between meditation and work: he voluntarily teaches certain subjects in the university. There is another sannyasi who is here as a pupil in the college. No one questions who they are or why they are here or how long they are going to stay—they are treated as honoured guests as long as they stay. One most noticeable feature of Sringeri is its attitude as host to whoever visits. The moment you are there you are freed from the concerns of food and shelter. As soon as you get down from the bus you are shown a room in the *dharmashala* or in the guest house. And then your hot water is ready for your bath, and as soon as you have bathed, your food is brought to you. There is an old cook, bent with age, who gets up every morning at four o'clock and goes to bed at eleven in the night, spending his waking hours in serving guests. I saw how deeply the spirit of hospitality had sunk in the people here when I caught the old man in a talkative mood: 'Before I came here I was a clerk in Trichinopoly jail. Through some adverse circumstances I became unhappy, very unhappy and then suffered from mental derangement. I came here, sought the guru, and begged him to permit me to wear the ochre cloth and become a sannyasi. He refused because I have a large family to support, and ordered that I should live here with my family and seek peace in serving the pilgrims. And now I have done it for forty years.' He collects the tips given to him, puts them by, and spends it twice a year in feeding the poor. Every day nearly two hundred persons are fed by the *math*, excluding the pupils in the university, the sannyasis, and others. This hospitality is not confined to human beings. In the niches of the temple towers there are thousands of pigeons living and breeding. From the stores of the *math* four seers of rice are scattered for the pigeons every day; they provide a grand spectacle when they sweep down for their rice at the feeding hour. In addition to this, five seers of rice are cooked and thrown in the river for the fish. There are numerous fish of all sizes in the river, sporting and splashing about, which come to the surface expectantly whenever any human being stands on the river step. The fish and the birds have lived and grown without knowing any fear of human beings.

There are numerous temples in Sringeri besides the chief one of Sharada. The temple of Vibhandaka in Sringeri itself and of his son Rishyasringa, which is at Kigga, six miles from Sringeri, built on a high hill, are two of the oldest temples here. Both are of the same type with an inner shrine in the middle, an open corridor around, and a roofed platform edging the corridor: the platform can accommodate thousands of persons at a time. It is believed that by praying at these temples rain can be called or stopped. Vibhandaka and his son are famous sages mentioned in the early portions of the *Ramayana*. Rishyasringa, like his father, was a man of great attainment, but he had grown up without seeing a woman. At that time there was a severe drought in Anga; the king was told that the drought would cease if Rishyasringa could be brought to his state and married to the princess. A bevy of young women disguised as hermits were sent in order to entice this sage. They arrived, stopped at Narve, a village near Sringeri, waited for an opportunity and appeared before the young man when his father was out of the scene. He felt such a deep interest in these strange hermits that it was not very difficult for them to decoy him. His approach to Anga brought rain. He married the princess and became the priest of King Dasaratha of Ayodhya, and officiated at the great sacrifice which resulted in the birth of Rama, the hero of the *Ramayana*. There is a carving on a pillar in the Rishyasringa temple at Kigga in which the young sage is shown as he is being carried off happily on a palanquin made of the intertwined arms of fair women.

Another important temple is Vidyasankara's built in about AD 1357. It is on the left bank of Tunga, of Chalukyan style, and built on a raised terrace. Round the outer walls are intricate carvings depicting scenes from the epics and Puranas. One of the most interesting figures carved is that of Vyasa discoursing to Sankaracharya. This perhaps illustrates the episode in Sankaracharya's life when the sage Vyasa came to him in the guise of an old man when he was teaching a group of disciples on the banks of Ganges. Sankaracharya was teaching a certain work of which Vyasa himself was the author. Vyasa objected to Sankaracharya's interpretation, and Sankaracharya would not admit the objection. A great debate ensued which went on for seventeen days, neither side giving in. At this the others grew alarmed. Sankaracharya's chief disciple appealed to them: 'Oh, great Vyasa, you are the incarnation of Vishnu, and oh, my master, you are Shiva. When you both argue and debate what is to happen to us, poor mortals? How can we bear to watch this mighty conflict?' And the debate was stopped. Vyasa blessed Sankaracharya for his grasp of the subject and his interpretation. And as Sankaracharya was about to complete his sixteenth year in a couple of hours, Vyasa conferred on him a further span of sixteen years.

The temple of Sharada is the most important institution here. This is the holiest sanctuary which any human being could be privileged to enter, the centre round which the life of Sringeri revolves. At the evening hour of worship the temple is transformed with lights, music, incense and flowers. Standing at the inner shrine one has a feeling of elation. At this moment the golden image of Sharada in the innermost shrine shining in the lamplight and the swaying flames of camphor, appears to be not a mere metal image but a living presence, and one gets a feeling that one can go on standing here forever looking at its tranquil and distinguished face.

WESTWARD BOUND

On the (rail) road to San Francisco, with Chamu and his wife in another compartment, four doors off. Life in train for the next forty hours. Food in the train, bath in the train, and neighbourly visits to and from Chamu with many occasions to narrate my new story, and discuss it with him. It is so comfortable that I enjoy having an illusion of being a permanent dweller here, and so arrange my little possessions around on that basis. Find a comradeship with all and sundry—including the very fat, crew-cut teenager, always tottering with drink. He is a nuisance, as he pushes the door of every compartment in the corridor and peeps in, much to the consternation of Mrs Chamu.

Our life is punctuated by movements to and from the dining car at various intervals—pushing and pulling the heavy doors all along the vestibule. Our biceps are greatly strained. Chamu and I have divided the labour, each doing in one-way. We march along as everyone in the lounge stares at Rukka's colourful sari, with open-mouthed wonder. We notice, however, a red-haired girl and two others being exceptions, who never look up, maintaining a concentrated gaze on their beer glass, all day. The steward is proud of being able to give us rice and butter-milk, and watches over us, as Rukka produces from her handbag South Indian condiments and spice-powder to help us through our meals. We form such a close community (although lasting only forty hours) that even the drunken teenager begins to say, 'Good morning,' 'how do you do?' and 'excuse me,' every time we pass.

I plan to do some writing but the hours pass unnoticed. I cannot take my eye off the window where grand mountain scenery passes. I think we are passing through an elevation of six thousand feet, farms and towns at night, the beacons on hilltops look mysterious; wayside towns with their streets, shop-windows, and above all the used-car lots, brilliantly lit all night although the population is fast asleep, and the lights of passing lorries and automobiles on the highway. At some small hour of the night we pass Reno—the haven of divorcees. I fancy I see the sign 'Court' on a building. I cannot help craning my neck to watch if any couple is getting down the steps and parting on the road in silence and tears. But it is an hour at which I suppose, even the turbulence in a divorcee's bosom is lulled into sleep.

Berkeley

Tuesday. Arrive Berkeley. We decide to get down here rather than go up to San Francisco. We climb down by means of a step-ladder. Professor David Mandlebaum and his wife are there to receive Chamu and wife and take us to a hotel. I have a feeling of being an intruder, the real expected guest being Chamu. I have got down here because Chamu is here, otherwise I should have gone to San Francisco and then on to Palo Alto which was really my original destination. But I never get there.

I think Chamu is the luckiest house-hunter in the world. Over lunch at Mandlebaum's he was suggested a house at Albany, a suburb of Berkeley. After lunch David went upstairs to his study and Ruth drove us to Albany. 1050, Peralta Avenue (the name attracted us). This was practically to be my second home in Berkeley for the next two months. Rukka saw the house, liked it, Chamu endorsed her view even without looking at the house, on hearsay, and there they were, ready to move in as soon as the lady of the house who had recently lost her husband and was going to live with her daughter in New York was able to move her things out. I never saw anyone make such a quick decision about a house. Chamu is a philosopher and a logician, a man who can specify what he wants. I sometimes envy him his clear-headedness and luck. What a contrast to my own management of my affairs. Having decided to stay at Berkeley, I was next involved in hunting for a flat or apartment for myself. With Ed Harper's help I am engaged for the next couple of days in house-hunting which Berkelians assure me is an exciting, unrewarding occupation. I find an apartment which is available for sixty dollars a month, which figure appeals to me instead of the seven dollar a day for a hotel room. But this apartment is too big, empty, and unfurnished, and I shall probably be obliged to spend all my time like a newly-wed equipping the pantry and bedroom and the front room. I shall have to be thinking all night about sheets and pots and pans, not to speak of grocery, which in any case I shall have to bother about. The heating primitive: you'll have to open a gawky apparatus and apply a match, and when it goes off apply it again and so forth. I never knew that a bare house could look so terrifying and discouraging—all due to its vast emptiness. To add to the emptiness, someone, a weird- looking woman, at the basement, a woman with seven or seventeen (as they seem) children, all in one room, a creaky staircase going up and up, full of thuds. The only reason that such a huge apartment is coming to me for sixty dollars is that the county council has marked it for demolition. Very wise of them. There is a beautiful elm tree in front of the house, which is a point in its favour. There is a spring settee in a landing on which I and Harper settle down to consider the matter. It's a crucial point; if I'm keen on an apartment, this is my opportunity. I shall not regret later that I didn't take it when it came. On the contrary we run over mentally all the things that one would have to do to make it habitable. Out of it a story develops. A helpless man like Dr A—an Indian anthropologist arrives at Berkeley on some important research assignment. He inherits this apartment, and starves for a day or two before he can make a cup of coffee for himself, and a friend like Ed Harper helps him and fills the house with labour-saving gadgets. Dr A—spends his time learning the technique of house-running with American gadgets and in tidying up the place. At the end of a month he finds he has not read a line nor written one—no time. He has all along been trying unsuccessfully to learn how to operate a can-opener, how to turn off the gas, and how to dishwash. He is helpless, incompetent and unpractical—until a girl arrives on the scene who is writing a thesis on his work and wants his help to finish her thesis. She starts running his household for him and complications arise.

'How old is she?'

'Twenty-six.'

'How about looks?'

'Charming.'

'Blonde or. . .?'

'Of course, blonde.'

After this refreshing dream we go out, and Harper drives me to another house—seventy-five dollars a month; which I reject for the opposite set of reasons, it's too full of gadgets and articles and equipment, which I shall be responsible for, the owner going away for a time. If I take this house, I fear, I shall become a care-taker, a sort of my man Annamalai, (who guards my Yadava giri home for thirty-five rupees a month) with the difference that I should have to pay a rent in addition to watching the house.

We come to the conclusion that it's no good deciding on a house in a hurry, and walk back to where Ed has parked his car. In all this preoccupation with fact and fiction, he seems to have forgotten the parking restriction, and when we reach the car, a long envelope is stuck at the windscreen—he has a police check, which means probably five dollars fine. 'I generally pay ten dollars a month in fines,' he confesses.

Today I create an unprecedented confusion for myself by checking out of my hotel at 2 p.m. I had all my baggage taken down to the lobby, and within half an hour came back to the hotel to ask for my room again. It had happened thus. After deciding against the ramshackle house, with Ed Harper's concurrence, I had decided to move to an apartment on Haste (sixty dollars a month). But at the last moment Rukka mentioned that David Mandlebaum did not quite approve of my taking a room there. When she said this, there flashed to my mind all kinds of defects in the apartment, which I had already noticed through a corner of my eye—its carpets were frayed, its towels were not fresh and were brought in by the hotel proprietrix herself, who also registered at the desk, there were cracks in the wall of my room, the place was full of old people moping in the lounge, the elevator was rattling and grill-ridden, and above all, the address was Haste and Telegraph, which sounded impossible as I feared I might have nightmares of 'Haste makes waste' or people might address my letters, 'Post and Telegraph'. And so I went back to tell them I'd not take the room and came back to my hotel much to the astonishment of my hotel manager.

Evening dinner at an Indian restaurant in San Francisco, our host being Ed Harper. Its elaborate and self-consciously planned Indian atmosphere, dim light, long coats, bogus Indian tunes out of gramophones hidden in the arras, more bogus bric-a-brac are deliberate, but I suppose, commercially successful. Chappati and Indian curry, are genuine and are not bogus. A waitress clad in sari, an usher in a long coat buttoned to the neck, create an Indian atmosphere, which seems to appeal to San Franciscans as, I find, all tables booked, and women dressed in caps and gowns, which outdo Fifth Avenue style, sit with an air of facing an impending adventure, while reading the menu card; and utter little cries of 'delicious, delicious', when they sample a curry. The story of Dr A goes forward in this setting. He decides to find a suitable bridegroom for the blonde—taking a fatherly interest in her (after taking time to realize that he is too much her senior and has a wife and children at home), being a busy-body and match-maker in his own country he has affection for John, a scholarly bachelor and makes it his business in life to 'arrange' a marriage between the two; he casts their horoscopes, compares to see if the stars match; all in correct Indian style; and thus imports into United States the first 'arranged' marriage! A promising theme, which I must take up immediately after *The Guide* is written. After dinner one half of the party returns to Berkeley while I stay back with John and others to see a little more of San Francisco. John takes us to a Bohemian place, where brandy served with coffee is a speciality. There are suggestive pictures everywhere on the walls, lewd sayings in glittering letters—framed gaudily; deliberate joviality, and girls who affect to be intoxicated and throw themselves on all and sundry.

John is a linguistic scholar, teaching Hindi in Berkeley, who sought me out a couple of days before at my hotel, offered to drive me around and show me the places of interest. He had spent some years in India and explained: 'When I was in Mysore, Mr——was so hospitable that I like to do anything I can for anyone from Mysore.' He is a gentle, sensitive, civilized and cheerful being. He drove me to San Francisco, over the Golden Gate Bridge at sunset, initiated me into the mysteries of photography with my box camera; and helped me to desensitize my first spool of negatives. With my camera he first took a picture of me standing below the Golden Gate Bridge, forgot to turn the film, and handed me the camera and allowed me to take a picture of him under the Golden Gate Bridge on the same film; when it was later developed I saw on the negative two Golden Gate Bridges with a double-headed, four-armed monster standing under it—my first photographic effort. He gave me a supper of pizza at an Italian restaurant, took me to visit Biligiri, who gave me scented betel-nut to chew and suddenly proposed that we go to Oakland to see the haunts of Jack London.

The inn where Jack London wrote and drank himself to death is still there. It is a shack made out of an old boat the entire floor sloping as in a ship's-bar, and the state of cleanliness and furnishing remaining unchanged since the days of Jack London. The waiter is a genuine admirer of Jack London's writing. Beer is served in bottle, and the man explains, 'It's anyway hygienic.' People drink straight out of the bottle as they do on a roadside soda-shop in Madras, tilting back their heads. Faded photographs of Jack London at various stages clutter the wall, and the waiter throws a torchlight on them while he lectures on Jack London's life and philosophy. He (the waiter) also mentions Raja Yoga, Gnana Yoga and the Bhagavad Gita. He confesses to being a book- lover, spending all his spare cash and time in reading. He is interested in Indian philosophy because Jack London was interested in it too. He quotes and explains the basis of various Jack London stories. I suggest that he become the narrator in a Hollywood picture on the life of Jack London but he says that his boss nurtures secretly such an ambition himself and so his own chances are poor. When he learns that I'm an author, he abandons the other guests to another waiter and sits up with us. He notes down the names of my books and he sees us off at the door with a simple good-bye; although his routine statement to every out- going couple would be: 'See you in the spring,' and after they say, 'Thanks,' he would add, 'if you get through the mattress,' full of double, treble, and shocking meanings, but no one minds it. And he generally utters this lewd quip mechanically, without any zest, as if it were an awful duty cast on him by his boss.

An Encounter

I loafed around San Francisco till 7 p.m. and returned to the Key-Station, in order to catch a street-car for Albany, where I was to dine with Chamu at 8.30.

I paid forty-five cents and took a ticket. I asked at the barrier, 'Where do I get the car for Albany?'

'Albany?' said a man standing there. He pulled out a time-table from his pocket, and said, 'There is one leaving in five minutes. Go, go. . . go straight *down* those steps.' He hustled me so much that I didn't have the time even to say 'Thanks'. I was in a hurry. I went down and saw ahead, on the road, two coaches with passengers, ready to start. As I hurried on wondering which of them I should take, two men standing at the foot of the stairs called me to stop, and asked, 'Where are you going?'

'Albany. If that is the bus. . . .'

'Where is your ticket?' I held up my ticket. One of them snatched it off, crumpled it into a pellet, and put it into his pocket. These men evidently liked to keep me at the San Francisco station. They were well-dressed, and looked like the presidents of a railroad or a college; one of them looked quite distinguished in his rimless glasses. I demanded an explanation for their arbitrary handling of my ticket but they strolled away and disappeared into the shadows around a corner of this grim building. Not a soul in sight. It was past eight. I dashed back to the ticket office and asked for another ticket of the woman (I purposely avoid the indiscriminate American usage 'girl') at the window. She said,'You took one now!'

'Yes, but I need another one for a souvenir,' I said.

She said, 'You don't get the next bus until nine o'five.'

'Is it a bus or a coach or a train or street-car? What is the vehicle one rides in for Albany?' I asked.

'Why?'

'Each time I hear it differently.'

'I don't know, ask there,' she said out of habit and went back to her work.

I went round the station asking for directions. No one was precise. It was surprising how little anyone here cared to know the whereabouts of Albany, only half an hour's ride away. They behaved as if they were being consulted over some hazardous expedition beyond uncharted seas; while the fact remained as any citizen of Berkeley Albany will confirm, 'F' trains and 'E' trains shuttling between Berkeley and San Francisco wailed and hooted all night keeping people awake.

This station was getting more and more deserted and I didn't want to miss a possible bus or street-car—that might start from some unsuspected corner of it. So I went round looking for a conveyance. At a particularly deserted corner, I was stopped by the two men who had misappropriated my first ticket. They blocked my way. I tucked away my new ticket securely into an inner pocket. I was not going to give it up again. One of them grabbed the collar of my jacket and said, 'Let us talk.' The other moved off a few yards, craning his neck and keeping a general look out. The nearer man said, 'Don't start trouble, but listen.' He thrust his fist to my eyes and said, 'I could crack your jaw, and knock you down. You know what I mean?' Certainly, the meaning was crystal clear. I knew at a glance that he could easily achieve his object. It frightened me. In a moment flashed across my mind a versatile, comprehensive news-headline, 'Remnant of Indian novelist near Key-Station. Consulate officials concerned—' I realized these were men of action.

'What do you want ?' I asked simply.

The one on sentry duty muttered something in the local dialect. The collar-gripper, took his hand to his pocket. I thought he was going to pull out a pistol, but he drew out a gold watch with a gorgeous gold band. He flourished it before me and said, 'How do you like it?'

'Don't hold it so close to my eyes. I can't see what it is. Take it back.' Yes, it was a nice, tiny watch. He read my thoughts and said, 'I'm not a bum, but a respectable member of the merchant marine. I'm on a holiday and have been gambling. I want money. Take this.'

It was of course an extraordinary method of promoting watch sales, but I had to pretend that I saw nothing odd in it. He said in a kind of through-the-teeth hiss, 'I don't like trouble, that's all. See what I mean?' His hand still held the collar of my jacket, and the watch was sunk within his enormous fist. It was very frightening. The lub-dub of my heart could be heard over other city noises. I'm not exactly a cowardly sort, but I am a realist. When I encountered a fist of that size I could calculate its striking force to the nearest poundal. I have always weighed 140 pounds, whatever I did, whether I starved or over-ate or vegetated or travelled hectically. My weight never varied. I felt, in my fevered state, that the man before me must weigh as much between his fist and shoulder. No police in sight. The entire force seemed to have been drawn away to meet a graver emergency elsewhere. I looked casual, as if it were a part of my day's routine, as if someone were always turning up doing this sort of thing to me every two hours. I tried to assume the look of a seasoned receiver of ladies' watches. The whole scene filled me with such a feeling of ludicrous staginess that I suddenly burst into a laugh. The man looked puzzled and annoyed.

'You think it funny?' he asked.

'S-u-r-e,' I said in the most approved drawn-out manner, dreading lest my tactics should misfire. He gave a tug to my jacket. I said curtly, 'I hate to have my jacket pulled. I hate anyone hanging on to my jacket. It shows an infantile mind and mother- fixation.'

'You are a professor, aren't you?' he said sneeringly.

I asked, 'Whose is that watch?'

'My own. I would not be selling it otherwise.'

The other man turned round to say, 'It is of course his. Should you ask?'

'I don't believe it,' I said. 'Maybe you are a guy with a slender enough wrist to wear that strap. Let me see how you manage to put it on! Seems to me it's a lady's watch.' At this he repeated his threat about my jaw. I had by now got used to hearing it; and almost said that if he broke one jaw another was sure to grow in its place. I still marvel why he didn't hit me. I took off my spectacles as a defence preparation. I didn't want splinters in my eyes. He ran his hand over the entire surface of my person, trying to locate my purse. Ignoring his action I repeated emphatically, 'It's a lady's watch.'

'It is Pat's,' said his friend.

'Who is Pat?'

'His wife,' he said.

'What does she do now to know the time?' I asked.

'I got her another one,' he said, 'that's why I want to sell it.'

'Does she know about it?' I asked.

'Sure. Peggy will do anything to help me.'

'Peggy?' I asked. 'Who is she and how does she get on with Pat?' I asked.

'What are you talking about?' he growled. We had now arrived at a level of conversational ease which must have looked like the meeting of three old school-ties around the corner. The only unsavoury element in it, if one peered closely enough, was that he still had his fingers firmly on my collar. He assumed a menacing tone suddenly, and asked,'So you don't appreciate our help?'

'Thanks a lot I don't. You are really mixed up. Your wife, if you have one, must be either Pat or Peggy, not both unless you are a bigamist who lets two wives manage with a single watch, or am I going to hear about Sally and Jane too? Are you a bigamist or a polygamist? Are such things allowed in this country?'

'Oh, stop that, you talk too much; that's what's wrong with you. Jack made a slip, that's all,' the man said with a touch of sadness.

'What's your time now?' I asked. 'I've a dinner engagement at Albany—' He looked at his own watch. He applied it to his ear and cried, 'The damned thing has stopped.'

'No wonder,' I said. 'All that clenching and flourishing of fist will reduce any watch to pieces,' I said. 'Why don't you look at the cute one in your pocket, Peggy's is it?' He pulled out the little watch, peered at its face and said. 'Can't see anything in this blasted place.'

'Why not we all adjourn to a better-lit place?' I suggested.

'And have a drink, eh?' he said.

After Jack had his laugh at the joke, the other one said, 'Professor, you are a good guy; learn to use an opportunity. You don't appreciate our help. Do you know what this watch actually costs?'

'Do you?' I asked.

He paused to think up a reply. His friend, Jack, turned round to say, 'It cost him one hundred forty dollars,' without taking his eye off the corner.

'What's your offer?'

'Not even the twenty cents that I am left with now,' I said. 'I would not accept it even as a gift. You know why?'

'Why, Doctor?'

'I've no faith in watches. I never wear one; I've never had a watch in my life. Only recently, for the first time in my life I bought a two dollar alarm clock, because—every morning I slept till twelve noon, and was in constant danger of missing trains and planes. So now I have a clock, which I look at strictly only once in a day; just to know whether I should get out of bed or continue to sleep.'

'How do you keep your appointments?' he asked.

'I never keep them. I should have been eating a dinner now at Albany. But where am I? What am I doing?'

'Now you know we want to help you.'

'I'll never buy a watch even if I miss all the dinners in the world,' I said emphatically.

'Perhaps you should take this to your girl friend,' he said.

'No such luck. Never had one in my life,' I said. 'Even if I had one, I'd never inflict a watch on her. It's a misleading instrument. What's a watch-time? Nothing. You don't even know how to look at Sally's or Pat's watch in your pocket. Your watch has stopped; I'm sure Jack's watch is showing some wild time of its own. It's a different hour now at New York; something else in Chicago; morning time in the other hemisphere, Greenwich time, summer time, and God knows what else. What's the use of having an instrument which is always wrong by some other clock?' He looked overwhelmed by this onslaught. His fingers slackened on the collar of my jacket, and I took the opportunity to draw myself up proudly, turn, and briskly walk away, with my heart palpitating lest they should grab me back. I walked off fast.

I don't think I overcame them by my superior wit and escaped. I cannot claim any heroism on that score. I think they let me go because they must have felt that they had caught a bankrupt and a bore. Or it may be Jack espied the police somewhere and they let me go. Although I missed my dinner that night, I was glad to be back at my hotel with my bones intact; and as long as I stayed in Berkeley, I took care not to visit the San Francisco Key-Station again.

VI: LEGENDS AND MYTHS

Editor's note: Narayan has always said that having firm roots in one's family and one's religion is an imperative for proper self-development. He himself had a strong and affectionate joint family that supported him during his years of finding himself. Religion is equally important to him, but a clear distinction has to be made. He was born a Hindu, he grew up in a Hindu family, and he has imbibed the Hindu culture, of which he has a profound knowledge, and from which he has derived strength, both as a human being and as a writer. But this does not for a moment mean that he indulges in the external acts that a devout Hindu is supposed to perform. He is unostentatious to an extreme. He never talks about going to a temple or being a devotee of a particular shrine. What being a Hindu means to him is being the inheritor of the rich culture it has to offer. Of the stories represented here, 'Yayati', deals with the age-old problem of growing old. The excerpts from the great epics, *Ramayana* and *Mahabharatha*, retell key episodes relating to their protagonists.

YAYATI

In the perpetual strife between the gods, led by Indra, and the *asuras*, or anti-gods, who were full of accomplishments and power, the gods were always losing. This caused much anxiety and self-examination in the world of gods. The worst of it was that when a demon was killed he revived quickly and got on his feet again, while a god who was killed was fit only for a funeral. The secret of survival of the *asuras* was puzzling, the more so because the gods were under the guidance of Brihaspathi, the presiding god of wisdom and acumen.

Eventually the gods discovered the secret of their enemies: they survived because they were guided by Sukracharya, the great sage who had mastered the Sanjivini mantra, an esoteric incantation which could bring the dead back to life. There were hurried consultations among the gods. They felt doomed to extinction unless they too could learn this mantra. It was known only to Sukracharya, and he was not likely to respond to an invitation from the gods. The gods decided to send down a disciple who could learn the Sanjivini from the master. They chose young Kacha, son of Brihaspathi. They sent him down to the country of the demon king Vrishaparva, where Sukracharya was kept as an honoured guest and teacher.

Sukracharya accepted young Kacha as his disciple, charmed by his humility and earnestness. The young man assured him that he would go through the novitiate, practise austerity, and adhere unwaveringly to a vow of celibacy. Sukracharya had a daughter named Devayani, who fell in love with Kacha. Kacha amused and enchanted her with music, stories, and talk, and she in turn attended to his needs, gave him fruit and flowers, sang songs and danced for him.

One day Kacha went into the forest to graze the cattle. The *asuras*, realizing that if Kacha learned the Sanjivini it might eventually lead to their own annihilation, attacked him fatally, cut his body into bits, and fed dogs and wolves with the flesh. When the cattle returned home in the evening without him, Devayani was distraught with grief. She told her father, 'I tremble to think what might have happened to Kacha. I assure you that I cannot live without him.' Her fond father immediately uttered the Sanjivini mantra and called the youth by name. At this call Kacha rent his way through the intestines of the dogs and wolves that had devoured him, became whole again, and joined Devayani.

Another day Kacha went into the forest to gather rare flowers that Devayani had asked him to fetch. The demons ambushed him, ground his body into a fine paste, and dissolved it in the sea. Once again Devayani appealed to her father, and he uttered the mantra and Kacha became whole again.

In their third attempt on Kacha, the demons burned his body, converted his ashes into a fine flour-like substance, and secretly dissolved it in wine that Sukracharya was about to consume. Sukracharya drained the cup and Devayani came again to implore him to find Kacha. Not knowing that the young man was in his stomach, he invoked the Sanjivini mantra and called Kacha aloud, whereupon Kacha answered from his bowels and explained how he had got there. Sukracharya was greatly upset at this callous, wanton murder that the *asuras* had repeatedly attempted, and swore that he would cease to be their patron if they misused their powers. But how to fetch the boy out? He told his daughter, 'I can revive Kacha by uttering my mantra, but he can come out only by bursting my belly. If you want him back I shall have to give up my life.'

Devayani said, 'I cannot live without my father. I want both you and Kacha. You will have to think of a way.'

Sukracharya thought of a way. 'I cannot help dying when Kacha comes out, but I will teach him the Sanjivini so that he may revive me after coming out of my body.' And so he called to the disciple in his stomach and taught him the formula. When he emerged from the belly of Sukracharya, Kacha uttered the mantra and made his master whole again. Sukracharya warned the demons, 'You have been stupid and overreached yourselves. Now Kacha has learnt the rare mantra. He has acquired the necessary knowledge and will be my equal hereafter.' The demons heard this and retreated in great bewilderment.

In course of time Kacha desired to go back to his own world, having completed his studies and training. When he approached his master for the final leave-taking, Devayani said, 'Marry me, don't go. I can't live without you.'

Kacha replied, 'I am under an eternal vow of celibacy and I cannot marry you. Moreover, the daughter of one's guru can never be other than a sister.'

She lamented, 'Remember all the anxiety I have gone through

for your sake whenever the demons tried to destroy you, and remember all the time we have spent together.'

He merely repeated, 'It's unthinkable. You are my sister forever; especially after, thanks to the demons, I was forced to sojourn within your father's belly—both of us are from his loins.'

She pleaded again and again, remonstrated, threatened to kill herself, but Kacha remained firm. He made ready to soar to the higher world. At which she cursed him. 'May the mantra you have learnt from my father prove ineffectual to you at all times!'

This was a terrible curse, frustrating his life's purpose. He was aghast at her viciousness. He merely said, 'You are blinded by lust, O Devayani, I love you as a sister, but you will not have it, O creature with those beautiful brows, and face like the full moon! How can you be so irresponsible? You are the daughter of a sage. I have admired you, loved you endlessly, but not through your attraction as a woman; nothing was farther from my mind. You care nothing for my vow of celibacy, you care nothing for my mission, you don't value my affection for you, and you curse me out of blind rage from frustrated lust. So be it. Let me tell you that the Sanjivini may prove ineffectual when I utter it, but I can still impart it to others and use it through them. As for you, you will never attain the hand of a sage or find happiness in marriage.'

So saying, he ascended to the higher realms, where he was welcomed by the gods. They rejoiced that he had brought with him the mantra that would save them from extinction. Now they felt that they should take the offensive and sent Indra down to the world of *asuras* in order to provoke them to a fight.

Indra planned first the disruption of the relationship between Sukracharya and the demon king, and he achieved it in a curious, roundabout way. In a forest glade he saw women sporting in a lovely little pool. Their clothes were on the bank. Indra piled up the clothes, carried them to a distant spot, and left them there. When they came ashore the women had to rush for their clothes and found them in a bundle of confusion; each wrapped herself in the first robe her hand fell on, not caring to whom it belonged.

One such person was Sarmishta, daughter of Vrishparva, the king of the demons, on whose behalf Sukracharya was employing his powers and talent. The sari that she picked up belonged to Devayani. At this Devayani lost her temper and cried, 'How dare you clothe yourself in my sari? You are, after all, in the position of a disciple and subordinate to me, as your father learns the art of war from my father. What foolhardiness on your part to touch my clothes!'

Sarmishta replied, 'Subordinate! We are the givers, you are the receivers. You and your father have your palms out always to receive the gifts we throw you in return for teaching. You teach because you need our support. Whereas we are a class who never ask support of anyone, we would rather die than ask a favour or a gift of anyone, and you think you are so superior that I should not touch your clothes even by mistake!'

At this Devayani swore, 'Your clan would be extinct but for my father's great help!'

Sarmishta cried, 'Great! Do you know how servile your father is when he stands before my father to ask for this and that, and yet you talk! I will teach you what it is to talk thus to a warrior girl.' So saying, she wrenched her clothes from Devayani, pushed her into a dried-up well, and returned to her palace without once looking back, and with no remorse in her heart.

As Devayani stood at the bottom of the deep well, crying, Prince Yayati, from the neighbouring country, came on horseback in search of a deer that he had been hunting. When he peeped in he cried, 'O lovely one, who are you? How do you come to be in this situation?'

She replied, 'Whom the gods kill, my father revives with his mantra. I am the daughter of Sukracharya.'

He reached down, gave her a hand, and helped her out, saying, 'Now go where you like without any fear.'

Devayani said, 'Take me with you. You have clasped my right hand, as you would during the wedding ceremony, and so you must become my husband.'

The prince gently put her off. 'I am a prince, of the ruling and fighting class,' he said. 'You are the daughter of a seer, a man who sees the events in all the worlds. I would not give him offence. I feel I am not worthy of you.'

'If you will not accept me yourself, through my father I will attain you, be assured,' she declared, and the prince went away. Then she stood under a tree, crying her heart out.

Sukracharya grew quite worried when Devayani failed to return home and sent out her personal attendant in search of her. After a long time, the attendant came back to report, 'Devayani was assaulted and thrown into the well by Sarmishta, and she has vowed never to set foot in this city again.' Sukracharya went after

Devayani himself, consoled her, and explained to her the importance of forbearance and tried to persuade her to return home. But she was adamant. He then went to Vrishaparva and declared, 'I feel I have made a mistake in supporting you and your clan. Your daughter called us beggars. My daughter will not set foot in this city again, and where my daughter is, is my place, none other. I must leave you to your own devices hereafter.'

The king replied with a lot of feeling, 'All that I own—palaces, wealth, treasures, elephants, and army—all are yours. You are truly the master of everything I possess and also master of me. I mean every word of what I say.'

'If you mean it, declare this to my daughter and personally comfort her.'

In response to the king's appeal, Devayani, who found it difficult to forgive the memory of the injury she had suffered, said, 'I desire that Sarmishta should become my servant, and that when I marry, she should follow me.'

The demon king said, 'Oh, let someone fetch my daughter immediately. Let her implicitly obey this young woman hereafter. To save a family an individual must be sacrificed, for the welfare of a village one family may be sacrificed, to save a country one village may be sacrificed, Sarmishta must be brought here at once.'

Sarmishta arrived, accompanied by a thousand servants of her own, and declared with all humility to Devayani, 'With my own one thousand attendants, I come to you as your servant to do your bidding.' And Devayani's shattered self-respect was now fully restored, and she consented to re-enter the city.

Months later Devayani went into the same glade to sport in the water and play games with her companions, her chief attendant this time being Sarmishta. While they were enjoying themselves there, once again, as before, Yayati appeared in search of a deer he had been chasing. He stood arrested by the spectacle before him—the battalion of beauties presided over by Devayani, and, sitting just a step below her, Sarmishta, whose beauty outshone that of the rest. He became involved in a conversation with Devayani, as he had before. At the end of it Devayani again proposed that he should marry her, as he had already grasped her hand.

He resisted the proposal, giving the same reason as before, namely, that she was too far above him in birth. Also, he felt drawn to Sarmishta. But he could not escape Devayani this time. She sent a messenger to fetch her father, explained the situation to him, and suggested that he should give her in marriage to this prince. Yayati accepted the situation, as all means of retreat were blocked. His last hope was that the father of the girl might object, but Sukracharya gave his blessing to the union, declaring that it was predestined and must be accepted without argument.

'You will be blessed in every way,' said the seer. But he warned the prince, 'This girl Sarmishta will also accompany my daughter. She is the king's daughter, and she will deserve all the honourable treatment you may provide for her, but take care of one thing; never call her into your sleeping chamber, and never seek to talk to her alone nor touch her. Devayani will be your wife and you will be blessed in every way.'

Yayati took his wife, with her retinue, including Sarmishta, to his own country, of which he was now ruler. In a beautiful spot outside the capital he built a mansion for Sarmishta and equipped it for her comfort.

Presently a son was born for Devayani.

Sarmishta was not happy at heart. She brooded over her lonely lot and began to think to herself: 'I am of an age to have a husband and a child. But he who might have been my husband is monopolized by Devayani. I cannot think of any other man as my husband. Will he ever come this way? I am Devayani's slave and whatever belongs to her belongs to me. She has a son and I must have one too. What is the good of all these gardens and flowers and food and marble halls, in this terrifying solitude? O trees, tell me, when will the king be here?'

Very soon the king, happening to pass that way, paused for a moment to have a word with Sarmishta. Straight away, as if to express herself fully before he should be gone, she confessed her love for him and demanded that he reciprocate.

He merely said, 'Ever since I met you, I have carried your image in my heart, but I have promised my father-in-law that I will never speak to you alone.'

Sarmishta replied, 'A promise made in jest, or under extraordinary circumstances, or to save a life or property, may be broken without any moral consequence. Truth is something more than that, and for all such lapses there are extenuations.'

The king was charmed with her speech. 'Ask for any gift,' he said. 'You want wealth, you want a kingdom? Ask for it and it will be yours.'

'O King, all such material gifts are of no value, they do not give one lasting satisfaction. I want a gift that will be a part of my body—that is, a child by you. It is said that a woman without a child goes to hell. Save me from hell. It is your duty. Devayani belongs to you, I belong to Devayani, whatever is a wife's may be freely used by the husband. Take me.' The king's defences were completely broken by this time, and when they parted for the day he had fulfilled her desire.

Yayati began to find Devayani less and less interesting. He left her alone, ignored her, and took extreme measures to keep away from her, spending all his time with Sarmishta. Devayani was unhappy and sent a message to her father complaining that the king had grown cold towards her.

Yayati often reflected: 'It is my good fortune that Sarmishta has come into my possession. She is like rain for the crops and nectar for thirsting souls. Devayani looks to me fierce like a serpent.'

Devayani was rather puzzled when she heard about the birth of a child to Sarmishta and went out one day to verify the fact. She confronted Sarmishta with her misgivings, 'What is this you have done? I had always thought you were so pure and innocent!'

Sarmishta answered, 'I am not the sort to run after mere pleasure. I came across a person of the utmost divinity and effulgence. I begged him to enrich me with a child, and he obliged me out of compassion; as anyone knows, it is proper and legitimate to acquire a child in this way when a noble soul acquiesces in it. The baby I have is a gift from a rare being.'

Devayani was somewhat appeased by this explanation, but she asked testily, 'Can you tell me where this great being lives, his whereabouts and his name? I also would like to know him.'

Sarmishta rose to the occasion by answering, 'His purity and spiritual eminence glowed like the sun, and I could not muster the courage to ask of him his name.' Devayani was satisfied with the explanation and went back to her palace.

Yayati had a second son by Devayani. As time passed he encouraged her to drink a strange beverage that looked colourful and tasted sweet, but was intoxicating. She grew accustomed to this drink and fell into a perpetual state of inebriety. Often she wept, sang, or was lost in prolonged slumber; sometimes she even failed to recognize Yayati and warded him off as if he were a stranger come to molest her. The king spoke severely to her, ill-treated her in many ways, and finally surrounded her with a company of deformed freaks, eunuchs, and senile persons, and took himself off to Sarmishta and was lost in the Elysium of her company, night and day. She now had three sons by this king.

Once when Devayani had passed through a phase of inebriation, she asked Yayati to take her for a change to a lonely garden place outside the city; there she found lovely children playing. She asked her husband, 'Who may these children be that have such a godly appearance and have some of your wonderful looks?' So saying, she approached the children themselves and asked who their father was. She was so gentle, persuasive, and insistent that the children pointed their fingers at Yayati standing beside her. He turned pale and remained aloof, and the children burst into tears and ran to the side of their mother, who was standing a little distance away, her head bowed in shame.

But her abashment lasted only a little while, until it received the full blast of Devayani's indignation. Sarmishta retorted, 'When I said my child was the gift of a person of great divinity I did not utter a falsehood, but meant it. Who could be more divine in appearance and accomplishments than the person at your side? When he accepted you, he accepted me too. When your worthy father gave you away, he gave me away to the same person. You and I have always shared everything.'

Devayani drew herself apart from the king, and declared to him. 'Let it be so. You may live with her and enjoy all the pleasures that you seek. I cannot stay here any more.' She plucked off her ornaments and threw them down and started to go back to her father. Yayati followed her, uttering many words of apology.

She reached her father's house and announced at the threshold, 'I have been wronged. The daughter of the demon has betrayed her true quality.' She concluded, 'I have two sons by this king. Sarmishta has three. You may judge him for yourself.'

Sukracharya told Yayati, 'You are one well versed in ethics and morality, and yet you have committed the sin of infidelity. Old age will overtake you in a few minutes in retribution.'

The king explained how he had come to have children by Sarmishta; he tried to represent it as an impersonal and altruistic act. Sukracharya was not taken in by this explanation; he merely said, 'A man who keeps up an appearance of righteousness and performs misdeeds under a false cloak is no better than an ordinary thief. You are already suffering for this duplicity.'

Even as they were talking, Yayati's appearance underwent a change. His flesh sagged, his hair turned white, he began to stoop.

He cried, 'Oh, forgive me, don't condemn me to senility. I still have longings and desires to fulfil.'

Sukracharya took pity on him and uttered a condition: 'If you find a youth who is prepared to take on your age, you will be free to effect the exchange. You shall have that power.'

Yayati approached the eldest of his sons by Devayani and offered him the kingdom immediately in exchange for his years. The son said, 'The senile man has no place in life; he is unable to enjoy anything in life, is laughed at by the servants and little girls. No, Father, let us keep our respective years to ourselves.' Yayati cursed him for his selfishness. 'You will never be a king.'

He asked his second son by Devayani, who said, 'Old age kills the power of love, to live, and it misshapes a man and destroys intelligence and judgement. No, I don't want old age yet.' The king cursed him. 'Your lineage will perish. You will find yourself leader of the lower grade of human beings, those that eat carcass and offal, adulterous and bestial creatures.'

Now he turned to his three sons by Sarmishta with the same request. The first one said, 'No,' and the king cursed him. 'Your lineage will perish and you will be the king of a desert, inaccessible by road, by water, or by a donkey-ride.' The next son also declined to take on his years.

He then turned to his last son, named Puru, and asked him to make the exchange. The young man said, 'I will do anything you like. All I have is yours, Father.'

The father embraced him with joy and said. 'I will give you back your youth in a thousand years.'

Yayati attained Puru's youth in every detail. He settled down to a life of the utmost enjoyment, never missing even a single moment of delight; and since he had youth and energy he also proved a just and good ruler. He fostered learning, honoured the saints, never missed a sacrifice or ritual that would please the gods, succoured the poor and the suffering, and punished evil-doers fearlessly. In private life he pursued a life of uninhibited pleasure, with women, wine, gold, possession, and comforts.

As he squeezed the utmost out of every second, a thousand years passed by uncounted, and suddenly, while enjoying the company of a semi-divine damsel, Yayati remembered that it was time to return his son his youth. He dropped the damsel abruptly and turned his back on the life of abandon. Returning the loan, he told Puru, 'You have been a wonderful son to me. Become young again and rule this kingdom as long as you wish. I have tasted every pleasure in life, and what I have realized is that there is no end to desire: it grows and keeps growing; there is no such thing as satiety. Gold, cattle, women, and food, you seek and attain, but the satisfaction each affords is short-lived, since you lust for more and more of them. After a thousand years of enjoyment, the mind craves for further and fresh enjoyments. I want to end this phase of life and turn to God. I want to live without the duality in mind of victory and defeat, profit and loss, heat and cold, pleasant and unpleasant. These distinctions I shall eradicate from my mind, divest myself of all possessions, and live in the forest amidst nature, without fear or desire.'

He kept his word. He was followed by his two wives. He ate the roots of plants and leaves; he overcame all desires and all moods and emotions, and his purity of mind helped him please the spirits of his ancestors as well as the gods. He lived on water alone for thirty years, completely controlling and suppressing his thoughts and words. One whole year he nourished himself by swallowing air and nothing else; he stood on one leg and meditated, surrounding himself on all four sides with fire and the blazing sun above.

By such austerities, Yayati attained enormous spiritual status and merit and was worthy of going to heaven in his physical body. He was welcomed in heaven by Indra, seated in the place of honour as befits a soul who has attained perfection, and was asked, 'You have attained salvation through great renunciation. Who is your equal in spiritual prowess?'

'None,' replied Yayati promptly. 'Among men, gods, saints, or divinities, I see none that has my attainments.'

Indra replied, 'Since you respect none, you shall fall back to earth; the weight of your ego must necessarily pull you back.' In consideration of his attainments Indra added, 'You shall, however, fall amidst good folk and return here in the ripeness of time.'

Yayati began his great fall from the heavens. When he reached the earth again, he was gently received by a group of saints in the forest. They said, 'Who may you be, resplendent one? In the dark clouds of the sky you shone like a meteor blazing down the path of the sun. May we know who you are?' They surrounded him and questioned him eagerly about heaven and hell, birth and death, and the good and bad life. After some time he went back to heaven; this time, with his ego controlled, he was fit not only to reach heaven but also to stay there.

THE WEDDING

Mithila, after all the forests, mountain paths, valleys, and places of solitude and silence through which we have travelled thus far, offers a pleasant change to a city of colour and pleasure, with people enjoying the business of living. The very minute Rama steps into Mithila, he notices golden turrets and domes, and towers, and colourful flags fluttering in the wind as if to welcome a royal bridegroom-to-be. The streets glitter with odds and ends of jewellery cast off by the people (a necklace that had snapped during a dance or a game; or had been flung off when found to be a nuisance during an embrace), with no one inclined to pick them up in a society of such affluence. There was no charity in Kosala country since there was no one to receive it. Torn-off flower garlands lay in heaps on the roadside with honey-bees swarming over them. The *musth* running down the haunches of mountainous elephants flowed in dark streams along the main thoroughfare, blending with the white froth dripping from the mouths of galloping horses, and churned with mud and dust by ever-turning chariot wheels.

On lofty terraces women were singing and dancing to the accompaniment of veena and soft drums. Couples on swings suspended from tall areca poles enjoyed the delight of swaying back and forth, their necklaces or garlands flying in the air. Rama and Lakshmana went on past shops displaying gems, gold, ivory, peacock feathers, beads, and wigs made of the hair of rare Himalayan deer. They observed arenas where strange elephant fights were in progress, cheered by crowds of young men; groups of women practising ballads and love songs under wayside canopies; horses galloping without a break round and round bridle tracks, watched by elegant men and women; swimming pools with multicoloured fish agitated by sporting in the water.

They crossed the moat surrounding Janaka's palace, with its golden spires soaring above the other buildings of the city. Now Rama observed on a balcony Princess Sita playing with her companions. He stood arrested by her beauty, and she noticed him at the same moment. Their eyes met. They had been together not so long ago in Vaikunta, their original home in heaven, as Vishnu and his spouse Lakshmi, but in their present incarnation, suffering all the limitations of mortals, they looked at each other as strangers. Sita, decked in ornaments and flowers, in the midst of her attendants, flashed on his eyes like a streak of lightning. She paused to watch Rama slowly pass out of view, along with his sage-master and brother. The moment he vanished, her mind became uncontrollably agitated. The eye had admitted a slender shaft of love, which later expanded and spread into her whole being. She felt ill.

Observing the sudden change in her, and the sudden drooping and withering of her whole being, even the bangles on her wrist slipping down, her attendants took her away and spread a soft bed for her to lie on.

She lay tossing in her bed complaining, 'You girls have forgotten how to make a soft bed. You are all out to tease me.' Her maids in attendance had never seen her in such a mood. They were bewildered and amused at first, but later became genuinely concerned, when they noticed tears streaming down her cheeks. They found her prattling involuntarily, 'Shoulders of emerald, eyes like lotus petals, who is he? He invaded my heart and has deprived me of all shame! A robber who could ensnare my heart and snatch away my peace of mind! Broad-shouldered, but walked off so swiftly. Why could he not have halted his steps, so that I might have gained just one more glimpse and quelled this riotous heart of mine. He was here, he was there next second, and gone forever. He could not be a god—his eyelids flickered. . . . Or was he a sorcerer casting a spell on people?'

The sun set beyond the sea, so says the poet—and when a poet mentions a sea, we have to accept it. No harm in letting a poet describe his vision, no need to question his geography. The cry of birds settling down for the night and the sound of waves on the seashore became clearer as the evening advanced into dusk and night. A cool breeze blew from the sea, but none of it comforted Sita. This hour sharpened the agony of love, and agitated her heart with hopeless longings. A rare bird, known as 'Anril', somewhere called its mate. Normally at this hour, Sita would listen for its melodious warbling, but today its voice sounded harsh and odious. Sita implored, 'Oh, bird, wherever you may be, please be quiet. You are bent upon mischief, annoying me with your cries and lamentations. The sins I committed in a previous birth have assumed your form and come to torture me now!' The full moon rose from the sea, flooding the earth with its soft light. At the sight of it, she covered her eyes with her palms. She felt that all the elements were alien to her mood and combining to aggravate her suffering. Her maids noticed her distress and feared that some deep-rooted ailment had suddenly seized her. They lit cool lamps whose wicks were fed with clarified butter, but found that even such a flame proved intolerable to her, and they extinguished the lamps and in their place kept luminous gems which emanated soft light. They made her a soft bed on a slab of moonstone with layers of soft petals, but the flowers wilted, Sita writhed and groaned and complained of everything—the night, stars, moonlight, and flowers: a whole universe of unsympathetic elements. The question went on drumming in her mind: 'Who is he? Where is he gone? Flashing into view and gone again—or am I subject to a hallucination? It could not be so—a mere hallucination cannot weaken one so much.'

At the guest house, Rama retired for the night. In the seclusion of his bedroom, he began to brood over the girl he had noticed on the palace balcony. For him, the moon seemed to emphasize his sense of loneliness. Although he had exhibited no sign of it, deeply within he felt a disturbance. His innate sense of discipline and propriety had made him conceal his feelings before other people. Now he kept thinking of the girl on the balcony and longed for another sight of her. Who could she be? Nothing to indicate that she was a princess—could be any one among the hundreds of girls in a palace. She could not be married: Rama realized that if she were married he would instinctively have recoiled from her. Now he caught himself contemplating her in every detail. He fancied that she was standing before him and longed to enclose those breasts in his embrace. He said to himself, 'Even if I cannot take her in my arms, shall I ever get another glimpse, however briefly, of that radiant face and those lips? Eyes, lips, those curly locks falling on the forehead—every item of those features seemingly poised to attack and quell me—me, on whose bow depended the destruction of demons, now at the mercy of one who wields only a bow of sugarcane and uses flowers for arrows. . . . ' He smiled at the irony of it.

The night spent itself. He had little sleep. The moon set and the dawn came. Rama found that it was time to arise and prepare himself to accompany his master to the ceremony at Janaka's palace.

At the assembly hall King Janaka noticed Rama and Lakshmana, and asked Viswamithra, 'Who are those attractive- looking young men?' Viswamithra explained. When he heard of Rama's lineage and prowess, Janaka said with a sigh, 'How I wish it were possible for me to propose my daughter for him.' Viswamithra understood the cause of his despair. A seemingly insurmountable condition existed in any proposal concerning Sita's marriage.

King Janaka had in his possession an enormous bow which at one time belonged to Shiva, who had abandoned it and left it in the custody of an early ancestor of Janaka's, and it had remained an heirloom. Sita, as a baby girl, was a gift of Mother Earth to Janaka, being found in a furrow when a field was ploughed. Janaka adopted the child, tended her, and she grew up into a beauty, so much so that several princes who considered themselves eligible thronged Janaka's palace and contended for Sita's hand. Unable to favour anyone in particular, and in order to ward them off, King Janaka made it a condition that whoever could lift, bend, and string Shiva's bow would be considered fit to become Sita's husband. When her suitors took a look at the bow, they realized that it was a hopeless and unacceptable condition. They left in a rage, and later returned with their armies, prepared to win Sita by force. But Janaka resisted their aggression, and ultimately the suitors withdrew. As time passed Janaka became anxious whether he would ever see his daughter married and settled—since the condition once made could not be withdrawn. No one on earth seemed worthy of approaching Shiva's bow. Janaka sighed, 'I tremble when I think of Sita's future, and question my own judgement in linking her fate with this mighty, divine heirloom in our house.'

'Do not despair,' said Viswamithra soothingly. 'How do you know it was not a divine inspiration that gave you the thought?'

'In all the worlds, is there anyone who can tackle this bow, the very sight of which in Shiva's hand made erring gods and godlings tremble and collapse—until Shiva put it away and renounced its use?'

'With your permission, may we see it?'

Janaka said, 'I'll have it brought here. It has lain in its shed too long. . . . Who knows, moving it out may change all our fates.' He called on his attendants to fetch the bow. . . .The attendants hesitated and he ordered, 'Let the army be engaged for the task if necessary. After all, this spot is sanctified by the sacred rites recently performed . . . and the bow is fit to be brought in here.'

The bow was placed in a carriage on eight pairs of wheels and arrived drawn by a vast number of men. During its passage from its shed through the streets, a crowd followed it. It was so huge that no one could comprehend it at one glance. 'Is this a bow or that mountain called Meru, which churned the Ocean of Milk in ancient times?' people marvelled. 'What target is there to receive the arrow shot out of this bow, even if someone lifts and strings it!' wondered some. 'If Janaka meant seriously to find a son-in-law, he should have waived this condition. How unwise of him!'

Rama looked at his master. Viswamithra nodded as if to say, 'Try it.' As Rama approached the bow with slow dignity, the onlookers held their breath and watched. Some prayed silently for him. Some commented, 'How cruel! This supposed sage is not ashamed to put the delicate, marvellous youth to this harsh trial!' 'The King is perverse and cruel to place this godlike youth in this predicament. . . . If he was serious about it, he should have just placed Sita's hand in his instead of demanding all this acrobatic feat. . . .' 'The King's aim is to keep Sita with him for ever—this is one way of never facing separation!' 'If this man fails, we will all jump into fire,' commented some young women who were love-stricken at the sight of Rama. 'If he fails, Sita is sure to immolate herself and we will all follow her example.'

While they were speculating thus, Rama approached the bow. Some of the onlookers, unable to bear the suspense, closed their eyes and prayed for his success, saying, 'If he fails to bring the ends of this together, what is to happen to the maiden?' What they missed, because they had shut their eyes, was to note how swiftly Rama picked up the bow, tugged the string taut, and brought the tips together. They were startled when they heard a deafening report, caused by the cracking of the bow at its arch, which could not stand the pressure of Rama's grip.

The atmosphere was suddenly relaxed. The gods showered down flowers and blessings, clouds parted and precipitated rains, the oceans tossed up in the air all the rare treasures from their depths. The sages cried, 'Janaka's tribulations and trials are ended.' Music filled the air. The citizens garlanded, embraced, and anointed each other with perfumes and sprinkled sandalwood powder in the air. People donned their best clothes, gathered at the palace gates and public squares, and danced and sang without any restraint; flutes and pipes and drums created a din over the loud chants and songs from many throats. Gods and goddesses watching the happy scenes below assumed human form, mixed with the crowds, and shared their joy. 'The beauty of our royal bridegroom can never be fully grasped unless one is blessed with a thousand eyes,' commented the women. 'See his brother! How very handsome! Blessed parents to have begotten such sons!'

Sita had secluded herself and was unaware of the latest development. She moved from bed to bed for lack of comfort, and lay beside a fountain on a slab of moonstone—the coolest bed they could find her. Even there she had no peace since the lotus blooms in the pool of the fountain teased her mind by reminding her of the shape of *his* eyes or *his* complexion. She grumbled, 'No peace anywhere. . . I am deserted. My mind tortures me with reminders. What use are they if I can't even know where to look for him? What sort of a man can he be to cause all this torment and just pass on doing nothing to alleviate it? A regal appearance, but actually practising sorcery!'

Her tortuous reflections were interrupted by the arrival of a maid. Instead of bowing and saluting her mistress, as was normal, she pirouetted around singing snatches of a love song. Sita sat up and commanded, 'Be quiet! Are you intoxicated?' The maid answered, 'The whole country is intoxicated. How would you know, my good mistress, if you lock yourself in and mope and moan!' She went on to explain in a rush of incoherence, 'The king of Ayodhya . . . son, broad-shouldered and a god on earth. No one saw it happen, he was so quick and swift, but he pressed, so they say, one end with his feet, and seized the other end with his hand, and drew the string and oh. . . !'

'Oh, intoxicated beauty, what are you saying?' When Sita understood what had happened, she stood up, her breasts heaving. She held herself erect as she said, 'Do you know if this is the same man who struck me down with a look as he passed along the street? If it is someone else, I will end my life.'

When the initial excitement subsided, King Janaka sought Viswamithra's advice. 'What shall I do next? I suddenly find myself in an unexpected situation. Is it your desire that I should send for the priests and astrologer and fix the earliest date for the wedding, or send a message to Dasaratha and wait for his convenience?'

Viswamithra replied,'Dispatch a messenger with the auspicious news immediately and invite Dasaratha formally.' Janaka at once retired in order to compose a proper invitation to Dasaratha, with the help of his court poets and epistle-writers, and dispatched it.

In due course, Janaka's emissaries presented the epistle of Dasaratha's court. Dasaratha ordered his reader to receive the epistle and read it out: The message gave an account of all that had happened from the time Rama had left Ayodhya up to the snapping of Shiva's bow. Dasaratha heaped presents on the messengers, and commented light-heartedly, 'Tell them in Mithila that we heard the sound of the bow snapping. . . .' He then passed orders: 'Let the announcement in appropriate language be made widely that King Janaka has invited for Rama's wedding every man, woman, and child in our capital. Let those able to travel to Mithila start at once in advance of us.' Professional announcers on elephants, accompanied with drums, carried the King's proclamation to every nook and corner of the capital.

The road to Mithila was crowded with men, women, and children. When the huge mass began to assemble and move down the road, the world looked suddenly shrunken in size. Elephants bearing pennants and flags, their foreheads covered with gold plates, horses prancing and trotting, and a variety of ox-drawn carriages and chariots were on the move, in addition to a vast throng on foot. The sun's rays were caught and reflected by the thousands of white satin umbrellas and the brilliant decorations of the army men. Heavy-breasted women clad in gossamer-like draperies sat on dark elephants, their necklaces swaying with the movement of the elephants, flanked by warriors bearing swords and bows on horseback.

The poet is especially happy and detailed when describing the mood and the activity of the young in this festive crowd. A youth followed a carriage at a trot, his eyes fixed on the window at which a face had appeared a little while ago, hoping for another glimpse of that face. Another young man could not take his eye off the lightly covered breast of a girl in a chariot; he tried to keep ahead of it, constantly looking back over his shoulder, unaware of what was in front, and bumping the hindquarters of the elephants on the march. When a girl inadvertently slipped down the back of a horse, another young man picked her up; but instead of setting her down after the rescue, he journeyed on with her in his arms. Another went along brooding and reflecting as he gazed on his beloved. Couples who had had a quarrel over some detail of the arrangements for this journey walked side by side without speaking, the woman not caring to wear a flower in her hair, but only a frown on her face, yet close enough to each other to avoid separation. One youth who was not spoken to but was agitated by the messages conveyed by the eloquent eyes of a damsel said, 'You won't speak? But surely, when you cross the river, you'll want my strong arms to carry you, and how shall I know if you don't speak to me? I know that you object only to speech, not to my touch, inevitably you'll need that when we come to the river's edge.'

Camels bearing enormous loads went along with parched throats until they could find the bitter margosa leaves—since they avoid tender greenery—and were thirsty again after chewing them, like men who look only for wine to quench their thirst, which again produces more thirst. Sturdy menfolk bore on their shoulders gifts and supplies for the journey.

Brahmins who practiced austerities followed, remaining aloof, afraid alike to walk amongst the elephants, for fear of being jostled, and in the areas where there were women, who might distract their inner vision. Some hopped along lightly on their toes, in order not to trample on any live creature on the ground; others held their fingers over their nostrils, both to perform breath control and to keep the fingers from touching their nether portions while their minds were fixed on God.

The noise of the rolling chariot wheels, trumpets, and drums, and the general din, made it impossible for anyone to hear what anyone else saying. After a while people moved along dumbly, communicating with each other only by signs, their feet raising an enormous trail of dust. Bullocks drawing wagons loaded with baggage, excited by the noise of drums, suddenly snapped off their yokes and ran helter-skelter, adding to the *melee*, leaving the baggage scattered on the road. Elephants, when they noticed a tank or a pond, charged away for a plunge, and remained submerged in the water up to their white tusks. Musicians sat on horseback playing their instruments and singing.

Behind this army, the king's favourites in the women's apartments followed. Surrounded by a thousand attendants, Queen Kaikeyi came in her palanquin. Next came Sumithra, accompanied by two thousand attendants. Surrounded by her own musicians came Kausalya, mother of Rama. She had also in her company several dwarfs and hunchbacks and other freaks. But her main companions were sixty thousand women of great beauty and accomplishment who followed her in a variety of vehicles. In a white palanquin studded with pearls, sage Vasishtha, chief mentor at the court, followed, surrounded by two thousand brahmins and priests. Bharatha and Sathrugna, also younger brothers of Rama, came next. Dasaratha, after performing his daily duties and religious rites and presentation of gifts to brahmins, started to leave his palace at an auspicious conjunction of the planets, ushered by a number of priests, men bearing in their arms golden pots filled with holy waters which they sprinkled on his path, while several women recited hymns.

When the King emerged from his palace, many rulers from the neighbouring states were waiting to greet him. Conch and trumpets were sounded, and loud cheering and the recital of honours, when his carriage began to move.

After journeying for a distance of two *yojanas*, the King with his army and followers camped in the shadow of Mount Saila. Next day the camp moved on to a grove beside a river.

The forward portions of the advance party, which had already reached Mithila, were received and absorbed into homes, palaces, and camps in the capital. As further contingents kept coming in, they too were received. The line of movement was continuous from Ayodhya to Mithila. King Dasaratha's party was the last to arrive. When the scouts who watched for their arrival flew back on horses to report that Dasaratha's party had been sighted, Janaka went forth with his ministers and officials and guards of honour to receive him. The two kings met, greeted each other, exchanged polite formalities; then Janaka invited Dasaratha to get into his own chariot and proceeded towards the capital. While they were entering the gates of the city, Rama, accompanied by Lakshmana, met them, greeted his father, and welcomed him. Dasaratha swelled with pride at the sight of his son, whose stature seemed so much grander now.

At this point Kamban begins to describe the preparations for the wedding of Rama and Sita. It is one of the most fascinating sections of the epic. The details of the wedding pavilion; the decorations; the arrival of guests from other countries; the flowers and gaiety, the citizens' joy and participation; the activities in the bride's house and then at the bridegroom's, and the preparation of the bride and bridegroom themselves: their clothes and jewellery; the moods they were in—all are described by Kamban in minute detail, running to several thousand lines of poetry.

At an auspicious conjunction of the planets suitable to the horoscopes of Rama and Sita, in ceremonials conducted by the high priests of Mithila and Ayodhya in Janaka's court, Rama and Sita became man and wife.

'Those who were together only a little while ago came together again, and there was no need for any elaborate ritual of speech between them,' says Kamban, describing the couple's first meeting at the conclusion of the wedding ceremonies.

Through Janaka's efforts, Rama's three brothers were also found brides and were married at the same time, in Mithila. When the celebrations ended, King Dasaratha started back for Ayodhya, with his sons bringing home their wives. On the day they left, Viswamithra told Dasaratha, 'Now I return to you Rama and Lakshmana. Their achievements are immeasurable, but there is much more ahead. They are blessed men.' Then he took leave of them and abruptly left northward. He was retiring into the Himalayas, away from all activities, to spend the rest of his days in contemplation.

BRIDE FOR FIVE

In the forest, Bhima maintained a watch, while his mother and brothers, overcome with fatigue, slumped down and fell asleep. His heart bled to see them lying on the bare ground. At the thought of their travails, he ground his teeth and swore vengeance on his kinsmen. But through his physical might and courage he was able to mitigate their suffering. He even carried them on his shoulder when one or the other was footsore or tired.

Once he encountered a *rakshasa*, hiding himself in a mountain cave, who waylaid and ate up any human being passing through the forest. Bhima destroyed him and made the forest safe for others coming after him. The *rakshasa's* sister, Hidimba, fell in love with Bhima, assumed a beautiful human form, and bore him a son named Ghatotkacha, who always came to his father's aid in any crisis and played a great part in the battle later.

The path ahead seemed endless as the one behind. The exiles had lost all sense of direction or goal. They ate roots and berries or hunted game. They had passed many forests, mountains, and lakes, with nothing clear except that they were going in the right direction, away from Hastinapura. Kunthi asked now and then, 'Do you have any idea when and where we shall stop?'

'No,' replied Yudhistira, 'but I have no doubt that we will have guidance at the right moment.' He proceeded along, and the others followed.

One day at dusk, when they were resting beside a lake after the evening ablutions and prayers, they had a venerable visitor. It was their great-grandfather Vyasa, the Island Born, and composer of the *Mahabharatha*. It was a welcome change from the monotony of trudging along in the same company.

Vyasa said, 'You see those two paths? Follow the one to your left, and you will arrive at a town called Ekavrata. There you will be quite safe from observation. You will have to behave like brahmins and live quietly and bide your time. Your fortunes will change and circumstances will change. But be patient. Ahead I see victory for your principles. Have no doubt that you will again live in your palace, rule the country, distribute gifts and alms to the needy, and perform grand sacrifices such as the *rajasuya* and *aswametha*.'

At Ekavrata, Vyasa introduced the Pandavas to a hospitable family who gave them shelter. They were at peace with themselves now, but for the gnawing memory of their cousins' vileness. Yudhistira always calmed them with his philosophy of resignation and hope. Their daily life soon fell into a routine. As became brahmins, they went round the town begging for alms, returned with their collection, and placed it before their mother, who divided it among them. Bhima's needs being greater than those of others, he was given the largest share of food. Thus life went on uneventfully until one day they found their hosts in great grief, arguing among themselves. There was much gloom and lamentation through all their quiet arguments, which were overheard by their guests. There came a stage when the Pandavas could not help asking for an explanation.

Their host said, 'On the edge of this town lives a *rakshasa* who leaves us alone only on condition that every home send up, by turn, a cartload of rice and two buffaloes, to be delivered by a member of the house. He is always so hungry that he consumes the food, the buffaloes, and finally also the person who has brought him the food. We dare not complain, since he threatens to destroy this town if there is any form of resistance. Every home gets its turn; today it is ours. I want to be the one to go and save the younger members of my family, but each one of them wants to be the victim to save the rest. I don't know. I think the best course would be for all of us to be consumed by that demon so that no one will be left to grieve for another. . . .'

After pondering the situation, Kunthi turned to Bhima and said, 'You take the food for that *rakshasa* today.'

But when Bhima readily agreed, Yudhistira tried to stop him. 'We cannot risk Bhima, nor Arjuna, nor the twins, who are very tender. . . . Let me carry the food for the *rakshasa*. Even if I perish, Bhima and Arjuna will be able to see you all through your difficult days.'

He was overruled by Kunthi. 'Let Bhima go; he will come back.'

Pushing along a cartload of food and two buffaloes, Bhima arrived on the edge of the town. He drove off the animals before entering the forest, and let out a big shout, calling the demon by his name. 'Baka, come out,' he called repeatedly, and started eating the food himself. 'Hey, you wretch,' he dared, 'come on and watch me eat. . . .

The demon came thundering out. 'Who are you to call me by name?' He was fierce and immense.

Bhima calmly continued to eat without even turning to look, as the demon came up behind him with all that uproar. Noticing his indifference, the *rakshasa* hit him from behind, but Bhima went on eating.

'Who are you, eating the food meant for me? Where are the animals?'

Bhima said, 'Animals? The buffaloes? They are grazing peacefully somewhere. I drove them off. You will not have them or anything else to eat today. You are on a fast today.' He was unconcerned even when the *rakshasa* belaboured him from behind. 'I don't like this disturbance while eating. You must learn to wait.'

The *rakshasa* felt rather bewildered at first, and gave him a few more knocks, but Bhima with his mouth full just flicked him off as if he were a bug on his nape. The *rakshasa* now tried to pull him away from the heap of food and grab it himself. He could hardly move Bhima from his seat, and when he tried to reach for his food, Bhima warded off his hand indifferently.

'I am hungry, how dare you?' screamed the *rakshasa* till the forests echoed with his voice. 'I will eat you.'

'Oh, yes,' said Bhima, 'I know you will do it, you devil, treating those who bring you food as if they were a side dish. Know that you can't do it any more. . . .'

'Or do you plan to eat me?' asked the rakshasa sneeringly.

'No, I wouldn't relish you, but I can tear you into morsels convenient for jackals and vultures to eat. . . .'

Every attempt that the *rakshasa* made to seize the heap of rice was frustrated by Bhima, who began to enjoy the game immensely. All the *rakshasa's* attempts to choke him were equally frustrated. Bhima did not budge until he had polished off every scrap of food he had brought, and then he turned to settle the score with his adversary. A grand fight ensued—they tore up immense trees, hurled boulders and rocks, and hit each other with fists. Finally Bhima lifted the *rakshasa* over his head, whirled him about, and dashed him on the ground. As he lay limp, Bhima placed his knee over him and broke his back.

The citizens of the town were filled with gratitude and asked in wonder how a brahmin came to possess such strength and valour, qualities which would have been appropriate only in a kshatriya. The Pandavas explained Bhima's talents away by saying that he had mastered certain esoteric mantras which enabled him to overcome even the deadliest adversary.

It soon became necessary for the Pandavas to move on from the hospitable home, where they were now in danger of being recognized. Moreover, a traveller had informed them that Drupada, the King of Panchala, had announced the *swayamwara* of his daughter, and that he had sent invitations far and wide for prospective bridegrooms to assemble in his palace on a certain day so that the bride might make her choice.

The Story of Drupada

Drupada, smarting under the defeat inflicted on him by the disciples of Drona, had wandered far and wide and found a guru, who instructed him as to how to beget a son who could someday vanquish Drona.

Drupada had performed prayers and sacrifices, and from the sacrificial fire arose a son and a daughter. The son was born bearing arms and encased in armour, and had all the indications of becoming an outstanding warrior. He was named Dhrishtadyumna, meaning 'one born with courage, arms, and ornaments'. The daughter was dark and beautiful and was called Draupadi and also Panchali.

Draupadi's *swayamwara* was not an occasion to be missed, so the Pandavas and their mother started for Panchala. There, they occupied an obscure house on the potters' street. At the start of each day they went round seeking alms, and brought home their collections to be divided among them by their mother.

On the day of the *swayamwara*, the Pandavas had left home early and joined the throng moving towards the palace. A vast ground had been cleared and built up with galleries to accommodate the visitors and the young men contending for the Princess's hand. Princelings wearing gaudy decorations and bearing imposing arms had arrived on horseback and chariots.

The day started with elaborate ceremonies performed by the royal priests. At the appointed hour, Draupadi entered the arena and looked around, sending all the young hearts racing. She was escorted by Dhrishtadyumna, her brother, the Prince of the house. He announced that those who would be eligible to be garlanded by the Princess must string a bow kept on a pedestal and shoot five arrows at a revolving target above by looking at its reflection on a pan of oil below.

The princes from the warrior class were the first to approach, but most of them withdrew after one look at the bow. One or two dropped it on their toes. Some could not even stretch the steel coil forming its bowstring.

Draupadi watched the process of elimination with relief. She saw the princes, in imposing battle dress, coming forward haughtily and retreating hastily, galloping away on their horses. Comments, jokes and laughter filled the air.

The Kauravas were in a group at one corner of the hall contemptuously watching the arrivals and departures. Karna, the most gifted master of arms and archery, was there with Duryodhana. His brothers and henchmen occupied the seats of honour and jeered at the candidates who failed. A lull fell on the assembly when their turn came, and the girl shivered instinctively and prayed to the gods to be saved from them.

She watched with apprehension as Karna approached the bow and lifted it as if it were a toy. He stood it on its end and stretched out the bowstring. But at the very moment when he took aim to shoot the mark, Draupadi was heard to remark, 'I will not accept him. . . .' At this, Karna dropped the bow and returned to his seat with a wry smile.

Duryodhana frowned and said in a whisper, 'She had no right to talk. If you string the bow and hit the mark, she must accept you. That is the condition. Otherwise, you may seize her and fly off. Go back and take the bow. We will support you.'

'No,' said Karna, 'I don't want her.'

In that assembly, unobserved, was a person who was to play a vital role in the *Mahabharata* later. It was Krishna, the King of Dwaraka, actually the eighth incarnation of the god Vishnu, who took his birth in the Yadava clan. He had incarnated as a human being as he has explained:

> For protecting the virtuous
> For the destruction of evil, and
> For establishing righteousness
> I am born from age to age.

He whispered to his brother, Balarama, at his side, 'These brahmins are none other than the Pandavas, who were supposed to have perished in a fire. This was all predestined, we will see a great deal of them yet. . . .'

Now there was a stir as Arjuna got up from the brahmin group.

There were shouts of protest. 'How dare a brahmin enter this contest, which is open only to the warrior class? Let brahmins stick to their scriptures.' But King Drupada ruled that he had mentioned no caste in his announcement. Anyone was free to try his luck at the *swayamwara*.

Draupadi watched anxiously as Arjuna approached the bow. He not only strung the bow, but hit the target again and again, five times. Draupadi approached him with the garland of flowers and slipped it over his neck, and they became betrothed. Arjuna clasped her hand and led her off.

There was a commotion at once. 'We have been cheated! How can a brahmin win a kshatriya bride? We will not tolerate it. We will kill King Drupada and carry away the girl.' Fighting broke out. Bhima, the strong brother among the Pandavas, armed with the trunks of two huge trees plucked out of the park, guarded the girl while she was taken away to their home in the potters' street.

Kunthi was in the kitchen when the brothers arrived. Bhima, wanting to sound light-hearted, cried from the doorstep, 'Mother, come out, see what *bhiksha* we have brought today.'

Without coming out, Kunthi answered from the kitchen, 'Very well, share it among yourselves.'

'Oh!' exclaimed Bhima. 'Oh! Oh!' cried everyone, and the loudest exclamation was from Arjuna, who had won the bride.

The mother came out to see why there was such an uproar and cried, 'Oh! Who is this? You have won, Arjuna?' She was full of joy, and clasped the girl's hand. 'Oh! Arjuna, you have won this bride, this Princess, this lovely creature! So you entered the contest after all. I never believed that you seriously meant to go there. What a risk you took of being discovered by your enemies! How happy I am to welcome this daughter-in-law! Tell me. . .what was the . . come in, come in.' Her joy was boundless. Her son had won the greatest contest and had come through it safely and gloriously. 'Come in, come in. . . .'

They trooped in behind her. She spread out a mat and told the girl to be seated, but, like a well-mannered daughter-in-law, Draupadi would not be seated when the men and mother-in-law were standing. Moreover, her mind was all in a whirl.

There was an awkward pause as the five brothers stood around uncertainly and Draupadi stood apart with down-cast eyes, trying not to stare at the five men who were to share her, if the mother's injunction was to be obeyed. What a predicament for the girl, who thought that she was marrying one man and found four others thrown in unexpectedly!

Now Draupadi studied the five brothers as unobtrusively as possible, wondering what freak of fate had brought her to this pass. Kunthi tried to make light of her own advice and said with a simper, 'Of course I did not know what you meant when you said you had brought *bhiksha*. I thought it was the usual gift of alms. . . .' Her voice trailed away.

Bhima the strong, incapable of the subtleties of speech, struggled to explain himself. 'I . . . meant to be jocular, I meant. . . .'

It was Arjuna who broke the awkward moment, 'Mother, your word has always been a command to us, and its authority is inescapable. How can it be otherwise? We will share Draupadi as you have commanded.'

'No, no, no . . . ' cried the mother.

Yudhistira said, 'Arjuna! What preposterous suggestion are you making in jest? A woman married to one man is a wife, of two, three, four, or five, a public woman. She is sinful. Whoever heard of such a thing!'

The mother said, 'Don't make too much of an inadvertent bit of advice. You make me feel very unhappy and guilty, my son. Don't even suggest such outrage.'

Arjuna pleaded, 'Please don't make me a sinner; it is not fair to condemn me to suffer the sin of disobedience to a mother's word. You, my eldest brother, you are a man with a judicious mind and a knowledge of right and wrong. We four brothers and this girl will be bound by your words. You must advise us as to what is good and fair. Advise us, and we shall be bound by your words, but bear in mind that we cannot go back on the command of a mother. . . .'

When he said this, all the brothers studied the face of the girl, and their hearts beat faster, for already Manmatha, the God of Love, was at work, stirring their blood and affecting their vision.

Yudhistira brooded for only a moment, recollected the words of a seer who had already prophesied the situation and to avoid heart-burning amongst the brothers, he declared, 'This rare creature shall be wife to all of us.'

The King of Panchala, father of Draupadi, summoned the Pandavas to discuss the arrangements for the wedding. The five brothers with their mother and the girl were invited to the palace to be honoured and feasted. They were taken through the palace and its grounds, where fruits, souvenirs, rare art objects, sculpture, paintings, carvings, gold-inlaid leather, furniture of rare designs, agricultural implements, chariots, and horses were displayed. When they passed through the hall where swords, arms, shields, and equipment of warfare were kept, the five brothers picked up the articles, admiring them and commenting among themselves, spending more time in this part of the palace than anywhere else.

Observing this, the King suspected that they might be warriors, although they were disguised as brahmins. When they repaired to the chamber and were settled comfortably, the King said pointblank to Yudhistira, 'I know you will always speak the truth. Tell me who you are.'

And Yudhistira declared his identity and that of his brothers, and explained their trials and tribulations since the time of their leaving their kingdom a year before.

Now the King said, 'Let us rejoice that this day your brother Arjuna, the man with the mighty arm, will marry my daughter, and let us celebrate this union of our families in style. Let us make everyone in this world happy today.'

Yudhistira replied, 'I am the eldest and still unmarried. I must be the first to marry, according to our law. Please give me your blessings to be married first.'

'So be it,' said the King, little dreaming of the implication. 'You are the eldest, my daughter now belongs to your family. If you decide to marry her yourself, you will be free to do so, or you may give her to whomever you like among your brothers. I have nothing more to say.'

'No,' said Yudhistira simply and quietly, 'Draupadi will have to be married to all of us.' He explained how it had come about and concluded, 'We have always shared everything and we will never deviate from the practice.'

The King was stunned on hearing this. When he recovered his balance, he cried, 'One man can take many wives, but one woman taking several husbands has never been approved anywhere, either in practice or in the scriptures. It is something that can never receive approval from any quarter. A man of purity like you, one learned and well-equipped in knowledge—what evil power is influencing you to speak thus?'

Yudhistira tried to calm him. 'The right way is subtle and complicated. I know I am not deviating from it. O conqueror of the worlds, have no misgivings, give us your permission.'

The King said, 'You and your venerable mother and my

daughter. . . please talk it over among yourselves and tell me what should be done.'

At this moment, the sage Vyasa arrived. When all the formalities of greeting were over, the King asked, 'Give us your guidance; can a woman marry five men?'

'Not always,' answered Vyasa, 'but in this particular instance, it is correct. Now listen. . . . ' He got up and walked into the King's private chamber. The others followed at a distance and waited outside.

The Lives of Draupadi

'Your daughter,' said Vyasa, 'was called Nalayani in her last birth. She was one of the five ideal women in our land. She was married to a sage called Moudgalya, a leprous man, repulsive in appearance and habits, and cantankerous. She was, however, completely indifferent to his physical state and displayed the utmost devotion to him as a wife. She obeyed all his erratic commands, accepted his fickle moods, submitted herself to all his tyrannical orders, and ate the scraps from his plate. All this she did without hesitation or mental protest, totally effacing her own ego. They spent many years thus, and one day her husband said, "O beautiful one, perfect wife on earth, you have indeed passed through the severest trial and come through unscathed. Know you that I am neither old nor diseased nor inconsiderate. I assumed this vicious and disgusting appearance in order to test you. You are indeed the most forbearing partner a man could hope for. Ask me for any boon you may fancy, and I will grant it."

'Nalayani said, "I want you to love me as five men, assuming five forms, and always coming back to and merging in one form." And he granted her the wish. He shed his unpleasant appearance in a moment and stood before her as an attractive, virile man—and he could assume four other forms too. The rest of their life was all romance; they travelled far and wide, visited beautiful romantic spots on earth, and led a life of perfect union, not in one, but several worlds. They lived and loved endlessly.

'She never got tired of it, but he did. He told her one day that his life of abandon was at an end and that he was retiring into loneliness and introspection. At this she wailed, "I am still insatiate. I have lived a wonderful life with you. I want you to continue it for ever."

'Moudgalya rejected her plea, warded her off as a drag on his spiritual progress, and departed. Whereupon she came down to earth from the dreamy elysium in which she had dwelt and prepared herself to meditate on Ishwara the Almighty. She meditated with great rigour, and when Ishwara appeared before her, she muttered, "I want my husband, husband, husband. . . ."

' "You will soon end this identity and will be reborn as a beauty and marry five husbands," said the god.

'"Five husbands! God! Why five? I want only one."

'"I cannot help it. I heard you say husband, and that five times," said Ishwara. And that proved the last word on the subject, since a god's word is unretractable.

'While it seemed as if the god had spoken in jest, he had his purpose. In the vision of a god there is no joking, everything works according to a scheme. Nalayani was reborn as the daughter of Drupada without being conceived in a womb, but out of a sacrificial fire. Justice and goodness have to be reinstated in this world. The Kauravas are evil incarnate; powerful, clever, and accomplished. For the good of mankind, they must be wiped out, and Draupadi will play a great role in it.'

Draupadi was wedded to the brothers. At the ceremony, the first to take her hand was the eldest, Yudhistira; next came the mighty Bhima; after him the actual winner, Arjuna; and lastly the twins, Nakula and Sahadeva, one after the other. The Princess was to live with each brother for one full year as his wife, and then pass on to the next. When she lived with one, the others swore to eradicate her image completely from their minds. A very special kind of detachment and discipline was needed to practise this code. Anyone who violated it, even in thought, exiled himself from the family and had to seek expiation in a strenuous pilgrimage to the holy rivers.

VII: THE WRITER AS CITIZEN

Editors note: Narayan has always taken his function as a citizen very seriously, municipal and other lapses evoking the gentle fairy in him which he gives expression to in the occasional speech and more often in letters to newspapers. Mindlessness in any form dismays him and in the following speech in the Indian Parliament, he takes up the cause of schoolgoing children in a minute of indignation, invective and sarcasm.

CRUELTY TO CHILDREN

In the stress of the concerns of the adult world, the problems or rather the plight of children pass unnoticed. I am not referring to any particular class but to childhood itself. The hardship starts right at home, when straight from sleep the child is pulled out and got ready for school even before its faculties are awake. He (or she) is groomed and stuffed into a uniform and packed off to school with a loaded bag on his back. The school bag has become an inevitable burden for the child. I am now pleading for abolition of the school bag, as a national policy, by an ordinance if necessary. I have investigated and found that an average child carries strapped to his back, like a pack-mule, not less than six to eight kgs of books, notebooks and other paraphernalia of modern education in addition to lunch-box and water bottle. Most children on account of this daily burden develop a stoop and hang their arms forward like a chimpanzee while walking, and I know cases of serious spinal injuries in some children too. Asked why not leave some books behind at home, the child explains it is her teacher's orders that all books and notes must be brought every day to the class, for what reason God alone knows. If there is a lapse, the child invites punishment, which takes the form of being rapped on the knuckles with a wooden scale, a refinement from our days when we received cane cuts on the palm only. The child is in such terror of the teacher, whether known as Sister, Mother Superior, or just Madam, that he or she is prepared to carry out any command issued by the teacher, who has no imagination or sympathy.

The dress regulation particularly in convent schools is another senseless formality—tie and laced shoes and socks, irrespective of the climate, is compulsory. Polishing a shoe and lacing it becomes a major task for a child first thing in the day. When the tie has become an anachronism even in the adult world, it's absurd to enforce it on children. A simple uniform and footwear must be designed and brought into force and these should be easier to maintain.

After school hours when the child returns home her mother or home tutor is waiting to pounce on her, snatch her bag and compel her to go through some special coaching or homework. For the child the day has ended; with no time left for her to play or dream. It is a cruel, harsh life imposed on her, and I present her case before this house for the honourable members to think out and devise remedies by changing the whole educational system and outlook so that childhood has a change to bloom rather than wilt in the process of learning.

Other areas where the child needs protection is from involvement in adult activities such as protest marches, parades, or lining up on road-sides for waving at VIPs; children are made to stand in the hot sun for hours without anyone noticing how much they suffer from fatigue, hunger and thirst. Children must be protected, and cherished which would seem especially relevant in this year of the Nehru centenary. How it is to be done is up to our rulers and administrators to consider—perhaps not by appointing a commission of inquiry, but in some other practical and peaceful manner.

VIII. ENVOY

Editor's note: The American Academy and Institute of Arts and Letters invited R.K. Narayan to join its fellowship, the second Indian to be so honoured, the first being the sitar maestro, Ravi Shankar. As Narayan could not make the journey to the U.S. to receive the award in person, the then U.S. Ambassador to India, Harry S. Barnes, presented it to him in a glittering function at the Roosevelt House, American Embassy, on 18 January, 1982. Excerpts from his acceptance speech:

'WHERE IS MALGUDI'

You (Mr Ambassador) have spoken of my writing with warmth and understanding. I am glad you have felt drawn to my characters and their environment. I am often questioned, 'Where is Malgudi?' which is the background of my novels and short stories. I'd like to take this occasion to answer it. I didn't consider too long when I invented this little town. It had just occurred to me when I started on my first novel, *Swami and Friends*, about fifty years ago, to be exact in September 1930, that it would be safer to have a fictitious name for the background of the novel, which would leave one free to meddle with its geography and details as I pleased, without incurring the wrath of any city-father of any actual town or city. I wanted to be able to put in whatever I liked, and wherever I liked—a little street or school or a temple or a bungalow or even a slum, a railway line, at any spot, a minor despot in a little world. I began to like my role, and I began to be fascinated by its possibilities; its river, market-place, and the far-off mountain roads and forests acquired a concrete quality, and have imprisoned me within their boundaries, with the result that I am unable to escape from Malgudi, even if I wished to. . . .